Manipulation

Mastery

6 Books in 1 : Dark Psychology, How to Analyze People, Cognitive Behavioral Therapy, NLP, Manipulation, Persuasion Techniques. Explore the Secrets of the Mind

Daniel Peterson

TABLE OF CONTENTS

The Most Comprehensive Guide

on Mental Manipulation

The trademarks that are used are without any consent, and the publication of the trademark is without permission or backing by the trademark owner. All trademarks and brands within this book are for clarifying purposes only and are the owned by the owners themselves, not affiliated with this document.

Dark Psychology

Learn The Secrets of Manipulation, Covert Persuasion and Mind Control Analyze and Emotionally Influence People Explore NLP and Brainwashing using Proven Psychological Techniques

Daniel Peterson

TABLE OF CONTENTS

Introduction

Congratulations on downloading Dark Psychology and thank you for putting faith in this book's capacity to educate you on the topic. Dark Psychology is an area of psychology, the study of the human mind, which few people are aware of. Dark psychology includes many topics, such as seduction, persuasion, depravity. It is effectively the underbelly of what we know about how human beings operate—what drives us, and why we sometimes do unsavory, or even unspeakable things, in order to achieve our goals. There are people all over who exhibit dangerous qualities and may try to harm you. Most of the time, we are so blind to what is happening to us, that is only have we have incurred emotional or physical damage that we realize we have been manipulated or abused.

This book seeks to arm the reader with all of the tools, tactics, and tricks of the trade of dark psychology. Knowing just what a manipulator or abuser looks and sounds like without having to become too involved with them is an invaluable skillset. This book will cover a range of topics from the motivations behind simple human pettiness to how some of the world's most deprave killers commit their crimes. In addition, this book covers how to spot and avoid harmful people and what sorts of tactics they may try to use on you. With all the options of books you had to choose from, we are pleased that you have chosen our offering to educate yourself. We hope you find this book useful in your future interactions with others and find yourself prepared to deal with even the cruelest and shadiest people.

Chapter 1: What Is Dark Psychology

Imagine this: Patrick and Nancy are married, but not happily. Patrick is generally callous towards his wife, who tends to his every need. He screams at her if his dinner is not prepared *just* so and regularly denigrates her for perceived shortcomings and faults. When Patrick is particularly angry, he may destroy an article of her clothing or lock the door if he is angry she has gone out with friends. In this relationship, Nancy is constantly afraid of incurring his anger or stepping out of line, lest she be subjected to one of his outbursts or punishments.

One day, Patrick becomes slightly annoyed that Nancy has left the house without taking out the garbage. She was in a hurry to get to work because she woke up a little bit late, and she mistakenly forgot about this simple home organization task that she does every day. Now the job is Patrick's, but he doesn't feel like doing it. Patrick thinks to himself, "Why should I take out the trash just because my wife forgot to do it. She always does it, so I shouldn't have to. She is so stupid for making that mistake. It's *her* job, after all!"

Patrick becomes increasingly annoyed at what has happened. Most people would think he is unreasonably angry over something so small —it's the garbage after all—it's not exactly difficult to dispose of. Patrick however, thinks this is an example of Nancy's persistent incompetence. Now he's really angry, sitting there clenching his jaw, getting more and more upset that Nancy did not do what he perceives to be solely her responsibility. He sits in his bedroom and wonders how he can teach her a lesson. He is unspeakably angry and has completely lost his temper. He decides he ought to shoot the dog they share so that Nancy will return from work to her slaughtered pet. *That* will teach her a lesson.

Patrick's pleasure in this action would be two-fold; he derives pleasure from how powerful he feels controlling the life and death of this animal and he is satisfied by the terror and pain in his wife's face. Nancy came home later that day and wept bitterly—she was sad for her beloved pet, slaughtered by the callous monster that is Patrick and afraid of his rage. He inspired fear and anguish in her, and thought he had won some sort of disagreement over who ought to take out the garbage. Despite how evil Nancy knows her husband to be, she is now extra careful around him. She hopes never to inspire his anger again, even though it is only a matter of time before Patrick will become aggravated over something else and act out violently, as abusive people often do.

Here, Patrick's thought process is an example of some extreme dark psychology tactics at play. His standard operating procedure and thought process are mean. He finds irrational justification for his actions, but they essentially serve no purpose other than to terrorize his wife and get what he wants—he found an opportunity to show off his authority and seized it by killing the dog. The infraction (not taking out the garbage) and the punishment (killing the dog) are almost meaningless. The mistake of not taking out the garbage was simply an opportunity for Patrick to satisfy his cruel urges. Patrick likes scaring people, manipulating them, and displaying his power over them.

What is Dark Psychology?

Generally and colloquially, dark psychology is the study of why some people are *really* bad. More specifically though, dark psychology seeks to elucidate how and why some people prey on others. It assumes that everyone has dark urges sometimes—as humans, we simply can't help imagining being mean to someone or ways we could emotionally manipulate them into doing what we want. When we get angry for example, we my exaggerate and say, "I just want to *kill* them" or "I'm so angry that I just want to hit them." Most of us would never really do those things though—we suppress these sorts of impulses and don't act on them. We know that taking advantage of others and mistreating them is fundamentally wrong. Dark psychology seeks to understand those who are *not* like us—those who act on their worst urges towards others, who steal, cheat, lie, and manipulate *constantly* in order to get what they want or think they deserve.

This is in stark contrast to the field of positive psychology, which studies which qualities and practices enable a person to live a happy, successful life. In general dark psychology, and its encompassed actions and behaviors, can be traced back to the fundamental drive all humans have somewhere in their psyche to put their own goals and needs above others'. Forensic consultant and licensed psychologist Dr. Michael Nuccitelli did the pioneering work to come up with this the concept of dark psychology as a separate field. He sought to understand the thought processes that lead human beings to prey on others. In Dark Psychology, there is an assumption that while some predators commit atrocious acts for sex, money, or some other goal, others do terrible things without a purpose. They simply want to hurt someone or feel powerful just for the sake of it.

Before we go into further depth on dark psychology, there are some concepts you should keep in mind. The first one is the **dark continuum.** Naturally, most callous, manipulative behavior exists somewhere on a spectrum. The dark continuum refers to the fact that these sorts of behaviors can range from being a slight nuisance to other people all the way to causing harm and death to them. Where one's actions fit in along the dark continuum is called the **dark factor**. Everyone has a dark factor to some degree or another, but it is not the same in everyone. A person's dark factor is the result of their experiences, genetics, and personality. For example, someone may develop a stronger dark factor if they grow up in an abusive household, because they have seen despicable behavior normalized and learned a lesson that hurting others is acceptable. The **dark singularity** is the theoretical place in a person's mind that allows them to commit terrible acts without a purpose. The dark singularity is the place in someone's mind that wants to hurt others simply for its own sake. As a dark factor, the dark singularity is on the rightmost end of the dark continuum, which no one ever reaches. However, the most extreme psychopaths, such as murderers and rapists, are unconsciously always on a quest to try to reach this place. No one can reach it however, because all behavior is purposive for to some degree or another. Hurting someone

15

for no reason other than to feel powerful still means there is a purpose to the offensive action.

When you combine the dark continuum and the dark factor, you get the dark singularity. Factors outside a person's control, such a circumstance and opportunity, either hinder or facilitate someone's ability to reach the dark singularity. The destructive person is always attempting to approach the dark singularity but never can. So, when you take the dark continuum, whose dark factors are affected by outside circumstances, you can see how close someone comes to the dark singularity.

For a brief introduction to what dark psychology may look like in your own life, I'll provide a few examples of what dark psychology looks like in everyday examples. Have you ever met someone who showers you with affection and tells you you're perfect for them, despite not knowing each other very well? This type of person will shower you compliments and gifts, and *constantly* remind you of their undying commitment to you. Then they reveal their true selves—as soon as you disagree with this person or give them any reason to doubt your reciprocity, they will turn on you. They may call you selfish or become very angry and abusive towards you. This is called love bombing. It works because showering you with affection will make you more committed to the relationship and more likely to entangle yourself with this person, giving you no way to leave them. Once you are trapped, the abusive person can reveal their true self; their inner core is manipulative, possessive, and downright nasty.

Choice restriction is another common tactic you have probably experienced. Choice restriction is when a person may give you certain choices about a decision in order to distract you from the choice they do not want you to make. An example of choice restriction may be speaking favorably about two choices a person may have, which are the manipulator's more desired outcomes, and ignore or speak badly of the third option. Objectively speaking, all three options are equally valid in the situation, but the manipulator seeks a specific outcome, so he or she will distort information about each of the three to push their victim in the direction they want them to go.

In addition, you've definitely experience covert emotional manipulation (CEM) or maybe even done it yourself. CEM is a tactic wherein the manipulator uses subtle cues and actions in order to manipulate someone. It may include the silent treatment or guilt tripping. Essentially, CEM unconsciously leads the victim to doubt themselves or feel more reliant or indebted to the manipulator. Over time, the victim may constantly second guess themselves, have terribly low self-esteem, or do anything they can to please the manipulator and not incur any more of their CEM tactics. CEM will be covered more in the next chapter, as it is a very important part of dark psychology and manipulative behavior.

So, why is dark psychology-- the science of evil, meanness, cruelty, and callousness—worth studying and devoting a whole vocabulary to? By knowing more about the worst individuals, we can protect ourselves—while we may not be able to empathize with those who seek to hurt us, and we shouldn't, understanding what their tactics may be, and the signs of a manipulative or cruel person, may help us avoid them.

From a more clinical standpoint, all humans have a lot to learn about ourselves from those among us who are most evil. Those with antisocial personality disorder (ASPD), known as psychopaths, can teach us quite a bit about responses to stressors and the reasons and mechanisms through which some people become impossibly cruel. ASPD can be thought of as consisting of two big pieces; one piece is a personality lacking in remorse and empathy with little emotional depth, callousness, and a lack of care and regard for others. The other piece of this personality disorder is antisocial behavior. Antisocial behaviors includes patterns such as poor impulse control, inappropriate displays of anger, and irresponsibility. The core emotional and personality traits of ASPD seem to be highly heritable, which means that having a close relative, such as a parent, with these traits significantly increases that likelihood that you yourself will have them. Higher levels of the personality traits associated with this disorder are fairly reliable predictors of the associated behaviors previously described.

Knowing these facts, there are a few others that may surprise you. For example, while the personality traits associated with ASPD may be highly heritable, the behaviors are not. In other words, having a cruel parent will not necessarily make you a cruel person. Instead of being a matter of genetics, the risk of engaging in antisocial behaviors seemed to be determined more by environmental factors a child may have been exposed to, such as trauma, poverty, or a delinquent group of friends. These risk factors however, tend not to precede the antisocial personality traits a child may possess. In other words, personality traits determined by genes in combination with an environment leading to antisocial behavior makes a psychopath.

What does this tell us about ourselves? From antisocial personality disorder, we can understand that darkness and evil can consume anyone, depending on their surroundings and upbringing. While those who have been mistreated by a parent and go on to develop this disorder don't have a choice, as adults we may surround ourselves with those who bring out the worst in us, even if we will never develop a full-blown personality disorder.

Dark psychology tactics are all over the place, not just in psychopaths and murderers—just think of stereotypes associated with the used car salesman. They are charming, enthusiastic, and persuasive, all so they can get a sale out of you. From their job, they learn a bit about how to lead people on, exaggerate and persuade—their livelihood depends on this, so they get good at it. Of course, not all used car salesmen are like this, but having some dark personality traits certainly helps. Let's look at some other examples of professions where dark psychology may be useful, and where there may be some incentive to engage in some morally dubious and manipulative, dishonest behavior.

Politicians are a great example. Every day, we see them campaigning and making speeches all to get our vote. Some use beautiful rhetoric and honest assessments of their policy agendas in order to garner votes but others appeal to emotion in unsavory was. A politician may make grandiose promises about wealth and prosperity for the nation that simply cannot be kept to. Other times, they may invoke unnecessary fears and bigotry and offer themselves as the sole solution to a country's problems, such that people vote for this candidate out of a sense of fear. Thus, a dark psychology tactic common among politicians is deception.

Another profession where dark psychology excels is, ironically, law. Lawyers often need to negotiate with other attorneys and persuade juries and judges. In this way, a lawyer may use effective persuasion tactics in order to swing a jury in their client's favor. An attorney may seek to play down their client's crimes for a lesser jail sentence or exaggerate the extent of a client's injury to increase their odds of winning a personal injury suit.

As many as 4% of CEOs may be psychopaths, which is astonishingly high. Why? Because running a successful, profitable company and pleasing shareholders may mean making a lot of people angry and making a decision completely amorally for the sake of maximizing profitability. A psychopathic CEO may see nothing wrong with demanding unreasonable work hours from a sick employee or laying off another who gets pregnant. A psychopathic CEO can focus themselves solely on the outcome they feel benefits them, and ignore the human cost of getting there, creating a successful company.

While certain dark psychology traits are not inherently evil or bad, they may certainly lead to bad outcomes. Of course, everyone lies every once in a while, or may use some CEM tactics, but a truly cruel person relies on these constantly. The object of this book is not to demonize all of dark psychology and specific personality traits, but rather to understand the logic of some of our worst impulses and drive to constantly satisfy ourselves.

Chapter 2: Covert Emotional Manipulation

Covert emotional manipulation, CEM, is a group of sly, sneaky methods of controlling other people. It includes all sorts of tactics, but the one thing all CEM has in common is that the person being manipulated often does not realize that they are being manipulated until it is too late.

As the name suggests, someone using CEM tries *emotionally* manipulation someone into doing what they want or as a way to punish them for a perceived misdeed. If someone is a chronic victim of CEM, he or she may come to suffer from low self-esteem, depression, anxiety, or even post-traumatic stress disorder. These people who have become emotionally worn down and vulnerable are even more susceptible to further abuse in the future. This means that they will continue to tolerate increasing abuse and dishonesty from their current abuser, or they will tolerate it from others in the future if their self-worth and self-esteem are not repaired and allowed to recover from the damage caused by CEM.

One of the hallmarks of CEM is that the victim often knows there is something wrong with their relationship to the abuser but can't quite identify what it is. The victim may constantly feel insecure in their relationship and feel like it is constantly about to fall apart. Another common trait among victims is that their relationship to the abuser seems more complicated than it needs to be—boundaries between the two people are often unclear and expectations can change at the drop of a hat depending on what the manipulator wants and what the victim is willing to do in order to stay on their good side.

While not necessarily as serious a crime as theft, arson, or murder, CEM most certainly fits into the study of dark psychology. CEM fits into dark psychology because it relies on the manipulator taking advantage of their victim's weakness. It involves deception and predatory behavior in order for the manipulator to meet their own needs and desires. Those who compulsively use CEM are unable to relate to others in a healthy way and lack the ability to communicate their needs properly. They do not so the need to communicate their needs straightforwardly and honestly, so they turn to manipulation in order to get what they want. If anything, they view their victim's humanity as a nuisance and obstacle to satisfying themselves; they feel entitled to CEM because it is not physically abusive, so "it isn't really that bad." This is what makes the manipulator able to justify their actions, and what often makes the victim feel trapped. CEM relies on the victim's shame, embarrassment, and their own minimization of what's happening to themselves, such that they feel uncomfortable confronting the manipulator about their underhanded actions.

Common CEM Tactics

CEM includes many different trick and tactics. The whole point is to make a victim submit to the will of the manipulator and to make the victim doubt their own reality. In this chapter I describe common ways an emotional manipulator may employ CEM.

Love Bombing

As previously described, love bombing involves grandiose displays of affection, often towards a new romantic partner, followed by extreme possessiveness and abuse. When someone is being love bombed, the relationship moves quickly. They start off flooded with constant praise and affection; their new partner may take them on fancy dates and want to be inseparably close all the time.

The person being love bombed is excited and overwhelmed at the same time. The ceaseless contact, flattery, and romance makes the person on the receiving end feel like they have found a unique romantic bond with a person who loves them endlessly. On the other hand, they become overwhelmed because they sense deep down that the relationship is moving too quickly and with too much intensity. They may feel smothered or like they have time for nothing other than their new partner.

Once this beginning phase wears off, the relationship can and will turn ugly. The manipulator often successfully elicits a reciprocal response of affection and commitment from their new partner. The victim feels confused—they do not know if they truly feel the same way about their new partner but felt pressure to say the feel the same way because it seemed like they had no reason not to. In addition, the manipulator will isolate them by taking up all their time, becoming their sole source of affection while also becoming increasingly controlling and manipulative in other ways.

The person who was love bombed feels trapped and confused about their own feelings towards the manipulative partner who bombards them with affection. They are isolated with this person now and by its very nature, love bombing can appear like a healthy but very intense start to a relationship, so the victim has trouble evaluating just how bad their situation is. It is not healthy though. A successful love bomb will isolate the victim, and blind them to surprise of how manipulative their partner will become in the future.

Reinforcement: A CEM Stacked Sequence

When has the manipulative person succeeded? A manipulator has succeeded when they have gained control of their victim's actions. When has a manipulator gained control of their victim? A manipulator has gained control of their victim when that victim is no longer excited and happy to be involved with them and becomes more fearful and distressed about the prospect of losing the manipulative person's approval and warmth.

Once the victim realizes this fear, they will do everything they can to ensure it does not come true—they want to make the manipulator happy and to appease them. Once this fear takes hold of the victim, the reinforcement can occur. Here is how it goes: the victim realizes that they ought to be afraid of losing the manipulator's love. The manipulator has *created* this fear in order to dangle security in the relationship just above the victim's head at all times. Every now and then though, the manipulator will relieve the victim's anxiety by giving them the love and decency they constantly crave and fear that they will lose. This creates a cycle—the victim practically *lives* for these fixes of approval. They begin to constantly crave it in hopes that the manipulator will offer it to them again. The victim will constantly do

23

their best to please the manipulator and get their fix, so to speak, and the rare occasion where they get it is the *reinforcement*.

Reinforcement is destructive because the victim keeps hoping the manipulator will go back to being the reliable, trustworthy person they were at the beginning of the relationship. It makes the victim think that they can somehow be good enough for their abuser, such that if they can just make the manipulator happy, they can get their approval back. Then, when on the rare occasion that the abuser shows them some approval, the victim believes that they finally changed the mind of the manipulator and made them realize their value! Unfortunately, they have only played into the manipulator's hands. The less frequently the manipulator reinforces, the more desperate the victim becomes for more reinforcement. The victim believes it is their own fault that the manipulator withholds affection—only realizing that they are being manipulated can stop the cycle.

Gaslighting: Denying and Distorting Reality

Chances are, you have experienced gas-lighting. Maybe it was in an argument. You told a friend, parent, or partner that something they did upset you or crossed your boundaries. You hoped to have a constructive conversation and address the problem, and that they would apologize for their mistake and amend their ways. At the very least, you hoped there would be a good explanation or a mild acknowledgment of your viewpoint. Instead, they outright deny any wrongdoing, or doing anything in the first place. They will say "No I didn't," or "I seriously have no memory of doing that. Are you sure it was me?"

You are slightly dumbfounded—you know they did it because you saw or heard it with your own eyes. You feel like you're going crazy—this manipulative person just told you not to trust your own eyes. If they're successful, you will doubt yourself and succumb to their distortion of reality. *This* is gas-lighting—when a manipulator distorts reality and makes a victim doubt themselves, such that they no longer trust their perception of an action by the manipulator which was truly offensive or mean.

Gaslighting is not limited to simply denying the truth despite the victim's evidence. It can also take the form of attacking your identity and things that are important to you. One would be that they tell you, "Your best friend is seriously ruining our relationship. I don't know why you're friends with him/her." While this may not seem like a distortion of reality, it falls into the category of gaslighting because such a statement is meant to make you doubt your own judgement. Hearing this, a victim may think to themselves that maybe they are not good at picking friends, or they may create distance between themselves and their best friend.

Gas-lighting works because, over time, the manipulator gets their victim not to believe their own eyes, ears, and perception. The first time it happens, it may seem like simply a difference of opinion. Once it starts to happen more and more though, the victim gets worn down. If they want to fight with the manipulator, they are forced into a position where they have to fight about reality itself, about facts and truth. These arguments always go nowhere, as the manipulator will get off topic and will continue to deny the truth or distort the perception of their victim.

Invalidation

This is one of the most painful CEM tactics to endure. Invalidation occurs when a manipulator belittles, ignores, insults, judges, rejects, and/or minimizes their victim's feelings. An example of invalidation at play is as follows. Sarah's father insults her new shirt and Sarah feels offended and insulted. Sarah says, "Dad, can you not insult my clothes, please? I felt really good going out today, and now I feel self-conscious that maybe I don't really look so good." Her father gives her an incredulous look and sneers, "I don't know why you think it's such a big deal that I was just expressing my opinion. Maybe you should just learn to take some constructive criticism. You're just so sensitive, so I can't say anything to you!"

Sarah's father invalidated her feelings—he was objectively rude to her and when she calls him out on it, he turns her feelings into the problem instead of his own rudeness. The whole point of invalidation is that is denies empathy to the victim. Empathy in relationships of any kind is important because it helps us know our feelings are valid and considered. We offer empathy to friends to let them know that they are not alone and that we have support for them—when someone expresses empathy, we feel like someone is in our corner. Invalidation flips that on its head, because not only are we deprived of empathy, but we are also made to believe that our own feelings are the problem.

A few examples of invalidating phrases are, "you have no reason to feel that way," "I'm not having this discussion again," "You don't realize how lucky you are," and "get over it." These phrases all have one thing in common—the person hearing them is being told that their feelings are invalid and unreasonable. Invalidation can make the victim feel guilty about their feelings or ashamed of themselves. Eventually, they may start ignoring their own emotions, for fear that there *is* something wrong with them. They may also stop trying to talk about their feelings with the manipulator, knowing it is a futile effort.

Victim Blaming

In victim blaming, the manipulator tries to convince their victim that a problem in the relationship is their fault. Victim blaming may make the victim feel guilty for harm that befell them or ashamed of themselves.

This tactic sound as though it would be completely obvious when it happens, but it can be more subtle than boldly shifting blame over to the victim. If the manipulator is begin subtle, victim-blaming may not be so obvious. For example, say a person's house has just been robbed and they are anxious, upset, and afraid. They go tell their friend, who's response is, "I told you that you need to start checking to see if you locked your doors! Why are you surprised this happened?" Here, the friend engages in victim blaming because they suggest that it was somehow the victim's responsibility to prevent their house from being robbed. It may be true that locking one's doors is safer than not locking them, this situation was not the place to remind someone of such a thing.

Accidentally forgetting to take precautions does not justify that a crime has been committed against someone. In victim blaming, the victim is meant to wonder or feel that they brought their harm onto themselves. This is common in domestic abuse situations and rape. Victims will become depressed and isolated by their shame that they did not prevent themselves from becoming victims of abuse or crime, and may become so ashamed that they stay silent, and do not tell anyone of what they have endured.

Extreme Anger

Remember Patrick and Nancy from Chapter One? Nancy made a small mistake and Patrick displayed his anger violently, aggressively, and cruelly by killing their dog. Out of fear and trauma, Nancy learned *never* to forget to take out the garbage ever again.

Extreme anger works by training the victim not to anger the manipulator; the manipulator will have such a huge outburst and get so angry that the victim will learn on the first try not to cross the manipulator ever again. This tactic controls the victim through fear. The display of anger by the manipulator can be so extreme and distressing to the victim that they will do anything possible to avoid evoking such intense anger from the manipulator ever again.

Passive-Aggression

We all know this one—someone does everything possible to know they are unhappy with you without actually saying it. Being passive-aggressive can include giving someone the silent treatment, giving them a dirty look, and can even include simple body language cues and tones of voice.

Passive-aggressive behavior usually evokes a feeling from its target— you will strongly suspect someone is mad at you, because they may be avoiding you or acting with some hostility, but you cannot quite put your finger on *exactly* what they are doing. Passive aggressive behavior can be stressful because the onus is on the victim to ask the manipulator what is bothering them. In a healthy relationship, instead of being passive-aggressive, someone will express their anger or dissatisfaction directly. This CEM tactic is damaging to relationships because both parties in the relationship wind up with a lot of pent up resentment and anger.

Do One Thing, Say Another

If someone you are in a relationship constantly says they love you or appreciate you, but cannot be bothered to do you a tiny favor, they are being inconsistent. An emotional manipulator will do this in order to keep you around. Often times, they are too last to go out of their way for their partner or too callous to treat them properly, but still want their company. The victim will realize that the abuser is not living up to the promises of the friendship or romantic relationship and confront them about it.

Here is where this CEM tactic finds its foothold. The manipulator does not want to lose their victim, so they will respond to their victim's confrontation with something like, "I do love you! If I didn't love you, I wouldn't spend time with you!" The manipulator may also make false promises, such as promising fidelity or emotional support in order to keep the victim around.

How Manipulators Choose Their Victims

Abusive relationships often require complete submission to the abuser from the victim in order to survive. We often ask, "why don't you just leave if he/she is so bad?" or "why don't you just ignore them?" This ignores the very real fact that abusers *know* whom they are dealing with.

Have you noticed that the worst abusers are often parents or romantic partners? Parents and partners have a pool of vulnerable people available to them. Parents have their children, for instance. Children look to their parents for comfort, advice, approval, and love. An abusive parent knows this and that their child cannot simply leave them if they become fed up with mistreatment. A child often cannot conceive that their parent is behaving badly, so they may blame themselves for abuse of any kind (whether it is emotional, physical, verbal, or sexual). Parents have an automatic victim, should they so choose to abuse their own children. Children cannot leave and are almost automatically reverent and loving towards their parents no matter what. They are weaker and smaller than parents and rely on them greatly.

A manipulative romantic partner will often choose people who are most open to being manipulated. They will choose partners who are emotionally vulnerable and have low self-esteem because they are more malleable—in their vulnerability these victims may already be more desperate for affection, and so more susceptible to the manipulator's tactics. For example, a victim of childhood abuse may be more susceptible to falling in love with a manipulative partner. Someone who is lonely or down on their luck may also become involved with someone emotionally manipulative.

If someone is desperate enough for love and approval, they will take it from anywhere. Manipulators can almost smell weakness in their victims. They want someone who is incapable of standing up for themselves, who is needy and desperate for attention. This is why once they find their vulnerable victim, they attempt to isolate them. The manipulator may nurture material, financial, and/or emotional dependence in from their victim in order to make it harder or even impossible for them to leave. A victim who has been isolated may feel that they cannot reach out to old friends or family for help because they have neglected those relationships in favor of the manipulative partner. They may also be unable to leave because they are financially dependent on the abuser—maybe they are married to each other and if the victim leaves, they will have no place to live or no food to eat.

Knowing the most common tactics of CEM and how they operate is extremely important. Emotional manipulation is present in *many* relationships, and it is one of the most insidious facets of dark psychology because it so easy for an abuser to get away with. Hopefully, this chapter has shed light on what CEM may look like in your life. Maybe you have experienced it in the past or are currently being subjected to it in a relationship you maintain. If you find yourself constantly on the receiving end of these tactics, constantly worrying that you are about to lose someone's love or affect—meaning that your partner or friend is manipulative—stick to your guns. They will try convincing you that you cannot trust your eyes and ears, that your opinions do not count. Do not fall for this. You can think for yourself, despite that a covert emotional manipulator would like you to think otherwise.

Chapter 3: Cover Emotional Manipulation, Part 2

Now that we know what CEM is, we can look at some ways it can be implemented on larger, more damaging scales. Mind games, hypnotism, and brainwashing are the most extreme forms of manipulative control that can result from CEM. These types of CEM tactics are more extreme than those described in the previous chapter and bend the reality of the victim even more than the first tactics we introduced. Mind games, brainwashing, and hypnotism come close to disarming a victim of agency and rationality. If these tactics are successful, the manipulator will have a victim who obeys their every command without much cajoling or persuasion needed.

Mind games

Mind games are a small-scale version of CEM, so they usually occur between two people, or one person turning two people against each other. The objective of a manipulator's mind games is to control your thoughts or actions using passive-aggression.

An example of a mind game is as follows. Michael has a disagreement with his friend José. Michael wants to go out to a bar with José, but José wants to go to the happy hour his friends invited him to at a different pub. In order to resolve the situation, José suggests that Michael join him and his work friends at happy hour, so that José can see Michael and also honor his plans with his coworkers. Michael however, wanted to spend one-on-one time with José because they have not seen each other in a while. Instead of explaining his feelings, Michael turns down José's invitation and tells him, "It's okay, I think I'll sit this one out. It's clear your work buddies are more important than me, your friend since *middle school*."

Because of Michael's comment, José feels terribly guilty. He thought he was helping the situation, because he would get to see José and get to honor his plans with coworkers, with the added bonus of introducing his coworkers to a dear friend of his. Here is the important part of this story—José does not, in reality, have anything to feel guilty about. Michael was playing a mind game in order to get what he wants or simply to make José feel guilty so he would be more likely to acquiesce to his requests in the future. By feeling guilty, José fell for Michael's mind game.

This is only one example, but mind games can take many forms. Gaslighting, invalidation, and reinforcement can be strategic pieces in a mind game. Think of it like chess, except the victim does not know they are participating in a game. The manipulator has many pieces at their disposal, such as common CEM tactics and circumstantial factors (whatever triggers their irritation or anger), and they use these pieces accordingly to manipulate others.

Although directly expressing feelings in an open and honest conversation is usually the best route to take in a conflict, people who play mind games actually have a lot of trouble with this. They may have grown up in emotionally repressive households or feel afraid of causing conflicts. Playing mind games often feels safer to the manipulator, who knows their victim will have trouble holding them accountable for their CEM tactics.

The best way to handle someone who plays mind games is to address them directly. Do not try to gain the upper hand by using CEM tactics. Instead, address the manipulator and say, "I don't like what you're implying," or, "It seems like you're angry. Can you explain to me what is bothering you? I can't help this situation if you don't communicate with me." In other words, be the bigger person. Sinking to the manipulator's level can leave both of you feeling frustrated and angry and make the problem even worse.

Hypnotism

When a manipulator hypnotizes you, they will most likely not do so by swinging a stopwatch before your eyes and pulling you into an irresistible trance. Hypnosis is a state of trance where a person is relaxed, more prone to hyper-focus, and more open to suggestion. A hypnotic trance can be caused by many things, particularly something with a monotonous and repetitive element—things like a very long drive down an empty road, watching a faucet drip or a candlelight flicker, or meditation.

Hypnosis can actually be a very useful therapeutic tool for the physically or psychologically ill. Using the power of deep relaxation and suggestion, an educated therapist can relieve pain in a certain part of the body or help a patient with chronic pain or physical discomfort, such as chemotherapy induced nausea. The scientific application of hypnosis began in the eighteenth century with Dr. Franz Mesmer. Her was a German physician who refined and tested hypnosis on his patients in Paris and Vienna. The famous Sigmund Freud also used hypnosis, to relieve his patients of childhood trauma and uncover repressed memories. Hypnosis has even been used as part of a treatment for social anxiety and as a weight loss aid!

A master manipulator can create circumstances to lull you into a trance or may generally take advantage of a relaxed state you already happen to be in. Perhaps they will make a request of you after you have had a bit too much to drink. They may even create ambient in the form of dim lighting and speaking softly to you while you are already sleepy and tired. Once a person is relaxed and more open to suggestion, the manipulator can strike. They can possibly get sex from you or change your mind about something. Afterwards, you may think you behaved out of character, but have no inkling that you were manipulated in any sort of way.

Those most susceptible to trance tend to be high in empathetic traits. Once someone is in a trance, time seems to pass very slowly or very quickly. They may be hyper focused on a long, complicated story the manipulator is telling. The high suggestibility and cooperation of the victim not only allows the manipulator to get what they want in the short term, but it also creates an enduring pattern of compliance from the victim.

If the victim and manipulator are in a romantic relationship, a trance will frequently take advantage of all the love hormones coursing through the target's veins—oxytocin, dopamine, cortisol. Exposed to these hormones and feeling more bonded to their manipulative partner, the victim feels more bonded to their partner. This attachment fosters

33

feelings of trust, such that the victim will let their guard down around their manipulative partner.

While not everyone you feel relaxed with is trying to lull you into a trance of manipulation, it is important to be on the lookout. If a new partner or friend asks a favor, *pay attention!* A good rule of thumb around any partner is "if it seems too good to be true, it is too good to be true." It is okay to take it slow in a relationship and maintain boundaries—if someone does not respect this wish, there is no reason to continue seeing them.

Brainwashing

This is one of the most famous large scale CEM tactics. We hear about it happening in religions, cults, oppressive governments, and captive kidnapping victims. It is an intense form of social influence that can change someone's behavior and thoughts without his or her consent, and often against their will.

Brainwashing requires the manipulator's total control over their victim, which is why is often requires total isolation of the victim such that their sleeping, eating, and basic needs are interrupted. The complete control required to brainwash someone is exactly the reason it occurs in cults and prison camps. In these settings, leaders have unfettered access to their vulnerable victims and can carry out their brainwashing techniques. In addition, those who join cults or are in prison camps are ideal candidates for brainwashing—they are vulnerable and because of their circumstances, are already prone to trying to find new ways of thinking. Due to the victim's circumstantial flexibility of thought, brainwashing can take effect.

After the Korean war in the 1950s, Robert Jay Lifton studied American soldiers who had been held as prisoners of war in Korea and China. He figured out that the men had been subjected to a process that started with breaking down their identity and ended with changes in their beliefs and thoughts. In addition, the sleep deprivation and malnutrition of the prisoners frequently facilitated this process. Under these circumstances, the POWs's critical thinking skills were seriously degraded. Almost no one can think on their feet under those circumstances, so they are more vulnerable to brainwashing techniques. Lifton identified ten steps of brainwashing from studying these men.

1. Assault on identity
In this step a leader tells their victim their identity is not valid—the prisoner is not who they think they are. In a cult, this may sound like, "Those who are not in our group are bad for you. You must separate yourself from them and devote yourself to our worthy cause. You do not belong in the outside world." This requires that the manipulator knows, at least to some extent, the core beliefs and identity of the victim. Once they know this, they can attack it, and make the victim begin to question and deny their former life.

2. Guilt
Once the victim's identity has been disturbed and confused, the manipulator can start using guilt as a weapon. The manipulator might tell the victim that their old identity is bad and sinful. During the guilt step, the manipulator will criticize the victim for just about anything, from breathing to loud to the job they used to hold. This constant criticism leads to guilt and shame in the victim—they really do begin to feel like everything they do is flawed, and they that need to correct themselves.

3. Self-betrayal
Now that the victim feels terrible guilty and ashamed, they can agree with the manipulator that they are bad and must change. Here, the manipulator may threaten physical harm or continuing mental abuse in order to make the victim comply. The victim just wants it to stop, so they will agree to denounce their family, friends, beliefs, or whatever else the manipulator may insist upon. In other words, they will betray their old beliefs and identity.

4. Breaking Point
Once the victim's identity has been severely disturbed and they feel terrible shame about who they are as a person, they reach their breaking point. The breaking point can include some serious psychological disturbances—they do not know what is true anymore, who they are, or what is happening to them. This is the point at which they are most vulnerable to having their identity molded by someone else. The victim

35

just wants some answers and is desperate to know who they are and what is happening to them.

5. Leniency

During leniency, the manipulator offers a helping hand. The victim has reached their breaking point, so the manipulator offers a solution and easy answers to resolve the anxiety and distress affecting them. Continuing the cult metaphor, we can expect a leader to say something like, "It's okay, I'm here and I can help you. I've seen this before and I've helped it," or maybe they will offer their victim salvation and comfort. During leniency, the victim feels some fleeting comfort and relief from the effects of the breaking point. The manipulator will not seem so bad, and may even appear to be a savior of some kind.

6. Compulsive confessing

The victim will begin to confess compulsively once they have experienced leniency. Compulsive confessing starts because the victim never wants to experience their breaking point again, and tries to attain and prolong episodes of leniency from the manipulator. When the victim believes they have done something shameful or wrong, they will confess it to the manipulator in hopes of forgiveness or more leniency.

7. Guilt channeling

When steps 1 through 6 have been going on long enough, the victim will stop knowing exactly what they feel guilty about. They have a general sense of shame and wrongness about themselves. The manipulator knows this and takes advantage of it by attaching the victim's newly imposed belief system to that guilt to make them increasingly compliant. When guilt is being channeled, the victim will associate their old belief with guilt and pain, and the manipulator's commands with salvation and relief.

8. Releasing guilt

The manipulator convinces their victim that it's their former beliefs that are wrong, assigning an external cause to the victim's pain. The victim comes to understand that they can end their own pain by fully dissociating themselves from their old belief system. Here, the victim denounces their old identity, leaving room for the manipulator to offer up a new one.

9. Progress and harmony

In this stage, the manipulator shows their victim a path to being "good"—"follow me, and you won't ever feel as badly as you did before." The manipulator will stop trying to destroy the victim at this point because this stage has already occurred. Without an identity and with a lot of overwhelming shame, the victim will believe in the promises and dreams of the manipulator and follow them into their way of thinking.

10. Rebirth

The victim fully chooses the path of the manipulator. Avoiding the old identity they believe led to their guilt and breaking point, the victim fully embraces the progress and harmony offered by the manipulator. They have a new identity now, and it involves following the wishes of their new leader.

It is important to recognize however, that brainwashing is relatively temporary if the complete isolation of the victim is interrupted. It is thought that although the victim's identity appears to have been completely decimated, it is still there inside the person. It only seems to have disappeared because of brainwashing tactics, but as soon as the victim feels (either consciously or unconsciously) that they are out of danger from the abuser, their old identity will begin to resurface.

One of the most famous cases of brainwashing has been immortalized by the Manson family. In the 1960s, Charles Manson gathered a group of young women, many with troubled pasts behind them, to join him in what he called The Manson Family. The Manson Family was a cult run by Charles Manson, whose followers were made to believe they were reincarnations of the original Christians and that Manson was the second coming of Jesus Christ.

Having convinced his followers of his spiritual relevance and replacing their old identities with that of members of the Manson Family. Manson often distributed LSD to his female followers, had sex with them, and convinced them to commit petty crimes, leading up to him commanding them to commit murder. In fact, the Manson Family killed actress Sharon Tate in 1969 under Charles Manson's command.

Ultimately, he received life in prison, as did his followers who actually carried out his heinous commands.

Chapter 4: The Dark Triad

There are many ways to describe the cruel and inconsiderate among us. We can say they are mean, callous, awful, immoral, rude, depraved, unfeeling, heartless, and shady. We can talk endlessly about the qualities about the worst among us, but in the science of psychology, three qualities have emerged that best describe these sorts of people. We call these qualities "The Dark Triad." The dark triad consists of narcissism, psychopathy, and Machiavellianism.

The dark triad is known to be the base of a lot of bad behavior, including lying, cheating, manipulation, impulsivity, and even murder and rape. It can be thought of as both a set of personality traits which can exist at varying levels in different individuals and also a device used by those high in these qualities to try to get away with mistreating others in all sorts of ways to satisfy themselves and get what they want easily and quickly.

The operative word here is quickly—while those whose personalities strongly exhibit personality components of the dark triad may get what they want often times, their relationships are strained, destructive, and fleeting. Naturally, those around them often catch on to their ways and, like a parasite, they need to find a new person or people to victimize. Now that we have some basic information, we can go into more depth about the three components—narcissism, psychopathy, and Machiavellianism.

Narcissism

At its most basic, narcissism describes a sense of extreme entitlement, lack of empathy, and excessive admiration of oneself. The word comes from the Greek myth of Narcissus, a young man who was so beautiful that he fell in love with his own reflection. He was callous and condescending towards those who loved him and drove some to commit suicide to prove their undying admiration of him. There are many signs an individual is narcissistic, and you have most likely met someone who displays this personality trait.

One of the most obvious signs of a narcissist is an excessive preoccupation with how they are perceived by others. They may spend an excessive amount of time grooming themselves and constantly presenting themselves in a light so positive that it treads on dishonest. The narcissist wants to be seen as a fabulous human being, constantly living it up and showing off their success and importance. They may exaggerate their achievements, social climb, or name drop about which important people they rub shoulders with.

In addition, the narcissist is an arrogant person who believes themselves to be more capable, important, and worthy than those around them. They are often exploitative and lacking in empathy, which means that they will use others to get what they want, with no mind that it may be hurtful to the victim. Narcissists are able to do this because they view others as extensions of themselves and are unable to fathom that others have priorities that are dissimilar to their own—no favor is too big to ask for, and the narcissist's self-centeredness makes them believe that they are justified in their actions. The narcissist believes his or her needs are above those of others—why *shouldn't* others be extra considerate of them.

Think you've seen anger? Just wait until you meet narcissistic rage. Narcissistic rage is the outcome of a narcissistic injury. A narcissistic injury afflicts a narcissistic person when their grandiose opinion of themselves is challenged or shown to be faulty. For example, a narcissistic injury can come from being rejected by a potential romantic partner or getting turned down from a job. Having this easily triggered response to rejection and disappointment frequently is the result of a childhood trauma, such as a neglectful or abusive parent. The child, who senses that their parent does not love them, developed a grandiose persona in order to hide their deep feelings of inadequacy and shame, and to convince themselves that they will be invulnerable to such suffering at the hands of another ever again. Essentially, the narcissist is constantly trying to cover up how insecure they really feel by pretending they are the greatest, most fabulous and accomplished human being of all time.

Once the injury occurs, the narcissist may fly into what is known as the narcissistic rage. They will be unable to regulate their emotions and actions. The actions resulting from narcissistic rage can range anywhere from the silent treatment and temporarily withdrawing from others all the way to physical violence and serious abuse. A narcissistic rage occurs because the narcissistic injury is simply too much to bear. To the narcissist, it calls into question how great they actually and exposes them as imperfect beings.

There are many telltale signs of a narcissist and knowing some of their common behavior can make them easier to spot. For one thing, they will take credit for good things that happen to them, and blame bad outcomes on others, no matter what the reality of the situation is. If they get a bad grade on a project, they will insist that the professor has it out for them or that the grading process was unfair. If they have a good outcome, say someone of their preferred sex being friendly, they may insist this person was flirting with them. The narcissist wants to bend every story to present themselves in the most positive light and will not entertain any possibility that they may be wrong about something.

A narcissistic person is also obsessed with perfection. Not only do they hold themselves to high standards, which they often believe themselves to meet, but they also hold entities external to themselves to such a standard. The narcissist expects the people around them to behave perfectly, for events they attend to be perfect, and their circumstances to be perfect. They will become irate if they feel others have not met their expectations, even if they are unreasonable.

Another sign you may be dealing with a narcissist is that they speak in extremes about those around them. For example, they may profess how "special" you are and how much they love you one day, but as soon as you irritate them, they will disparage, insult, or neglect you. Despite a close relationship, a narcissist will always seem fairly uninterested in you as a person. You may tell them you had a bad day, or an interesting story about your day, and they will respond by talking about themselves. We have all had conversations like this—it's almost jarring. There you are, drinking coffee with a friend and believing both yours and your friend's needs hold equal weight in the conversation, when they suggest otherwise by talking about themselves nonstop. They will ask you few questions about yourself and if they do, they seem to lose interest once you being to reply. In short, what's the biggest sign someone is a narcissist? A narcissist will make you wonder if their life motto is "It's all about me!"

Psychopathy

We often picture a psychopathic person to be a serial killer or career criminal. In fiction, Patrick Bateman of American Psycho is seen as the quintessential psychopath—charming, brilliant, and unfathomably evil. Most psychopaths though, will seem pretty normal to us. They are our coworkers sometimes, have been our classmates, and maybe even our lovers and friends.

Psychopathy is referred to as Antisocial Personality Disorder (ASPD) in clinical settings. Psychopathy can exist along a spectrum; it is not an all or nothing quality. If someone were to take a personality test, they may score significantly higher than the population average on psychopathic tendencies, but may still fall short of the necessary criteria for an ASPD diagnosis or may not exhibit antisocial behaviors sufficient for a diagnosis.

So, what characterizes psychopathy? First of all, psychopaths seem normal. They can be perfectly pleasant in conversations and give no hint about who they truly are. Underneath the normal exterior though, a psychopath is wicked. The psychopath lacks conscience, empathy, and remorse. Because these qualities are absent, they are manipulative, self-serving, and exploitative. Some even become criminal.

Another quality which defines psychopaths is a very high sensitivity to reward—when they want something they want it *badly*, and they will do whatever is necessary to satisfy themselves. Many psychopaths are promiscuous and have many one-night stands. Being extra sensitive to reward combined with callousness and insensitivity means that psychopaths do not care about who gets hurt when they seek whatever appeals to them at the moment. Speaking of rewards, psychopaths will frequently use others to get what they want. They are keen to develop

42

intimacy and trust, but once the main goal has been achieved, the psychopath discards the person they used, sometimes leaving a trail of emotional or financial devastation. Most psychopaths do not get into treatment for the ASPD. Not only do they believe there is nothing wrong with them, but their traits seem fairly fixed. Therapy and medication do not help change their thought patterns or often sadistic methods of controlling others. Consider yourself lucky if you have not been affected by a psychopath. They often wreak havoc on the lives of those they get close to.

In general, psychopaths will often seem to lack emotion. If a tragedy occurs they may seem impossibly unaffected. They are also practically fearless compared to the rest of us—they are afraid of neither getting hurt nor getting caught. Overall, their emotions are shallow. They may enjoy someone's company, but they do not really care about this person. The psychopath often lives for pleasure and power—human connection and emotion means little to them.

Like narcissists, the psychopath also has a hard time accepting responsibility. Because of this and their lack of fear, they are often reckless and irresponsible. Not only do they behave irresponsibly, they also insist that whatever they have caused is not their fault. Eventually, even if a psychopath is forced to accept blame, they will seem not to care. They do not see their irresponsible ways as an indictment of their skills, character or ability. They see no reason to change because *it's always someone else's fault*.

Last but not least in the most important traits to look out for is the psychopath's intense selfishness and egocentricity. The psychopath often lives a parasitic lifestyle, which is to say they use others to meet their own needs without thought about how this may affect the victim being bled dry. What does this look like? A psychopath may get close to you and then constantly ask you for money, whether or not they have enough of their own. If you are married to a psychopath, you are probably the one who constantly cleans up the house and cooks dinner unless your psychopathic spouse sees incentive to complete those tasks. Often, this is how psychopaths destroy lives. They may have children with a partner who feeds and cares for them and abandon this family eventually. They often take and take and take until their partner is completely broke and financially destitute. This is the parasitic lifestyle at play—the psychopath will suck your blood without you even noticing until you have none left. Once there is nothing for the parasite to take, they cut and run because you have nothing left to give them. It is estimated that up to twenty five percent of incarcerated individuals suffer from ASPD.

Machiavellianism

Before we get into Machiavellianism, let us understand the word's namesake, Niccolò Machiavelli. Nicolò Machiavelli was an Italian statesmen during the Italian renaissance during the fifteenth and sixteenth centuries. He was a diplomat, politician, secretary, philosopher, poet, historian, humanist and playwright. He is known today for his book, "Il Principe," or "The Prince." The book is a deep analysis into the acquisition and maintenance of political power, written so Machiavelli could return to Italian politics from exile and hopefully be appointed a political advisory position by the Medici family. The book was so shocking at the time that Machiavelli was labelled and atheist. Machiavelli advocated for ruthless, cunning, and strategic methods of gaining and keeping political power. He is often credited with the saying, "the ends justifies the means."

Given this introduction of Machiavelli the man, a deeper discussion of Machiavellianism as a member of the dark triad is appropriate. Machiavellianism includes low empathy, prioritizing power over others, strong ambition, and exploitation of others for personal gain. Machiavellianism is different from psychopathy because of the Machiavellian's emphasis on exploitation for *personal gain*, whereas a psychopath's very nature is insensitivity and callousness no matter what.

The Machiavellian believes human nature is inherently evil, and that deception is a justifiable way to attain goals and success. They generally undervalue human connection and overvalue wealth and power. The believe depending on others and cultivating meaningful emotional relationships is a worthless endeavor. When they manipulate or exploit others, they believe they have acted with reason and can justify their actions. They will do something terrible to complete a goal and when confronted, they will say, "Hey, I got the job done, right? It all worked out."

So, how do you know you're dealing with a Machiavellian? The Machiavellian is notoriously low on empathy; human connection always comes second to achievement and personal gain. To the Machiavellian, people are often conduits to other things—money, power, sex, or whatever else may seem worthwhile to achieve. Machiavellians are known to lie and exploit when necessary in order to get what they want.

Another common quality of Machiavellians is their penchant for strategy and calculation. A Machiavellian is good at sizing up others. They can read the room so to speak, and are perceptive of others' thoughts, feeling and weaknesses, despite the low empathy that accompanies Machiavellianism. Due to this calculating nature, these people tend to be patient. They are constantly collecting information and analyzing it to use to their best advantage. They know how to plan and wait for their rewards.

The demeanor of a Machiavellian often falls into one of two camps. They either seem aloof and emotionally distant or charming and friendly. Note that both of these demeanors may be present in the same person; someone may be charming and friendly but reveal so little about themselves that you may become suspicious or realize well into a relationship of any kind with the Machiavellian that you know little about them. This is deliberate, as the Machiavellian generally prefers not to share their true intentions with others.

With respect to their morals, Machiavellians are unlike psychopaths. While the psychopath simply lacks morals, the Machiavellian's are scattered, inconsistent, and ill-defined. The Machiavellian may claim to have certain ethical principles they value highly, but they are certainly willing to ignore them if they can justify doing so. Generally speaking, they have little respect for humanity as a whole. They think it is inherently evil, or at the very least not good, and are usually cynical.

How to Spot These People

The dark triad can take shape in numerous ways. Generally, the actions that result from these qualities can have a seriously damaging effect on others. All traits of the dark triad have one important thing in common —they lead the narcissist, psychopath, or Machiavellian to believe other people do not matter as much as themselves. Because they believe this (consciously or unconsciously), they consistently place their own needs above the needs of others, often being hurtful, harmful, and inconsiderate in the process.

When it comes to the specifics of how a Machiavellian behaves, you have probably encountered a Machiavellian leader before. They may be a politician, a boss, or a high school mean girl. Your Machiavellian leader probably attempted to inspire fear and respect among subordinates. They wanted admiration but not as much as they lusted for loyalty and fear-induced deference from others. They were also probably ruthless in their question for power; perhaps their ascent required humiliation or betrayal of someone. Maybe your boss used some dirty tricks to get their job, or the high school mean girl spread a vicious rumor about a social rival to eliminate her as a threat or competitor for social capital.

Psychopaths, while similarly lacking in empathy, tend to be a bit more pleasure-driven than Machiavellians and may be a little bit less calculating. Psychopaths are not reliable or predictable per se, but most engage in some pretty typical behavior for their personality.

They tend to be promiscuous and enjoy casual sexual encounters. They are not above lying or using sneaky seduction tactics, including dishonesty, in order to achieve this. More importantly, those who commit violent crimes, regardless of whether they are sadistic, are more likely to be psychopaths. Why? Because psychopaths lack empathy and are incapable of caring that they may hurt another human being. In addition, they have low impulse control. If a psychopath gets angry enough, they may harm another human being simply because their rage drove them to do so, and they have no empathy serving to slow them down and reconsider the consequences of their actions.

46

Psychopaths are generally as manipulative as narcissists. They will engage in many CEM tactics like guilt tripping and gas-lighting to get what they want.

Sadism

Sadism is a trait common among those who are high in narcissism, psychopathy, and/or Machiavellianism. Sadism is the tendency to find enjoyment in causing pain to other living beings, human or otherwise. While sadism is commonly associated with sexual pleasure derived from inflicting pain on another human being, it can certainly be non-sexual.

Sadistic individuals are low on empathy, which is why they would not have the same internal cringe as a non-sadist when they inflict pain. They are unable to feel the secondhand pain they cause to their victim, so they do not get the twisted, nauseous feeling most of us would experience if we were to hurt an innocent person.

Usually, when we imagine a sadist, they are a murdered slowly torturing their victim before finishing them off. This is not the case in everyday life though. Plenty of sadistic individuals do not need to go to such extremes to satisfy their urges. Sadists get off on the power they have over someone else by hurting them. This is why a sadist may seem like they enjoy humiliating others in person. They want to watch their victim suffer.

For example, a sadist may also create problems at work or in their social circle to watch the rest of the group gang up on someone. Here, the sadist enjoys the difficulty and pain they cause to the individual while also creating unrest and chaos in the group. They like that they can stir up so much pain. They also make mean "jokes" at someone's expense. They like making jokes about their friends', family's, or partner's biggest insecurity to watch their confidence be undermined. Once again, they live to see people feel small and helpless so they can feel powerful themselves.

At their most extreme, sadists can be violent and cruel. They often have a high threshold for disgust, so watching pain does not disturb them. The most extreme sadists tend to be those high in psychopathy. These people are the ones often covered in the news for heinous, bloody crimes—the serial killers who started off torturing and killing small animals when they were children.

The three traits of the dark triad covered in this chapter—narcissism, psychopathy, and Machiavellianism—represent the worst humanity has to offer. They are the three prongs of a nasty pitchfork of hostility and antisocial behavior. Beware of those you believe to match the descriptions of these personality types, if possible. As the biggest takers and cheaters in the world, they have serious potential to create damage and pain in your life. If you cannot avoid contact with them, at least attempt not to cross their bad side. This does not mean completely foregoing your own needs to placate them but try not to argue with them too much and avoid them when possible. Once again, get out of these relationships as quickly as possible or minimize your contact and dependence on them.

Chapter 5: Shedding Light on Dark Persuasion

Persuasion in general is the act of convincing someone to do something or to change their mind. Persuasion is not always evil or manipulative, people do it all the time. In fact, it can be a good thing sometimes. Say, your friend recently went through a hard breakup—they are sad and refusing to leave their house or socialize. You, a good friend, know that getting out and having fun may cheer them up, so you convince them to come join you at an art museum or a cool new restaurant that just opened. To get them out, you had to *persuade* them. You did it with good intentions though, knowing that your friend would need a subtle push to feel better and take care of themselves. This chapter, however, concerns itself with a more sinister side of persuasion.

Dark persuasion is persuasion, but with more self-serving interests or general lack of concern for the person being persuaded. A dark persuader will use all sorts of mental tricks to push you in the direction they want. They may undermine your judgment or ask you for a favor so many times that you give in simply so they will stop asking.

Who Is The Dark Persuader?

How can you tell if you're dealing with a dark persuader? The dark persuader understands your motivations, intentions, and desires to convince you to follow their wishes. The dark persuader will tend not to be transparent. Normally, if you were trying to persuade a friend for good reasons, you would be open and honest about your intentions. The dark persuader however, will make sure the process is opaque. Unless you know what to look out for, you will probably not realize with whom you have been dealing until you are persuaded to do something with little benefit to yourself. The good news is that dark persuaders usually have a set of techniques they rely on and if you know them, you can protect yourself from the dark persuader.

Dark Persuasion Tactics To Watch Out For

Dark persuaders usually have a handy set of tricks to get you to agree to whatever it is they need for themselves. They often obfuscate, keep secrets, manipulate, and even coerce and intimidate. Knowing what dark persuasion looks like can help you avoid it yourself.

The Long Con Strategy

The long con is a bit like what it sounds like—when the persuader takes their time learning all about their target and earning their trust. Once again, earning someone's trust is part of any normal, healthy relationship. In the long con though, this gaining of trust is for more nefarious purposes. The persuader wants to learn all about their target in order to use this information to serve themselves.

The long con involves building rapport with the target and gaining their approval. This makes the target lower their defenses; they have built what they believe to be a bilateral cooperative relationship with someone reliable and interested in their well-being. This works because gaining someone's trust requires that they have a positive opinion of the persuader. The manipulator would have no chance of successfully persuading someone who does not have at least an inkling of trust in them. Gaining someone's trust makes it more likely they will do favors and such for the persuader, and the more time the persuader spends gaining their victim's trust, the larger the favors they can ask for. Think about it, you may do a coworker you don't know very well a favor by picking them up a cup of coffee on the way to work. Would you lend this coworker five hundred dollars though? Probably not. Such favors we usually reserve for close friends.

While the long con game is common, it's not easy to spot, as building rapport is always a component of building healthy relationships. Usually, you will realize you are being long conned because of *other* tactics the dark persuader will use on you.

Graduality

A dark persuader who uses graduality knows very well that they cannot just come out and ask you to pay their rent or commit a crime for them.

They need to create a path of little favors of increasing value to get you to do them big favors.

This may look like a partner who gets you to pay for increasingly expensive things. For example, may one day your partner will ask you to pick them up a soda on your way back from work. This is perfectly reasonable—a soda costs three dollars at most. You love your partner; you have no reason *not* to spend the measly three dollars. The requests keep getting bigger though. Next time, they will ask you to pick up take out. They may ask you to give them the fifty dollars they desperately need. Then it will become asking you to pay their cell phone or car bills.

Graduality works because the victim's standard of acceptability become lower and lower with the increasing stakes of the persuader's requests, and the persuader can refer back to former favors their victim did in order to justify new requests. Once the victim has lent the persuader the fifty dollars, it may not seem like such a big deal to give them one-hundred, or to constantly pay for their meals. If the victim chooses to say "no," the persuader can say, "oh come on! You did it last time, right? And it wasn't really such a big deal!"

This is how graduality takes place—the requests get increasingly bigger, so the victim has little idea that what they will do for the persuader is completely unreasonable and even comes at an expense to themselves.

Masking True Intentions

A master manipulator can hide what they really want in many ways. Masking their true intentions is just another tool, and there are many ways a dark persuader can be opaque about their intentions to extract whatever it is they need from their victim.

A good example of how a dark persuader may hide what they really want is using a classic bait-and-switch. A bait-and-switch is when a persuader presents one request and as soon as the victim agrees, the persuader changes the terms of the agreement or tacks on a bigger request to the smaller request. For example, your mother may ask you to make a dessert for thanksgiving. This sounds easy enough to you. You simply show up to her house a bit early to prepare and plate the

51

dessert, and then the task will be done. As soon as you agree however, she says, "Great! Get to my house at 8 AM they day of and clean up the house and do some grocery shopping too. Can you also take care of that?" See what she did there? The original request was just to make a dessert, but your mother's true intention involved significantly more work than just that. You probably will not feel like fighting back too— she is your mother, after all, and you feel to guilty and awkward denying her request.

Another way a dark persuader may mask their intentions is using some reverse psychology. What does this involve? It is a little bit like CEM. Maybe a manipulative romantic partner wants to move in with his girlfriend. He does not want to ask her about this directly, so he tells her during a conversation one day that he thinks moving in together would be a terrible idea. His girlfriend is stubborn and he knows this, she will ask "Why do you think that? I think we would get along together just fine." The persuader is simply pretending to think this would be a terrible idea, because he knows it will get his girlfriend to argue with him about why it *would* be a good idea. Now that he has gotten his girlfriend to insist moving in together is a good idea, he can suggest they move in together. By pushing his girlfriend in the no-go direction, the manipulator has gotten her to go the way he secretly wants, which is to move in with him.

Although reverse psychology in this circumstance does not seem like a huge harm, it is actually detrimental to building a trusting relationship. The persuader should have simply told his girlfriend directly that he wants to move in together in the name of honesty and openness. Instead, to protect his own ego, he uses a mind trick to get her to suggest what he wanted all along. This ultimately undermines trust and communication, because in this story, the girlfriend is being lied to and the persuader gets away with being sly and hiding what he actually wants. Healthy relationships cannot be built on deception and secrecy.

Leading questions

Leading questions are common sales tactics, and you have probably been on the receiving end of one. Think of a commercial whose first words are, "Are you sick of feeling bloated, tired, and fat?" Now the commercial has your attention and has convinced you that you *should* pay extra close attention to however you feel. Then, the commercial describes a new diet pill that will "change your life" or "make you feel twenty years younger." What you do not realize when you answer "yes" to the question, is that it is totally normal to feel fat, bloated, or tired sometimes! But now, the commercial has gotten you to admit to a negative feeling, and you are seriously considering buying this product.

In general, leading questions are questions phrased or spoken in a subtle, certain way to get you to respond how the manipulator wants. The whole idea is that if a persuader successfully uses leading questions, then the victim will have no choice but to agree to their ultimate request.

Another example is in order—imagine Jessica and Joe are on a date. Jessica asks, "Joe, you're attracted to me, right?" Joes responds in the affirmative, that of course he is attracted to her, otherwise he would not go on a date with her. Jessica goes in for her next questions; "You want to make me happy, right Joe?" Joe says that of course he wants to make her happy. Jessica goes in for the kill now: "Okay, so if that's the case, do you think I could sleep over tonight?" Jessica knows that Joe has a meeting he wants to be awake and well rested for tomorrow, but she wants to have sex with him and sleep over at his apartment.

Joe certainly likes Jessica and wants to make her happy, but he wants to perform well at his meeting the next day. Because of her leading questions though, he feels more uncomfortable saying no to her request than he would if she had not introduced her request with some leading questions. So even though he has a meeting the next day, he agrees to let his date sleep over. Never mind that they could have just rescheduled for a time better for both of them, Joe already felt as though he has said too much to deny Jessica's request.

Authority

One of the most intimidating and effective dark persuasion techniques is misusing authority. Why? Someone is simply more likely to do a favor for someone in a position of power, regardless of whether that person actually has the right to make such a request of them. For example, maybe you are a paralegal and your boss asks you to work

53

extra hours on a Friday night to make some appointments related to his daughter's wedding. This clearly puts you in an uncomfortable situation —normally, you would not mind doing a little bit of extra work. Except this time, it is a Friday and your boss is asking for a favor that is not even work-related. He is your boss though, and you feel as though you cannot deny his request without possibly incurring consequences. Maybe cuts are coming to the law firm and some people will be let go, and you fear that not following through for your boss will result in the loss of your job. In this way, your boss's authority over you has left you feeling as though you have no choice but to work overtime on a Friday and do work that is not appropriate for a paralegal.

Reciprocity

This is another dangerous trick. Like some of the other previously describe tactics, it involves making you feel like saying no is not an option. What is it? Basically, the persuader will give you what seems like a gift. They may take you out to dinner or give you a place to stay the night. Once you have accepted the gift, they will make a request of you. You are more likely to give in to the persuader because you may feel like you *owe* them something. If you seem doubtful, the persuader may even remind you of the nice favor they did you in order to intimidate or shame you into completing the reciprocal transaction they had in mind. Reciprocity is a great example of how persuasion works because it involved one of the most effective persuasion techniques— masking true intentions. Reciprocity usually works because the victim has no idea that the persuader's generosity come with a price.

Reciprocity is actually a common tactic pimps use in order to traffic women into prostitution. This happens when a young woman, usually disenfranchised and hungry meets a seemingly generous man. He will offer her a roof over her head and place to stay, and they may begin a sexual relationship with this man (or they may not). Eventually, the man will tell them that he needs money because he has been so generous to her, and she owes him a favor. The pimp will then intimidate the young woman into having sex with one of his friends for money in order to pay him back for the food and shelter. When she agrees once, the pimp will probably get her to agree to sleep with a few

54

more of his "friends." By now, she has become reliant on this pimp and she cannot leave—he provides her shelter and abuses her and transforms her into a prostitute to rake in money her can take from her.
Dark persuasion is one of the most powerful techniques for a manipulative person to get you to do what they want. Usually, the best way to spot a dark persuader it is to observe how angry they get if you seem as though you will not meet their request. They will likely continue to push and cajole you and may eventually get angry at your lack of acquiescence. In addition, someone has been manipulatively persuading you if you have kept completing their requests with no benefit to yourself, unless it is incidental. A good way to deal with someone you suspect may be self-serving or manipulative it to project an air of confidence and self-assuredness. As mentioned in previous chapters, manipulative people can almost smell weakness in their victims. Project an air of confidence and know-how and develop these qualities in yourself. Remember: knowledge and self-confidence are power.

Chapter 6: Undetected Mind Control

Undetected mind control tactics are the smoke and mirrors of manipulative people and organizations. They are tiny little tricks to get you to buy this, eat that, subscribe to that other thing, and start thinking of something you have never thought of before. It is so subtle and discrete, that we can be completely unaware of it while it occurs, even though we are flooded with these tactics as soon as we look at our smartphones or turn on our televisions.

Undetected mind control is one of the most useful tools of governments, media, and companies. Think about a time you had low self-esteem. You left your house feeling very good that day—at least until you saw an underwear advertisement with an impossibly slim yet curvaceous woman with a guy whose abs are better than you could ever have the time to develop. The couple in that ad looks so happy and sexy. They are *cool*, and they are wearing the brand of underwear in the advertisement. You begin to feel ever-so-slightly insecure the rest of the day after comparing yourself to the two beautiful models. Later that night, you see an ad on Facebook or on TV for this same brand. You remember how cool the ad was, and how you yourself want the happy, sexy life presented in the advertisement. You buy a few pairs of underwear online from this brand by the end of the night.

Undetected mind control can be pretty much anything that gets you to think and do what someone else wants, and it is one of the most dangerous methods in dark psychology. This is because if someone does not know they are under the influence of mind control, they have no power to break themselves free of it and think for themselves about what is actually happening to them.

It can be carried out by one manipulative individual on another, or it can be a large-scale project by a big corporation or government. Individuals who engage in undetected mind control to be manipulative and cowardly. They want what they want, but without having to ask or having to cooperate with the person they are trying to control. When undetected mind control occurs in an interpersonal relationship, the manipulator usually chooses a victim who *needs* something. Someone in need is almost always more open to undetected mind control tactics because having those needs unmet make them more reward focused. The corollary to this is that being more reward focused makes the victim less aware of consequences; they will be more compliant towards the manipulator because they are focusing on the possibility of being relieved of their unsatisfied needs.

Individuals trying to get away with undetected mind control will often use choice restriction to get what they want. Remember, choice restriction is a common CEM tactic. See where this fits in? Undetected mind control in interpersonal relationships is a more subtle form of a lot of CEM tactics. As previously discussed, choice restriction is when a question is phrased so the manipulator will be almost guaranteed to get what they want out of their victim.

Imagine buying furniture with a spouse, and they say, "We are getting this couch or that couch. Choose right now." Here, the spouse makes sure you will choose one of the couches that they would prefer. They avoid asking an open-ended question on purpose in order to limit the scope of your thinking and possibilities.

When the media engages in undetected mind control, they do not need to use interpersonal tools of manipulation—it can reach you through your smartphone, laptop, television, billboards, magazines, newspapers, and radio. The media engages in undetected mind control by enticing you to spend your money on all sorts of products and services. The ad usually isn't really about the product though—otherwise it would be a short informational clip about all of the technical specs of what exactly you are about to buy. Remember the underwear ad? That advertisement was not *really* selling you underwear; that ad was selling you the dream of beauty and affection. The same goes for cosmetic advertisements telling you that the specific product being advertised will make you happy, glamorous, and beautiful. If advertisements did not work, most people would save a lot of money and have higher self-esteem, as they would not see any need to spend money on expensive diet pills or skin creams sold with dubious claims.

Why Don't We Realize It's Happening?

Most people's initial reaction to this news is to argue, "Hey wait! I know when someone is trying to trick me! I am no fool!" You are probably not a fool, but undetected mind control is almost impossible to escape.

Let's zoom in on choice restriction. In choice restriction, all the thinking is done for you. The choices are made available, and all we have to do is choose one or the other. The same goes for what happens when you watch an advertisement for a new product—the person on television tells you a little bit about the product, why you need it, and how it can make you hotter/cooler/richer/taller. Most of the ad is spent proving the latter two points. Sitting in front of the television, practically on autopilot, you are unlikely to think critically about what is being presented to you. All your brain will absorb is "I am flawed. I need to change and I need to have this product in order to get what I want out of life." See what happened? In both choice restriction and watching an advertisement, you did not have to do any of your own thinking, so you simply accepted what was presented to you.

Another tactic common in undetected mind control is complete shamelessness by the parties attempting to control you. They will present what they are doing as though it is bettering the world. Think again of the diet pill advertisements—they show many before-and-after photographs of young beautiful people, who say that when they lost weight, their marriages improved and they received promotions at work. These companies are not just trying to sell you a product, they are trying to sell you a product *by promising you a happier life*, which they convince is only possible by using X product.

Who is most susceptible to undetected mind control? The unhappy, the lonely, the forgotten. Think of your newly single friend consoling herself with some retail therapy and ice cream. She has fallen victim to the ice cream advertisements telling her that ice cream will "make the afternoon so much sweeter" and the clothing advertisements telling her "He won't be able to resist you in *this* dress."

You should be sensing a theme here: the people most susceptible to manipulation and most likely to believe pie-in-the-sky promises tend to be having a hard time and be in need of love, support, and self-esteem. This is why many advertisements prey on insecurities they know most of us have and problems many of us face. They bring up fatigue, or body weight, crumbling marriages and disorganized homes—these are issues no one wants to have that drive many of us crazy, and an advertisement that subtly suggests a product to cure us of these ills will subconsciously register as a saving grace of sorts.

Why Would The Media Want To Control You?

It's simple—the more the media controls your thoughts and beliefs, the more money you spend on just about anything. The companies that control your mind the most are the companies that get the most of your paycheck. In advertising, as previously discussed, this can be manipulating you through the promise of a happier life. But there are other forms of media as well, like cable news. Cable news engages in undetected mind control by providing news-as-entertainment with all sorts of graphics and editorialized stories, and often has a political agenda which is right- or left-leaning. Presenters will often feign outrage or elation just to get you to agree with them, and it works—they certainly *look* knowledgeable, so you see no reason not to take what they say as true.

A news presenter on TV may demonize a current of previous president without providing much evidence about what they are actually doing wrong, for example. So long as they inspire outrage or passion within you, they have done their job. The average American watches almost five hours of television per day—that's quite a bit. This means that we are constantly inundated with images of violence and messages to make us feel afraid and confused. While we watch TV, we often go into a more relaxed state of mind, meaning we are more suggestible and open to agreeing with whatever we see on television. Once we are relaxed, we are more receptive to all the advertisements and messages thrown our way to make us change our beliefs or buy new products.

How The Media Controls You With Images

The two senses we have that are the easiest means for undetected mind control are sight and audition. We are most likely to use these senses to appreciate beauty—we gaze at a lover or beautiful piece of art and find great joy in listening to a great song. We often remember the visuals of our dreams in vivid details, and daydream without vision as well. While these sound like obvious statements, they are worth stating explicitly because the special privilege awarded to sight in how we process the world explains how the media can engage in undetected mind control using images.

In our lives, this can mean subliminal messaging by quickly flashing an image across a TV or computer screen. The flash is milliseconds long, so we are unable to consciously process it, but our subconscious can certainly get an impression from it, and it can influence how we perceive the parts of the screen we *can* see. The image flashed across the screen could be sexual, to convince you a character is attractive. It could be a fearful image, to prime you for suspense building up in a movie's plot.

Generally, mind control by the media using image can be fairly devastating. Remember the underwear ad. We *constantly* are flooded with images of whom and what we ought to aspire to be—if we see these images frequently enough, we begin to compare our own lives to them and are perpetually dissatisfied with ourselves. You can guess where this leads—the constant imagery makes us feel low or afraid, so we spend money or change or beliefs.

How The Media Controls You With Sound

Audition is another extremely important way for undetected mind control tactics to reach us. It works more or less the way sound does, given that sound has the ability to inspire emotions in us because it how most language occurs between people, and because we associate different patterns of sound with certain emotions. For example, a song can make us happy because of its lyrics or its fun beat while the sound of a crying baby can make us anxious or feel concern for the infant.

A famous and fun example is from the movie "Jaws." Every time the shark is about to attack a victim, a specific soundtrack plays and the audience begins to unconsciously become anxious every time that music plays—even though it does not always precede a shark attack.

A funny example of media control using sound occurred in a psychological experiment involving customers at a liquor store. Researchers hypothesized that if they played French music in the store, even at low volume so customers would be less likely to notice that any music was playing at all, would result in higher sales of French wine during the hours that the music was playing. Can you guess how this experiment ended? That's right! The store sold more French wines while they played French music.

Chapter 7: Don't Say A Word—Body Language

Everyone, to one extent or another, has one language in common—body language. Body language is subtle cues relayed by our body about our innermost thoughts, emotions, and intentions, and are often called non-verbal cues. Body language can show up in how we sit, stand, walk, and gesticulate. While our voice may say one thing, "Oh, I'm so happy!" our bodies can convey our true feelings—maybe you were not as happy as you claimed.

Nonverbal communication is much more important than most of us realize. It is one of the first forms of communication we experience, when we are infants. When we are newborns, we cannot communicate or understand speech. Our parents and caretakers understand this, and instead they cuddle us and make frequent eye contact in order to offer us communication through means we can understand. In addition, adults can pick up on how an infant might feel by how much they squirm and how much they smile. As adults, we also take more cues about others' emotions than we realize. For example, we may notice our friend seems to have her back turned toward us a rather large portion of the time on a particular day; perhaps she is slightly annoyed at you or feeling hostile. A woman may notice a man leaning in close to speak to her, suggesting that he is sexually attracted to her. Ever found yourself suddenly adjusting your clothing and hair in front of someone? You might have been nervous about impressing this person, whether you are going on an exciting first date or walking into a job interview.

Intuitively and unconsciously, most of us understand the importance of body language and how we can use it to our advantage. When we walk into a nightclub in a cool new outfit, we may walk with some extra spring in our step with our shoulders back and head up. We feel that we look good so we act accordingly to show others just how confident we feel. Sometime we lock eyes with a friend when someone else says something silly, sharing a moment of amusement. Body language is possibly one of the most forms of communication we as humans have. Without body language, we would have serious difficulty understanding what other mean when they speak and would have a significantly harder time forming a first impression of some. While words can tell us where to be or what happened, body language conveys some of the most important information about the person we are talking to—whether or not they like us, feel attraction, hate us, are nervous, or are lying.

Nonverbal Cues Associated With Sitting

Sitting sounds like a fairly simple activity, which it is. The way we sit, however, can reveal quite a bit about ourselves. If you know what to watch out for in the way someone sits, you will have some insights about their mental and emotional state and how they actually feel about you.

Proximity

Have you ever had a nice cup of coffee on a bench with someone and realized how close they are sitting to you? They are leaning in to hear what you say and seem to have moved closer than they were in the beginning of the conversation. If someone is sitting close to you, this is a sign that they enjoy your company and want to feel close to you (either platonically or romantically). Sitting a little bit far however, or moving away when you move closer, suggests that they do not trust you very much or they do not particularly enjoy your company.

Legs Crossed

Plenty of people cross one leg over the other when the speak. When someone crosses their ankle over their knee and rests is on top, they are dominant and self-confident. In general, there are three body parts someone will expose if they are confident and relaxed; the belly button, the neck, and the crotch. These are vulnerable areas so if someone exposes them, they convey that they feel safe and secure. In contrast, crossing the legs at the ankles, locking them together, may indicate some shyness or apprehension. Crossing legs at the ankle is common in interview situations or when someone may be nervous, like meeting their partner's parents.

The most common way people cross their legs, one knee over the other, can go either way. If someone crosses their leg toward you, they are more likely to be fond of you and enjoy your company. Crossing a leg away from you can mean that they are uninterested in you sexually or want to create some distance between the two of you.

Tapping And Shaking Of The Feet

This is a classic example of fidgeting. Someone who is jiggling their leg on the ball of their foot or shaking their foot is most likely anxious or impatient. This is why we so often see this action during exams or in waiting rooms—they are both circumstances often full of expectations!

Legs Spread

Someone who sits with their legs spread is trying to be dominant. This position takes up quite a bit of space and opens up the bodies. If a man does it to a member of the preferred sex, it could also signal attraction, as he is exposing his crotch area to that person.

Nonverbal Cues Associated With The Arms

Ah yes, the arms! We use them to hug, wave at others, exercise, and dance. The arms are an interesting way our body can speak to others because they are almost like a gateway to our torso, which is a fairly vulnerable part of our bodies. With this in mind, the arms can convey all sorts of information about how a person feels and knowing what to watch out for can be very useful.

Arms Crossed

When someone has their arms crossed in front of them folded in front of their chest, be prepared for a possibly tense conversation. If you ask someone a question and they do this, they may be feeling stubborn, irritated, anxious, or insecure. They may also be trying to create emotional distance from you, putting up a barrier between yourself and the other person. Fear not though, sometimes, this gesture also means someone is thinking deeply about what you just said or asked, especially if the rest of their body language looks relatively relaxed.

One Or Both Hands On The Hips

Standing in this position often exudes dominance and confidence to the point of hostility or aggression. The pointy elbows serving as a barrier to the torso almost scream, "don't come any closer!" Someone who stands with a hand or two on the hips may be trying to come off as confident and independent—why else would fashion models use this pose so often?

Waving The Arms While Speaking

This gesture can go in either direction, emotionally speaking. Someone may wave their arms and wring their hands in either aggravation or excitement. With that said, the person doing this is either *very* aggravated or *very* excited.

Nonverbal Expressions Associated With Fingers And Hand Gestures

We use our hands and fingers for just about anything requiring precision and attention to detail. The hands can grab small objects and move the finger to point at things we see. Babies first experience their own agency through their fingers and hands, just look at strong their little grasp can be!

The Handshake

Let's introduce ourselves—most people would reach their hand out to grasp the other person's and hold it firmly, trying not to be uncomfortably tight while also trying not to hold so loosely that shyness or aloofness is conveyed. In general, someone initiating a handshake with you is a sign of warmth and friendliness. They want to get to know you and look forward to speaking more.

Touching The Nose

Sometimes when you ask a question, someone who is lying may begin touching their nose. This may seem random, but there's some biology facts that back up why this happens. When people lie, the body releases chemicals that cause some of the blood to rush to our face. This can cause some itching of the slightest bit of tingling, and anyone tends to touch areas that feel this way. The liar will not only realize they are doing but also not even register that they have a little itch on their nose.

Hands Behind The Back

The most obvious quality of this pose is how vulnerable it leaves the torso. If someone allows for such vulnerability, take note. Having the hands behind the back can signal submission to another person. On the flip side however, it can also convey confidence, as leaving the torso so vulnerable suggests that someone trusts that they will not be hurt.

Exposing the Palms

Exposing the palms and wrists is a way of exposing oneself. Just think of how sensitive the palms are and how many delicate veins are in the wrist. Exposing these areas conveys more trust and openness than you may realize. If someone expose their wrists and palms to you, they are communicating openness and trustworthiness. By exposing the palms, someone is unconsciously showing you that they have nothing to hide.

Clasping And Fidgeting With Hands

The person who is clasping their hands, rubbing them together, and fidgeting with their own fingers may need a hug. This is a self-pacifying action, meaning that it is an attempt to calm down and relax. Someone who does this may be in distress, anxious, or afraid of something. If you see someone doing this, be friendly to them—they may need it more than they want you to know.

Nonverbal Gestures Of The Head

The face and head possibly convey the heart of our emotions. There is a lot more than a grain of truth to the saying that goes, "they eyes are the windows to the soul." We can tell someone's emotions and interest in what we are saying based on their facial expressions and their physical orientation toward us.

Nodding Up And Down

When someone nods up and down, this signals approval or agreement about whatever you may be saying. If accompanied by eye contact, the person is meaning to convey that they are paying close attention to what you are saying. In general, this is a good sign; someone who listens is being polite and giving you the time and attention that you deserve during an interaction.

Raised Eyebrows

Raised eyebrows are a sign of interest, sexual or otherwise. If someone's eyebrows raise slightly when they see you, there is a good chance they have the hots for you. If it is a friend or more platonic relationship who does this while you are speaking, they could be expressing surprise or shock. Think of it this way—by raising the eyebrows, they are opening the eyes up more, almost as if to show you something in themselves (attraction) or to take in more information (like what you are saying and showing).

The Closed Smile

A big, toothy smile signals genuine happiness and agree-ability, but what about the tight, closed-mouth smile? This type of smile is a little bit less happy. Someone smiling like this may be trying to hide something or may be faking a friendly smile for appearances' sake. Think about having to say hi to someone you do not particularly like; you want to be polite, but it is hard to bring yourself to do so. You may have unconsciously given this person a smile with your mouth closed to be friendly without revealing to much about yourself.

Microexpressions

A microexpression is an ultra-fast display of a particular emotion that flashes across someone's face. It is so quick that an untrained observer is usually unable to catch it. Even the person who exhibited the microexpression is unaware that they did it. The seven universal micro-expressions are contempt, disgust, happiness, surprise, anger, sadness, and fear. These expressions are so primal that they are expressed the same across people no matter where on earth they were raised. An Inuit person's microexpressions will look identical to those of an American person or a Japanese person's or a Haitian person's.

Body Language And Attraction

Very rarely do we find out someone is attracted to us based on their words, at least initially. Sometimes we just walk away from a conversation with a feeling that this conversation was somehow a little bit more flirtatious than most. Perhaps the person made more eye contact than usual or touched our arm at some point.

We often have trouble ascertaining whether someone is interested in us romantically or sexually because some many body language cues can be easy to miss, and we are often unsure of ourselves in romantic situations. With that said, men and women may express attraction through their body language very differently and knowing how the two genders express themselves sexually can be useful and clear up a lot of confusion.

How Women Display Attraction

Often, when women display attraction to you, they do so by showing off the most feminine parts of their body. Keep this in mind when you are scratching your head wondering whether she likes you.

Touching Her Hair

This is the classic movie moment where the male protagonist is gazing into his crush's eyes while having a mundane conversation with her and she tucks some hair behind her ears or twirls a little bit around her fingers. She may also toss her hair behind her shoulder. She does this to draw attention to a feminine part of herself and also as an unconscious grooming technique to look her best for you.

Standing At Attention

this is a woman's sexiest posture, and she is most definitely doing it on purpose. What does it look like? It is all in the arch of her back. When a woman arches her back, she is showing off her breasts and buttocks, making them appear prominent, larger, and perkier. She is doing this to get your attention and show off the goods. Enjoy the view, then go ask her if you can buy her a drink.

Touching Herself

When a woman rubs her neck, shoulders, or legs in your presence, consider yourself lucky! These gestures are an invitation to intimacy sometimes. By rubbing these areas on her body, she is unconsciously suggesting she wants you to touch her too. With that said, do not proceed to pounce on this poor woman. Instead, take these gestures as a small invitation to come closer and get into her space. She will appreciate you taking it slow.

The Gaze
Is she looking at you a lot, and then looking away? If she returns your gaze and holds it when your eyes meet, there is a good chance she is intrigued. Prolonged eye contact between two people is an intense and vulnerable moment. For most people, such a look conveys either aggression and intimidation or attraction. If she keeps looking at you and does not seem to mind all the eye contact, she wants you to initiate contact.

Clothing Adjustment
This one is cute. If she keeps touching her jewelry and adjusting her clothes, especially in ways that expose her body more, she wants to expose more of herself to you. For example, rolling up her sleeves or removing her sweater, even if the room is cold, are signs she wants you to see more of her body. In addition, if it seems like she is fidgeting with her clothes and continuously readjusting, she is engaging in some grooming to make herself as attractive as possible for you.

How Men Display Attraction
Fear not! Men certainly communicate with their bodies too, but in ways that are more assertive than women. Men will often use physical displays of dominance to display their attraction to you. Most male body language of attraction is an unconscious signal of strength and power, unlike women who tend to draw attention to characteristics of their beauty. Next time you want to know whether you should talk to that guy across the bar, think about these tips before shooting your shot.

Foot Position
If a guy is interested in you, he will want to angle himself towards you in one way or another. If his body or face are not turned at you but his feet are, that's a good sign. If he likes you, he will angle his feet in your direction to signal interest.

He Is Comfortable Touching You
Picture yourself on a bench with your cutie when your knees accidentally touch. Does he pull away or let them stay there, continuing to touch? If it is the latter, congratulations! He likes you and craves

your touch. He is comfortable enough to have you in his personal space.

Showing Off The Package

This is *quite* the move. It occurs when a guy stand confident, legs slightly apart, with his thumbs resting in his belt loops or his hands in a similar area. By doing this, he is showing off the goods and showing a more sexual side of himself, drawing attention to his sexual organ.

Preening

Men and women have this in common actually! Like women, men will also unconsciously adjust and fidget with their clothing in order to look their best.

Touching You

Men are sometimes a bit more forward than women when it comes to initiating touch. If he is into you, he may touch your back, shoulder, or knee (if you seem comfortable already). By breaking the touch barrier, he is making it clear that he wants you in his personal space and is thinking about touching you even more later. With that said, if he goes straight for grabbing your but, run away! This man may lack boundaries or feel ownership over you if he gropes you too early.

Looking You In The Eyes

Once again, men tend to be a little bit more aggressive than women when it comes to body language and attraction. Unlike women, who may look towards their interest and then look away, men will attempt to hold prolonged eye contact. They will also check out your body, moving their eyes up and down to more thoroughly drink in the sight of you.

Chapter 8 : Seduction And Dark Psychology

Flirting, at its most basic, is a form of interaction where two people interact closely to convey sexual or romantic interest. Flirting can include all sorts of behaviors. It can be one of the behaviors from the signs of physical attraction in the previous chapter, it can be witty banter, lots of compliments, sitting very closely, and many other sorts of exchanges between two people. Flirting is often a gateway to seduction. Once a person flirts with someone of interest, and they reciprocate interest, the flirting can escalate—it can become more sexual in nature. Over multiple episodes and over time, it may escalate into an invitation to someone's apartment or asking someone out on a date.

So now—what is seduction? Seduction is persuading someone to have sex with you or make them more excited to do so. Seduction is often simply part of attraction between two people, as it sets the stage for the sex to come. It may include a woman wearing lingerie to greet her partner after his long day at work, or a man buying his date a fancy dinner and whispering in her ear how beautiful she looks in her dress. Among good-intentioned people, seduction is a normal, specific mode of communication appropriate for indicating desire and hoping the person of interest feels the same way. Ideally, the process of seduction is never dishonest or misleading. The person being seduced knows what their pursuer wants, and they can have a mutually satisfying sexual encounter or start a romantic relationship.

How does seduction fit into dark psychology then? Seduction can be to help the person being seduced, to hurt that person, or to benefit the person doing the seducing. All three of these motives have one thing in common though; all seduction, to some degree or another, requires at least some affection of the desired person's mental state.

Why Use Dark Seduction?

Dark psychology seduction is often an effective seduction technique because it can make the person of desire feel intrigued and excited. In some ways, it is almost a form of persuasion. At its most ethical, persuasion is beneficial to the person being seduced and the persuader has good intentions. At its worst, the persuader causes harm to their victim and only thinks of possible rewards to themselves. The same goes for seduction.

A person with good intentions may use dark psychology seduction techniques gets the most out of their love life. They harbor no will to harm others, but know how to have fun. When this person decides to marry, it will most likely be a happy marriage, as they have created excitement and joy in their partner.

Someone who seeks to harm through dark psychology may choose to do so because of the thrill they derive of letting someone down so spectacularly. When this harmful person seduces someone, usually a vulnerable person, they feel pleasure in watching the partner's excitement turn into fear and anguish. This person has no regard for the person they have seduced and is often promiscuous, with a long trial of failed relationships and angry exes behind them.

If someone is completely self-serving with their dark seduction, then their results will fall somewhere between those of the good intentioned seducer and of the maniacal seducer. The completely self-serving seducer may cause harm but mostly out of selfishness and lack of awareness. In general, this person will often be dissatisfied because their intentions lead them to neglect their relationships with those whom they seduce.

Using some dark psychology when trying to seduce someone is not innately good or evil. Instead, it simply a tactic that has proven more successful that others. The only absolute truth about this method is that it is an efficient way to seduce someone, that maximizes one's chances of finding someone they actually find attractive and enjoy. With that said, dark seducers are more likely to get what they want *because they know what they want*. Dark seducers usually get the most attractive, most successful partners because they see what they want and go for it. They are not wishy-washy, and they do not settle out of convenience or loneliness.

The Dark Seduction Techniques

There are many techniques to dark seduction, but at the core of this method is creating excitement and joy in whomever you wish to seduce. Be sure to entice this person, make *them* want *you*. These techniques are all about creating witty banter and showing off how fun and attractive you are in a suave, smooth, swoop.

The Friendly Opener

This technique involves doing anything but asking "what's your sign" or "come here often?". In this technique, an open-ended question is best. Something like, "Hey there, could you help my friend and I? We have a disagreement over who the most overplayed artist on the radio is right now." See what's happening? The seduce asked a friendly question that opened the floodgates for a funny, friendly conversation. The person being seduced does not feel overpowered or intruded upon. Instead, a friendly stranger asked an interesting question.

The strength of this technique is that it simply invites friendly conversation without mentioning any sex. It is impossible to be rejected, because this is not even a sexual advance. It is simply a way of meeting a new person and having some fun banter.

This also works because it avoids coming on too strong. The object of your desires is less likely to feel defensive, suspicious, or intruded upon if you present yourself in a friendly, non-aggressive way. You will not seem to overtly sexual or creepy, so this person will not feel the need to avoid you or shut down conversation as soon as it ends.

Show Off (A Little Bit)

This tactic is all about demonstrating, not just bragging about, social capital and success. The first step is to simply look the part—wear a nice, noticeable watch or jewelry. Dress unlike everyone else, as it is a sign of a confident, independent thinker. Another important way to show off is not to seem too desperate for company; show up to a bar with a group of friends, or flirt with *two* women at a time who are friends with each other. This demonstrates to both women that you are not only a bit of a challenge but also that you are a friendly, confident person in general.

Be Mean (But Again, Just A Little Bit)

If the person you are trying to seduce is acting a little bit haughty or clearly playing hard to get, pretend you are about to walk away. They will be wowed by this one because they expected you too keep playing along with *their* little game. Showing that you are not so desperate that you will put up with game playing from them show you are confident and not in need of their attention because you can simply go seek attention elsewhere. Once they want your attention back, you have practically won, because now the person you are interested feels like they are working a little bit extra for *your* attention, not the other way around.

Send Some Mixed Signals

It can work in your favor not to seem *too* interested. Do not pick up their call every now and then. Maybe once whomever you are interested in seems to reciprocate, hold back just a little bit and cut back contact. Why? Seeming just a tad aloof can create a sense of depth about you, leading your target to wonder even more about you or maybe even become fascinated. This is all about creating an air of value about yourself. Everyone wants what they can't have, right? Playing just a little bit hard to get can make someone's interest in you pique.

Give The Ego A Nice, Long Stroke

To stroke someone's ego, do not simply flatter them until you turn blue in the face. Instead, agree with them a lot—go along with what they say, get to know them and come to understand how this person's emotions work. In doing this, you will comply with the person's belief that they are the main character of their own story. Everyone believes this about themselves because it is true; each person, in their own story of their life, is the main character of that story. By playing along with someone else's story of their own life, you satisfy and validate them, making them trust you and enjoy your presence.

Be A Little Bit Taboo

Most people are, at least to some extent, thrill seeking. This does not mean that we all seek out dangerous situations or abuse hard drugs in order to feel alive, but rather that we all crave a little bit of excite, and the taboo inspires this in us.

Another important facet of dark psychology is know that *you miss one hundred percent of the shots you do not take.* Why is this important? A little bit of arrogance and psychopathy is actually useful here. Most people suffer from an overwhelming fear of rejection when they are trying to flirt. They are so afraid in fact, that they will avoiding going after those they find attractive because they fear how much pain they may feel as a result of rejection. The dark seducer knows a secret, which is that there are billions of fish in the sea, and rejection is not all that bad.

Simply put, learn to take rejection—avoiding it simply makes flirting an even more daunting prospect and adds even more anxiety to dating. Instead, flirt enough that you get some practice with rejection. Once you survive it a few times, it will seem way less intimidating. The dark seducer knows a rejection is a blessing in disguise, because it simply frees up time in the future to pursue other, more interested prospects.

Rejection creates resilience and will let you figure out what your flirting and seduction style may be. Some people go for a more structured approach, by asking questions and knowing the emotions to evoke in a specific order in the object of their desires. Others, however, may like to go for it more organically by asking an open-ended question or "going with flow"—of course, projecting confidence and ease throughout the interaction.

While you may have already made up your mind about dark seduction, it is important to ask, "When does dark seduction turn cruel and unethical?" Dark seduction becomes malevolent when it involves dishonesty, deception, and coercion. There are many ways one may wield dark seduction morally dubiously but knowing what this looks like can prevent you from experiencing a great deal of pain.

Of course, not everyone can be lucky in love. Some people were raised in chaotic households and find themselves in dysfunctional relationships as adults because they were not taught as children how healthy relationships function. Others are young, naïve, and impulsive; the prospect of love is so tempting to them that they are willing to ignore obvious red flags about their dates and dive headfirst into sex and relationships.

There is a different type of serial dater though. This person does not seem naïve, and has a string of failed relationships behind them. Many of us know someone like this—an uncle on his fourth wife or a friend who dates men for short periods of time, all of whom seem similarly different and meek, before discarding them and finding the next one. The serial dating dark seducer, unlike a normal person who has simply dated many people, will often take no responsibility for why their past relationships failed. This is the guy who says, "All my exes are crazy," or "I won't break up with her now even though I don't like her. I'll leave her when I line up someone else to date afterwards." Avoid this person. They discard people callously and use dark seduction to either harm others or benefit only themselves.

Another common sign of a malevolent dark seducer is sexual coercion. Sexual coercion is when one person pressures another person to have sex with them using non-physical methods. This can mean a person is pressured, tricked, threatened, or scared into having sex. Sexual coercion can include threatening to end a relationship if someone does not have sex whenever the coercer wants or simply badgering someone into sex after they have already said no.

This form of dark seduction often occurs in situation where the dark seducer has power or authority over the person they want to seduce. For example, a tenant may be late on rent, and the landlord may insist that the only way to mitigate his anger and avoid eviction or a late fee would be if the tenant had sex with him. The tenant may feel extreme pressure because she is in a dire financial situation and cannot lose the apartment which she and her children live in. Thus, she may be coerced into having sex with her landlord, to whom she feels no attraction and does not want to have sex with, in order to keep living in her apartment. Sexual coercion is a sign that this dark seducer does not respect you or your boundaries. If someone uses this tactic on you, separate yourself as soon as possible.

In addition, dark seducers with ill will often like a particular type of prey. Most of these people have a particular type of emotional or material need, and possible an empty space inside themselves needing to be filled with romance and affection. The malevolent dark seducer knows this and uses it to their advantage.

One type of common victim of the wicked type of dark seducer is the prude. The prude is excessively concerned with standards of goodness and morality. This victim goes to great pains to seem perfect—never licentious or overindulgent, the prude wants to maintain a pristine reputation, especially about their sexual morals. One frequent stereotype of the prude is "the good girl." She would *never* sneak out of the house or have a one-night stand. The predator knows this and can sense that this prey is secretly tempted by forbidden pleasure and the possibly of breaking one of their own strict and self-imposed rules. If this predator knows what to do and how to flatter, charm, and *tempt* their prey, they will have successfully seduced them.

The intellectual is another target for a dark seducer. This type is constantly analyzing, weighing, calculating and thinking. They are most likely afraid of rejection and they know they are a bit too nerdy for most people's taste. The predator can pick up the insecurity this bookish prey be harboring. To seduce this type, the dark seducer must make them feel more like a stud than they actually are. Once this happens, the intellectual will be putty in their hands.

Another common prey is the pseudo-loner. Who is the pseudo loner, you ask? The pseudo loner is that person at the bar wearing a leather jacket and combat boots, but is somehow exceptionally sanitary and lacking any tattoos. This person wants to be *viewed* as a badass lone wolf, but in reality they crave intimacy. They want someone to break down their walls and show them affection and interest. A dark seducer can do this by showing interest in this person, asking them about themselves, and actively expressing that they want to transverse all of those careful, excessive emotional boundaries put up by the loner. When a malevolent dark seducer finally gets into the heart of the loner, they can wreak havoc. This person is usually very afraid of heart break, and is extra sensitive to manipulation. The often do not know how starved for love they are until they finally receive some.

While dark seduction can be a useful, ethical way to entice a potential date or sexual partner, note that romance and sex of any kind are domains of life with the potential to cause both parties great pain. While it is important to know when someone trying to seduce *you* may have some nefarious intentions or a sketchy past, it is in your best interest to avoid certain types of people you yourself may be interested in.

Try to stay away from the dramatic type, for example. The dramatic type may also be a narcissist, but one thing is certain—these people will become irate or upset over just about anything that does not go their way. A simple missed call or any perceived slight can set off a serious rage. How can you spot this person? They will most likely be exceptionally self-centered and complain about their friends' flaws frequently. They make a mountain out a molehill and refuse to compromise over what is important. The dramatist will fight over just about anything.

Avoid someone desperate as well. This person is very lacking in self-love and needs constant reassurance and company from their partner, no matter how inconvenient or unreasonable. This person may only be dating you to avoid loneliness. They are not a challenge to seduce and will generally put up with anything you throw at them. They will be clingy and needy, and be prone to outbursts about their insecurities in the relationship. This sort of relationship is fun for neither party involved.

Hopefully, this chapter on the dark art of seduction has enlightened you on how sex fits into dark psychology and has shown you that not all of this field is rooted in absolute evil and maleficence. In general, seduction always takes on a dark hue—it is, after all, about temptation and pleasure. Knowing whom to avoid, how to get what you want, where to draw the line, and how to protect yourself are all extremely useful skillsets when it comes to love. It is important to strike while the iron is hot, but not to play with fire, lest you suffer a bad burn. While seduction may seem like a complicated game of eyes, lips, and hearts, avoid taking yourself too seriously. Romance and sex are supposed to be fun! Take rejections and successes simply as part of the process, and you will enjoy your love life endlessly.

Chapter 9 : Cons Worldwide And The Dark Psychology Behind Them

What is a con artist? A con artist cheats and tricks others out of something, usually money, in order to make a profit themselves. The most successful notorious con artist of modern to is the Infamous Bernie Madoff. Mr. Madoff was an investment adviser and financier who swindled his 4800 clients in the largest Ponzi scheme in world history—he almost made off with about 65 billion dollars.

How did he do it? He gained the trust of his clients, who expected him to invest their money wisely. Once he gained access to their money, he would put it in a bank account as his own. He would lie about the returns he was making on his clients' investments, saying they were producing huge profits. In reality however, almost no client's money was invested. Retirement funds, charities, and pensions were destroyed by Bernie Madoff's actions. How did he keep getting return customers, then? Other than lying about what a successful investor he was, Madoff built relationships with his investors. He touted himself as successful, responsible, and knowledgeable so people would give him their money to invest.

Cons regularly employ tactics like these, presenting themselves as legitimate business men while ripping people off and causing financial catastrophes to them. Much of the time, con men make their escape just before their victim realizes the destruction that has befallen them—by the time the con has taken the money and run off, there may be no route to rectification and no chance of compensation for the victim.

Embarrassment

How do conmen get away with what they do for so long? How do ludicrous pyramid schemes keep attracting customers with seeming impunity? Easily—many of their victims feel terribly ashamed and silly for having had their information stolen. While the prudent, responsible action would be to call authorities, it can be humiliating for someone to admit they were scammed or fool.

In retrospect, many victims of a scam can identify in retrospect each of the red flags about the con man whose promises they fell for. Perhaps the con continuously asked for money or seemed dodgy when the victim began asking perfectly reasonable questions about what exactly was going on. Even in the process of being conned, a victim may have some awareness that the agreement they have with the con man seems sketchy, but they ignore these fears because they focus on the possible reward. The figure that because the con man looks trustworthy, he must be offering a legitimate deal or service.

Appearing Trustworthy

Appearing trustworthy is the most important skill of any con man willing to swindle others out of their hard earned money. It is in their facial expression, their clothing, and how they speak of themselves.

Many con men lie about their past achievements—they will say they were former marines or served in the army, forge diplomas and awards, anything to make you believe that they are a knowledgeable, trustworthy person. Con men know we instinctively trust people who look like they know what they are doing, especially if we ourselves feel a little bit ignorant of a process. Con men prey on this, and use victims' naiveté and ignorance to cheat them.

Con men also use more subtle tricks, such as in their facial expression. Con men know that in order to be perceived as knowledgeable and trustworthy, they must look relaxed and interested in their victim. According to studies, a trustworthy face has high cheekbones, eyes opened wider (as opposed to narrow), with relatively high inner eyebrows. They will use friendliness, charm, and intimacy to make you trust them and believe in them.

Another subtle, nonverbal trick of the conman is to mirror your body language. For example, a con man may take a sip of his own drink when you take a sip of yours, or cross when leg over the other when you do so. This is a successful trick because the victim unconsciously processes this copycat behavior as a signal of empathy from the con. In general, when someone feels that they are empathized with, they will trust the person showing empathy. They feel understood, heard, and paid attention to. To further evoke trust, a con man may also use your name a lot in conversation. When someone remembers our name, we often feel validate and important. We are pleased that a new person we have met thinks we are important enough to remember. It is almost impossible not to have a positive opinion of someone who remembers you name, and the con man knows it. The more he drops your name in conversation and the more special he makes you feel, the more likely you are to trust him and follow him into whatever plan he devises. Using someone's name is even successful when pulling a card trick! Essentially, the card hustler distracts a person by using their name, giving them just enough time to make a card appear or disappear, seemingly like magic.

Conmen cannot simply rely on psychological tricks and trustworthiness to gain your trust. They must also look the part, which is to say that they must dress and act accordingly and meet your expectations as to what a trustworthy person would look like. For example, if a conman is telling you he is a banker and he can invest your money wisely, he will likely not wear a construction uniform and a hard hat. If a person in such attire told you they could invest your money, you likely would not believe them; you would question their credentials and ask them what sort of education they have in economics and accounting. If a conman attempted to present himself as a banker had a great haircut and an expensive looking suit, a victim would be more likely to believe him. Think about it—how often do you actually question whether a surgeon is actually a surgeon? Simply seeing someone in scrubs and glasses, looking studious and serious, makes us assume that they are whoever they say there are, which in this case is a doctor. Conmen know that they must look totally and completely as expected for the job they are expected to do (be it yard work, banking, or closing a sale) so as not to arouse your suspicions.

The Conman And Your Emotions

Once a conman looks and acts the part, the mind games can begin. One of the most important tactics of the conman is getting you to trust and confide in him. The benefits to a conman of getting you to talk about yourself are practically limitless. First of all, asking you many questions about yourself provides the conman with a lot of information about you—they find out how much money you may be willing to trust them with and how gullible or desperate you are. In addition, getting you to talk about yourself gives the conman an inner look at your innermost desires. Once the conman knows this, they know which false promises to make to get you to trust them. With knowledge of your desires and hopes, they can illustrate a fantastic future full of promise and get you believing in even your wildest dreams.

Talking about yourself to someone also gets you to trust the conman because it can make you feel as though you have discovered a new confidante. Someone who really cares, who really understands you. Once you feel this way, you are more likely to keep giving money and time to the conman who promised you success and wealth. You will probably feel some sort of emotional intimacy towards a successful conman because getting you to trust him is all about building rapport and a sense of reliability.

When trying to cheat someone, the easiest target is someone vulnerable. The con man will most likely want a victim who is in financial need or very insecure about themselves. The insecure and financially embattled desperately want a solution to their problems. Someone desperate for cash is more likely to fall for a get-rich-quick scam because the conman offers them a little bit of hope that their problems will be solved easily and quickly if they can follow instructions and hand over a bit of money to the conman. This works on the insecure as well. An insecure person loves the attention they get from a conman, who asks them endless questions about themselves and seems genuinely interested in their answers. An insecure person will feel important around a conman and believe in their promises of success and wealth.

Dreams and weaknesses are the conman's greatest weapon. This is also why they use a victim's greed as a weapon. All of us have *some* greed deep down, and a conman knows that finding out just how badly you want to be wealthy or comfortable helps a conman tempt you. When you become aware that the person you have entrusted with your money may bit at least just a bit shady, the conman will tempt you. They will remind you of the reward to reaped from following through with them. "What about the money?" he might say, "I promise, just hold out and I'll get you what you want." By reminding you of what you want so badly, the conman can get you to stick by him and keep giving him money and loyalty.

Conclusion

Now that you have made it to the end of this book, we hope sincerely that you walk away feeling assured of your skills in spotting possible psychological trick out to get you. Hopefully, you feel confident in your abilities to size up people and situations around you in order to keep yourself safe and secure.

From here on out, resolve to treat yourself kindly by associating with kind people, and being decent yourself. Surrounding yourself with positive people who are not high in dark triad traits or cutting off relationships with those who use CEM tactics can be the biggest favor you ever do for yourself. Finding a group of people with good intentions who are not out to use or abuse you can build up your self-esteem and make you feel confident of your place in the world. No more lying, no more fear, no more "It's my fault I made them angry." Now you have the skill-set to value yourself and call out bad intentions when you see them.

How to Analyze People

The Ultimate Guide to Understanding Body Language, Influencing Human Behavior and Speed Reading People with Emotional Intelligence and Proven Psychological Techniques

Daniel Peterson

TABLE OF CONTENTS

94

Introduction

Congratulations on downloading *How to Analyze People: The Ultimate Guide to Understand Body Language, Influence Human Behavior, Read Anyone with Proven Psychology Techniques*, and thanks for doing so.

The following chapters will discuss techniques that you can use to assess and make accurate judgments about people's thoughts and emotions based on observing their body-language and analyzing the things they say. The book will look at all the basic elements of analyzing people and introduce you to the art of reading people like an open book. You will learn the rules for analyzing people, and you will learn various tricks that can instantly make you a better observer of human behavior.

The book discusses in detail how to analyze people based on the nonverbal signals that are related to the hands and the palms. It teaches you how to tell a lot about a person just by shaking his or her hands. It also explains how you can use hand signals to your advantage when you want to convince people of certain things.

The book also teaches you everything you need to know about nonverbal signals that are related to the face and the eyes. It teaches you how to read facial expressions as well as micro-expression in order to discover the emotions that people try to hide.

The book also teaches you tried and tested techniques for telling if someone is lying to you, or if they are withholding the truth. It also teaches you to analyze the people you date to tell if they are genuinely attracted to you.

The book looks at the different personality types out there, and it teaches you how to identify people's personalities based on the things they say and do.

There are lots of books on analyzing people in the market right now, so thank you very much for choosing this one! Every effort was made to ensure that this book is filled with useful information and insights that can help you improve your life, so please enjoy!

Chapter 1: Understanding the Basics

The human need to communicate predates the ability to speak. That means that we have been using body language to communicate our emotions and to convey our thoughts longer than we have been using verbal communication. We all have a natural ability to read body language; it's just that most of us don't pay much attention to it. The idea that you need to have advanced degrees in psychology to understand non-verbal communication is a myth. You have an inherent ability to comprehend it.

When you were a baby, before you could even talk, you were able to mirror the emotions of your parents and other people around you. From an evolutionary standpoint, the innate ability to read body language is crucial for one's survival. The ability to perceive slight changes in the body language of the people around us is written in our genetic code, so all we need to do is learn to be better observers, and to sharpen our ability to interpret whatever it is that we are observing.

The point here is that anyone can master the art of analyzing people because we all have that natural ability, it's just that most of us don't sharpen it, so it lays dormant inside of us. To awaken the behavioral analyst inside of you, in this chapter, we will help you understand the basics aspects of how to analyze people. When you are done with this chapter, you will have a baseline understanding that can help you start analyzing the people around you, and we can then build from there.

How does body language reveal your emotions and thoughts?

When we have certain thoughts, or we feel certain emotions, we subconsciously convey those thoughts and emotions through body language. Body language is natural to humans and other animals. Anthropologists believe that body language naturally evolved in humans to serve a very crucial social need. The theory is that people (or even animals) in a society are able to get along with each other a lot better if they can be able to detect each other's feelings and make fairly accurate guesses as to what others are thinking.

Since much of our body language is subconscious, it's much more difficult for one to mislead you through body language than through verbal communication, anyone can lie outright about anything, but body language often reveals the person's real thought and emotions, because it's much more primal. A friend can say that he is not worried about a given situation, but you will be able to see the worry in his eyes, his face, and the rest of the body.

Body language reveals our emotions and thoughts because the body is naturally inclined to react to both internal and external stimuli, even when our conscious minds aren't paying attention to the stimuli. If we perceive certain threats in our environment, the subconscious mind will register those threats, and the body will react accordingly. Most of those reactions will be visible to the people around us if they are keen.

When we experience emotions or have thoughts, they tend to affect our facial expressions, our posture, our gestures, our tone of voice, and our ability to maintain eye contact with others. These subtle reactions in our bodies can be either innate or learned. Innate body language tends to be universal; it's the same in pretty much every culture in the world (for example, people who are angry tend to scowl, no matter what part of the world they live in).

Learned body language tends to be specific to certain cultures, and we tend to acquire it during the developmental stages of childhood (for example you probably learned certain postures and gestures by watching your parents or other people around you).

As you learn to analyze people, you will realize that there are certain signals that mean the same thing for everyone, but there are other signals that mean different things in different cultures. The constant fact, however, is that body language is a direct result of one's emotions and thoughts. This means if you understand a person well enough, you can be able to connect the dots and figure out the real meaning of their body language signals.

Why are women more intuitive than men?

There's a lot of misunderstandings as to what intuition really means, but there is a general consensus that women are more intuitive than men. So, it's important to clarify that it's not that women have some sort of psychic ability that makes it possible for them to discern the thoughts and feelings of others. It is just that they are better than men when it comes to spotting and interpreting subtle body language and emotional signals.

There are several research-based explanations and logical theories that explain "women's intuition." One such theory has to do with social power. It argues that in most societies, women have historically had lower social power than men, and so they developed a natural tendency to keenly observe those in power (in this case, men), which made them more attuned to subtle non-verbal cues.

Another such theory has to do with the fact that women are the caregivers in most societies. The theory argues that since women took care of everyone else (men and children), they developed the ability to correctly interpret subtle cues so that they could anticipate other people's needs.

From an evolutionary standpoint, intuition is a great trait for human females to have because it increases the probability that their offspring would survive.

Another research-based explanation for women's intuition has to do with the testosterone hormone. Scientists have discovered that exposure to testosterone at the prenatal stage can predict how intuitive a person is going to be. Women who are exposed to lower levels of testosterone tend to be more intuitive than men who are exposed to high levels of the hormone. Interestingly, the study also found that men who were exposed to lower levels of testosterone than normal seemed to be more intuitive than the average man.

Even though there is a correlation between testosterone and intuitiveness, the fact is that in general, intuition is something that can be learned. Irrespective of your gender, you can learn to be more intuitive and to analyze people. The science says that women may be faster learners than men in this specific area, so if you are a guy, you might be a little behind on the learning curve here, but don't give up!

Universal gestures

Most gestures tend to be culture-specific, but there are a few gestures that are universal. Universal gestures are those that are part of the human biological makeup. In other words, they are wired in us, and they mean the same thing no matter where in the world you go.

Smiling is a universal gesture. Newborn babies have reflexive smiles from the time they are born, and they start having "purposeful" smiles when they are around two months old. There are different reasons why people smile, but those reasons are all cross-cultural. People smile when they are pleased, when they are slightly embarrassed, when they want to reassure others, to convey affection, or they smile in complicity. Some smiles can be fake, and others can be genuine, but even those factors that distinguish between real and fake smiles are also universal.

Shrugging is an involuntary gesture that appears to have the same meaning in all cultures of the world. People shrug to protect themselves somehow. Shrugs can often indicate uncertainty, indifference, embarrassment, or even disdain. A full shrug involves bringing one's shoulders up, pulling the head inwards, and often time, turning one's palms upwards (this indicates that the person has nothing to hide) shrugs often mean "I don't know" or "I submit," or even "I don't understand."

Blushing is a universal gesture that conveys embarrassment. When a person is embarrassed in one way or another, blood flows to their cheeks, turning them red, and they often try to avoid eye contact at that moment. The interesting thing about blushing is that it's an outward manifestation of involuntary reactions that are occurring internally.

Pointing is universally used as a gesture to indicate direction or to stress a point that one is making. There are minor cultural variations in the way people of different communities and backgrounds point; most cultures use the index finger for pointing, but there are few that use the middle finger or even the thumb. In most cultures, pointing at a person (particularly a stranger) is considered rude and confrontational.

It's important to note that even though there are cultural variations in the use of most gestures, the world is increasingly becoming a smaller place and thanks to the spread of western pop-culture to other parts of the world, there are certain gestures that are becoming more universal by the day. For example, the "thumbs up" gesture used to mean lots of different things in different cultures, but thanks to the internet, movies, and TV shows, cultures across the globe are increasingly accepting it as the conventional symbol for approval.

Rules for analyzing people

Analyzing people is both an art and a science. That means that you can understand the meanings of certain non-verbal signals in principle, but when it comes down to actually interpreting what those signals mean, you have to take certain liberties and look at the specific situation at hand. Because of this, it can be difficult to come up with a set of rules or a rigid instruction manual that you can use for analyzing people in all situation.

Ultimately, your instincts are better than any "playbook" when you are trying to read people, so we are going to focus on imparting you with skills that are going to sharpen your instincts. However, before you start analyzing people, there are a few ground rules that you first need to keep in mind in order to increase the accuracy of your interpretation. Here are six rules you should always follow:

Don't read individual gestures

You can learn a lot from the gestures and the body language signals that a person is using, but you shouldn't make conclusions about a person's thoughts or emotions based on just one signal. To analyze people accurately, don't look at individual gestures. Instead, try to observe all the gestures that one is displaying, and you can then infer meaning from the combination of cues.

One individual gesture can have a hundred different meanings. Take the example of a smile. When someone smiles at you, and you jump to conclusions based on that individual gestures instead of looking at the totality of the gestures that the person is conveying, you can easily assume that the person is happy, or interested in you. However, if you pay attention to all the body language signals he/she is sending out (particularly the more subtle ones), you could end up realizing that the smile has a whole other meaning; maybe it's a sarcastic smile or a closed smile (where the teeth are concealed) which could indicate that the person is hiding certain secrets from you.

You should learn to observe and read the totality of one's gestures, a person's facial expressions can show positive emotions; but his/her hands, torso, feet, posture, etc., could be telling an entirely different story. As a body language analyst, you need as many data points as necessary to make a more accurate assessment of the individual's body language.

There are certain emotions and thoughts that are depicted using pretty much the same major body language signals, so it's the minor details that will make it possible for you to do proper readings. When analyzing people, you are like a doctor who is trying to diagnose a patient, and the body language signals are the symptoms; the more symptoms you can observe, the more accurate your diagnosis.

Search for harmony

You want to make sure that there is harmony between all the body language signals that the person is putting out, as well as the verbal signals. Lack of harmony across all signals is often a sign of deception or a sign that someone is hiding something. A person can say one thing, while his/her body language tells you something else. A person can fake a smile, but his posture, arm positions, and legs, can reveal what he/she truly feels at the moment. If there is no harmony or congruence in a person's body language, it always means something is wrong, so you have to pay close attention once you make note of this.

Disharmony can be detected in mismatched body language signals, but one of the easiest ways to spot it is through a person's tone of voice. For instance, you could detect a hint of anger when a person answers your question. Think back to all the times that you have asked people, "How are you doing?" Most people say "I'm fine" in response to this question, but you can tell a lot by the tone of their voice and the body language that accompanies this answer.

They could answer after a slight hesitation, they could use a tone that indicates a slight irritation with your question, they could do it with arms crossed, or plaster a half-smile on their faces to reassure you, but in all these signals, there is a mismatch between what the person says and what you can observe.

You also need to understand that there are people who are practiced at the art of deception, so they may be able to convincingly fake certain body language signals to the point of convincing a novice analyst that their verbal and non-verbal signals are in total harmony. With such people, you are going to need to learn to observe their micro expressions in order to detect disharmony.

Read gestures in the context

As we have mentioned, a gesture could mean a hundred different things, so the context of the gesture is extremely important if you want to understand what it means. When you take certain gestures out of context, you could make serious mistakes in your judgment. With time, you will learn that body language reading is not an exact science, and there are lots of environmental or contextual factors that could cause a person to convey certain signals; as part of your training, you have to learn to identify the contextual elements that affect the accuracy of your readings.

For example, you may have heard that people who cross their arms or legs during conversation are being defensive. While that may be true in many cases, there are lots of other reasons why someone you are talking to would cross his/her arms or legs. If you are in a cold environment, the person could be crossing his/her arms to keep warm. If you are talking to a lady in a skirt, she could be crossing her legs out of habit. If you are talking to a plus-sized person, he/she may be defensive, but you won't see him/her cross his/her legs because it's uncomfortable.

If a man gives you a weak handshake, you may assume that it's because he has a weak character, but in actual sense, it could be because he has arthritis, which affects the strength of his arm. A person may sweat a lot because they are nervous, but it could also be because he has a glandular issue, he ate something spicy, or the room temperature is high.

As you can see, the presence or absence of certain body language signals could merely be the result of special or prevailing conditions. Before you judge the meaning of any body language signals, make sure that you have a full understanding of the context.

Recognize and decipher quirky nonverbal cues

There are people who have certain quirks, which make their non-verbal cues somewhat different from what you would expect in the conventional sense. As we have mentioned, most non-verbal cues are subject to social context. Because of a person's unique experiences, or physiological conditions, he/she may have certain idiosyncrasies in the body, so you have to take that into consideration when you are performing your analysis.

You probably know someone who always looks like they are smiling, or you have that one friend who has "resting serious face." The point is that people look different, and they have different mannerisms, so if you are not familiar with them, you could easily misinterpret some of their body language signals. This fact explains why it is so hard to come up with a standard rule book for reading body language even if you correct for cultural context.

There are idiosyncratic body language signals that are merely habitual. For instance, there are people who use their hands a lot when they are talking. It doesn't mean that they are more open or honest than their counterparts who don't move their hands as much.

Some mannerisms could also be related to a person's training or experiences. For example, a person with military training may have better posture than a person without that kind of training, but it doesn't necessarily mean that the former is more confident than the latter.

This also applies when it comes to tone of voice. When you start analyzing people, you will realize that the sound of their voices is one of the most misleading things you will have to deal with. Studies show that most humans have inherent biases when it comes to judging people based on how they sound; this explains why women with "shrill" voices are often thought of as "unlikable" in political discourse. Unless you learn to overcome such biases, your interpretation of body language won't be accurate.

Try to establish baseline behaviors

If you watch cop shows, you have probably come across one of those scenes where a person is given a lie detector test. After the machine is set up, you always see the detective start by asking obvious questions that have nothing to do with the case in question; the point of this is to establish a "baseline." When you are analyzing a person, you have to do something similar (you won't be interrogating them, but you will be observing their behavior). In psychology, baseline behavior is simply the way a subject act or behaves normally when they don't have a reason to behave otherwise. It's the way a person reacts to garden-variety situations before he/she puts his/her guard up.

Establishing a baseline help you to calibrate your expectations when it comes to a person's behavior so that when they deviate from that expectation, you know that something is off. When you are trying to analyze a person, you have to spend some time with them and observe their mannerism. For example, if it's an absolute stranger, having a conversation about the weather wouldn't set off any alarms in the person's mind, and he won't modify his behavior. You can take this time to make a mental note of how he uses his hands, how he smiles, if he maintains eye contact, his posture, the position if his feet, and so on.

Once you have a baseline of the person's behavior, you can introduce a test to see how the person reacts; a reaction is anything that deviates from the baseline. Any difference in the tone of voice, facial expressions, hand gestures, posture, or leg position has a certain meaning, and you should try to interpret it.

Study behavioral changes that could lead to a decisive conclusion

There are many ways to test a person after you have an understanding of his or her baseline behavior. You could ask them a question, bring up a certain topic of conversation, or introduce some other form of sensory stimulus. In the context of criminal investigations, trained experts can learn a lot just by showing a person a picture and watching the way he or she reacts. If you are analyzing people in your personal or professional life, you can use the same technique in many different ways. You have to keenly observe any changes in the person's behavior that could be conclusive indicators of thoughts or emotions that the person may be having. In subsequent chapters, you will learn about behavioral changes and behavior clusters that could lead you to make certain conclusions about a person's reaction to a given topic or situation.

Tricks to becoming a better reader

Although body language signals are subjective, and there are lots of contextual aspects to consider, there are still some quick tricks that you can use to become a proficient body language reader almost instantly. Here are a few quick tricks:

When you want to tell the difference between a genuine and a fake smile, you have to look at the eyes. A real smile tends to crinkle the eyes. Don't look at the person's mouth; look at the eyes. As we have mentioned, people tend to smile when they are hiding something or when they are anxious. The eyes will, however, show you if the smile is genuine, or it's being used to disguise something. Look straight into the person's eyes and pay attention to the corners; if there are no wrinkles, then the person is smiling to conceal something.

When you are talking to someone, and they cross their arms or legs, it's often an indicator that they are resistant to the ideas that you are passing across. When a person is mentally, emotionally, or even physically resistant to something that is right in front of them, then they tend to cross their arms or legs to protect themselves subconsciously. Of course, as we have mentioned, you have to rule out the possibility that the person is crossing his arms or legs because of its cold or out of habit.

If a person you are conversing with is mirroring your body language that is always a good sign. If you take certain actions and the person subconsciously copies you, it means that he/she feels that there is a bond between the two of you. If you are talking to someone, you can try leaning your head in a certain direction and waiting to see if he/she does the same thing. You can also try crossing your legs, touching your upper lip, or even slowly bobbing your head. If the other person mirrors you, it often means that he/she is receptive to your message, and in the context of a negotiation, it could mean that things are going well.

You can tell if a person is lying by the way they hold eye contact with you. It used to be that lairs tended to avoid eye contact, but because this indicator is common knowledge, many lairs try to beat it. Experienced liars know that people check for eye contact, so they tend to overcompensate by holding eye contact for too long to hide the fact that they are lying. Lairs these days tend to hold their gaze with you to the point that it becomes uncomfortable. Studies have shown that under ordinary circumstances, people in Western nations hold eye contact for 7 to 10 seconds, so anything longer than that could indicate that the person is deceptive.

If a person nods more than usual when you are talking to him/her, it often means that they are anxious, and they are dying for your approval. The fact that a person is seeking your approval could be a positive or a negative thing, so you have to consider the situation at hand or the dynamic between the two of you before you infer any further meaning.

When a person raises his or her eyebrows, it often means that they are uncomfortable about something, people tend to raise eyebrows when they are worried, fearful or surprised. If you are talking to someone, and you observe that he/she is raising his/her eyebrows, reflect back on the conversation that you are having; if there is nothing that either of you has said that would logically cause any fear, surprise or worry, then something else is afoot.

Understanding the limbic brain

The limbic brain is part of the brain that supports functions such as emotional reactions, behavior, motivation, smell, and long-term memory. The limbic brain is a system of brain structures that controls certain behaviors that are crucial to the survival of all mammals. The limbic brain is present even in the less advanced brains (such as those of reptiles) and it controls the sense of smell, but in humans and other primates, it is more involved when it comes to regulating emotional behaviors and motivation.

To be good at analyzing people, you need a basic understanding of how the limbic system works. Because it's responsible for emotions and behaviors, understandings its functions can help you understand how and why people react the way they do in response to threats and other stimuli.

How the limbic system helps you to deal with threats and recover from stress

The limbic system is often referred to as the "feeling and reacting brain." it's responsible for dealing with all sorts of threats. The limbic system has a rather complex structure, and it includes components of the brain such as; the amygdala, the cingulate gyrus, the fornix, the hippocampus, the hypothalamus, the olfactory cortex, and the thalamus. For the purposes of understanding the way the limbic system deal with threats, we will only look at the parts that deal with the threat response process.

The hippocampus is responsible for memory, so it stores a running list of the situations and sensory stimuli that the brain considers to be dangerous. When you encounter a potential threat, the hippocampus will instantly compare that threat to its "registry" of threats and properly identify or categorize it. The hippocampus will then send a high-priority signal to the amygdala, and this will trigger your fight/flight response.

The amygdala activates the limbic system so that it can be ready to tackle the threat. It triggers the adrenal glands to release hormones such as epinephrine, which cause an increase in heart rate and blood pressure. When the heart rate goes up, more blood is pumped into muscles and other organs, and the breathing often increases.

When the limbic system reacts to threats as described, there will be certain physical signs that one might be able to observe in a person who is undergoing such reactions. In our modern world, the threat response could be set off by pretty much anything, including an uncomfortable question. The reaction is usually involuntary, so even if a person works hard to conceal it, you may be able to observe some outward signs if you are good at analyzing people.

How the limbic system relates to non-verbal cues

When the limbic system sets off certain reactions in your brain and body, there are outward manifestations of those reactions. The limbic brain is in charge of your survival behavior, which means that the reactions it triggers are beyond your control, so it's hard for someone to completely conceal those reactions from a keen observer or analyst.

Studies show that even children who are born blind are able to exhibit the same limbic reactions as everyone else, which is conclusive proof that such reactions are hardwired into us. The body language signs of limbic reactions are always immediate, and they are never misleading.

Limbic reactions include things such as pupil dilation, frowns, and plenty of other behavior that we naturally tend to exhibit when we experience certain comforts and discomforts. When a baby sees its mother, its pupils will dilate, indicating that it is delighted. This will happen, irrespective of the cultural context. When that baby turns into a grown up, his/her pupils will dilate at the sight of someone he/she is attracted to. This is a limbic reaction that can't be faked or controlled.

In response to bad news, people tend to press their lips together. People also tend to clench their jaws when they are angry. These are both limbic reactions that you can observe in people even if they are working hard to hide their true feelings from you.

Limbic responses are primal, involuntary, and fast; they happen even before the person has had the chance to think through a situation consciously or to rationalize something. The next time you ask someone for a favor, try to observe him/her closely. Even if they try to conceal their displeasure with a smile or an affirmative statement, you just might be able to catch a glimpse of their limbic response, and it could reveal the truth to you.

How to analyze people via non-verbal behaviors of the arms

The way people use their arms tells a lot about what they are feeling or thinking at that given time. The way we use our arms is so primal that anthropologists have observed similarities between humans and other primates in this area.

In the study of body language, arms are often seen as devices that can expand the amount of space that one occupies. With the use of our arms, we can make ourselves seem bigger or smaller. When a person extends his/her arms laterally, it makes him/her occupy a much larger space, and it can often indicate that the person is showing confidence, either in a casual and friendly way or in response to a threatening situation. Spreading one's arms is a way of saying "I'm big," and it can either show that a person is feeling confident, or he is aggressive.

People also use arms to "shape things" during conversations, and it's normal for us to wave arms as we talk. However, if someone seems to be waving's arms more frequently or more vigorously than usual, it's often an indicator that he/she is excited about something.

Raising one's arms up during conversation could be a sign that the person doing so is frustrated about something. It could mean that the person feels as though there is something weight down on him; the motion of raising one's arms provides him with a certain amount of relief. If one raises his arms as part of a shrug, it could be a sign of confusion.

When a person reaches his arms forward during the conversation, it could mean that he is offering you support and affection, and it could mean he has an underlying desire to touch you or to connect with you in one way or another.

If a person suddenly pulls back his arms or crosses them over his chest during a conversation, it could mean that he has been put on the spot and is feeling defensive.

When someone hides his arms behind his back, it could indicate that they are trying not to be a threat to you (this could be genuine, but in some instance, it could mean that they are trying to hide something that you may find threatening). When one's arms are hidden, the torso is exposed, and that makes the person vulnerable. This could mean that they are submitting to you, or they feel comfortable in your presence.

Defensive arm display

There are many arms displays that could indicate that one is defensive. We have mentioned that crossing one's arms in front of the torso could indicate defensiveness. It means that one is trying to create a barrier between him/herself and an aggressive person.

When one places his/her arms next to the torso and presses them inwards, it could be that they are trying to appear smaller and less threatening to a person or people who are domineering. This arm signal is often accompanied by lowering of the shoulders and looking downwards.

The fig-leaf position is another sign of defensiveness. This is where a person puts the arms close to the torso and clasps their hands over the lower abdomen or the crotch area. This gesture is often displayed when one is trying to appear confident or respectful, but deep inside, he or she feels vulnerable.

Self-hug

The self-hug is often referred to as the self-administered hug. It's done by grabbing one's arms across the front of the torso, and holding onto the opposite elbows, upper arms, or even shoulders (in extreme cases).

The self-hug means that one is feeling the need to be comforted at that particular time. It can often mean that one is feeling a bit awkward in a social situation. If you are talking to someone and they self-hug, it could mean that you have said something that has made the person self-conscious. It indicates defensiveness, or it could mean that one is closed off to your ideas.

Self-hugging tends to remind us of the comfort and the care that we received from our mothers when we were children. As grownups, when we self-hug, it could mean that we need to be comforted by someone, but we are afraid to seek that comfort because it doesn't feel appropriate. If you are good at reading body language and analyzing people, you can look at the other signals that accompany the self-hug and pinpoint whatever is making the person uncomfortable.

Territorial arm displays

As humans, we tend to subconsciously stake some sort of physical claim on objects we believe to be ours. People, particularly men, use the arms in different ways to either lay claim to other people or objects or to intimidate actual or perceived rivals.

Types of territorial arm displays

Putting one's arms up and crossing one's fingers behind the head while leaning back on a chair can indicate a territorial sense of ownership over the space around a person. Putting one's arms on a desk or table and leaning forward can show that one feels that he is in charge, and he wants everyone else to acknowledge it.

Putting your arms around someone in public is an obvious territorial display, but there are other more subtle arm displays that are driven by the same underlying motive. For example, if two people are sitting on a sofa and one puts his arms on the headrest in the general direction of the other person that too could be interpreted as a territorial display.

How to spot insecurity in the rich and famous

You can use both verbal and nonverbal indicators to assess whether a certain celebrity or public figure is insecure, even if you only get to see the person on TV or read about them online. The verbal indicators of insecurity are pretty straight forward, and often times, when you listen to, watch, or read interviews of the rich and famous, you will be able to spot certain characteristics that could indicate to you that the person in question is insecure.

One verbal indicator of insecurity is bragging. If you spot a rich and famous person who can't stop bragging about his or her accomplishments, you can be certain that the bragging comes from a place of insecurity. The second verbal indicator is denigrating others in order to appear superior. If you see a rich and famous person defames a rival, you can be certain that this action is a reflection of the celebrity's insecurities.

Other verbal cues of insecurity include dismissing of compliments (when a person downplay compliments, he/she clearly deserves), apologizing excessively and unnecessarily, deferring one's decisions to other people, using self-deprecating humor, seeking the validation of others, and using an upward inflection when talking.

There are many nonverbal signals that could indicate that a rich and famous person is insecure, and based on these signals, you could make a fairly accurate assessment of the source of the person's insecurity even if you only base your assessment on a photo or some video footage.

The most obvious signs of security are facial cues. If you see a famous person who tries to avoid eye contact with an interviewer, chances are the person is insecure. When the person lowers his or her eyebrows, it could indicate that he/she is having some sort of internal conflict that stems from insecurity. When the person licks or bites his/her lips, it often indicates that he/she is nervous.

When one feels insecure, he/she instinctively tries to make the body seem smaller than it is, so if the person tucks his/her chin, it means that he/she is feeling insecure. You should also pay close attention to the way the person is breathing. Labored breathing indicates insecurity.

There are also a number of indicators that are tied to the upper body. If the person turns his/her body away or tries to shield the torso using the arms, it often indicates that he/she feels vulnerable at the moment. Crossed arms and legs could be indicators of insecurity. However, most women tend to cross their legs when they are wearing skirts, so don't jump to conclusions if you see a famous lady crossing her legs during an interview.

Other upper body signs of insecurity include putting one's hands between the legs, or inside one's pockets, walking with a hunched posture (often indicates stress, which could be the result of insecurities), biting or picking on one's nails, wringing one's hands, and quivering of the hands.

There are also other indicators that are associated with the lower body. They include jiggling of the feet and interlocking one's feet.

The legs reveal the intentions of the mind

There is a simple reason why the legs reflect the intentions of the mind. When we find ourselves in a threatening situation, our natural "fight or flight" response is subconsciously activated by the limbic system, so our legs react to the threat accordingly. Minor threats such as nervousness, fear, shyness, stress, and anger can set off the response system. Even if we won't run away or start a fight, technically, the legs will show signs or such reactions. You may not flee from an uncomfortable conversation, but your legs may point towards the exit because you subconsciously want to flee.

How to analyze the nonverbal signals of the legs

When someone's legs are pointing towards the exit, it means that they are uncomfortable with the situation, and they want to get out of there. When a person stands at a parallel stance (with legs closed), it often indicates that he/she is not completely sure about his/her position on a subject, which often means that the person can be persuaded.

Standing with a broad stance gives the person a firmer foundation, and it often indicates that he/she is either vigilant or self-assured. Men tend to stand with their legs apart more often than women, and this stance can be seen as a way of asserting one's dominance or putting one's masculinity on display.

When a person is standing with one foot forward, the foot in front almost always points in the direction in which the person wants to go. Standing with legs cross could indicate that a person is being closed off, defensive, or even submissive, depending on the accompanying cues. Crossing one's legs is a symbolic and subconscious denial of access to one's genitals.

If you are having a conversation with someone and he/she crosses both the legs and arms, you can be certain that the person has emotionally withdrawn from the conversation.

Men who tend to make the "leg clamp" when they sit and those who sit at the "figure 4 crossed legs" position are often very confident, competitive, tough-minded, and self-assured. These sitting positions are less common with women, but they are still observed in women who prefer to wear pantsuits; such women often thrive in male-dominated fields.

Why are leg accurate reflections of our emotional state?

Legs are accurate indicators of our emotional states because we are less aware of them. One study showed that when people set out to be deceitful, they are aware of their facial expressions, their general posture, their upper body, and their hands, and they may consciously modify their behavior as it relates to these body parts. Legs and feet are however out of sight, so even the most practiced deceivers often forget to control the signals that their legs are putting out. The professionals who analyze people often point out that the signals they observe in the lower body are more reliable than those of the upper body.

Chapter 2: How to Analyze People via the Non-Verbal Signals of the Hands and Palms

We were born to speak with our hands. Even babies who don't yet have the ability to talk, use hand gestures to point towards things, to indicate excitement, and for lots of other reasons. Because hand gestures are a primal part of the way we communicate, people tend to listen to you more closely when you make use of hand gestures.

Some psychologists and anthropologists have asserted that hand gestures aren't just an add-on to the languages we speak; they are an integral part of that language. For example, if you are indicating the location of an object in your vicinity, the word "there" would be meaningless if it weren't accompanied by a pointing gesture. There is also evidence that we just can't help but use hand gestures; scientists observed blind people conversing with each other, and they found that they all used hand gestures even though none of them could see.

Hand gestures can also help you to access certain memories, and they can boost your understanding of complex concepts and aid learning. Most importantly, you can learn a lot about the people you interact with based on how they use their hands as they talk.

Let's begin with touching. As a gesture, touching comes in many different forms, but in most cases, it is used to indicate affection or fondness. Then a person touches you during a conversation it means that they are fond of you, or they are attracted to you. However, if the touch is aggressive and unwelcome, it could be a sign that the person is trying to manipulate you.

When it comes to holding hands if a person makes full contact with your palm, it indicates warmth and familiarity, but when one holds your hands with just the fingertips, it can be a sign of doubt or discomfort on their part (this often happens during first dates). The temperature of the person's hand also tells you a lot about what they are thinking or feeling. A cold, clammy hand could be a sign that the person is tense, while a warm hand often indicates that the person is at ease (remember

117

that a cold or warm hand could just be the result of the current temperature conditions so don't jump to conclusions).

Open palms often have a positive effect on people; there is a wide variety of open palm gestures that can indicate a number of positive emotions. Open palms with outstretched hands are a gesture that indicates openness, acceptance, and trustworthiness. If it's part of shrug, it could indicate resignation (or that a person is admitting a certain weakness or lack of knowledge). Salespeople often use open palm gestures to build trust with their customers.

The palms down gesture often indicate that the person is confident. It's the kind of gesture you would use to indicate to a crowd of people that they need to calm down, relax, and let you deal with things. On the flip side, these gestures can also indicate that the person is rigid in his opinions, and is unwilling to be persuaded by you.

If the downward palm gesture is accompanied by fingers that are stretched out straight, it could be a sign of dominance, authority, or even defiance. If the gesture is accompanied by a downwards chopping motion, it could indicate that the person emphatically disagrees with you, and is unlikely to budge, so if you are trying to persuade him about something, it might be time for you to change your tactics.

Clenched fists often indicate resolve. A clenched fist is essentially a battle stance, so when a person clenches his/her fists during the conversation, it could mean that they are firm and unyielding, and they are willing to defy you if you hold some sort of authority over them. Usually, the fist would be clenched with the thumb on the outside. If on the other hand, someone clenches his/her fists with the thumbs tucked on the inside of the palm, it could mean that they are anxious or uncomfortable, and they are trying to harden themselves so as to gain the courage to confront the situation at hand.

Putting one's hands behind one's back can be a sign of confidence or openness's because the person leaves his vulnerable parts (the belly and genitals) exposed to whoever he is conversing with. This gesture is more commonly observed in men than in women.

When a person talks while moving his/her hands in a chopping motion, the aim is usually to emphasize the point that he/she is trying to make.

It often indicates that the person is authoritative and that he has made up his mind about the topic under discussion and he is unlikely to change it.

Putting one hand over one's heart is a sign that the person wants to be believed or to be accepted. The person making this gesture wants you to perceive him/her as sincere, but it doesn't always mean that the person is honest. This sign indicates that what the person is saying is coming from the heart, whether or not it's factual. Be careful when you observe this gesture in everyday conversations because it could mean that the person is trying to manipulate you.

When a person points the finger at you as he/she speaks, it means the person is authoritative. Pointing also means that the person is imposing himself on you (this might be okay if it's a parent pointing at a child, or a teacher pointing at a student). When a person points at you, it could mean that he/she is talking down to you, and it can happen when the person is angry or just aggressive. When a social equal does it to you, it could be a sign of arrogance, or it could be that he/she is making an accusation. It's considered more polite to point with your entire palm instead of just the index finger. There are also other instances of pointing which don't imply aggression (for example, playful finger pointing can be a sign of approval while pointing into the air could be used to emphasize certain words during regular conversations.

When someone rubs their hands together, it means that they are eagerly awaiting something and that they may be anxious about it. It implies that they are anticipating or they relish something that is about to occur. Some people tend to crack their knuckles in place of rubbing their hands, and this often indicates that they are ready for action (knuckle cracking is more common among men).

Standing with hands akimbo can in, rare occasions be seen as a sign of unfriendliness, but in most cases, it is really an indicator that one is ready to do something. It's often observed in athletes, and highly productive people (especially those who work in fields that require physical exertion). It can also be a sign of confidence or authority; it shows one is assertive or in control of a given situation.

Pocketing is more common among men than women. It's often an indicator of reluctance or lack of trust. When someone keeps his hands in his pockets, it often means that he is unwilling to act the way you want him to, so you have to gain his interest first before he can consider trusting you.

When a person clasps his hands or squeezes them together, it often means that he/she is uncomfortable and feels the need for some reassurance. It's a self-pacifying gesture, and it's a way of telling oneself that everything is going to be okay. When the fingers are woven together, it can be a sign of frustration or anxiety.

When one uses his/her hands to support the head, it is often a sign of boredom. The higher the degree of support the head receives from the hands, the more bored the person is. Stroking one's chin with a hand could mean that the person is thinking. Supporting one's head with a closed fist can mean that a person is paying keen attention to what you are saying. Tapping one's fingers can be a sign of impatience or even anxiety. The steeple-hand gesture is a sign of confidence and introspection.

Women tend to use their hands to frame their faces during dates (by putting the elbows on the table, intertwining their fingers, and resting the chin on top of the downwards facing palms). This is a sign of attraction; the person doing this is attracted to you so she puts her face on display so you can admire it. It's always a positive sign during the early stages of a relationship.

How hand movements boost your credibility and persuasiveness

Hand movements and gestures can go a long way in making you appear more credible and persuasive as you navigate through your personal life and your career, there are many gestures that you can use to assure the people you interact with on a daily basis that you are open, trustworthy, and an expert on the subject that you deal with. Let's look at some of the hand gestures that you should be using more regularly.

You should use numerical hand gestures to list things when you are having discussions with people, especially when you are in a professional context. For example, when you a giving a presentation, whenever you say a number out loud, you should use your hand to show the numerical gesture that corresponds to that number; this will make people pay attention and remember whatever you are saying.

When you are trying to come across as assertive or determined, you can use the "shaking solid fist" hand gesture to stress the point that you are making. This gesture can be perceived as threating in some cases, but if you use it while your voice is calm but firm (without a hint of irritation), it can make people take you more seriously.

When you are asking for a small favor, you can use hand gestures to stress how small that favor is. You are probably familiar with the gesture used to indicate that something is tiny (pushing your index finger and thumb towards each other while the other fingers are folded). The person whom you are asking for a favor is more likely to comply if you offer them a visual demonstration of how minor that favor is; that's just how the mind is wired.

When you are sitting down and having a discussion with someone, you can bring your hands together in such a way that the tips of your outstretched fingers touch each other (this works best when you are in a relaxed posture in a chair with armrests. This posture indicates to the people around you that you have everything under control. As you do this, you can tap the tips of your finger lightly as you talk and respond to people's questions; this often indicates that you are wise and introspective. If you are nervous and you start using this gesture, you will find that it calms you down. Remember not to overuse this gesture because it could lose its charm if people see you doing it all the time.

When you are speaking in public, and you are making an extremely important point, you could usc the gesture where your hands are spread apart, and your palms are facing your audience. Analysists describe this gesture as "God-like" because it's used in many religious depictions of Christ, and other divine figures. If you are a leader, it makes you seem somewhat magnanimous.

Bringing your hands in towards your chest or your heart is a way of indicating to yourself, so it can make your audience associate what you are saying with who you are as a person. Body language experts advise using this gesture whenever you say something positive during a conversation or during public speaking. It works like neurolinguistics programming— in their minds, your audience will associate you more with the things you say while making these gestures, and they will like you more if you only perform the gesture while saying positive things.

There is also the "stop" gesture which is performed by flashing your arm at someone. This gesture tells someone to either pause or to stop talking. This is a "power gesture," and it can work on almost anyone. It's okay to use it regularly if you are the boss or the parent, but it can be considered rude if you use it with someone who is your social equal or higher than you in the social hierarchy. You should use it sparing, or only when you have an extremely important and urgent point that you want to make. The gesture makes you appear commanding and confident, but only if you use it in the proper context.

The appearance of hands speaks volumes

You can learn a lot from the appearance of one's hands. There are researchers and scientists who even believe that measuring the lengths of one's fingers, the relative strength of different fingers, inclinations or minor deformities, and other parameters can help to predict certain aspects of one's personality.

There are many published papers that prove a correlation between the characteristics of people's hands and their behavior or occupation, but most of them are not yet conclusive (plus there are other scientists who detest this theory, and they have been working hard publishing papers to disprove it). Since we are not dealing with exact science, when you analyze a person based on the appearance of their hands, make sure you have other cues to back up your observations before you arrive at any conclusions.

Researchers have come up with something called 2D:4D (which is the ratio of your index finger to your ring finger). People have different 2D:4D ratios, and there is evidence that this ratio can reveal a number of things about a person.

If a person's ring finger is longer than the index finger, he could be more prone to having multiple sex partners. If the index finger is shorter than the ring finger, studies show that a person might be nicer and more agreeable, more willing to make compromises, more likely to have a higher number of children, and more likely to be a good listener. There are some other obvious things that you can observe just by paying attention to some's hands. If the person has calluses, it could mean that he has a job that involves hard manual labor. If a person has nails that are torn or bitten, it could be that he/she has an anxiety disorder, which he/she copes with by biting the nails. A person with carefully manicured fingers could be affluent and refined (although in some cases, it could be that the person just wants to be perceived as affluent).

Analyze people through their handshakes

Shaking someone's hand can tell you a lot about him/her. A handshake can be analyzed using several parameters. The next time you shake someone's hand, you may rate the person according to how complete the grip is, how strong the handshake is, the vigor of the handshake, the temperature of the person's hand, the dryness of the handshake, the texture of the hand, the duration of the handshake, and whether or not the person maintained eye contact during the handshake. Expert analysts can be able to infer a lot of meaning based on all of these parameters.

A strong handshake indicates a strong character and good health. It's easy to assume that this is just conjecture, but there is real scientific evidence to back up that fact. In a study done in Sweden, more than one million adolescent boys were observed over several decades, and the researchers found that those who had lower hand-grip strength were more likely to die young as a result of pretty much all cause of mortality! They were more likely to develop cardiovascular diseases or even to commit suicide.

Some studies have shown that people with strong handshakes tend to be extroverted, to have a generally positive outlook in life, and to be less shy in social situations. In fact, it is even possible to gauge to a certain degree of accuracy if a person has a decent job based on a mere handshake. Studies have shown that interviewers are more likely to hire candidates with firm handshakes when every other factor is constant.

A firm handshake can be a sign of virility in a man. Studies have shown that men with firm handshakes tend to have more sexual opportunities than their counterparts with weak handshakes. Men with strong grips also seem to be more dominant and aggressive. Unfortunately, if you are a woman looking for a trustworthy man, you should know that some of those studies also indicate that men with firm handshakes are more likely to have a high number of sexual partners.

In older people, (retirees) a firm handshake could be a sign that the person is well educated and that he had a white-collar job; people with white collar jobs tend to age slower than their counterparts who have labor-intensive jobs, so their handshakes stay stronger for longer.

Analyzing non-verbal signals of the arms

We briefly discussed the non-verbal cues of the arms when we looked at the basics a body language analysis, but it's worth mentioning that there are some arm display signals that accompany hand signals. One of the most common ones is the shrug. The shrug is such a complex signal because it involves many parts of the body. In a full shrug, the arms are bent at the elbow, and the hands are open with the palms facing upwards. This kind of shrug can mean that one is lying, he is sorry, or he just doesn't care about the subject you are talking about.

When someone says they are sorry and the apology is accompanied with a shrug, they often press the arms inward and tuck the head downwards to make themselves seem smaller and less threatening so that you can forgive them. People also shrug when they are uncertain about something. Often, they shrug without knowing it, so if someone assures you of something but you notice that he shrugs slightly, it could be that he is lying, or he is making an assumption.

We have also talked about crossing one's arms, but when this is combined with clenching one's fists, it means that the person is aggressive or angry in addition to being defensive. If the person crosses his/her arms but grips tightly at the upper arms near the elbows, it could mean that he/she is tense and is working hard to restrain himself from reacting in a highly emotional and inappropriate way.

If during the course of the conversation, the person with the folded arms opens up the palms, lets one arm pop out or even starts using the arm to make gestures, it could mean that you are reaching him/her and he/she is starting to open up to you. Once the ice is broken, the person may release the crossed arms altogether.

Chapter 3: How to Analyze People via the Non-Verbal Signals of the Face

The ability to read people's faces is very crucial in human communication, and to some extent, it's innate in all of us. Even without any form of training, you might be able to tell if someone is in a bad mood or if they are delighted, just by looking at the person's face. However, to become competent at analyzing people, you have to look beyond the obvious outward signs. That's because people are deceptive, and they are quite good when it comes to faking certain emotional reactions. That is where the concept of micro-expressions comes in.

In order to become a competent analyst, it's not just enough to tell what the expressions on someone's face mean, but also to discern whether those expressions are real (genuine) or fake (forced).

Micro-expressions are defined as brief and involuntary facial expressions that appear on a person's face when they experience certain emotions. We have talked about the limbic system and how the emotional reactions that relate to it are mostly involuntary. If a person intends to conceal how he or she feels about something, micro-expressions can betray him, because the person doesn't have control over them.

For example, if say someone is disgusted by something, but he wants to hide it, the moment he encounters the sensory stimulus that disgusts him, he is going to flash a micro-expression that indicates the disgust for a very brief moment, but once the situation fully registers in his conscious mind, he may then try to hide that disgust with a smile.

To be good at reading micro-expressions, you have to be extremely observant so as to avoid getting deceived. If you are not fast enough to catch the micro-expressions, you will only be able to see the facial expression, which can be controlled by the conscious mind, which means it can be altered to conceal the person's true emotions.

The good news is that even if you miss the micro-expressions and you are only stuck with the facial expressions, there are ways to tell if those facial expressions are real or fake. In this chapter, we will discuss those two concepts; how to read micro-expressions, and how to tell the difference between real and fake facial expressions. We will also take some time to look at the non-verbal signals that are specific to the eyes. The first thing to understand about facial expressions and micro-expressions is that there are seven different universal ones, and as long as you understand those 7, you could infer a lot of meaning depending on the context of your interaction with the person who you are analyzing. The seven facial expressions and micro-expressions are; anger, disgust, fear, contempt, sadness, surprise, and happiness. Once you are able to identify these expressions, you can combine them with other non-verbal and verbal signals to get a full picture of what the person is feeling.

Experts believe that micro-expressions occur in less than 1/15 to 1/25 of a second, which means that they are very easy to miss. This is going to be one of the more difficult lessons to learn, but once you have mastered it, reading micro-expressions could be the most important tool in your arsenal, so it's worth it to take the time to understand each one.

We should also make a note of the fact that these expressions are universal (meaning no matter where in the world you are, or what someone's cultural background is, the expressions will be the same, and they will have the same meanings. In fact, micro expressions have even been observed in people who were born blind, which means that they are rooted in our genetic code.

The best way to learn to identify each of the facial expressions and micro-expressions we are about to discuss is by practicing them in front of the mirror on your own. You can look at images or videos of all these expressions online, but when it comes to understanding and internalizing the signs associated with them, you have to practice them on your own in front of the mirror; it may seem silly, but it works. For each of the seven universal facial expressions, we will discuss both the signs associated with the genuine facial expression and the signs associated with the corresponding micro-expression.

Here are the seven facial expressions and micro-expressions, and the signals that are associated with them:

Anger

The genuine facial expression for anger includes eyebrows that are lowered and drawn towards each other to form a "V" shape in the area above the nose. Wrinkles are also formed on the forehead, in the area above the nose and the eyebrows. The eyes are narrowed in such a way that they create an intense stare, and the upper eyelids are usually raised. The lower eyelids appear tense, or they too may be slightly raised, as if the eyes are trying to focus on something. The nostrils flare, and wrinkles may appear on the nose as a result. The lips could be either open or closed, depending on whether the anger is accompanied by surprise. In instances where the lips are closed, they are pressed together, and they appear thinner than usual, and wrinkled in some cases. In instances where the lips are open, they form a rectangular or square shape, and the teeth are exposed. The lower jaw is pushed slightly forward in some cases. In other cases, the jaws may be clenched together for a fleeting moment, forming a depression on the cheeks. When you see all or most of these signs, it means the person is very angry, but if you see a few of the signs, it could mean that the person is either starting to get angry, or he is working hard to suppress the anger he is feeling.

The micro-expression for anger can be detected using the following signs: the eyebrows move downward, and they are drawn towards each other; vertical lines appear in the area between the eyebrows and above the nose; the lower eyelids tense up; the eyes form a hard stare, and it appears as though they are bulging out; the nostrils are dilated; the lips are pressed together, and the corners of the mouth move downwards, or they form a square shape; the lower jaw protrudes outwards.

Disgust

When someone is highly disgusted the eyebrows are lowered, and they form a "V" shape in the area above the nose. Wrinkles appear on the forehead. If the person is only slightly disgusted, the eyebrows are slightly lowered or they stay the same.

129

The eyelids are brought close together, and the eyes will be narrowed; the higher the level of disgust, the closer the eyelids come together, and in cases where the person is extremely disgusted, it could look as though the eyes are almost totally shut (this reaction occurs because the mind tries to block the sensory stimulus that is causing the disgust).

The person's nostrils are drawn upwards, and this produces wrinkles in the bridge of the nose and where the nose meets the cheeks. The cheeks are raised, and you may be able to observe an inverted "U" wrinkle in the area around the nose.

When the person is extremely disgusted, both lips are raised as high as they can go, and the corners of the lips turn in a downward direction. If the person is only slightly disgusted, the lips are mildly raised, and in some cases, the corners of the lips may not turn at all. In some cases, the chin will pull backward, and a circular wrinkle may appear (this is hard to observe in man with facial hair).

The micro-expression for disgust is characterized by the following signs: the upper eyelids are raised; lines form under the lower eyelids; the nose is wrinkled; the cheeks are raised; the lower lip is raised slightly.

Fear

When someone expresses fear, you will notice that the eyebrows are raised and drawn towards each other, causing wrinkles to form on the forehead. The eyes are very expressive when it comes to portraying fear. The natural reaction is to have the eyes as wide open as possible, so the upper eyelids will be raised as high as they can go. When one is afraid, the brain conditions the eyes to open wide so that the person can optimally perceive the threat in question so as to assess it effectively.

The lips are horizontally stretched out, and the corners of the mouth move towards the ears. The stretching of the lips occurs whether or not the mouth is open. You can gauge the extent of the fear based on how far the lips are extended towards the eyes; the higher the level of fear, the more stretched out the lips will be. The chin is usually pulled backward in most cases (this naturally occurs when people feel threatened).

130

The fear of micro-expression is characterized by the following signs: the eyebrows are raised and drawn towards each other, forming a straight line; wrinkles form in the forehead in the horizontal direction, as though they are parallel to the eyebrows; the upper eyelids are raised alongside the eyebrows, while the lower eyelids are tense; the white part of the eyes show more on the upper side, but they barely appear on the lower side; the mouth opens slightly, and you can observe some tension on the lips, which are usually stretched and drawn backward.

Contempt

In the contempt facial expression, you should be able to notice that wrinkles appear on the surface of the nose. The upper lip is usually raised in such a way that it forms a sneer. The eyes become narrow but still mostly open. The lips are usually pushed forward, and the mouth is generally tight, with the corners slightly raised. If the mouth is open, you will notice that the teeth are clench (or at the very least, they are not parted). The chin either lifts or drops and the head is almost always slightly turned to one side.

The contempt facial expression can be accompanied by a smile; in such cases, it could be that the person making the expression is enjoying someone's misery or just looking down upon someone.

The contempt micro-expression flashes by very fast, but it's easy to spot. Usually, the person's mouth is momentarily raised on one side, pushing upwards on one cheek. In some cases, it can appear in the form of a tight-lipped smile that doesn't reach the eyes.

Sadness

When someone gets sad, you should be able to observe an upwards movement on the inner corners of the eyebrows, and it often appears as though the brows are forming an inverted "V" above the eyes. Wrinkles are formed in the forehead; you can observe vertical wrinkles between the eyebrows and horseshoe-shaped wrinkles above the eyebrows. Even in a person who has permanent wrinkles, you will notice that those wrinkles seem deeper and darker when he is sad.

131

When it comes to the eyes, you'll notice that the upper eyelids will droop, and often times, the person will look down.

The lips are stretched in a horizontal direction, the lower lip is slightly pushed upwards, and the corners of the mouth will be turned downwards. When the person is extremely sad, you'll notice that the chin muscle pushes the lower lip far up; the sadder the person, the higher the lower lip is pushed, and the more curled the corners of the mouth will be (if you have ever seen a child cry, then you have a clear mental picture of the lip shape that we are describing).

The cheeks are raised, and an inverted "U" wrinkle forms around the nose. Depending on the person's bone structure, if the cheeks are pushed upwards too much, it could appear as though the lips aren't curled at all (that explains why when some people are crying, they look like they are grinning).

The micro-expression for sadness includes the following signs: the inner ends of the eyebrows are drawn inwards and then upwards; a triangular shape forms on the skin between the eyebrow and the eye, usually with the inner corner of the eyelid coming upwards; the corners of the lips are pulled downwards; the lower lip forms an outward pout; the jaws move upwards.

Surprise

The facial expression for surprise is similar to the one for fear in lots of ways, and novice analysts often confuse the two. The surprise expression is triggered by external events that are unexpected, the same as the fear expression. The only difference is that surprise can be a result of pleasant events, while fear is invariably a result of unpleasant events.

When someone is surprised, the eyebrows are raised, and the eyes are opened as wide as physically possible (this is somewhat similar to what happens when one is afraid). The difference is that when someone is surprised, the eyebrows are not drawn close together the way they are when someone expresses fear. In some cases, the surprise expression includes wrinkles, which are a direct result of the raised eyebrows. The wrinkles that appear when one is surprised are horizontal and fairly straight, unlike those that appear when one is afraid (as we have mentioned, those include vertical lines between the eyebrows).

People who are surprised also tend to drop their jaws and to open their mouths. Unlike those expressing fear, people who are surprised don't stretch their lips horizontally.

The micro-expression for surprise includes the following signals: the eyebrows rise up, and they are curved downwards; the skin underneath the eyebrows stretches; horizontal wrinkles may form on the forehead; the eyes are open extremely wide, and the whites of the eyes show both above and below the iris; the jaw drops open, the teeth part, and there is no stretching or tension on the lips.

Happiness

The facial expression for happiness is pretty straight forward; people smile when they are happy. However, as you analyze people, your biggest challenge here will be to tell the difference between smiles that are real and those that are fake.

When a smile is real, the eyes tend to sparkle; the eyes water a little bit, and as a result, you will notice a twinkle in the person's eyes. If you don't notice the twinkle, it could mean that the person is faking the smile, or he is using it to disguise a different emotion.

In a real smile, there are certain muscles around the eyes which are activated, and this causes the eyebrows to dip down slightly towards the eyelids. This can be hard to spot, but with practice, you will learn to tell if it's there. Wrinkles also tend to form in the corner of the eyes when a smile is real. A real smile makes use of both upper and lower facial muscles, while a fake smile only makes use of the lower facial muscles, so the wrinkles in the corner of the eyes won't form if the smile is fake.

When a smile is real, you also notice that the cheeks are raised. People are able to fake this sign when they make a conscious effort to fake a smile, but sometimes, they forget to do it, and if you are keen, you may be able to notice it.

Fake smiles are characterized by straight lips. One example of a fake smile in this instance is the "smug look," which involves pulling one's lips into one's mouth and forcing a smile. This also happens when someone smiles to conceal anger. Fake smiles are also characterized by the showing of the bottom teeth. When someone smiles and you notice that a large area of their bottom teeth is visible, it can often mean that the person is deceptive. It indicates that the person is going out of his way to seem enthused, even though he isn't. Sometimes the bottom teeth may show if the person has a relatively large mouth, so don't jump to conclusions if you spot this sign.

The happiness micro-expression is characterized by the following signals: The corners of the mouth are pulled backward and upwards; a wrinkle is formed from the outer part of the nose to the outer edge of the lip; the mouth could be parted, and the lips could be exposed; the cheeks are raised; the lower eyelids either tense up or show wrinkles; "crow's feet" form on the outer edge of the eyes.

Non-verbal gestures of the eyes

When analyzing people, you can tell a lot by observing their eyes. There is a reason why people believe the eyes are the windows to the soul; they have an uncanny ability to reveal people's thoughts and emotions. Even without any training, we naturally tend to look into people's eyes to figure out their intentions; both humans and animals do this. This also explains why people who want to conceal their intentions (e.g. law enforcement officials, security personnel, and even criminals) tend to wear dark glasses in public; they don't want others to learn certain things about them just by looking at their eyes.

Here are some eye signals and what they mean:

When people look upwards, it often means that they are thinking. It could also mean that they are trying to remember something. Looking upwards and to the right means one is engaging his imagination, so if someone is doing this, it could mean he is making stuff up. Looking upwards and to the left means someone is recalling past events, and it often indicates that one is telling the truth. In some people, it could be the other way around, so if you want to use this trick to detect if someone is telling the truth, you might want to start with some control questions to figure things out.

Looking downwards can be a sign of submission. When you stare directly at a person, and he/she looks down, it could be that they are intimidated by you, and if they do this during an argument, it could mean that they are about to concede.

Looking sideways often means one is distracted by something in his/her peripheral vision, so if you are on a date and someone keeps looking sideways during a conversation, it could mean that he finds other people or objects around more interesting than you.

Lateral eye movements are often a sign that someone is deceptive or conspiratorial. It could be that the person is shifty and wants to get away from you, or it could be that he is secretive and he doesn't want anyone else to hear your conversation.

Gazing at something or someone is a clear sign of interest. However, there are many types of gazes, and they vary in meaning depending on the facial expression and body language signals that accompany the gaze. Gazing softly into someone's eyes often indicates sexual attraction or love. Looking up and down at a person could mean that you are sizing him up because you think of him as a threat (either a sexual rival or there is a power dynamic at play). Gazing at someone's forehead indicates disinterest (it means the person is only paying attention out of obligation).

Glancing at something or someone often indicates a hidden desire. When someone glances at the door, it means he has a desire to leave the room, or he is expecting someone more interesting to walk in. Glancing at someone indicates a desire to talk to that person. Glancing also often means that one has an urge to gaze, but it feels inappropriate or forbidden. A sideways glance accompanied by raised eyebrows indicates attraction, but if the eyebrows aren't raised, it's often a sign of disapproval.

Eye contact generally indicates one of three things; dominance, affection, or interest. A prolonged doe-eye gaze accompanied by dilated pupils is a sign of attraction and sexual desire. Making eye contact with a person is a way of acknowledging them.

You can also look into a person's eyes to figure out what the person is looking at, so if one person in a relationship keeps looking into the other's eyes, it could be a sign of insecurity. If someone looks into your eyes after you have said something, it means you have grabbed his/her attention.

When a person holds eye contact for long, it shows he is paying attention. Long eye contact also indicates that you like someone or you are attracted to them.

Eye contact is also used in persuasion, so if you are asking someone for a favor, you should know that holding eye contact with him increases the odds that your request will be granted.

Squinting eyes usually means that someone is evaluating the person or object that he/she is looking at. If they are not looking at anything, in particular, it could mean they are evaluating an idea they have just heard. It could also indicate that the person is uncertain about something. Squinting is often used by liars to conceal deception. It could also mean that someone is trying to avoid forming a bad mental image.

Blinking occurs naturally (it's a way for the eyelids to clean the eyes), but the frequency with which it occurs can tell you a lot about someone. When someone blinks faster than usual, it could be a sign of stress, and it often indicates that he is lying. Blinking can also indicate that two people have formed a rapport; if the person you are talking to is blinking at the same rate as you, it means there is a good rapport between the two of you. A single blink can often be a sign of surprise.

Rapid blinking is a somewhat confusing signal. If someone blinks rapidly during casual conversation, it could be a sign of arrogance. However, in some cases, it could be a shy romantic invitation. You can make the distinction based on the other signals that you observe.

Winking can either be a suggestive greeting, or it can be a sign that someone is conspiratorial.

Closed eyes could mean that someone is dismissing you or is disinterested or uncomfortable with what you have to say. However, some people are visual thinkers, and they tend to close their eyes when processing certain thoughts.

Dilated pupils indicate attraction. Constricted pupils indicate disgust. However, it's important to note that light affects pupil size, so you have to account for it when using pupil size signals to analyze someone.

Chapter 4: How to Determine If Someone Is Lying

Being able to detect when someone is lying is probably the most important skill you will need as an analyst. In this chapter, we will look at both verbal and non-verbal signals of lying, but before we do that, let's explain why it's easy to spot a lair, and why it's difficult for someone to conceal their lies completely.

Why lying is difficult

Lying is difficult because it actually takes a lot of work. The way the brain is designed, it's far easier for someone to tell the truth than it is for him to lie. For example, let's say you walk into a room and someone asks you "Where have you been?" when you tell the truth, the brain doesn't have to do much work; it just has to recall where you've been and then enable you to say it out loud.

However, if you choose to lie in that instance, your brain will be juggling a number of alternative narratives; there is the true narrative, there is the narrative that you want to be true, there is the narrative that you think the other person wants to hear, and then there is the narrative that you finally choose to present. As you juggle those narratives, you will also be dealing with several emotions that result from the deception; you will be feeling fearful, hopeful, guilty, or even angry. At the same time, you will be thinking about how to modify your body language so as to make yourself seem more credible.

Because of all of these internal struggles, your brain will be going into overdrive trying to keep everything together, and you might even experience some physiological reactions, including changes in heart rate or breathing. As you can see, lying is a lot more complex than you ever imagined, and in most cases, if you do it, there will be some outward sign of deception, which a well-practiced analyst should be able to spot.

Psychologists call this phenomenon "leaking." When someone lies, no matter how smart they are, some signs are going to leak. These signs could be subconscious reactions, or they could be the result of conscious efforts meant to conceal the deception.

Nonverbal signals of deception

When you are detecting lies, you have to analyze the verbal and nonverbal elements together, and the first thing you need to look out for is a mismatch between what the person is saying, and the body language that he/she is putting out there. Naturally, when we converse with others, we tend to use verbal and nonverbal language in a harmonious way, so if there is any disharmony, it's a clear sign of deception.

For instance, in Western culture, we nod our heads when we say "Yes" and shake them sideways when we say "No." so, if someone denies something but you notice a slight nod, it could be a sign that he is lying. Experts reviewed videos where people denied doing certain things (and were later proven to have been lying), and in most instances, they seemed to be nodding their heads while denying allegations.

This also happens often when people claim that they are fine, but their body language seems to indicate that they are worried, angry, sad, etc. This often means that not only is the person lying to you, but he also doesn't even admit the truth to himself.

Unusual gestures can also indicate that someone is deceptive. People tend to use unusual gestures when they are lying because they are under scrutiny, and their anxiety response mechanism kicks in and interferes with the normal use of gestures. You might observe that when a person lies, he may look at his nails, lick his lips, or even show a slight tremor in the hands. Of course, you have to make sure that you have observed the person under normal conditions to make sure that the unusual gestures aren't just idiosyncrasies.

You also have to look out for fake smiles. In the previous chapter, we discussed who you can tell the difference between a genuine and a forced smile—a fake smile often indicates that a person is lying, and the smile is meant to help sell the lie. If someone makes a certain assertion, and he smiles at you, pay close attention and try to see if you can spot any signs of deception.

You can tell if a fake-smile is meant to conceal a lie if the timing is a bit off. A deceptive person may hold a smile for longer than you'd expect, or sometimes, the smile might be combined with other emotional expressions (for example, one might fake a smile, but if you are keen you might notice signs of anger beneath that smile).

You have to pay attention to the way the person is making eye contact with you; lairs either make too much or too little eye contact. Before you set out to determine if someone is lying, spend some time with him and determine his baseline regarding eye contact. When you have a casual conversation with no stakes at all, the person will make normal levels of eye contact. When you test the person to see if he is lying, try to determine if he is making less or more eye contact than usual. If it's an absolute stranger that you are analyzing, some experts believe that the 7 to 10 seconds range is normal when it comes to making eye contact.

If the person tries to avoid eye contact, breaks it too soon, or if he holds eye contact for 10 seconds or more, chances are he is lying. Inexperienced lairs tend to break eye contact too soon, while the experienced lairs are more likely to hold eye contact beyond a point where it's comfortable (because they know that eye contact instills trust, but they tend to overdo it).

The direction of eyes can also help you figure out if someone is lying. We explained earlier in the book that when people engage their imagination, they tend to look to the left. Lying requires a lot of creativity and imagination, while truth-telling requires recollection (so a truth-teller would look to the right). The direction could be reversed in left-handed people, so make a note of the person's dominant hand before you use this trick.

The appearance of the eyes can also indicate if someone is lying. When the whites of one's eyes are more exposed than usual, it often indicates that the person is afraid of something, so if it happens in the context of a conversation, it could mean that he is afraid of you finding out that he is deceptive. In some cases, the eyes may even dart around, and he may keep glancing towards the exit; this often means the person has been put on the spot, and he is afraid of prolonged inquiry.

When you notice that a person has become perfectly still, sometimes it can mean that he is lying. Studies have shown that when people lie, they become anxious and nervous, so they tense up. When a person tenses up, he will try to keep as still as possible so as not to reveal his tension to the people around him. During a casual conversation, where there is nothing to worry about, most people are very relaxed, and there is a certain fluidity to their posture and body movement. When something is wrong (even when they are just telling a white lie), their body movements tend to become stiff and rigid.

When a person starts literally pointing fingers, it could be a sign of deception. When we point fingers during conversations, it's often to direct the other person's attention towards something else. If you notice that someone is suddenly using more pointing gestures than they were a moment ago, it could be because the person is trying to direct your attention away from him. You need to observe the person for a while to understand whether or not the gestures are just a part of his baseline behavior, or if they are an actual deviation from the norm. Also, if the person points his fingers one way while his eyes are looking in a different direction, it could be another sign of deception.

People also tend to cover their eyes or their mouths more often when they are lying. It's a subconscious reaction when someone is telling a lie — he is inclined to cover his lips or his eyes to keep you from detecting whether or not he is deceiving you.

Lips can also reveal when one is deceptive. When a person folds his lips before speaking, it could be a sign that he is lying. Folding lips literally indicates that the person is holding back whatever information he has, and he has a real fear of blurting it out before thinking things through. Folded lips mean that the person is editing his thoughts before speaking out loud.

Verbal signals of deception

The verbal signals of deception include both the words that a person chooses to use and the way the person sounds as he speaks. When a person lies, his voice or manner of speaking may change ever so slightly, and if you pay keen attention, you will be able to notice it. Law enforcement experts make use of this trick when interviewing suspects and persons of interest. They usually start by asking the typical person questions that are easy to answer to get a baseline of what the person's voice sounds like when they are not under stress. They then proceed to ask the important questions, and they pay attention to tonal variations.

Now, we are not suggesting that you should go out and start interrogating your friends and family, but you can use this technique is a subtle way. You can start a casual conversation with someone (maybe talk about the weather) before you bring up the topic you really want to find out about. If the person's voice or speaking mannerisms change, you might be on to something.

When a person offers lots of details when providing a response to a simple question, it often indicates that he is lying. Liars tend to be very generous when it comes to offering details because they know that people tend to buy stories when they are overloaded with details. When someone gives you a lot of details or seems to have an answer for almost everything, it means that he has put a lot of thought into what he is going to say, and he has anticipated every possible line of inquiry that you might take. It means he has been rehearsing the whole thing in his head, which is why those details are just at the tip of the tongue, ready to roll off.

When people are honest, they tend to offer answers that are short, and clearly stated; they don't put much thought into what they are saying because all they have to do is recall it. Lairs, on the other hand, offer answers that are heavily editorialized. Lairs use sentences that are convoluted, and they add a lot of qualifying phrases into what they are saying (they are more likely to say things like "to tell you the truth").

Sometimes, lairs will keep adding details to their stories because they are trying to take up all the time, and therefore keep you from having to ask them any more question. In other cases, they do it because they want to preempt all the information so that you don't have the chance to frame your questions in a certain way; this gives them a loophole and allows them to feed you what they consider to be white lies.

143

Lairs also tend to tell stories in the same exact way that they did before. That's because the stories lairs tell are memorized in a specific order, and they are likely to freeze if you ask them to tell the same story in a different order altogether. Lairs have to stop and think when you ask them to tell a story backward. In a social context, it would seem strange for you to ask someone to recount the story he just told you, but there is a way to use this technique without revealing to the other person that you intend to catch him on a lie.

After someone has told you a story for the first time and you have your suspicions that he might be lying, you can ask him an unexpected question about something that occurred in the middle of the story, and then, immediately ask a different question about something that happened close to the start of the story. If the person has to stop and think long and hard before responding, it means that he made up the story.

Even though liars tend to share plenty of details to seem credible, when they lie, they are likely to explain things in very simple terms. That's because the human brain struggles when it comes to creating and recalling complex lies, so lairs try to keep things simple in case you ask them to repeat the details later on. They know that if they make the lie complicated, the odds of slipping up will increase.

Liars also tend to repeat questions as a way to stall you while they try to concoct a believable lie. For instance, if you ask someone, "Have you been smoking?" and he answers with "Have I been smoking? No" chances are he is lying. In some cases, when the person can't come up with a believable lie, after repeating your question back to you, he could feign outrage and accuse you of not trusting him.

Outrage is often a sign of a lie. When you ask someone a question, and instead of providing a straight answer, he reacts as though your question is the most insulting thing in the world, it could be a sign of a lie. Of course, there are people who will be honestly outrage with your line of questioning, but most of them would answer your question in the process of conveying their outrage, and they won't blow things out of proportion.

Lairs also tend to talk about themselves in the third person because they are trying to distance themselves from the lie, they are in the process of telling. They subconsciously try to avoid referring to themselves in the same statement they know to be a lie. They often do this when defending themselves against allegations.

People tend to use formal language when they are lying. In casual conversation, people are more likely to use contractions such as "I'm" and "didn't" but when lying, people are more likely to use the full form of those contractions (like "I am" and "did not"). Again, you need to have a baseline understanding of a person's behavior before using this technique on him. Talk to him casually and figure out if he is the kind of person who speaks formally all the time (some professionals speak formally out of habit).

Long pauses can also be a sign of deception. When someone tells you a story, and he takes long pauses before continuing, it could be because he is making things up, and he needs the time to come up with additional details to advance his storyline. The only exception to this is when someone is talking about a topic that is highly technical; when dealing with hard topics, most people have to stop to think before coming up with a rational statement to make, so they may take long pauses (for example, President Barrack Obama was known for taking long pauses when answering complex policy questions).

Chapter 5: Analyzing People in Dating and Love

Being an astute observer of human behavior can go a long way in helping to improve your dating and love life. The fact is that we tend to miss other people's body language signals all the time, and this has lots of negative implications for us. If you can't read the people you meet, you could waste your time pursuing someone who isn't attracted to you, or you could miss the fact that someone you like likes you back. If you can't read the people you know, you could miss your partner's non-verbal signals, and that could put a strain on your relationship in the long run. The fact is that relationships only work if we are able to understand the other person's body language to some extent. In this chapter, we will discuss how you can analyze people in dating and love.

What happens when you meet the opposite sex?

There are lots of physiological and psychological reactions that occur in the body when you meet the opposite sex, especially when it's someone you are immediately attracted to. However, these reactions are often subtle, and not as pronounced as they are depicted in pop culture (you have probably seen a few romantic comedies where people freak out and start stuttering when they meet a potential love interest—while this may occur in real life, it's rarely the case). Let's look at what really happens when you meet someone.

Dilated pupils are very reliable signs of attraction. When you spot something or someone that you are particularly interested in, your brain tells your eyes to collect as much information about that person as possible; therefore, your pupils dilate so that you can see the person more clearly. Pupil dilation has a dual purpose. Studies show that people appear more attractive when their pupils are dilated (because they seem to have big round eyes). In as much as dilation helps you gather more visual information about the person you are attracted to, it also increases the chances that the person will also find you attractive.

When you are attracted to someone, you experience a "dopamine high." Dopamine is a neurochemical, and is often referred to as the "feel-good neurotransmitter." When you spot someone of the opposite sex, you feel an "attraction" towards that person. Everyone has experienced that feeling at one point in his/her life; it's a feeling of bliss and a sense of yearning. The dopamine in your brain is what causes that feeling. It's a way for your brain to indicate to you that it's expecting to be rewarded in a certain way. Unfortunately, dopamine is thought to contribute to addiction, which would explain why we tend to be obsessive when we are in love. Because of this, it's technically possible to be "addicted" to someone.

Your heart races when you meet someone you are attracted to. You have probably heard all the clichés about someone making your "heart skip a beat," and that love is a "matter of the heart." There is a reason why people believed love was associated with the heart before they came to understand how the brain works; the heart is the one organ that reacts most noticeably when you are attracted to someone (you will not notice your eyes dilating, but you'll certainly feel your heartbeat increasing).

You get flushed, and you blush when you meet someone to whom you are attracted. This is a reaction that no one can control. When you come face to face with the person you have a crush on, blood will flow to your face at an increased rate, and it will cause your cheeks to get red. This is an evolutionary way for your body to try to attract potential mates; when blood flow increases in your facial area, you appear more attractive and fertile (if you are a woman) and more virile (if you are a man).

You may sweat more than usual when you meet someone you are attracted to. Now, there are plenty of reasons why people sweat; it could be that they are stress or anxious, or that they have been doing something physically strenuous, but sometimes it could also be because they are aroused. Sweating is a way for the body to release pheromones, which are basically natural chemicals that are designed to attract and excite the opposite sex. So, next time you worry about how much you are sweating during a date, it might be useful to remember that the sweat might actually be working in your favor!

When you meet the opposite sex, and there is an instant attraction, your body will find ways to synchronize with the other person's body. If you are talking to the person, you may find yourself starting to mimic him/her on a deep level. This phenomenon is referred to as interactional synchrony, and it's a natural way for people to bond on a subconscious level. You will start mirroring the other person (or he/she may start mirroring you) in various ways, including copying your facial expressions, and even your speech patterns.

How to analyze indicators of attraction

We all want to know when other people are attracted to us. In fact, that is probably the reason you are making an effort to learn how to analyze people. People are naturally guarded, and even when they like us, they tend to try to conceal it, but if you are keen, you may be able to observe subtle cues that indicate attraction. The next time you see the following signs in someone you are interested in, consider it your lucky day because it means that he/she is interested in you as well.

Eye contact is one of the most obvious signs of attraction. When a person is attracted to you, he/she will make more eye contact with you and will try as much as possible to keep you within his/her line of vision. You will notice that their eyes widen and sparkle and their eyebrows will be raised when they're speaking to you. Some people tend to give those they are attracted to the "intimate gaze" (starting at their lips).

In some cases, if they are shy (or playing hard to get), they may look you straight in the eyes, but they'll break eye contact and smile/blush when you link eyes with them. Whatever the case, some level of eye contact, glancing, or gazing is necessary where sexual attraction is involved. If someone doesn't look at you at all, it's because the attraction isn't there, even a person who plays hard to get will at least try to steal a few glances when you aren't looking.

You should also pay attention to any preening gestures the person might display when you walk up to them. When we are around people to whom we are attracted, we subconsciously try to look our best. When you enter the scene, whether you are alone or out in a social gathering, if the person is interested in you, they might try to straighten themselves up somehow. If it's a woman, she might try to adjust the way her hair frames her face, or adjust her top. A man might subconsciously touch his tie or dust imaginary lint off his jacket.

When a person is interested in you, he/she may tilt the head slightly during conversations. This signal is more common with women than men, and it often indicates that the person is very interested in you (there might be other reasons for that kind of intense interest, so make sure that other signs are present before you conclude that its attraction).

Head tilting and hair tossing gestures tend to expose the neck, which is a part of the body that is vulnerable, and we are anthropologically programmed to protect. When a woman performs these gestures during an interaction, it means that she likes you and trusts you to some extent. Women also tend to flick the hair when they are particularly interested in you. Some also play with their hair when they are on dates; this is a conscious indicator of romantic attraction. It's a subtle sign of flirting. It could mean that your date is either feeling playful, or she is a bit nervous, both of which are good signs when it comes to predicting attraction.

You can also figure out if someone is attracted to you by observing their feet, we have already discussed why feet reveal the brain's subconscious intentions. When a person is attracted to you, they have this desire to turn their whole body towards you, but if they are standing or sitting close to you, they would appear obvious and desperate, and it would be awkward for everyone. In such situations, they may consciously condition their bodies to face away from you (and towards whatever direction is appropriate), but they will almost invariably forget to do the same thing with their legs. The result is that while their body is pointing away from you, their feet will be pointing directly at you.

In social gatherings, if they are in a different group from yours (say you are sitting at different tables during a party), you might notice that one foot is pointing towards you while the other foot points to their group.

This could mean that they secretly want to leave their group and join you.

The orientation of the person's body could also reveal a secret attraction to you. Even in situations where the person is standing far away from you, paying attention to the general orientation of their body can tell you if the person wants to engage with you somehow. If they are fidgeting, it could mean that they want to approach you. Even if they are conversing with someone else, they'll subconsciously orient their shoulders in such a way that they are parallel to yours. If the person is standing still you can try to figure out in what direction they would move if they started walking; if it's towards you, then subconsciously, that is where they want to be.

We all have a pretty decent sense of personal space. We tend to value our own personal space, and we subconsciously respect other people's personal space. When we get more comfortable with other people, we tend to let them into our personal space, and they do the same with us. When someone is attracted to you, they'll let you into their personal space or make subconscious attempts to occupy yours, even if you haven't known each other for long. You will find the personal space between the two of you keeps narrowing until it's pretty much non-existent.

You can test whether a person is into you by slightly infringing on their personal space (in a socially acceptable way). Most people will immediately step back if you stand too close to them, but if a person is attracted to you, they may let you stay close at least for a while. Be very careful when you use this test; you don't want people thinking of you as a creep.

As the personal space between you narrows, a person who is attracted to you will find excuses to touch you. Physical contact is important for breaking the ice when two people are headed towards intimacy. When physical contact is reciprocated, it registers the minds of both parties that there is something between them that's worth pursuing.

If you touch someone and you notice that it negatively affects their mood, or that they don't seem to want to reciprocate, it could mean that the attraction is only one way. However, if you read some of the other

151

signs that we have discussed, then it's possible that they are attracted to you, but they just aren't on the same page as you. In that case, you might want to slow down a bit.

When you are hanging out with the person you are attracted to (even if it's not a date), you might notice that they are leaning towards you. If it's a colleague at work, you may notice that they move their seat closer to you during meetings. You also notice that the person removes physical barriers between the two of your whenever there are any (for example, if you are sitting on a table across from each other, they may move coffee cups and plate settings aside, and lean on the table in your direction. Watch out for such minor signs, because they are clear indicators of attraction.

Constant and consistent communication is also a sign of attraction. If someone seems to want to be in constant communication with you, it could be that they want you to notice them. Someone who keeps texting you, asking for your help with things that they could just handle themselves, asking you questions they know the answers to, etc. usually has a crush on you. They are trying to keep the lines of communication open so that you form enough of a rapport, and you grow closer to each other. It could also mean that they are too shy to ask you out right away. Finally, if someone laughs hard at your jokes or finds your somewhat silly ideas amusing, it could be a sign of attraction. We all tend to overestimate our sense of humor, so, some objectivity is required if you want to use this technique to assess a love interest. When you tell a joke or make a silly off-hand comment, you may draw a few laughs, but if the person reacts as though you were Chris Rock, they are attracted to you.

Chapter 6: Analyzing People via Their Verbal Statements

The words we choose to use can offer a lot of insight into how we think and feel. Throughout the book, we have been focusing on non-verbal cues, but the fact is that verbal statements are just as useful when analyzing people. People who speak the same language have access to the same set of words, so the words they choose to use at any given time reveal something about each one of them.

In as much as you want to use verbal statements to analyze people, you have to be careful because you want to retain your objectivity. There a people who end up obsessing over each and every word other say, looking for some hidden meaning where none exists. When you interact with someone, you want to make a quick assessment of their verbal statements on the spot, not spend the whole day replaying the conversation in your head.

How words reveal your personality

If you have studied linguistics, you are probably aware of the difference between function words and content words. Content words are those that name real things and describe tangible qualities. Function words, on the other hand, are those words that express the grammatical relationship between other words in the sentence. When we make verbal statements to express certain ideas, we have little choice in the kind of content words we use, but we have lots of choices when it comes to kind of function words we use. Function words are pronouns, articles, conjunctions, prepositions, and auxiliary verbs. Linguists refer to function words as the "connective tissue" of language.

While content words communicate ideas, function words shape those ideas, which is why they reveal something about the person who chooses to use them. For example, when a person says "I don't think I want to do it" and another one says "I don't want to do it", it may seem that they are saying the same thing, but that difference in choice of words actually reveals a lot about each speaker's state of mind. The use of function words reveals people's sense of self, their level of honesty, and their emotional stability. All you have to do is listen closely.

Analyzing verbal statements

First, you can tell if someone is an introvert or an extrovert within a few minutes of meeting them by estimating the number of words they are using as they talk. Extroverts are chattier than introverts; they use more words, and they speak a lot faster. Psychologists have also observed that extroverts tend to use language that is loose and abstract, while introverts use language that is more concrete. Extroverts seem to be vague, while introverts seem to be specific.

Introverts tend to express more caution and conscientiousness in the way they phrase their statements, while extroverts seem more direct. Introverts also speak in terms that are more quantifiable, but they also tend to use "hedging words" in their speech. Extroverts seem to be more liberal in the way they use their words, while introverts are noticeably reserved.

For example, where an extrovert would say "let's go out for drinks," an introvert might say, "maybe we could go to the pub for a beer." These statements indicate the way the person saying them perceives the world; one lives life in the fast lane, and the other one stops to figure out the details and doesn't make assumptions about what others want to do. While the extrovert's statement sounds like a command, the introvert goes out of his way to make his statement sound like a suggestion.

There are also certain "word clues" that reveal the characteristics of a person. Researchers have found that the human brain is wired to process thought in the most efficient manner possible; that means that people think only in nouns and verbs. However, when we speak out those thoughts (or write them down), we tend to add things like adverbs and adjectives, and we do that with a specific subconscious intention.

For example, when you ask someone for a favor, he might turn you down by saying, "I'm busy" or "I'm very busy." The former is a mere statement of fact, while the latter is a bit editorialized. The person who says, "I'm busy" has less empathy than the one who says, "I'm very busy."

In its most basic form, a sentence consists of a subject and a verb, so any modification beyond that could be a clue that indicates what the person is thinking.

When one person says "I'm buying a new car," and another person says "I have decided to buy a new car" you can tell that the second person is more introspective than the first one. Based on the choice of words, it's evident that the second person makes a habit of weighing his/her choices before taking action. The word "decided" is an example of an "action word," and it is indicative of a trait that the person possesses.

When it comes to word clues, the "royal we" is perhaps the most important one for analysts who want to discover a person's thoughts or emotions, especially as it relates to his/her relationships or other social dynamics. The "royal we" refers to the use of plural pronouns such as "we," "us," and "our" to refer to oneself. It indicates a sense of belonging in the person who uses it. For example, a guy who says "I'm going out with her" and one who says "we are going out" may seem to be expressing the same idea, but if you look deeper, you will realize they have different mindsets regarding the relationship they are in. While the first one makes a distinction between himself and the girl he is seeing, the second one seems to think of himself and his date as one entity; it could mean that the second guy feels a stronger sense of commitment at that point in time. Couples who use "we" when talking about their relationship tend to be more satisfied and to have a stronger bond.

The "royal we" can also reveal a person's attitude towards his/her career, family, friends, or teammates. Research shows that employees who refer to the institution they work for as "the company" tend to be less productive than those who refer to it as "our company." Other studies have also shown that CEOs and managers who use the word "I" frequently when talking about their work turn out to be bad team leaders, and they are more likely to run the company into the ground.

When a person uses "I" a lot, it often means that he is very focused on himself. This usually has two implications; it either means that the person has a self-centered personality, or it could mean that he is going through certain emotional issues that are making him focus more attention on himself at the moment. Studies have shown that when people are depressed or anxious, they tend to use the word "I" more often than when they are emotionally stable.

"I" can also imply that certain people have an innate need to seek credit for small contributions that most people don't care about. For example, when you ask someone, "How's the weather?" one might answer by saying, "It's cold" or "I think it's cold." The "I think" part may not appear to be significant at first glance, but in this case, it shows the person is focused on himself.

You should also pay attention to whether the person uses words or phrases that indicate anger, or if he tends to talk about violence. You can tell if a person is prone to anger just by the way he talks. Even in casual conversation, there are people who tend to express irritation at mundane things, and there are others who tend to use words that seem like threats. A person who makes a habit of snapping at people might have anger management problems. The same goes for people who tend to use curse words in inappropriate contexts.

You can also tell if someone is likely to take responsibility for his actions or to pass the blame to others from the way they talk. If it's a person that you have started dating, pay close attention to the way they talk about their exes. People who like to blame others will likely describe their exes in derogatory terms, and they may even tell you that their exes are the ones who caused the relationship to fail.

In a professional setting, you can find out who a person's nemesis or rival is, then bring up the name in the middle of a conversation, and wait to see what he/she says. People who like to pass blame won't have a single positive thing to say about their rivals.

As you pay attention to the words a person uses, try to discover any underlying patterns. You might be able to notice if the person has certain biases on specific topics. Depending on your reason for analyzing the person, you might want to initiate discussions that steer the conversation in a certain direction. If it's a person you are dating, and you want to know his stand on certain political issues, such information is very easy to elicit.

Try to understand how the person used hyperbole during conversations. We all tend to exaggerate a little, but there are some people who use hyperbole to pathological degrees. You can direct the conversation towards a topic that allows the person to brag about a recent accomplishment, then pay attention to how generous he is when it comes to self-praise. Be wary of people who exaggerate their accomplishment too much.

Words can also reveal secret interests or hidden agendas that a person has. For example, a friend who brings up the name of a certain girl at every chance is probably romantically interested in her. This is something you should watch out for when you are in a relationship. If your partner can't seem to shut up about a person, he/she has met, you should pay more attention to the dynamic between them, and you should take action to strengthen your relationship so as not to lose out. As for hidden agendas, if a person keeps bringing up a certain topic, or he keeps "sucking up" to you, it often means they want something out of you.

Also, pay attention to the assumptions the person seems to make, and the misunderstandings he seems to have. People who make lots of assumptions about others tend to have a sense of entitlement, and that is something you need to watch out for, especially in a new relationship.

Word choice and deception

Word choice can also reveal when one is lying. When people lie, they tend to avoid using first-person pronouns in the answers they supply. Instead of saying "I didn't eat your cake" a lair might say something like "that is not the kind of thing a considerate person would do." this way, they get to deny doing something without going on record. People who tell the truth tend to make frequent use of negations (words such as "no," "never" and "none") and exclusive words (such as "without" and "but") without any hesitation. Lairs, on the other hand, go out of their way to avoid using such words in sentences.

157

When people are truthful, they use the pronoun "I" more often because it is a sign of commitment. The word "I" doesn't leave anything open to interpretation, so the person doesn't have any loopholes in case they are caught on a lie. The more impersonal a statement seems, the more likely it is to be a lie.

When people use words that indicate a lack of conviction, it can mean that they are lying, or they are telling a half-truth. When people use phrases such as "I believe" and "I think" when they are recounting events which are supposed to be factual, it often means they are being less than truthful. When people use phrases like "kind of" and "sort of" when recounting supposed facts, it introduces an element of uncertainty in the statements they are making, and it can be a sign of deception.

Words have a way of revealing a person's insecurities.

When people who talk about themselves in self-promoting terms, it is a way to overcompensate for an inferiority complex. Some studies have shown that people who tend to emphasize their membership in certain groups are usually on the edge of those groups, which is why they feel a need to remind people that they belong in those groups. For example, people who go around bragging about being millionaires usually don't have tens or hundreds of millions of dollars, in most cases, they are the guys who are worth 1 or 2 million dollars.

People who are insecure about their ability to perform in their jobs are more likely to bring up their credentials unprompted during conversations.

You can pinpoint a person's insecurities based on the words they use to project those insecurities on other people. For example, if a person keeps pointing out others' physical faults, they are definitely insecure about their own physical appearance. Someone who criticizes others' body weight, attractiveness, or sense of fashion has a deep fear of being perceived as unattractive, overweight, or lacking a good fashion sense.

A person who calls others names is bad at dealing with high-pressure situations. If you have a minor argument with someone and he quickly resorts to calling you "stupid," or using other derogatory terms, it indicates a profound lack of confidence on their part.

Words reflect character

Sarcasm reveals that people are deeply cynical, and it can be deeply rooted in their character. Everyone uses sarcasm from time to time, so as you interact with someone, try to gauge the rate at which they react to situations in a sarcastic manner. Also, make a note of whether they do it in a light-hearted way, or if they do it in situations that are serious. If you want to start a relationship with someone, deep-rooted cynicism can be a red flag because it might be difficult to connect with a person who is that cynical.

You can also tell if a person is generally impatient after listening to the way he talks. Impatient people tend to interrupt you during conversations in a way that most people would consider to be rude. They could keep finishing your sentences for you instead of letting you tell your story to completion. They might also Segway into different topics while you are in the middle of talking about something that is important to you.

The missing words

When you are analyzing people's verbal statements, the things they don't say are almost as important as the things that they say. This is particularly true if you are trying to understand someone you have started dating, and you are trying to figure out if you are compatible in the long run.

For example, when you go out on a first date with someone, there is an expectation that he/she will ask meaningful questions about you; if this doesn't happen, it could mean that they are not invested in making the relationship into something more than it is.

When you share upsetting information with someone, and he doesn't do anything to soothe your worries, it could be a sign of a lack of empathy. The same could be true if a person dismisses your feelings or laughs them off. When you share bad news, and you don't even get an "I'm sorry to hear about that," the silence speaks volumes about the person's character.

Chapter 7: Understanding Personality Types

Psychologists have used different systems to categorize personality types over the years, but it seems that only one method has stood the test of time; The Myers-Briggs Personality Type Indicator. Now, we should note that there is a lot of debate in the field of psychology on the accuracy of this indicator, and some professionals have even argued that the whole system is based on pseudoscience, but there is no denying that understanding the Myers-Briggs indicator can go a long way in helping you sharpen your skills when it comes to analyzing people. For that reason, in this final chapter, we will discuss the 16 personality types.

The Myers-Briggs indicator assumes that people experience the world in 4 main functions, which shape their personalities. The indicator is based on a theory that was postulated in the early 1970s by Carl Jung. He believed that people are characterized by a preference of general attitude; they were either Extroverted or Introverted. He also believes that people could be categorized into two functions of perception; they either perceived the world by Sensing or through Intuition. Additionally, he believed that people processed information based on two functions; Thinking, or Feeling. About a decade later, Isabel Briggs Myers came up with a 4th criterion which reflected the way people implemented information after processing it; she believed that people processed information either by Judging or Perceiving it.

In the end, Myers came up with 16 personality types that would reflect:

• A person's energy expression; either they were Extroverted (E) or Introverted (I).

• A person's preferred method of perceiving information; Sensing (S) or Intuition (N).

• A person preferred method of processing information; Thinking (T) or Feeling (F).

• A person preferred method of implementing information; Judging (J) or Perceiving (P).

If you put together the four characteristics in all possible combinations, you come up with a total of 16 personality types as shown in the chart below.

ESTJ	ISTJ	ENTJ	INTJ
ESTP	ISTP	ENTP	INTP
ESFJ	ISFJ	ENFJ	INFJ
ESFP	ISFP	ENFP	INFP

Now, let's take a brief look at each of the 16 personality types, and describe how to identify people who fall under each category.

ISTJ aka The Doer or The Inspector

When you meet ISTJs, you might feel a bit intimidated by them at first. That is because they always seem to be serious. They tend to dress and act in a very formal manner. It's in their nature to be very proper in the way they conduct themselves. They also tend to uphold traditional values, and they are fairly old-school in the way they perceive the world. They are very hardworking, and they have a heightened sense of honor. They also tend to be very patient with the people in their lives. They contribute to their societies out of a sense of duty, so they end up being pillars of the communities they live in. They are generally interested in living in an environment that is peaceful and secure. They are very dependable, and they are the kind of people that you always know you can lean on. They have the ability to concentrate on the work they are doing, so they tend to be successful in life. Often times, they end up accomplishing tasks once they have set their minds on doing them.

ISTP aka The Mechanic or The Craftsman

They are generally very quiet, and they tend to be reserved, so to the outside observer, they can appear to be a bit mysterious. They have a very keen interest in how things work, and why they are designed that way, which is why they end up being good at fixing things or even designing them. They are the kind of people who will figure out how to repair things around the house without ever being taught to do so by anyone. They tend to have a high-risk tolerance, which means that they tend to be adventurous, and they live in the moment. They are more likely to express interest in extreme sports, and they are often talented in areas that require physical exertion. Their desires seem to be straightforward and uncomplicated. They tend to be loyal to their friends, and they have their own system of values or personal code which they adhere to. In fact, they care more about their own personal code than they do about the laws of the land or even the rules that are imposed on them by institutions. They may consciously break the rules if they seem arbitrary and obstructive. As a result, they are good at finding practical solutions to problems.

ISFJ aka The Nurturer

They tend to be very kind towards others, and they are conscientious. They tend to put the needs of other people before their own, and sometimes, it can be to their own detriment. They are generally quiet. They are the kind of people you know you can depend on, and when they take on certain responsibilities, they almost always follow through. They have stable personalities, and they tend to be very practical. They uphold traditional values, and they work hard to create a sense of security for the people in their lives. They are very perceptive when it comes to understanding the way others feel, and they go out of their way to help others overcome negative emotions. They observe others closely, and they tend to come up with theories about the emotional states of others. They are inclined to dedicate their lives to serving others, and they are likely to end up in vocational careers or areas

163

where service is valued above personal enrichment. They are also more likely to give to charity. They tend to bring out the best in others.

ISFP aka The Artist or The Composer

They tend to be quiet and serious, but they are also very kind and sensitive. They will try as much as possible to avoid conflict, so they will avoid confronting others or doing things that could cause others to confront them. In relationships, they tend to be loyal and faithful. Their senses are highly developed, so they have a unique ability to appreciate aesthetic beauty, which is why they tend to be artistic. They have no interest in controlling the actions of others, so they try to avoid leadership positions. They are likely to venture into careers or pursuits that require a lot of creativity and originality. They also tend to be very open-minded and flexible, so they are good at adapting and appreciating other cultures. Although they are introverts, they tend to warm up to people and become approachable, so if you have known them for a while, it might not even occur to you that they are introverted. They tend to be spontaneous and fun, and they are the perfect friends to have if you want to explore new experiences. Unlike other introverts, they actually value meeting new people.

INFJ aka The Counselor or The Protector

They are creative, original, and idealistic. They are also very sensitive. They have a quiet demeanor, but they tend to be forceful when it comes to asserting for themselves or for those they care about. They have a high sense of duty, so when they take on certain responsibilities, they tend to stick with them until they are done, no matter how hard it gets or how long it takes. They are very good at reading other people, and they tend to care about the welfare of others. They have their own value systems, which they tend to stick to; their value systems don't infringe on the comfort of others. They are the kind of people who always do the right thing. People tend to respect them because of their moral compass and their ability to persevere. They tend to be individualistic, so they are neither leaders nor followers. Their outlook is usually different, but it's very profound. They don't take things at face value;

they always look deeper, and they are good at finding hidden meaning in things.

INFP aka The Idealist

Their defining characteristic is that they are very interested in serving humanity. They have very lofty ideals and value systems, and they work very hard to live according to those ideals. They are generally quiet and reflective, which contributes to their idealism. They tend to be laid back, and they adapt well to different social environments. However, they can react in radical ways if their strongly-held values are threatened. They are loyal to the people in their lives. They tend to be very good writers because it's the best way for them to share their ideas with the world. They are mentally sharp, and they tend to identify possibilities that others seem to overlook. They avoid talking about themselves, especially with people they don't know well. They would much rather spend time alone in quiet reflection because it helps them make sense of the world around them. They like to attach meaning to a lot of abstract things; they are likely to spend time figuring out the meaning behind random events. They also tend to get lost in their imagination; they tend to have deep thoughts, ideas, and fantasies, and they can daydream even in the presence of others.

INTJ aka The Scientist or The Mastermind

They tend to be very analytical, independent, and determined. They are good at coming up with original ideas. They have an uncanny ability to transform mere theories into well thought out plans of action, and then to execute those plans and bring forth unprecedented results. They value knowledge and competence both in themselves and in the people around them. They also tend to be very structured and methodical in their approach to life. They tend to perform well in school and in their careers, and they have very high standards for themselves. They are natural leaders, but they can also be followers. However, they are only likely to follow other people if those people prove to them that they are competent, and they share their values. They can be team players, but they prefer to work alone. They are very self-sufficient, and they need minimal supervision if they are working under you. They are keen observers of the world and the people around them. They always question why things are the way they are, and they deeply dislike uncertainty. They like to be in control of their environment.

INTP aka The Thinker

They are very logical, but they are also creative thinkers. They are good at coming up with original ideas and solutions to problems. They are very excited about their ideas and theories, and they can dedicate a massive amount of time pursuing their ideas. They tend to be quiet and reserved, and they value competence, logic, and knowledge. They are hard to get to know well because they tend to keep to themselves and to have interests that others find strange or surprising. They are neither interested in leading nor following; they are highly individualists and are likely to march to the beat of their own drums. They are very good at reading people, so it's hard to get away with lying to them. They like patterns, and they are good at picking up on discrepancies; they find logical inconsistencies to be disturbing. They are disinterested in day to day routine activities, and they are more interested in the bigger questions in life; they flourish in areas that require the application of creative genius.

ESTP aka The Doer

These are action-oriented people. They are very social and highly adaptable. They have great people skills. They also tend to get immediate results. They live in the moment, and they are the kind of people whose lives are in the fast lane. They have a higher tolerance for risk than most other people, and they tend to jump before they look. They also tend to be very impatient, especially around people who like explaining things in too much detail. They quickly lose interest in theories and abstract ideas; they would much rather act immediately and find out later if they were right or wrong. Because of this, they tend to be rule breakers. They aren't very respectful of the kinds of laws that keep them from doing the things they need to do. They are governed by a need for freedom, so they don't go into fields where they are highly restricted. They are prone to making mistakes, but they fix their mistakes as they go. They don't sit by and make idle plans; they figure out their plans along the way. They tend to be logical and pragmatic, and they are loyal to the people in their lives.

ESTJ aka The Guardian or The Supervisor

They are very organized, and they tend to be practical. They have traditional values; they have a very clear idea of how things ought to be, and they dedicate them to doing what they think is right. They are likely to be athletic or in good physical shape. They only care about theories and abstract ideas if they contribute towards practical and applicable solutions. They are loyal to their communities, and they contribute to the society however they can. In fact, they are the epitome of good citizenry. They value security and prefer to live peacefully, so they are unlikely to question rules and laws. They like to take leadership roles in their communities, and they are good at organizing and running social activities. They are very dignified, and they are likely to sacrifice their own time or their comfort to help others. They are likely to volunteer their time and other resources towards non-paying community activities. They are the leaders of the pack, so others are happy to follow them because they know that what they are doing is not out of self-interest.

ESFP aka The Performer

They are very outgoing, and they are people-oriented. They love having fun, and they are the life of the party. When you hang out with them, they make things more fun for you. They live in the moment, and they value new experiences. They don't like to overthink or over-analyze things. They like to serve others because they are more fulfilled when they bring joy to others. They are natural entertainers, so they often end up being the center of attention in social situations. They also love the spotlight, and they value the approval of others. They have advanced interpersonal skills, and they can bring introverted people out of their shells. They are very generous and warm towards others. They have a deep concern for the well-being of others, but they can be competitive with those who try to steal their spotlight. They are also very observant, and they have a good barometer for detecting people's feelings and interests. They are often admired by others.

ESFJ aka The Caregiver or The Provider

They are very conscientious and warm-hearted towards the people in their lives, and as a result, they tend to be popular. They have a tendency of putting the needs of others before their own because they are driven by a strong sense of duty and responsibility. They like traditional values and security. They derive a lot of satisfaction from helping others, and they need positive reinforcement. In fact, they live for the expressions of gratitude which they receive from the people they help. They are stereotypical outgoing people. They are considered to be social butterflies, and their need to socialize is central to their identity. They yearn to be popular, and they get lonely pretty fast when they are left alone. They tend to be the sports heroes and cheerleaders in school, and they choose career paths and social activities that allow them to stay in the spotlight. They are more inclined to organize social events for their friends and families. They are generally well-liked and easy to get along with.

ENFP aka The Inspirer or The Champion

They are very creative and idealistic, and they are enthusiastic about their ideas. They are able to take on anything and achieve it, as long as they are genuinely interested in it. They have great people skills, and they are outgoing, but they also have personal value systems which they have a need to live by. They are fascinated with new ideas, but they are disinterested in too many details. They tend to be flexible and open-minded, and they have a broad range of abilities which seem to come naturally to them. In as much as they like attention, they are individualistic, and they like to chart their own courses. They prefer to create their own methods of doing things and to execute their own ideas, so they hate it when others try to define them. They don't like people who try to force them to live inside a box, which means they are not great followers. They tend to act impulsively on their feelings.

168

ENFJ aka The Giver

They tend to have exceptional people skills, so they are very popular as a result. They are sensitive to the needs of others, and they are very concerned with helping others feel better about themselves. They worry a lot about what others think of them, so they go out of their way to act decently. They often dislike being alone, so they pack their calendars with social activities. They tend to see things from a human angle, and they are less likely to go along with impersonal analysis. They are quite good at managing interpersonal issues. They are very effective regulators when it comes to leading group discussions because they tend to treat everyone equally. They also like serving others, and at times, they tend to put the needs of others above their own needs. They are charismatic, highly ethical, and very outspoken. They connect with people very well because they are open communicators.

ENTP aka The Visionary

They tend to be very sharp, highly creative, and extremely resourceful. They have broad talents, which they explore with passion. They like vibrant debates, and they tend to one-up people in their personal lives and in their careers. They have a need to prove that they are smarter than others. They are always excited to pursue innovative ideas, and they tend to take up a lot of new projects. They get easily bored by the mundane and routine aspects of life, and they may end up neglecting such things. They tend to be quite outspoken, and they are very assertive when it comes to advocating for their ideas. They thrive in the company of others, although they aren't always well-liked because of their competitive nature. They are good at applying logic to come up with solutions to complex problems. Even though they are extroverted, they don't like small talk; they prefer to discuss complex subjects with their intellectual equals. Without constant mental stimulation, they easily get bored.

ENTJ aka The Executive or The Commander

They are highly driven natural leaders. They are extremely assertive and very outspoken. They are able to comprehend the most complex organizational problems, and they come up with practical solutions. They are usually smart and knowledgeable. They are great at public speaking, even when they are improvising. They like competence and efficiency, and they dislike disorganization. They have a logical and rational approach to leadership, and they often rise high in their career ladders. They are good at identifying the strengths and weaknesses of others, which makes them great team leaders. They tend to look at challenges and obstacles as opportunities to test their own limits, so they tend to thrive in the face of adversity. They are also very decisive; even though they make quick decisions, they always deliberate carefully. They hate sitting around and waiting for things to happen; they like to take charge of every situation.

Conclusion

Thanks for making it through to the end of *How to Analyze People: The Ultimate Guide to Understand Body Language, Influence Human Behavior, Read Anyone with Proven Psychological Techniques*. I hope that you have learned a lot of useful techniques for analyzing people, which you can now apply to improve your personal or professional life. The next step is to start observing people more keenly so that you can spot their cues and start analyzing them to your advantage. Spotting the cues, we have talked about in this book is more challenging than you might assume, so you have to be as keen as possible to avoid missing subtle changes in people. However, don't worry; it's a skill that you will sharpen with practice.

You want to practice analyzing people wherever you go in order to be truly competent at it. To do this, you have to practice people-watching. If you take public transportation to work, spend that time observing the people around you. If you watch a lot of TV shows, you can try to pay close attention to the mannerisms and the facial expressions of the people you see.

We have cautioned time and again throughout the book that you shouldn't jump to conclusions based on just one or two cues. The accuracy of your reading depends on the number of cues you observe, so if you have a theory about what someone is feeling or thinking, keep observing them for a while until you are absolutely certain about your theory.

Finally, if you found this book at all useful, a review on Amazon will be greatly appreciated!

Cognitive Behavioral Therapy

Strategies for Retraining Your Brain, Managing and Overcoming Depression, Anxiety, Stress, Panic, Anger, Worry, Phobias.
Live in Happiness

Daniel Peterson

TABLE OF CONTENTS

Introduction

Cognitive behavioral therapy deals primarily with addressing the negative patterns in the way that a person sees himself or herself and the world. This is an issue of perception on the part of the person who has a diagnosis of an anxiety disorder or of a depressive disorder. It also focuses on the distortions that may emerge as a result of these negative patterns of thoughts and perceptions. The goal of cognitive behavioral therapy is to adjust the thought patterns and behaviors that cause a person to perceive things in a negative manner, that in turn cause the person to experience the difficulties that he or she possesses. In changing these patterns of negative perception, the person can change the way that he or she feels and then will be able to begin to make changes in his or her patterns of thoughts and behaviors that will continue the cycle of more positivity in his or her life.

How Does Cognitive Behavioral Therapy Work?

Cognitive behavioral therapy is a very commonly used form of psychotherapy. This specific form of therapy treatment can sometimes be even more beneficial when it is combined with other types of treatments such as with the use of antidepressants or other prescribed medications. A central focus in cognitive behavioral therapy is to assist people in becoming aware of when they perceive things in a negative manner and to make interpretations of what has happened based on these negative perceptions. In general, patterns of behavior will reinforce the distorted thought processes and thus continue the cycle of distortion. The goal of cognitive behavioral therapy is to break this cycle with the introduction of behavioral changes that the patient will be able to utilize in all future interactions that occur.

Cognitive behavioral therapy is a therapeutic treatment option that aids people in understanding the negative feelings and thoughts and the distorted ways in which they influence their resulting behaviors. It assists people in developing different ways of perceiving situations, achieving different thought processes, and learning different behaviors, which all have an end goal of reducing the overall psychological distress that the person feels. This type of psychotherapy is one that is educative in nature. The patient learns how to observe and analyze his or her own behaviors and how to replace them with more beneficial behaviors that will help him or her to reach their goals. It relies on the person or patient to have an understanding of himself or herself and to have the ability to be his or her own therapist.

Cognitive behavioral therapy works because of the focus on the individual and of his or her knowledge of his or her personal needs and goals. The person or patient needs to have a strong understanding of the disorder he or she possesses, as well as the ability to understand how it affects him or her on a daily basis and the course that the disorder may follow. This includes things such as self-doubt and negative self-talk and the likelihood of potential for relapses in the illness. He or she will also learn about the way in which cognitive behavioral therapy works, the process to follow to successfully complete the therapy, and the cognitive model from which the therapy was originally developed.

The cognitive model is based on the theory that your thoughts influence your feelings and emotions and that through these emotions, they will also influence your behaviors. So, before a person begins cognitive behavioral therapy, he or she perceives a majority of the things that happen in the world around them in a negative manner. He or she begins to have negative thoughts. The negative thoughts lead to negative feelings and then the negative feelings eventually lead to negative behaviors. As the cycle continues, the person either continues to perceive things in a more negative manner than what they are presented with, or the person's behaviors actually do lead to a more negative environment. In either case, this is a cycle that must be broken and the thoughts and behaviors need to be replaced with more suitable responses to meet the given occasion.

Once in cognitive behavioral therapy, the person will learn to recognize the patterns of his or her negative thinking and the emotions and behaviors that his or her thoughts and perceptions will lead him or her to display. He or she will learn how to allow himself or herself to be able to tune out the negative perceptions and thoughts by determining and utilizing new ways of thinking.

A person typically will work with a therapist in order to break the problems down into separate parts that are easier to analyze. The broken down portions usually consist of thoughts, emotions, physical feelings, and finally, actions or behaviors. Once broken down as such, the smaller portions are able to be much more easily analyzed. Then the patient can begin the evaluation process. He or she must look at everything, beginning with the thoughts and perceptions to determine if they are accurate and realistic. In most cases, the patient will discover that he or she has been perceiving things in a more negative way than those in which they really occurred. At this point, the rest of the sections can also be analyzed for accuracy. Homework is an essential part of completing cognitive behavioral therapy in a traditional clinical setting with a licensed therapist. This is because the patient will generally only see the therapist between two and four times monthly and each session is usually only somewhere between 30 and 60 minutes in length. The new skills that are learned in therapy sessions must be utilized on an everyday basis for the therapy to be successful in the replacement behaviors becoming second nature to the person. Also, in the long term, these new skills will continue to be utilized by the patient long after the therapy has concluded in order to maintain his or her mental wellness.

Many times, especially when dealing with anxiety or depression, once an unrealistic negative perception enters the mind of the patient, the thoughts and feelings that occur as a result are also unrealistically negative as well. Once each section has been analyzed, new patterns of thinking and behaving can be learned by the patient. Eventually, with practice, the patient will be able to implement the new patterns of thought processes and behaviors in his or her everyday life until they become automatic and replace the prior more negative thoughts and behaviors.

Chapter 1: What Is cognitive Behavioral Therapy

What is CBT?

Cognitive Behavior Therapy (CBT) is a type of talk treatment that involves focusing on emotions, thoughts, and behavior of an individual while teaching them skills to cope with various challenges and issues in life. It is based on the idea that how we think (thoughts), feel (emotion), and act (behavior) are closely interrelated.

This type of treatment combines examining thoughts (cognitive therapy) and things a person does (behavior therapy). The underlying concept behind CBT is the fact that human thoughts and emotions play a significant role in their behavior.

Negative and unrealistic thinking can bring us stress which causes us to get distressed or depressed. This ultimately becomes a problem if not given attention. Once a person suffers from psychological distress, the way they see thinks become twisted and distorted and can have a negative impact on their actions.

To illustrate, a person who spends a lot of time watching horror movies and reading books about suspense and thrillers are more likely to be afraid to sleep alone or without lights on. They can easily get paranoid over nothing.

It is CBT primary aim to let people became aware when they are into this situation – e.g., making negative interpretations and likewise making them aware of an existing behavioral pattern that reinforces this negative thinking. CBT helps us develop alternative ways of thinking to reduce psychological distress brought about by negative and unrealistic thinking.

The goal of the treatment is to teach us that while we don't have much control over some situations we come across to, we can take control of how we interpret and deal with them.

Simply put, CBT teaches you to take charge of your thoughts, emotions, and behavior for a better experience. By targeting your responses and reactions to situations, CBT can help you react more effectively to challenging issues and situations. This way, you will learn how to feel better when situations become uncontrollable.

Cognitive Behavior Therapy is gaining increasing popularity among health consumers and treatment providers in recent years due to its affordability. Because it is generally a short-term treatment, it more cost-efficient compared to other types of therapy.

Psychological Issues Where CBT Can be Applicable

Pieces of evidence suggest that CBT can be used for an effective treatment for a wide range of psychological issues and disorders including:

• Chronic Anxiety

• Phobias

• Panic attacks

• Borderline personality disorder

• Anger issues

• Depression

• Post-Traumatic Stress Disorder (PSTD)

• Drug and alcoholism

• Obsessive-compulsive disorder (OCD)

• Psychosis

• Sleep problems

• Sexual and relationship issues

• Eating disorder

• Schizophrenia

CBT can likewise help you discover new ways to cope with physical health issues such as:
• Chronic pain

• Chronic fatigue syndrome

• Habits

• Facial tics

• General health problems

Where Did CBT Originate?

Cognitive behavioral therapy talks about how our thoughts influence how we feel. I'm sure you can relate and think of several examples where you've thought of something and it instantly changed your mood.

Beck proposed that how we think influences how we feel and how we feel determines how we behave. And how we behave influences how we live our daily lives and the choices we make in it.

A perfect example of this would be to consider any phobias you may have. How have those phobias influenced your behavior and your choices? What's unfortunate is that what we fear limits us. If you have a fear of insects, it isn't likely that we'll spot you outside in the jungles of the Amazon hiking. If you have a fear of flying, you're probably going to travel mostly by car, right?

In many cases, this fear can become debilitating and limit our quality of life. For that reason, we might want to work with someone to get over this paralyzing fear. They want to be able to push past their fear and regain full quality of life.

It's for this reason that people seek therapy. They want help from a professional who has the answer to help them release their fears. One of the ways of working with anxiety including depression is cognitive behavioral therapy.

It's for this reason that people seek therapy. They want help from a professional who has the answer to help them release their fears.

The Theory Behind

Cognitive Behavioral Therapy is based on the idea that the way an individual thinks about a certain situation can affect the way he feels and behaves. So if you have this tendency to interpret a situation in its negative point of view, then this can lead you to experience negative emotions. These negative emotions will eventually affect your behavior.

Emotional problems were recognized to stem from irrational beliefs. So if you are experiencing negative emotions such as unhappiness, anger or rage, it is because of irrational beliefs. Ideas that are faulty becomes real because we believe they are the truth.

Take, for instance, there are children who hate their parents because they believe that their parents favored other siblings more than them. It could not be the reality but because they believe them, they perceive this negative as reality. As a result of these misconceived ideas due to faulty beliefs, these children grow up developing bitterness and hatred in their heart towards their parents and siblings.

When a person has ill feelings, the behavior likewise becomes negative and so the development of a behavioral disorder that needs to be treated. In such a case, the person has to see the value of seeing a therapist.

In accepting the fact that something in your needs to be changed, you must work hard to counteract irrational beliefs, dysfunctional feelings, and bad behaviors. In other words, you have to be responsible for making the change yourself and practicing the new behavior until it becomes second nature.

Irrational Ideas from the CBT Perspective

Irrational ideas lead to self-defeating behavior. For example, you yearned for the approval, love, and attention of significant people in your life. However, it does not necessarily follow that all these people will give you what you yearn for. In fact, there are those who will never give you their attention and approval and much more with their love. This may be unlucky of you but this is life. We can't have all in life. We can't get everything we want.

How logical is it that everybody will love our approval of you. It isn't. There are people who will never give you their approval. That's life. People have to get used that idea so as not to be negatively affected when rejected.

Another example is when you believe that you need to perform perfectly everything that you will be doing. This idea can stem from your childhood when you have perfectionists parents who kept on telling you to do or behave perfectly. This kind of idea has long been ingrained into your thinking that you believed it's the reality so that when you commit a mistake, it creates in you a great emotional impact. Such behavior could either result in your avoidance of socializing with others or expecting others to do everything perfectly.

Such an idea is absurd as no one is perfect. Even coaches, teachers, and therapists commit a lot of mistakes which makes learning a continuing process. That's fine. We all have our own share of imperfections. What counts here is the idea that we are all working hard for perfection even when it seems unattainable.

Negative thinking can start from your childhood days onwards. So, if you lack the attention or appreciation you need from your parents or teachers at school, you are most likely to think that you aren't good enough. Over time, this assumption will become your belief which will become automatic as you grow to be an adult. This way of thinking will then affect how you feel at work or in the university, and even in your daily life.

If these negative assumptions aren't challenged, then these negative thoughts, emotions, and behavior will become a normal cycle and integrate with your normal routine.

Efforts in CBT treatment is geared towards **changing thinking patterns**. Strategies used may include:

- Recognizing distorted thinking that triggers issues and reevaluating then in light of reality.

- Gaining awareness and a better understanding of the behavior

- Utilizing problem-solving skills to resolve issues

- Developing a greater sense of confidence in one's abilities

- On the other hand, CBT treatment likewise involves efforts to **change behavioral patterns**.
- Behavioral pattern changes are likewise considered and strategies may include:

- Facing your fears instead of avoidance

- Role-playing prepares you for potentially problematic interaction with people

- Learning to calm your thoughts and senses

However, not all those strategies mentioned are utilized. Collaboration is required between the psychologist and the person seeking treatment or assistance. This is to develop an understanding of the issue and together developing a treatment strategy that can work effectively for the specific condition.

General Assumption

The cognitive approach believes that a person unusual behavior (abnormality) is a result of faulty cognition's (misconception) about life, people, and self. This misconceived thinking may be due to cognitive deficiencies because of lack of planning or cognitive distortion. Cognitive distortion occurs then information is processed inaccurately).

Such cognition's distort the way we see things and while we interact with the world through our mental representation, any inaccuracy in our mental representations or any inadequacy in our ways of reasoning will result to an emotional and behavioral disorder,

Through CBT, therapists are teaching clients' ways to identify distorted cognitions via a process of evaluation. The clients then learn to separate thoughts from reality and eventually learn the influence of cognition on their emotions. They are also taught to recognize, analyze, and monitor their thinking patterns.

This behavioral therapy involves setting home works like keeping a journal of thoughts and a series of activities that will help them challenge their own irrational thinking and beliefs.

The bottom line is for the person to identify his own negative thoughts and unhelpful beliefs and prove them wrong. As they begin to shift to a more positive belief, their outlook in life changes as well.

Types of Cognitive Behavior Therapy

There are specific types of therapy regularly used by mental health professionals that involve CBT.

Rational Emotive Therapy (REBT)

This type of treatment approach is focused on identifying and changing beliefs that are quite irrational. The process of REBT involves:

• Identifying these irrational beliefs

• Challenging these beliefs

• Learning to recognize and alter negative thought patterns

Cognitive Therapy

Cognitive therapy is centered on pointing out and altering distorted and inaccurate thinking patterns, behaviors, and emotional responses.

Multi-modal Therapy

In this CBT approach, psychological are initially treated by addressing the following seven different but interconnected modalities:

• Behavior

• Imagery

- Sensation

- Affect

- Interpersonal factors

- Emotional responses

- Medication and biological considerations

Dialectical Behavior Theory

This CBT approach addresses behaviors and thinking patterns while incorporating strategies like regulation of emotions and adopting Mindfulness technique.

Each type of CBT offers an approach that is unique to them and centers on addressing the underlying thinking patterns contributing to the psychological distress.

Advantages of adopting CBT
CBT is Goal-Oriented

In contrast to other forms of talk therapy, CBT is geared towards helping you achieve your goals which can be anything from finding a suitable career to getting away from depression and anxiety. Once your goal is achieved, you can decide along with your therapist to end the treatment if there's nothing left to work on.

CBT is focused on the Present

CBT is generally focused on current situations and difficulties that are somehow distressing. By focusing on the here and now, it allows you to solve current problems more effectively and quickly. When you are able to identify specific challenges and focus on them in a structured and consistent manner, this can result in achieving greater treatment gains in a shorter period compared to traditional talk therapy.

CBT is Active

CBT requires you to collaborate with a therapist and work as a team in identifying issues and solutions. Instead of waiting for the situation to improve using repeated talks about the issue, you are allowed to take an active role in the treatment with the aid of CBT tools and assignments in between sessions to speed up the treatment. Each of those sessions is focused on determining ways to think differently while unlearning unwanted responses.

CBT is Time-Bound

Other types of therapy are open in terms of time-frame and have no definite end date established especially talk therapy. With CBT, the goal is to cease therapy at a certain point which is usually 14-16 months. Generally, it takes eight weeks for an individual undergoing therapy to become competent at the skills provided to them in therapy sessions and to reasonably understand how it works. While undergoing those sessions, the person usually observes a significant reduction of symptoms. So between 8-12 weeks, those undergoing CBT treatments often experience a remission of symptoms. From there on-wards, they continue with the practices learned skills and address issues related to ceasing the therapy.

More severe cases though take a longer duration to resolve. To help reduce the risk for relapses and provide them with refreshers to make use of core CBT skills, booster sessions are sometimes recommended.

Once you feel significant relief from symptoms and you have developed the skill to do it on your own without the help of your therapist, you can end your CBT which makes it shorter in duration compared to traditional talk therapy which usually lasts for years.

People who are using CBT were able to end their CBT after just a few months of using it. However, not all are making the same significant progress. There are some who still need additional therapy to create lasting change or reduce symptoms.

There are those who need more than six months to years of continuous CBT. They are usually those with chronic psychological issues. However, even in such a case, CBT is generally more effective and of less duration than in traditional talk therapy.

CBT is Science-Backed

More than 500 studies have demonstrated the effectiveness of Cognitive Behavioral Therapy for myriads of medical and psychological issues – and is one of the few treatments that are science backed.

Supportive

Achieving something that is different from what is considered normal for a long time is quite hard. With this in mind, cognitive behavior therapists are dedicated to assisting the client along the process at their own pace while providing them with a warm and caring relationship. With such type of environment, the client feels more comfortable stepping outside their comfort zone in order to achieve their goal.

Major Steps Involve in CBT Process

Typically, Cognitive Behavioral Therapy includes these steps:

Identifying Underlying Issues or conditions

Issue such as a medical condition, grief, divorce, anger or symptoms of mental illness can be underlying causes for a behavioral illness. At the start, you need to provide your therapist with personal information as well as medical history to help identify the possible underlying cause for the behavioral issue.

Becoming Aware of Thoughts, Emotions, and Beliefs

After you are able to identify the problems to work on with the help of your therapist, you are encouraged sharing your thoughts on these matters. Remember that CBT is talk therapy and so you are encouraged to tell more about yourself even those which you think is not related to the issue. But primarily, your self-talk should include though not limited to sharing your thoughts about yourself, experiences, interpretations, and beliefs about yourself, other people, and events. With this, your therapist will be asking you to keep a journal of your thoughts and actions on a daily basis.

Identifying Negative Thoughts and Faulty Beliefs

This is to help you recognize patterns of thinking and behavior that may be contributing to the behavioral issue. Your therapist will encourage you to concentrate on your physical, emotional, and behavioral reactions of responses in various situations.

Thoughts or emotions that reinforce faulty beliefs can result in problematic behaviors which ultimately affect numerous areas in life including career, family, relationships, and study.

This is evident in a person suffering from low esteem which lacks self-confidence arising from negative thoughts which created faulty beliefs about his abilities or appearance. As a result, this negative thinking can lead to problematic behaviors like the person might end up being anti-social and passing up opportunities for advancements in all areas of life.

To combat such destructive thoughts and behaviors, a cognitive behavioral therapist may start by allowing the person identifies the underlying reason for his suffering such as pointing out a problematic belief. At this stage of functional analysis, it is an important part of the learning process to know thoughts, emotions, and situations contribute to maladaptive behaviors. Though the process is not easy especially for those who are struggling with introspection, it can ultimately result in self-discovery and insights that are significant to the process of the treatment.

Focusing on Actual Behaviors

What comes after the functional analysis is to focus on actual behaviors that serve as the underlying cause of the issue.

At this point, the person starts to learn and execute new skills that can be applicable to real-life situations. So if a person is suffering from depression, then must start practicing new coping skills to deal with social situations that can potentially trigger a relapse.

In most cases, Cognitive Behavioral Therapy is gradually implemented to help the individual take incremental steps towards a behavioral shift. For those suffering from anxiety, they may begin by simply visualizing themselves in an anxiety-provoking situation.

After the person is able to cope with the visualization exercise, he may proceed by getting into conversations with family, friends, and acquaintances. Through a progressive exercise working towards a larger goal, the process seems less daunting, making the goal easier to achieve for the person suffering from a specific psychological issue.

Reshaping Negative and Inaccurate Thinking

At this point, the therapist will be asking on your views of the particular situation based on an inaccurate perception. This can be a difficult step after gaining long-standing thinking patterns about yourself and your life. However, with enough practice, helpful thinking and behavioral patterns will soon become a habit and it would no longer take much effort to implement or practice.

CBT is a useful tool to address emotional challenges, so if you are in need of the following, then CBT is for you.

• To cope with grief, loss, or death of a beloved

• Prevent a relapse of mental illness symptoms

• Cope with a medical illness

• Manage chronic physical symptoms

• Overcome emotional trauma related to violence or abuse

• Resolve relationship conflicts for better communication

• Manage symptoms of medical illness

• Identify ways to manage emotions

• Learn techniques for coping with stress and stressful situations

• Manage eating problems

Chapter 2: Goals of CBT

Two most essential CBT methods are the practices of self-monitoring and examining progress, by raising self-awareness and most times assess the state of one's being, individuals are also able to discover the faulty cognition's, limiting the core values, patterns of dysfunctional thinking, and behavioral hindrances. With this powerful insight, CBT therapist will guide the parents in taking steps that will prevail whether a behavior or mental obstacle.

The practices of self-monitoring and evaluation are the heart of CBT, just as every individual can prevail over mental illness by becoming conscious of the challenging behaviors and improving the probability for success by enhancing and monitoring the actions and thoughts. Great practices that can widely increase the awareness of the inhibiting thoughts, harmful behaviors and limiting beliefs that act as roadblocks on the path of success is the third strategy of mindful meditation.

While undertaking practices of SMART goals, self-monitoring, action plans, and self-evaluation, it is typically enough to make individuals achieve success and decrease the amount of time it takes to achieve goals by using several CBT tools. Basing decisions on and attaching to general psychological governing principles like the mind-body connection and the law of effects and cause, just as the CBT practitioners assist their patients to do, we can confidently transform our lives in the most necessary ways. After we begin to spin the positive spiral of personal growth with the CBT methods, the following will be used to build our starting momentum.

The CBT Toolbox

There are a wide variety of CBT tools that therapist use to improve the mental health of their patients, unlike some treatment methods, cognitive behaviors therapy helps to limit the way parents rely on the medications rather than focusing on establishing a behavioral and cognitive change through various modes of exercise and activities. After establishing a case formulation gotten from initial therapeutic communications with their patients, a CBT therapist will start recommending several cognitive and behavioral practices that are found within the toolbox of CBT. The exercise from the toolbox is vital due to the long-term necessity to give patients the resources to act as their therapist later in the future.

While there are several activities and exercises that may be used for a specific medical case, or favored by a particular therapist, there is an accepted range set for CBT methods based on their effectiveness and popularity. It is with standardized tools and techniques that can be used to enhance the success of achieving our aim or goals. We will examine, but it will be useful to gain more understanding of how CBT therapists frame their treatments methods.

Using CBT to Achieve Success

Since the basis of CBT is upon several psychological truths that are applied to everyone, they all can use the CBT methods to improve our level of wellbeing. Also, a CBT therapist assists their patients to change their downward spiral mental health; it is possible to use CBT tools as a springboard to success. One ideological way to meditate on using CBT for personal growth is to envision a scale that ranges from -5 to 0, represent every individual who has mental illness while the range of 0 to 5 represents healthy minded individuals that pursue high levels of life satisfaction. It is obvious to note that implementing CBT methods to improve your self-worth, you will learn fast on how positive emotions and thoughts can spiral you towards great success.

Defining Success

While there is an endless number of a personal growth goal that you can use CBT methods to achieve, the first step is to know which one will guarantee you success. Unfortunately, many people fall victim to assuming that materials, money, possessions, and social status will give them the satisfaction that is needed only to discover that limited happiness is achieved from them.

SMART Goals & Action Plan

The therapist and clients work together to establish a SMART goal that is (Specific, Measurable, Achievable, Relevant & Time-Bound) and make an achievable plan that assists towards accomplishing their desire. Typically, both the patient and therapist will meet together on a scheduled basis to review, update the client's formulations, goals, and action plan.

We know what success is all about; we can establish the SMART goals. Generally, we may consider having goals in a number of the following steps; Personal & Intellectual, Health Fitness, Spiritual, Financial & Professional Developments and Communication. Also, personal qualities like social intelligence and emotional may be difficult to measure; these are some of the most vital and rewarding goals to help because they are needed to achieve some extraordinary things. Just by committing yourself to also focusing on targets that are intrinsic and desires, in addition to this external success, you will be able to discover the life-satisfaction that is craved for. Before moving to the action plan, you need to consider your objectives using SMART goals. There is no reason to feel discouraged if you have the aim to achieve something monumental, you will have to put the bigger aspirations down into smaller, time-bound and measurable. You will have to reduce the bigger goals into smaller, time-bound and measurable goals.

The next step in using the process of CBT for success, which is to be considered the final step in the initial phase, would be to establish a management plan that might allow you to monitor your progress. While deciding on the methods that will be used to break down specific objectives will be for a particular individual option that is mainly based on situations and plans, the most necessary thing to do is to review and update your appropriate measurable and time-bound action plan.

Chapter 3: Common problems that CBT addresses

Who hasn't been depressed? Chances are you've been down in the dumps a time or two. Maybe you're not sure what to call it. Maybe it's just a phase, or maybe it's something that lasts longer than you'd like.

Depression is also called Major Depressive Disorder. It is commonly defined as experiencing a depressed mood which could mean feeling sad or empty or hopeless, or a loss of interest in almost everything including pleasure.

Needless to say, it's no fun. A person who suffers depression could experience weight loss or weight gain, insomnia, physical agitation, fatigue, difficulty focusing or making decisions or concentrating on any one thing. In more extreme cases, thoughts of death or suicide occur and feelings of guilt or worthlessness are also present.

Although we can't find any resources citing who discovered depression, yet there are many who had contributed and still contributing to the growing understanding of this psychological disorder. To begin with, let us go back to the early accounts of depression.

Early Accounts and Beliefs about Depression

It was during the 2ⁿᵈ millennium in Mesopotamia where the earliest written accounts of depression first appeared. Depression was taken in a spiritual viewpoint rather than as a physical condition. At that time, depression, along with other mental illnesses, are believed to be caused by demonic possession. It is for this reason that depression cases are dealt with by priests rather than by psychologists.

This concept of depression as being caused by evil spirits and demons had long existed in many different cultures like the ancient Romans, Chinese, Egyptians, Greeks, and Babylonians. Because of this misconception, treatment of sufferers includes physical restraint, beatings, and starvation in an attempt to drive away evil spirits which they believe resided in the body of the sufferers. Greeks and Romans physicians, however, considered it as a biological and psychological illness. Accordingly, treatment methods like massage, gymnastics, diets, baths, and music were applied. Some medication treatment made use of poppy extracts and donkey's milk.

Ancient Beliefs in Physical Causes of Depression

On accounts of physical causes, Hippocrates, the Greek physician was credited with the concept of depression as caused by an imbalance of four body fluids:

• Yellow bile

• Black bile

• Blood

• Phlegm

Melancholia or depression at that time was specifically attributed to the excess of black bile in the spleen. Treatment applied by Hippocrates when dealing with melancholia included:

• Bloodletting

• Diet

• Baths

• Exercise

Contrary to Hippocrates practice on the treatment of depression, Marcus Tullius Cicero, a Roman philosopher and statesman believed that melancholia was caused by psychological factors such as grief, fear, and rage. So during the lasts years prior to the Common Era, there are many – including some highly educated Romans – who believed that depression and other mental illnesses were caused by demons and wrath of gods.

How it works

Depression Causes and Treatment in the Common Era

Around 25 BC-AD 50, Cornelius Celsus is reported to recommend treatment of shackles, beating, and starvation in cases of mental illness. However, a Persian physician named Rhazes in AD 865-925 didn't find mental illness as arising from the brain so instead recommend baths for treatment. Remember that baths are a very early form of behavior therapy that also includes positive rewards for appropriate behavior.

During the middle Ages when Christianity is at its peak, mental illnesses are attributed to doings of the devil, witches, and demons. Drowning, exorcism, and burning became popular treatments at that time and many were locked up in asylums for lunatics. Although there are some physicians who continue to search for physical causes for depression and other mental illnesses, there were only a few of them.

In the Middle Ages, religion influenced European thinking about mental illness and attributing it to works of the devil, demons, and witches, At the time, popular treatments were in forms of burning, drowning, or locking up in a lunatic asylum. There are even stories of people with mental illness thrown in snake pits. While some doctors continued to seek physical causes for depression and other mental illnesses, they were in the minority.

During the Renaissance period beginning from the 14th century, people who were mentally ill were hunted and executed. This practice which is common at that time started in Italy and spread throughout Europe. Still, there are doctors revisiting the idea that mental illness is due to a natural cause and not a supernatural one.

It was in 1621 when Robert Burton published a book outlining both social and psychological causes of depression such as fear, loneliness, and poverty. The book is titled "Anatomy of Melancholy". In this book, his suggestions for treatment for depression include:

• Travel

- Exercises

- Diet

- Purgatives (to clear the body of toxins)

- Herbs

- Bloodletting

- Music therapy

Depression in The 18th and 19th Centuries

In the 18th-19th century or what was considered the Age of Enlightenment, depression was considered a weakness in temperament which is in the genes and therefore can't be changed giving rise to an idea that people with such mental condition must be locked up. It was during the latter part of this age when doctors began suggesting the idea that aggression was at the root of this condition. Exercises, diets, medication, and music were advocated with doctors strongly suggesting the significance of talking about the problem with your friends or a doctor. One doctor suggested that depression is a result of an inner conflict between what you want and what you know is right.

Depression treatment at the Age of Enlightenment included immersion of people underwater and tying them up in a spinning spool. They believe that by inducing dizziness, the brain will be put back to its original position. It is also at this time when Benjamin Franklin is said to have developed his own electroshock treatment. In addition, suggested treatments also include horseback riding, enemas, diet, and vomiting.

Recent Beliefs about Depression

In 1985, Manic Depression or what is known to us as Bipolar Disorder today was first identified by Emil Kraepelin, a German psychiatrist and distinguished it as a kind of illness that is different from Dementia Praecox or Schizophrenia. At this point in the history of psychology, psychoanalysis and psychodynamic theory were developed.

Sigmund Freud, who was considered the father of psycho-dynamic theory and psychoanalysis in 1917, wrote about melancholia and mourning. Freud considered melancholia as a response to any loss which can either be real or symbolic. Death is a close example of real loss and the failure to achieve the desired goal is an example of something symbolic. Freud further explained that psychoanalysis could help reduce a person's self-destructive thoughts and behaviors as well as resolve unconscious conflicts in an individual.

Treatments for Depression in the Recent Past

From the early part of the 19th century to the early 20s, many people were desperate for relief from severe depression to the extent that they are willing to undergo lobotomies or surgeries to destroy frontal lobes of the human brain. Although such operations were said to produce a calming effect, it can create changes to personality such as loss of the ability to make decisions and poor judgment. It could sometimes lead to a person's death. Sometimes, electroconvulsive therapy which uses an electric shock to the scalp is sometimes utilized for people with severe depression.

Present Concept of depression

Depression today is assessed as being a combination of many factors which are social, psychological, and social. Treatments for depression may be in various forms including medications targeting neurotransmitters and psychotherapy. CBT is one form of psychotherapy used in the treatment of transmission although electroconvulsive treatment may also be used in some cases such as in severe cases where immediate relief is needed and in treatment-resistant form of depression.

Since depression and its causes are more complex than what is understood by many, some newer therapies were developed in recent years in an attempt to provide a solution to those who failed to respond to therapy and medications. Some of the new therapies are Trans cranial Magnetic Stimulation and Vagus Nerve Stimulation.

Depression and Negative Thinking

We all have our dark thoughts when we are in our worse mood. With depression, however, these thoughts can go extremely negative that they can invade and distort your outlook in life.

To diffuse these negative thoughts, CBT can be effective as it provides a mental tool kit to challenge these negative thoughts. Over time, CBT for depression can realign an individual's thinking and get it back to normal.

Types of Depression

Unfortunately, there are several types of depression that a person can acquire. Some situations in life along with chemical changes in one's brain can cause depression. Regardless of the cause, you have to let your doctor know what you feel so he can refer you to a mental specialist to help you figure out if you have depression and what type of depression you have. Diagnosis is crucial in deciding the right kind of treatment for you. CBT has been known to treat all of these effectively.

Major Depression

This means that an individual suffers from five or more depressive symptoms for at least two weeks. Major depression is very disabling and it will interfere with your ability to eat, work, study, and sleep. These episodes may only happen a few times a year but they are awful to go through. Not only that, but they can pop up out of nowhere, after a life trauma like a death in the family or a relationship breakup.

Symptoms of Major Depression

• Weight loss or gain

• Difficulty in making Decision

• Lack of concentration

• Loss of interest or pleasure in your activities

• A shift in sleeping pattern

• A feeling of unexplained physical tiredness

- Mental tiredness

- Restlessness and feeling agitated

- Feeling a sense of unworthiness or guilt

- Thinking of suicide

With major depression, one can find it difficult to study, eat, work, and socialize with friends. Once in a lifetime, some people experienced having major depression or clinical depression while others can have it several times.

Major depression can occur from one generation to the next but generally, it affects people with no family history of the sickness.

Women are more at Risk of Having Major Depression

Women who are affected with clinical depression are almost twice in number compared to that of men due to the following factors:

- Menstruation

- Pregnancy

- Menopause

- Miscarriage

- Hormonal changes

Other factors that increase the risk of clinical depression in women include increased stress at work or at home, caring for aging parents, and balancing life-family with career. Even raising up a child is enough to increase the risk.

Persistent Depressive Disorder

This used to be known as **dysthymia**. PDD is a type of depression that lasts more than a year, typically at least 2 years. This isn't as severe as major depression, but you can experience many of the same symptoms.

Irritability, stress, and the inability to enjoy life, in general, are just some of the symptoms that may present during PDD.

This type of depression lasts for two years or more which is why it's called persistent depressive disorder. This is used to describe two conditions: dysthymia - chronic major depression and low-grade persistent depression.

Symptoms of Persistent Depressive Disorder

• Change in appetite (either overeating or not eating at all)

• Sleeping too much or too little

• Fatigue

• Feeling of hopelessness

• Low self-esteem

• Hard to make decisions and concentrate

Bipolar Disorder

This type of depression can butt into your life like a roller coaster that involves massive highs and drops in emotions. It can be extremely frustrating to experience this and not understand how to make it stop.

Warning Signs of Depression

Although only licensed and qualified mental health practitioners can correctly diagnose depression, yet there are certain early signs that may help you identify when someone is suffering from it.

Because depression varies in different people, they likewise differ in signs and symptoms. When there are some who would hide in a nutshell, some can manage to go on with their daily routine making it hard to detect the signs.

There are times when symptoms may appear like signs of depressions when they aren't. Symptoms observed in substance abuse issues, medication side effects, medical issue, and other mental health conditions may appear to be somehow the same to symptoms of depression.

The Diagnostic and Statistical Manual of the American Psychiatric Association (DSM-5) recognizes many different types of depressive disorders with Major Depressive Disorder and persistent Depressive Disorder as the most common ones. But the good news is the fact that depression is treatable. If you spot the following signs of depression, consider CBT (or other talk therapies), medication or a combination of these two to reduce depressive systems before it gets too late.

Low Mood

Low or depressed mood is apparent in both major depression and persistent depressive disorder.

In major depression, the person is depressed most of the time or almost every day which is apparent and observed by people around them. A person suffering from this type of depression is more irritable than lonely.

An adult person with a depressed mood normally reports having a sense of sadness or emptiness which is the reason why they are frequently in tears. Being in a low mood is one of the two basic or core symptoms used to diagnose the presence of depression in an individual.

People with a persistent depressive disorder will be experiencing depressing moods most of the time for at least two years while in children, they are more likely to experience irritability for more days at a minimum of one year. Although it may be less chronic and less severe compared to major depressions, yet it could represent symptoms of a major depression that have persisted for more than two years.

Difficulty Concentrating

In both major depressive disorder and persistent depressive disorder, symptoms are difficulty in making decisions and lack of concentration. As the individual with these symptoms struggles to think clearly, the change can be noticeable by those around them.

Decreased Interest or Pleasure

Next to low mood, having a decreased interest or pleasure in things that you enjoyed before is the second core symptoms of Major Depressive

Disorder. A person with these symptoms will display significant diminished interest or pleasure in almost all daily activities.

Sleep Disturbances

One may experience the inability to have quality sleep which may include difficulty in sleeping and feeling sleepy even after sleeping the whole night. Feeling sleepy at daytime is also an indication of either persistent depressive disorder or major depressive disorder.

Changes in Appetite

A loss or gain in weight of more than 5% in a month when you're not attempting for any weight change is significant and may indicate the presence of Major Depressive Disorder. In children, this may present as a failure to gain weight.

The persistent depressive disorder may either be apparent in loss of appetite or overeating although there may not be the same dramatic change in weight as observed in those with major depressive disorder.

Significant changes in weight (a gain or loss of 5 percent or more in a month) while not attempting to gain or lose may be indicative of the major depressive disorder.

Fatigue

The chronic feeling of fatigue or significant loss of energy can be symptoms of both major depressive disorder and persistent depressive disorder. When you are feeling tired most of the time, this can greatly interfere with your ability to function normally as an individual.

Psycho-motor Agitation or Retardation

When you are experiencing restlessness, agitation or lethargy that is affecting your behavior, daily routine or appearance, it could be an indication that you have a major depressive disorder. Such symptoms can be apparently shown in body movements, reactions or speech which are likewise seen by others as a significant change in your character.

Feelings of Worthlessness or Guilt

Common symptoms of major depressive disorder may include inappropriate and excessive guilt as well as feelings of being worthless. This sense of guilt can get severe and become delusional.

Recurrent Thoughts of Death

When a person is constantly thinking of death which is beyond the fear of dying, then it can be a symptom of a major depressive disorder. The individual may have suicidal tendencies or think of ways to kill themselves.

Why is it effective?

There is a wide range of Cognitive Behavioral Therapy techniques which you and your therapist can choose from. You may mix and match these techniques to work for you and to suit your preferences. Here are some of these techniques that are commonly used for people with a behavioral disorder.

Behavioral Experiments

Behavioral experiments in CBT aim to test thoughts. For example, your therapist may test your thoughts like, "If I kindly tell myself not to buy anything on impulse, then I can minimize my spending" or "If I criticize myself for impulsive spending, then I may stop myself from unnecessary spending."

To find out which approach will work best: self-criticism or self-kindness, then you have to do some behavioral experiments. Try doing each approach on different occasion and monitor your responses. This will allow you to have objective feedback on whether criticizing or being kind to yourself will be more effective in dealing with your impulsive buying behavior.

Thought records

You will be asked to record your thoughts like when your boss said commented something on your performance and you jump to the conclusion that your boss hates you or that you are stupid to do something good.

As you record your thoughts, make an evaluation based on evidence – weighing the pros and cons. So at times when your boss would be praising you for a job well done, then it allows you to assess your previous thoughts like, "If my boss didn't like me and believe I am stupid, he won't be giving me a positive feedback today!"

Once you are able to weigh the thoughts based on evidence, you will come up with more balanced thinking. So from there, you can tell yourself that it is always possible to make mistakes and that you will be doing better next time!

Thought records will teach you to be more logically reasonable and will be changing your faulty beliefs about yourself.

Pleasant Activity Scheduling

You would probably be asked to write down 1 -3 activities you will enjoy doing for certain days in a week like Friday to Sunday. So you will be making your daily planner Friday to Sunday, listing down pleasant activities you would not normally do like writing a poem, taking good pictures or doing some DIY crafts. This will develop in you a sense of competence, accomplishment, and mastery.

The aim here is to indulge in activities that produce higher levels of positive emotions to keep your mind less-thinking about negative emotions.

Situation exposure Hierarchies

This approach involved giving priority on things you would normally avoid. That is when your therapist would ask you to list, let's say things you wouldn't want to do when you have this social phobia, you will have on top of your list, "Going out with a friend tonight." Staying at home to read a book or watch TV would be at the bottom of your list.

Imagery-Based Exposure

An imagery exposure aims to provoke negative emotions by bringing to mind a recent memory. A good example would be about a woman who caught his boyfriend dating another woman. In the imagery exposure, the memory brings back all the details like how the cheating partner is holding the other woman's hand while looking deeply into her eyes. Even the smiles of the two are deeply engraved into her memory which solicits negative emotions of anger and bitterness. She could even still remember their voices.

The person is encouraged to keep visualizing until the feeling of distress and remorse are reduced to about half or more than its original level.

Chapter 4: Depression, Anxiety, and Anger Management

Anxiety and depression are two of the most common mental health problems that people face. There are so many mentions and conversations that revolve around the topics of anxiety and depression. But even with that, no many people understand them well. In fact, a majority of people still struggle to distinguish anxiety and depression from each other.

Anxiety and depression are closely related. Actually, almost half of the people diagnosed with depression are, also, found to have an anxiety disorder.

Understanding Anxiety

It is normal for people to feel anxious when they are faced with certain situations. With life as it is today, there are so many factors that may lead bring you stress and worry. But these are just normal ways that anyone would respond when they are under pressure. But anxiety is more than just feeling stressed and worried.

A person is said to have anxiety disorder when the anxious feelings they experience persist. It is when the feeling of anxiety doesn't go away and they occur to you for no particular reason. The feeling cannot be controlled. Anxiety is dangerous as it greatly lowers your quality of life.

Types of Anxiety

There are different types of anxiety. The difference comes in the triggers and the charactcristics that one exhibits when they are feeling anxious. Most people always exhibit symptoms for more than one type of anxiety and some may even experience depression as well. It is important to understand the type of anxiety condition that one is facing for the correct treatment measures to be undertaken.

Here are some of the most common types of anxiety

Generalized Anxiety Disorder

Generalized Anxiety Disorder is where a person experiences the feeling of anxiety almost every day for a period of about 6 months or more. They tend to worry a lot about so many things and not just specific situations that may cause stress. The worries are usually very intense and persistent to the extent that they interfere with a person's personal life.

The triggers are pretty much the normal things that people go through in life. Work, family, health or even financial matters. Any little variation or slip up can lead a person to imagine the worst and worry that something terrible with happen.

People with GAD tend to have other related disorders like social phobia, depression or other anxiety conditions.

Social Phobia

Social Phobia is a type of anxiety that causes one to have a very intense fear of receiving criticism, being embarrassed or receiving any form of humiliation. They tend to fear eating or to speak in public, making small talk and having casual conversations with people and being assertive with their decisions and choices at work.

Social phobia can, also, be specific. This means that a person may be comfortable doing some things but they get anxious when they are faced with certain specific situations.

The symptoms of social phobia are both physical and psychological. The symptoms, particularly the physical symptoms can be very distressing to a suffering person. Some of the common symptoms people with social phobia exhibit include trembling, excessive perspiration, stammering or blushing when they are trying to speak, nausea and/or diarrhea.

You know that a person has social phobia if they exhibit these characteristics and they persist for more than 6 months.

Specific Phobias

Just as the names suggest, specific phobia is the fear or the phobia of encountering a specific activity, object or a person/animal. It actually is pretty common for people to have a phobia for certain things. You could get very anxious when you see a spider or snake. It, also, can be that you are just scared of heights. This fear is natural. However, people with specific phobia tend to exaggerate the danger that they feel exposed to when they encounter the specific things they are afraid of. They end up panicking and feeling extremely terrified by simply thinking about a certain thing that they are afraid of.

Specific phobias trigger panic attacks. A person may experience choking, increased heartbeat rate, dizziness, hot and cold flushes, chest pain and perspiration. These sensations can be quite overwhelming.

You are said to have specific phobias if you experience these symptoms for 6 months or more.

Panic disorders

Panic disorders refer to the situation where panic attacks are recurrent and, possibly, disabling. They can be characterized by unexpected panic attacks that are recurrent, worrying that you will experience another panic attack after the previous one, worrying about the consequences of the panic attacks and significant change in behavior due to fear of amplified reaction.

Panic attacks often reach their peak after about 10 minutes, but they tend to last for about half an hour. A person often ends up feeling really tired and exhausted when the attack subsides.

Another unique thing about panic attacks is that they are very random. They can occur more than once in a day or just once in a few years. The attacks happen when one least expects it. You can even experience it when you are asleep.

Obsessive Compulsive Disorder

Obsessive-compulsive disorder is a condition where people's behaviors are extremely influenced by their anxious thoughts. They get obsessions or compulsions which lead them to repetitively act in order for them to alleviate a worry they have.

A person with OCD will feel intense shame about their need to satisfy their 'need' to act. This shame can lead to the problem being exacerbated.

Some of the common behaviors associated with obsessive compulsion disorders include obsessive cleaning due to increased fear of contamination, hoarding or counting items, constant safety checking to counter the fear of being harmed, having a sense of disgust for sexual activity or being overly religious and feeling the need to pray multiple times to an extent that it affects the person's performance in other aspects of their lives.

People with obsessive-compulsive disorders may experience other anxiety disorders, eating disorders, substance-use problems or depression.

Post-traumatic Stress Disorder

Post-traumatic stress disorder (PTSD) refers to a set of reactions that certain people experience as a result of being through a life-threatening or dangerous event in the past. It could be a sexual assault in the past, an accident, torture, war or being affected by a disaster. These events cause a person to experience intense fear, horror, and helplessness.

A person with Post-traumatic stress disorder tend to re-live the traumatic event, they are very alert and always looking for signs of danger in their surroundings, they tend to avoid anything that would remind them of the event and they tend to be emotionally numb. They lose interest in most things and often feel cut off from their close ones.

People with PTSD may, also, experience additional problems and may end up being depressed.

Chapter 5: Depressive/ Mood Disorders

There are many people all over the world who suffer from some form of depression. There are many disorders that fall under the umbrella category of depression. In this chapter, we will discuss what exactly depression is, as well as who it affects. We will also outline the various types of depression and the process of how depression is diagnosed.

What is Depression?

Depression is a common mood disorder. It is perhaps the most commonly diagnosed mental illness. However, although it is common, it can also be quite serious. Depression can be the cause of many severe symptoms that a person experiences. These symptoms can affect a person's daily life in the way that he or she thinks, feels, and even how he or she goes about his or her daily activities in life. Even the most mundane of daily activities such as eating, sleeping, and going to work or school can be affected by the disease of depression.

Depression is commonly diagnosed as clinical depression or as major depressive disorder, but these are just the two broadest terms used in the world of psychiatry in diagnosing depressive disorders. In order to receive a diagnosis of depression, the symptoms a person experiences must be persistent, nearly every day, for most of the day, for a minimum of a two week period of time. Symptoms and signs that may point to a diagnosis of depression include persistent anxiety or feelings of sadness or emptiness. This can include feelings of loneliness, low self-worth, and apathy. Feelings of intense pessimism or lingering hopelessness can also be a part of depression. A person who is depressed may lose interest in activities that he or she previously enjoyed or might no longer feel pleasure from spending time in previously much-loved hobbies. A depressed person may find that he or she is struggling with feelings of guilt, has become more irritable than normal, or feels helpless or worthless. A patient with depression may begin to talk and move in a slower manner than he or she did previously. This could be due to fogginess of fatigue that has enveloped the person or because of decreased levels of energy that have occurred. This can be related to the fact that many people suffering from depression have difficulties associated with sleep. These patients may experience insomnia, may often wake in the early morning hours, and often oversleep past the time they need to be up and functioning for work or school responsibilities. On the other hand, a person who is experiencing depression might have difficulty sitting still or feel restless and move about much more than what is normal for him or her. Another symptom that shows up commonly in cases of depression is the development of a mental fog that causes the person to have difficulty in remembering things, often lose his or her train of thought in conversations, have trouble concentrating, and unable to make even the most inconsequential decisions. A person with a depressive disorder often experiences changes in their appetite and therefore can have weight gains or weight losses. Some people lose their appetite altogether and find that they are only picking at their food if they even remember to eat and may experience weight loss, while others might eat more out of emotion or feelings of anxiety and so will see an increase in their weight. Both of these instances, although at extreme opposite ends of the spectrum, can be seen in people who have depression. Achiness and a variety of pains such as cramps, headaches, and digestive system issues are often found to be complaints of depressed patients. These pains often occur with no clear cause in a physical sense and often are not successfully treatable. Some of the most troubling concerns that may occur in patients with depression include uncontrollable thoughts of suicide and death that in some cases can even lead to attempts of suicide.

Major depressive disorder or clinical depression is a diagnosis that is given when the symptoms discussed above cause distress to the person or cause a significant impairment in occupational or social functioning. The symptoms cannot have a relationship to the use or abuse of drugs and alcohol. There is a high mortality rate associated with major depressive disorder. The majority of these deaths are a result of suicide. It is of the utmost importance that anyone who thinks that he or she may have symptoms of depression is seen by a doctor, therapist, or psychiatrist in order to receive treatment for his or her condition. Depressive disorders are one of the most commonly diagnosed mental illnesses and in most cases are highly or completely treatable. Cognitive behavioral therapy is a short-term treatment that is highly effective when utilized to treat depressive disorders. The tools and strategies that are developed and learned in therapy can help a person to manage his or her mental conditions for a lifetime.

Major Depression

Over 15 million people suffer from depressive disorders worldwide. Depression has been cited as one of the most common disabilities. Sadly, however, only approximately 10 percent of the millions of people who suffer from depression will receive adequate treatment.

One-quarter of adults in the United States live with a diagnosis of clinical depression also known as major depressive disorder. Although depression is a disorder that affects mental wellness, it can also take a toll on physical health. The cardiovascular system is especially vulnerable to the added stress placed upon it as a result of depression. The risk of suffering cardiovascular issues increases with a diagnosis of depression. This is mostly because the stress of depression causes the blood vessels to constrict, which makes the heart to work harder. People who have depression are also more likely to die as a result of a heart attack than their counterparts who do not have depression.

Depression can have a direct impact on nutrition especially in the form of fluctuations in appetite. Some people with depression do not eat enough, although it may seem an unpleasant side effect, it can actually contribute to anorexia nervosa, an eating disorder that can often time be quite severe. Many times, people who experience depression also have deficiencies in at least one of the following categories: B vitamins, amino acids, minerals, and omega-3 fatty acids. Without adequate amounts of these nutrients, the brain is unable to work as it is supposed to. In other cases, people with depressive disorders tend to overeat, even binging. This can lead to extreme weight gain, along with other physical health disorders such as the onset of type II diabetes, high blood pressure, and other illnesses that are a direct result of obesity. It may be difficult, but for these reasons, it is essential to maintain a healthy and nutritious diet while experiencing depression and while undergoing treatment for depressive disorders.

There are many factors which lead to worse overall health in those people who have a depressive disorder. These include poor sleeping patterns, poor eating habits, and a lowered immune system. It is just as important to receive treatment for one's physical health as for one's mental health when suffering from a depressive disorder.

Depression has an impact on every aspect of an individual's daily life. It affects your ability to eat and sleep. You may not be able to sleep well, you may have insomnia, or you may sleep away your entire day. All of these can be symptoms of depression. As far as eating goes, a person with a depressive disorder may eat too much or too little. Depression can rob a person of the ability to understand when they need to eat. Due to these factors, as well as the suppression of a person's immune system, depression can also have a negative effect on your health.

Depression can also take its toll on your relationships. The correlation between your moods and emotions and the health of your relationships is strong. When dealing with a mental health disorder such as chronic depression, it can be difficult to manage relationships. When your mood is often low, your behaviors can cause distance to occur between you and those with whom you have relationships. You may not even realize that you are behaving in a manner that can cause issues within your relationships. This is one way in which learning replacement behaviors through the use of cognitive behavioral therapy can be of great benefit to people who are suffering from depressive disorders.

There are multitude ways that depression can affect a person that may not be visible to others. One of the most common and extreme feelings that a person with depression may experience is guilt. Too often, a person with depression just does not feel the ability to do the things that need to be done. This includes showering, eating, cleaning his or her home, walking his or her dog, and more. A person with depression knows that these are things that should be done, but may not have the ability to complete them. The resounding feeling that follows the inability to complete these daily tasks is often guilt. Studies have shown that due to variances in the brain, people with depression feel guilt in a much more intense way than people who are not depressed.

Some people with depression have a much more difficult time dealing with their lives in the morning than at any other time of day. This is when it can be a tremendous struggle just to make it out of bed. Frustration, fatigue, anger, and extreme sadness are some of the feelings that can compound so-called morning depression when the mornings contain the most severe depression symptoms.

People with depression are often good at hiding things from the outside world. This can be due to the guilt that they feel. A person with a depressive disorder may actually be totally exhausted at any time, yet be able to pull himself or herself together in order to prevent causing distress to others. Some people who are experiencing depression might be great at acting like they are alright, even when they are not. This is why it is not always possible to look at a person and decide if he or she is depressed.

A behavior that is often displayed by people dealing with depression is canceling plans. This is especially common in cases of bipolar disorder. Many times a person feels that they can go through with the past when the time comes, however, when dealing with depression, once the time comes, the person is unable to participate or even to leave his or her house. Just the thought of preparing for a scheduled activity can be too much to deal. Entering the outside world, where it appears that everyone else is able to easily function can be extremely stressful for a person struggling to deal with the side effects of a depressive disorder. One of the most difficult things for a person with depression to understand is that even though he or she knows logically that his or her life is great and he or she thinks that he or she should be happy and grateful, is that it is not always possible to use logic in terms of feelings. Even if a person does not think that there is any reason to feel depressed, the feelings are not necessarily on board. Feelings are not something that can be controlled and this can be one of the most frustrating circumstances a person with a depressive disorder must endure.

What Causes a Person to be Depressed?

In the United States, depression remains one of the most commonly diagnosed mental conditions. There are many factors at play in how a person can have a diagnosis of depression. These factors can be singular in nature or occur in a combination for the cause of depression in any one individual person. Depression can be genetic, meaning that it can be found in a person's DNA to have a higher risk of developing a depressive disorder. In many cases, a diagnosis of major depressive disorder is not merely a psychological effect, but may also be linked with biological factors as well. In some of these cases, a biochemical background of higher depression risk can contribute to the development of the disease of depression. Environmental factors can also be at play in the onset of depression. This is most commonly seen in cases of seasonal affective disorder which will be discussed in depth later in this chapter but can also include events like divorce or the death of a family member. Lastly, psychological reasons may be a causation of depression in some cases. In this case, pessimists and people who already carry conditions such as having low self-esteem may develop depression.

Some people develop depression as a co-morbid diagnosis, along with another serious physical or mental medical condition. It is not uncommon for patients who experience cancer, diabetes, heart disease, or Parkinson's disease to develop depression as well. Any of the previously listed diagnoses can completely change a person's life and limit daily activities, which in turn, can lead to depression.

Some people carry higher risk factors for developing depression than the rest of the general population. As stated above, experiencing major life changes can predispose a person to be at a higher risk of developing depression. This can include anything from a job change or a move to a different city to the death of a loved one or going through a divorce. Trauma and stress can also cause depression to more easily occur in some people. Even high levels of stress on the job can contribute to a diagnosis of depression. People who experience post-traumatic stress disorder have a very much increased likelihood of depression. Post-traumatic stress disorder is often seen in soldiers who have been in active duty. It can also occur in other situations such as after an abduction, assault, or car wreck. Depression and post-traumatic stress disorder are often co-diagnosed in individuals. A patient who has a personal history of depression is more likely to have concurrent relapses of the disease, especially when medication or therapy has been discontinued. Likewise, a family history of depression allows for a higher incidence of depression to occur in an individual with this background.

Many medications carry potential side effects that include a possibility of predisposing a patient to become depressed. In addition to this, as discussed previously, certain diagnoses of physical illnesses can cause a person to more likely to develop depression. Sadly, in many of these cases, not only does the disease itself lend a higher incidence of depression, but in addition, the medication prescribed to treat or control the disease can carry depression as a potential side effect as well.

Depression often co-exists with the abuse of substances such as alcohol or illegal drugs. Since the two diseases share many of the same symptoms, sometimes it can be difficult to discover whether a person began to abuse substances because he or she was depressed or if the substance abuse led to depression. A propensity substance abuse is quite similar to that of depression. There can be a genetic link, as both depression and substance abuse tend to occur generationally in families. Issues with mental health can at times be found as the reason that a person began to abuse substances. Conversely, substance abuse can be a cause for later mental health issues to develop. Both depression and the abuse of alcohol or other illegal substances have an effect on the human brain. They both affect the same portion of the brain which is the one that is in charge of a person's response to stress.

This combination of depression and addiction is often referred to as a dual diagnosis. A dual diagnosis can be any form of mental illness that coexists in combination with any form of addiction. The instances of dual diagnoses in the US are rising in number. Another worrying fact is that both mental illnesses and substance abuse can down a person's immunity, causing them to more easily become susceptible to illnesses. One safety measure that can be taken is to avoid the use of alcohol and medications that have not been prescribed for you if you have depression or any other form of mental illness.

Depression can become so severe that it can be considered a disability. Depending on how well a person with a depressive disorder continues to function in daily life or how much impairment it creates will determine whether or not it is a true disability. Both major depressive disorder (and clinical depression) and bipolar disorder are considered to be disabilities by the social security administration.

Persistent Depressive Disorder

Anyone can potentially have a depressive disorder. Depression is not a disease that occurs only at a typical age, to a standard stereotype. Age, fitness level, wealth, race, or religion makes no difference in who can develop a depressive disorder. Depression can be mild or major. Mild depression typically has less severe symptoms and it mostly interferes with motivation. Major depressive disorders as previously stated is also called clinical depression is the most commonly diagnosed form of depression. It interferes in a person's daily life and with his or her daily activities.

Under the diagnosis of depression, many forms of the disease exist that have some degree of variance from each other. Some types of depression may be slightly different from each other, while others will develop only under certain unique circumstances. In addition to clinical depression and major depressive disorder, here we will discuss five other forms of depression that exist under the umbrella of the depression diagnosis.

The first type of disorder we will look at is a persistent depressive disorder. This is also termed as dysthymia. A persistent depressive disorder is a mood of depression that persistently lasts for a period of at least two years. This is a continuous, chronic, and long-term type of depression. Although the level of depression may not be as deep as it is with some other types of depressive disorders, the key component with the persistent depressive disorder is the length of time that it lasts. Similarly to clinical depression, the patient may experience symptoms such as feelings of inadequacy, hopelessness, and a lack of productivity.

The person may lose interest in their typical daily activities and even in completing personal hygiene tasks on a regular basis. People who have a diagnosis of this disorder often feel gloomy and down, finding it difficult to be happy even in circumstances and occasions that would typically warrant higher spirits. This particular depressive disorder can cause impairments that range from mild to severe.

Next, we will discuss postpartum depression. This is a type of depression limited only to women who have experienced pregnancy or delivered a child. Postpartum depression is viewed as a complication of giving birth. It is a separate phenomenon from the typical "baby blues" that many women experience in the first few weeks after giving birth that includes difficulty in sleeping as well as some mood swings. Although this disorder has a certain event of causation, women who experience postpartum depression have full symptoms of a major depressive disorder that begins at any point during the pregnancy or after the delivery has occurred. The woman may experience anxiety, severe feelings of sadness, and extreme exhaustion. Many women who experience postpartum depression have a difficult time bonding with their new baby. Due to these symptoms, the woman experiencing postpartum depression may find it difficult to care for themselves or to complete daily care for their newborn babies. Many women with postpartum depression feel intense emotions of anger, sadness, and irritability. They may feel that they are not or are unable to be a good mother to their child. In some of the most severe cases, the new mother can have recurring fantasies of hurting either herself or her baby. This can include uncontrollable thoughts of suicide and death. There are cases of postpartum depression that can occur in new fathers as well as new mothers. Men experience the same symptoms as women, but they are typically focused on the lack of sleep they now endure, feelings of being unworthy as a father, and a lack of energy. Other symptoms may include insomnia, difficulty in bonding with the baby, and a withdrawal from friends and family members.

The third disorder we will outline is psychotic depression. This term is used when a form of psychosis is present in addition to the diagnosis of severe depression. It can also be referred to as major depression with

223

psychotic features. Depression with accompanying hallucinations or delusions qualifies for this diagnosis. A delusion is defined as holding a false, disturbing fixed belief. Hallucinations can be auditory or visual in nature. Auditory hallucinations occur when a person hears things that are disturbing that no one else is able to hear. Likewise, visual hallucinations occur when a person sees upsetting things that are not seen by anyone else. Typically, the theme of the hallucinations and delusions are of a depressive nature. An example of this is a person with depression who experiences delusions of illness, poverty, or guiltiness. This is what occurs when the psychotic features are mood congruent. This means that they comply with typical depressive features. When the psychotic features are termed mood-incongruent, it is considered more dangerous for the patient and the other people in his or her life. With this type of hallucinations and delusions, the risk of suicide, harm to others, and self-harm are much increased. The hallucinations and delusions not only cause people to hear and see things that are not real but also to believe in them. Approximately one out of every five people who have a diagnosis of depression also has a psychotic diagnosis as well, making this disorder far from uncommon. This type of depressive disorder is more serious than some other types. Behavior, mood, sleep, and appetite are among the many areas of a person's life that this depressive disorder can affect. It typically requires immediate attention from a doctor and immediate medical treatment.

Seasonal affective disorder is a type of environmental depression that is commonly experienced to some extent by many people, particularly in the northern hemisphere where there are prolonged seasonal periods of darkness. This disorder is most commonly characterized by depression symptoms that have an onset in the winter months while lifting in the spring and summer months. The onset generally occurs due to the lessened availability of natural sunlight. Symptoms of seasonal affective disorder include an increased amount of sleeping, a withdrawal from social activities, and weight gain. Seasonal affective disorder usually has a predictable return each year as the months grow colder and darker. Some reasons that may potentially be behind the cause of seasonal affective disorder include a disruption of the body's natural circadian rhythm and an imbalance in the hormone melatonin which is caused from the decrease of natural sunlight.

The last type of depressive disorder that we will discuss in this chapter is bipolar disorder. This illness was previously named manic-depressive disorder, referring to the extreme highs and extreme lows that the patient could reach. People who experience bipolar disorder have extreme shifts in mood. On end of the spectrum, extremely sad moods that meet the diagnosis criteria of major depressive disorder. These low moods are labeled as bipolar depression. On the other hand, patients with bipolar disorder also go through periods of extreme highs, called mania. These moods are unstable and can cause the patient to feel either irritable or euphoric. Manic episodes of a lesser severity are called hypomania. Some of the symptoms that people with bipolar disorder experience include changes in activity levels and sleep patterns, unusual behaviors, and intense emotions. While displaying signs of depression or mania, the moods and behaviors are quite different from what would typically be expected from the person. Manic episodes can consist of increased levels of high energy, feelings of elation, difficulty in sleeping, speaking very quickly, having difficulty staying on topic, being jumpy and irritable, engaging in risky behaviors, and thinking that many things can be handled at the same time. Periods of depression can consist of decreased levels of energy, feelings of hopelessness, sleeping too much, sleeping too little, forgetfulness, difficulty concentrating, eating too much or too little, and thoughts of suicide or death. Bipolar disorder is actually able to be divided into four distinct subcategories. All four of the categories have commonality in that mood, activity, and energy levels are variable. The first of the subcategories is bipolar I disorder. Manic episodes lasting for at least one week are a characteristic of this category. Sometimes the manic symptoms can be so intense that the person will require hospital care immediately. The time frame for depressive episodes can last for as many as 14 days. Some patients with this diagnosis can experience mixed features during their depressive episodes which means that manic and depressive symptoms can exist at the same time.

Bipolar II disorder is quite similar to bipolar I disorder. The main difference is that instead of reaching the intensity of the manic period that can be experienced in bipolar I, bipolar II is consist of hypomanic periods, along with periods of depression. Cyclothymia which is also known as cyclothymic disorder is quite an interesting category. With this diagnosis, symptoms must last for a period of a minimum of at least two years. There are depressive and hypomanic symptoms present, but they are not at a level of severity as to be diagnosed as either bipolar I disorder or bipolar II disorder. This is because the diagnostic requirements have not been met to see the episodes as truly depressive or hypomanic. The last category of bipolar disorder is labeled as "other specified and unspecified bipolar and related disorders." This serves as a category for people whose symptoms of bipolar disorder do not meet the requirements to be diagnosed as any of the other three categories. In some cases, people who are having switches from depression to mania may not notice the shifts themselves, but they can be picked up on by family members or friends. Bipolar disorder is famously difficult to diagnose due to the similarities of symptoms it shares with types of psychosis and other mental conditions.

Depression can take on many forms. A similarity among each type of depressive disorder is the theme of feeling low, sad, empty, or sad. Due to the similarities of symptoms and the number of diagnoses that fall under the umbrella term of depression, finding the right diagnosis and treatment option can be difficult. However, in most cases, if a person has a diagnosis of depression, cognitive behavioral therapy can be a key to successful treatment.

At this point, you can skip ahead to chapter four if you wish to find out how cognitive behavioral therapy can help you to overcome your depression.

Chapter 6: Anxiety Disorders

Short-Term Anxiety Disorders

A short-term anxiety disorders usually takes as little as 6 sessions, or even up to 20 sessions. All through every session, you and your therapist might identify situations and circumstances within your life that might have caused your low mood, or contributed to it. This is when your current way of thinking and your distorted perception can be tackled and identified. You might be encouraged to save journals to keep records of each of your life events and your reactions to them.

Long-Term Anxiety Disorders

If the anxiety is caused for long term, the person usually experiences a host of other experiences. When anxiety is caused due to a single event or so (like writing an examination), it will eventually fade away as the event passes by. If the reason for anxiety is a tussle between you and your mother-in-law, then it is likely to be caused for a brief period (till whenever you both see each other). Such cases are usually accompanied by other symptoms, including diarrhea, irritability and constipation.

If the anxiety is caused due to some problem at work, then it is likely to be a long term problem. You may fear getting up in the morning or going to the bed at night (as you will need to go to work). You will feel anxious on the weekends (as once it is over you will need to go to work). If the root of anxiety always hangs around, you may experience certain other symptoms chest pain, loss of appetite, loss of sleep as well as sexual desire.

All these situations described above, will lead to anxious moments day in and day out. Even though such anxiety is pretty common and part of our everyday life, it impacts our health mentally, physically as well as emotionally.

Generalized Anxiety Disorder

One of the most prevalent anxiety disorders around, Generalized Anxiety Disorder (GAD) is characterized by an excessive worry about almost everything in a person's life with no particular cause or reason as to why.

Individuals who have GAD tend to make a big deal out of everything. They become anxious about everything in their life — are it their financial status, work, family, friends, or health — and are constantly preoccupied with worries that something bad might happen. They expect the worst case scenario about everything and always try to look at things from a negative point of view.

With that said, it's easy to see how GAD can make it difficult for someone to live a happy and healthy life. It can come as a hindrance for their day-to-day life and become an issue with regards to their work, family, friends and any other social activities. Some of the most common symptoms of GAD include: excessive worry or tension, tiredness, inability to rest, difficulty sleeping, headaches, mood swings, difficulty in concentrating, and nausea.

Fortunately, however, CBT has worked wonders in treating all these symptoms and more. With the help of CBT, individuals suffering from GAD can change these negative thoughts into positive ones, which will ultimately change their behaviors for the better as well.

There are a number of CBT techniques that people with GAD can apply to better manage their symptoms. For example, if you have GAD and want to feel relief from all the muscle tension in your body, you can try yoga; whereas meditation can help you stop over thinking; and breathing exercises are good to practice when you start to feel yourself getting anxious again.

Yoga has been proven to help lower a person's stress, which in turn, relaxes their muscles as well. There are a number of different yoga poses and routines you can find on the internet tailored to relieving your stress and anxiety. Some examples include: the eagle pose, the headstand, child's pose, half-moon pose, and the legs up the wall pose.
If you need help getting started with how to use yoga to ease some of the distress you may feel from GAD, here is a quick rundown of how you can do it:

• Go to the gym and sign up for their yoga class.
• Or if you prefer, you can stay at home and do yoga by yourself.
• It's often best to do yoga in the afternoon or at the end of the day, as a way to decompress.
• Set up your mat, and if you want, play some relaxing music.
• Breathe in and out, deeply.
• Be aware of your breathing as you move through each pose.
• Take your time going through all the movements.
• Most importantly, enjoy yourself and keep your mind clear.

On the other hand, if the most problematic symptom of your GAD is overthinking and emotional turmoil, not muscle tension and chronic pain, then meditation just might be the CBT technique for you. Here's how you can do it:
• Download some guided meditation videos online (there's plenty on YouTube)
• Listen to them on a regular basis, preferably everyday (as you wake up or before you go to sleep is the most ideal).
• Find a quiet place to do this, where you can be alone and away from distractions.
• Devote all your attention to these 10-30 minute mediations and do not think or worry about anything else while you're doing so.
• Make it a rule that once you start meditating, you need to forget about everything else going on in your life and just focus on the present moment.
• Repeat everything the instructor is saying in the guided meditations

By meditating, you are giving your anxiety a healthy and positive outlet and releasing your physical tension from your body. The more you do it, the more peace of mind you will feel, and the easier it will be for you to overcome your anxiety.

When using CBT, a person with GAD will have a much more favorable perspective in life. Instead of always worrying and thinking about the worst case scenario, CBT reinforces an optimistic and reasonable outlook on life, which will then have a positive impact on their behavior as well. Most of the time, they'll change from a tense and edgy person to a relaxed and easygoing one that doesn't assume the worst out of everything.

Chapter 7: Panic Disorder

Panic attacks are characterized by out-of-the-blue emotions or feelings of trepidation when, in fact, there is no real reason to be afraid. Having recurrent panic attacks for seemingly no reason at all is what is known as a panic disorder. This is mostly found in young adults aged 20 and above. However, it can also be experienced by other children who also have panic-like symptoms.

Anxiety disorders can greatly affect a person's life. Always being at risk of spontaneous panic attacks may lead them to avoid going out, and thus, isolate themselves from others. Individuals with panic disorder typically live their lives in fear of getting another panic attack, so they try their best to control it or maybe even hide from other people.

Individuals with panic disorder often spend most of their time fearing the possibility of having another panic attack (a fear known as "agoraphobia"). Agoraphobia is when individuals stay on high-alert for potential panic attacks and always keep their guard up in case real danger arrives. This can cause them to avoid certain places like shopping malls, festivals, movie theaters, grocery stores, and the like.

With different types of indications, panic disorder typically includes symptoms like sweating, rapid heart rate, chills, trembling, or always sensing potential danger in every situation. In order to control symptoms like these, there are a lot of different treatments created for panic disorder. Cognitive Behavioral Therapy is also commonly used by therapists in treating patients with a wide variety of mental problems, including panic disorder.

CBT deals with a person's thought patterns, emotions, and behaviors. It deals with the cognitive and behavioral factors of psychological problems and seeks to transform a person's negative ideas and behaviors into more positive ones. When dealing with panic disorder, it is important for CBT to eliminate their constant fear of being in danger and replace them with the assurance that not all situations will lead to an untimely death.

There are several CBT techniques that can help individuals with panic disorder overcome their condition or calm themselves whenever a panic attack arises. Developing your calming skills is one of the most notable techniques. If you're struggling with panic disorder, try this basic guide on how to ease your mind and prevent a panic attack from escalating once you sense anxiety knocking on your mind's door.

• Take long, deep breaths.
• Are you anxious? Be honest with yourself about what you feeling and identify your emotions.
• Work towards accepting these feelings, even the negative ones like fear.
• Once you've accomplished this, remind yourself that your thoughts only have power over you if you let them. Your feelings do not control you, but rather, you control them.
• Assess your thoughts and ask yourself if these are actually realistic or reasonable (much like what you did before, in dealing with social anxiety).
• Visualize a calming scenario and go to your happy place. This can be a pristine, white sand beach with the cool sea breeze in your face; or a lush, green mountain top overlooking a beautiful sunset. Wherever it is, go to it.
• Repeat a positive, self-affirming mantra in your mind. Examples include:
This is only a trick played by my brain; I am more powerful than these negative thoughts.
I am strong and powerful and I will not surrender.
I am getting stronger and healthier.
I can do this. I believe in myself.
No matter how terrible this feeling may be, it will pass. And I'll be okay again.
• Focus on the things on hand and the positive side of everything.

Social Phobia/Social Anxiety Disorder

Another common type of anxiety is social anxiety, characterized by an immediate distress whenever you meet or interact with unfamiliar people. Affecting over 15 million different American adults, this can be considered to be one of the most prominent types of anxiety that in the country.

Also known as "social phobia", those with social anxiety often displays visible signs or symptoms that indicate their discomfort towards the situation. Some of those symptoms may include blushing, stuttering, increased heart rate, sweating, being awkward or boring, and, worst case scenario, experiencing a full-blown anxiety attack.

If you are one of the many people suffering from social anxiety, than you'd understand how much of a disturbance it can be in your life. Because it hinders you from a lot of social interactions, you may have a hard time in connecting with other people and making new friends. This may also affect your personality, as it can keep you from enjoying yourself when you're out with friends since you don't really have the courage to stand up and talk for yourself. You fear becoming involved in social situations and you try your best to keep to yourself as much as possible and avoid interacting with other people at all costs.

Although individuals with social anxiety know that their reaction to the situation may be over-the-top or unreasonable, they just can't seem to keep the anxiety and emotions at bay. They often seem powerless when battling this emotion and sometimes, in the end, anxiety takes over their lives. Due to these symptoms, they may try their best to avoid situations where they might get pressured into socializing with other people at all costs.

In order to overcome social anxiety, many individuals have turned to therapy. Cognitive Behavioral Therapy (CBT) is one of the most common and used treatment for this certain problem. With an array of different methods and techniques, CBT can help you overcome your social anxiety by getting to the heart of the problem: your thoughts.

Everything we feel and do stems from our thoughts. So, CBT alters the way individual's process information and turns negative thoughts into positive ones. In turn, it generates positive moods that may also lead to favorable actions or behavior. When relating CBT to social anxiety, it tries to get rid of all the negative thoughts that may pop up into your mind when you're about to interact with other people.

For example, when you're meeting new people, you might instantly think that they might hate you or dislike the way you talk or act immediately. However, with CBT, it eliminates this type of thinking and keeps an open and positive mindset of the things that may happen. CBT can also help individuals calm themselves down when experiencing a panic attack or when having an inner conflict colored with anxiety.

There are some CBT techniques that are specially designed to help individuals overcome different types of situations. For example, Cognitive Restructuring can be used in treating social phobia. It can be crucial in understanding your triggers, controlling your mood swings and keeping a positive mindset on everything.

Typically, individuals would have to go to therapists for their own CBT treatment. However, there are some ways that it can still help you when you're on your own. You simply have to follow a series of steps in order to overcome the situation.

• Make an effort to calm yourself down before you interact with someone else.
• Look at the current situation you're faced with. Describe it to yourself.
• Assess how that particular situation made you feel and identify those feelings.
• Go through your thoughts about that certain scenario and scan through what your mind immediately thought of when you faced that situation. The first few thoughts that pop into your head are your "automatic thoughts."
• Narrow in on your negative automatic thoughts. Ask yourself what triggered these thoughts.
• Now, are these triggers reasonable? Is it your negative view of yourself or the situation justifiable? Be as objective as you can and try not to let your emotions get in the way.

• Soon, you will realize that your thoughts are only misguided and aren't actually true at all. They're just the lies you sometimes tell yourself which feed your insecurity.
• Work on erasing these thoughts from your mind by replacing them with the truth. For example, whenever you think, "Nobody likes me," automatically reply with "Hey! That's just not true! [This certain person] likes me!"

Cognitive restructuring can be extremely helpful for those individuals who are trying to control or assess the way they react to certain scenarios. It can help them lighten their mood.

As for those individuals who still need to calm their nerves whenever they are faced with a situation they dread so much, they can also try relaxation techniques. While we've already talked a lot about yoga, meditation, and breathing exercises to help you relax, here is another technique you can use to calm yourself down:

• Take a seat and sit with your back straight.
• Place one hand along your chest and the other one on your stomach.
• Inhale through your nose. You will notice your hand on your stomach area moves more while your other hand should only move slightly.
• Breathe out with your mouth. This will cause your stomach to move in while your chest will still move slightly.
• Repeat this process and count each deep breath you take. Imagine that with every exhale, you are releasing negative energy from your body.
• After a while, your muscle tension will decrease and you will feel a lot calmer than you were beforehand. Keep doing this until you no longer feel any distress or anxiety.

Chapter 8: How CBT can Help

Now that you've been acquainted with a brief history of CBT and how it has developed and changed throughout the years, it's time to move on to the many different ways CBT can help people. Enumerated below are just a few of its many benefits and advantages, such as:

It can solve a specific problem

As we've mentioned before, CBT is actually a general term for a classification of a number of different therapeutic techniques, all of which are guided by the same underlying principle, and that is: when we change our thoughts, we change our lives. This makes CBT an incredibly versatile approach and enables it to address a wide range of issues just by identifying the maladaptive thought or behavior the client would like to correct the most.

For example, someone suffering from anorexia will need to change the way he/she feels about himself/herself and his/her body; whereas a patient struggling with social anxiety must resolve his/her feelings of insecurity and social isolation and target the thoughts that trigger them. These two clients have different presenting problems, but CBT can benefit them both because it can be tailored to fit any problem in particular, so CBT techniques can help just about everyone.

It is goal-oriented

It's been said many times that CBT is a goal-oriented therapy. This means that there is a clear and definitive objective in mind that the client and the therapist must define at the start of their relationship. During every session, they will work towards realizing this goal step by step, and both parties understand what it is that they ultimately want to achieve.

This is an advantage because it clarifies the purpose of the therapy and makes sure that both the therapist and the individual are in agreement about what they are looking to achieve. Sometimes, with other kinds of therapy like psychotherapy or behavioral therapy, this is not the case. In

CBT, what the client wants to achieve is often what the therapist will do for them.

It gives the client more freedom

Similar to the previous point, another advantage that CBT has over other psychotherapeutic approaches is that it is more collaborative than most. CBT practitioners often work together with their clients to help them overcome their problems and alleviate their psychological distress. It is directive and focused, but it also allows the client more freedom and control over the therapeutic process.

CBT is also more interactive and requires mutual effort from both parties for the therapy to succeed. The therapist's role is to listen and guide them through their thoughts and experiences; while the client needs to be open, honest, and expressive. So while the counselor's guidance is important, the client's participation and involvement is equally as integral...

It deals with current problems

Unlike other therapeutic approaches, CBT mainly deals with present-day problems and experiences. It addresses thoughts and behavioral patterns that are currently detrimental to the client. It doesn't dig deeper into their past or analyze their childhood experiences and subconscious drives. Rather, it is firmly rooted in the here and now, and it emphasizes the client's current issues at hand.

This is part of the reason why it is the least time-consuming of all the therapeutic approaches, and also a factor for why it is so practical and efficient. Clients can start to see positive results and progress quicker because CBT helps them deal with their issues and improve their current state of mind. It doesn't waste time trying too hard to uncover the deeper or hidden meaning behind things.

It is faster than other forms of therapy

This brings us to the next advantage of CBT: it is a time-limited approach. As stated before, it is the least time-consuming of all the kinds of psychotherapy and takes only one to two months before clients can start to see some progress. On average, most clients will often need

20 hourly sessions on a regular basis, usually once a week, so the therapy can be completed in over five to six months.

This is why CBT is the most recommended form of therapy for clients looking for a simple and effective solution that can alleviate their psychological distress and better enable them to deal with their problems. It is quick and efficient, and most people have a good idea about what to expect.

Moreover, clients can also benefit from CBT in the sense that less sessions means it's less costly. It's a great help for people who are seeking professional help and counseling, but cannot afford to spend more than 6 months in therapy (be it due to time constraints or financial reasons).

It is easily accessible

CBT is perhaps the easiest to understand and apply of all the psychotherapeutic approaches. It's highly structured nature lends itself well to several different mediums, which makes it one of the most accessible and widely available forms of counseling. From individual counseling, to group counseling, to self-help books like this one — almost anyone can learn and practice CBT.

It can help with many different mental health problems

An evidence-based therapy, thousands of studies to date have documented and demonstrated the effectiveness of CBT in dealing with a wide range of mental health problems.

From clinical diagnoses like post-traumatic stress disorder (PTSD), generalized anxiety disorder (GAD), social anxiety disorder, borderline personality disorder, and eating disorders like anorexia nervosa and bulimia; to more common problems like overcoming addiction, recovering from substance abuse, dealing with depression, relationship problems, and anger management — CBT can help with quite a number of things, as you can see.

It helps you grow as a person

When you begin to seek help through CBT, it will promote positive behavioral change and personal growth in you. Through this process, you will be able to identify the root of your problems and understand your role in perpetuating your own unhappiness.

CBT can help you see the impact of your negative thoughts and beliefs, and once you do, you will begin to work towards changing them. This will make you more kind, forgiving, and accepting of yourself and your shortcomings, as you will start to correct your own negative self-concepts.

It will make you more positive

You might remember that earlier ago we said that Dr. Aaron Beck, the founding father of CBT, was able to identify three major kinds of automatic thoughts: negative ideas about the self; negative beliefs about the world; and negative views of the future.

In line with this, CBT is geared towards helping people overcome this negative mindset and instead, encourage them to adopt more beneficial ways of thinking and behaving. In this way, CBT can do a lot to help a person become more positive, as it addresses their negative views of the world and the future.

Cognitive-behavioral therapy (CBT) has the power to transform an individual's way of thinking, so they can replace their negative thought patterns with a more positive outlook on life. Clients will learn to stop jumping to conclusions, stop seeing things as purely all-good or all-bad, stop comparing themselves to others or blaming themselves too harshly for mistakes, and many other different kinds of maladaptive mindsets.

It promotes mental wellness

The main goal of psychotherapy is to promote mental wellness, and CBT is no different. It has countless of different benefits that can do this (many of which we've already named on this list). It can be as effective as medication in treating certain mental health disorders and doesn't put you at risk of dependence or can be helpful in cases where medication alone is not effective.

Other benefits include: helping a person reduce their stress, overcome their past trauma, stop over thinking or ruminating, calming their mind, and learning to regulate their emotions better.

The last part has become a focus of many psychotherapeutic efforts of recent years (such as positive psychology and mindfulness). It's important that a person knows how to control their thoughts and emotions instead of letting it control them.

It makes you more rational

In order for CBT to be successful in treating a client's psychological distress or dysfunction, the person must first learn to be aware of their own maladaptive thoughts in order to correctly identify the root of the problem and resolve it. They can do this through mindfulness training, meditation, and practicing emotional self-awareness, all of which helps them to become more objective and reasonable in their thoughts.

Cognitive-Behavioral Therapy (CBT) teaches your mind to see things from a new perspective and consider the truthfulness of your beliefs. It helps you think more clearly and makes you more resilient against negative thinking and feelings, thus allowing for better judgment and decision-making.

It makes you more empathetic

With the previous point in mind, CBT can also help you to become more empathetic by training you to be more level-headed in dealing with your problems. It encourages you to see past your own point of view and helps you see things better from other people's perspectives. You become better at distinguishing facts from irrational thoughts, and you gain more insight into the motivations behind the actions of others.

You can become your own therapist

The last and most important way that CBT can help a person is by training them to become their own therapist. The ultimate goal of CBT is to guide its clients as they overcome their personal dilemmas and teaches them how to change their perceptions for the better, to see things more clearly and constructively.

It shows us how to approach our psychological distress with calmness and peace of mind, which makes us better equipped to handle negative or stressful situations. Moreover, the ability to resolve our problems on our gives us a better sense of control over our lives and builds our self-esteem and feelings of self-efficacy.

Cognitive-Behavioral Therapy (CBT) instills its clients with better coping strategies to help them deal with a wide variety of everyday challenges and overcome the hardships of life on their own. The skills you can acquire in CBT are useful, practical, and helpful in everyday life. It has also been proven to keep people from relapsing into their old, self-destructive ways and improve their overall quality of life.

Is CBT Right For You?

With all that said, now it's time to ask yourself whether or not trying Cognitive-Behavioral Therapy (CBT) is right for you.

With so many different options available when it comes to counseling and therapy, it's easy to feel confused and not know which one is best for you. Sometimes it's all a matter of trial-and-error, or simply asking your therapist for their professional opinion about which treatment option is suitable for you. However, if you can't afford to do either, then you can at least do some research and try to find out for yourself.

Thankfully, over here most of the research has been done for you. Now all that's left is for you to do some confirmatory checks and ask yourself the following questions:

What is my diagnosis?

Most of the people seeking therapy have been diagnosed with serious mental illnesses, and while it's not entirely necessary, it's best to ask for a psychological assessment from a trained professional to determine whether or not you have one, too.

In a nutshell, most mental illnesses are gauged on the level of the distress they cause the individual; how much they deviate from normal behavior; whether or not they cause significant impairment in a person's social, mental, or emotional functioning; and whether it makes the individual a danger to themselves or others.

Knowing your diagnosis can do a lot to help you figure out which type of psychosocial treatment is best for you. Each mental illness responds differently to each kind of therapy, so you should go for the one that's been proven to be the most effective in treating your specific diagnosis and symptoms.

However, if you don't have a diagnosis or feel that you don't have a serious mental illness, but rather, personal problems that you would just like to resolve, then CBT is the best answer for you. And as we've said many times before, it's also effective in treating anxiety disorders (i.e., GAD, social phobia), eating disorders (i.e., bulimia, anorexia), and mood disorders (i.e., bipolar disorder, major depression).

How serious are my problems?

Similarly to the last question, the seriousness of your mental health problems is an important consideration to whether or not CBT will work best for you. If you suffer from panic attacks, general anxiety, insomnia, specific phobias, substance abuse and addiction, relationship problems, anger management problems, or any of the disorders we've mentioned above, then CBT can help you.

However, if your problems are more severe or complex, then you might need a more long-term treatment plan, especially if you have multiple diagnoses or have a chronic or recurrent mental illness (like a personality disorder or an intellectual disability).

Are my problems rooted in my thoughts?

The fundamental idea behind CBT, as you already know, is that our thoughts direct our behaviors, so it's specially designed to treat problems wherein the individual's automatic thoughts play a crucial role in their problems. With the help of CBT, you will be better able to control and reframe your mindset ("I'm no good, I'm always messing up. Nobody likes me."), which will alleviate your emotional distress and help you eliminate your dysfunctional behaviors.

However, if your problems are not rooted in your thoughts, but rather your environment, physiology, or things that are out of your control, then CBT might not be the best choice for you. Someone suffering at the hands of an abusive partner or family, for example, can only be able change the way he/she feels and responds to the abuse, but still have to live with it. So as long as there is abuse, there will always be some degree of unhappiness in his/her life.

Do I have a clear problem to solve?

CBT is a solution-focused, goal-oriented therapy. Because it's only a short-term process, there needs to be a specific problem that you want to work on resolving. If you want to quit smoking or get over a bad breakup, for example, then CBT is a suitable option for you.

On the other hand, if you're just generally unhappy or dissatisfied with your life but can't think of a particular reason why (i.e., no past trauma, no abuse, no significant failures), CBT might not help.

If you're also interested in exploring your dreams and unconscious memories, or want to understand the meaning of life, then you're better off with psychoanalytic therapy than CBT, because CBT is more practical, direct, and focused on the here and now.

Am I ready to confront my personal issues?

Because you will be spending so much time analyzing and understanding your thoughts, you might learn or recall some uncomfortable things about yourself and your life. You will need to talk about your problems openly with your therapist in order for them to help you, as therapy cannot work if the client isn't ready to be emotionally vulnerable and confront their personal issues.

So before you go on, ask yourself: am I comfortable thinking about my feelings? Can I handle my emotions and my anxiety? It might be a bit upsetting at first, but if you really want to solve your problems, the best way is to face it head-on.

Can I dedicate time to therapy?

Even though CBT is quite a short-term process by most standards, 5-6 months is still a considerable period of time. You will have to go to hourly sessions once a week and sometimes even come home with homework and exercises for you to do outside of these sessions. This can be time-consuming, but you have to commit to the process in order to benefit from it.

Some people go to therapy and don't come back because they feel it wasn't effective or that it wasn't worth the time. People like this often expect therapy to happen overnight, but it doesn't. Not only will you need to dedicate your time to the healing process, but you must be emotionally invested, committed, and motivated as well.

So if you can't dedicate this time to allow yourself to get better and work through your problems patiently, then CBT will not be effective for you.

Do I believe in the power of therapy?

Before you try CBT, be honest with yourself first about whether or not you really believe that it can help you. If you're not at least open to trying it or willing to commit yourself to the process, then therapy is really not for you.

Therapy is a collaborative effort. Your therapist will help you get better, but they're not going to do the work for you. They're only there to guide you and help you through it. You need to be the one who wants to change and actually make an effort to improve your life with more positive thinking and healthier behaviors. If you don't, then you're just wasting your time. There really isn't any magic pill to be the cure-all for the mental distresses that we may face over the course of our lives.

So is CBT really right for you? It's a difficult question to grapple with. In summary, those who will benefit from CBT are generally people who: know what their problem is and want to fix it; are willing to work hard and put in the effort to do so; and know that their issues can be solved with a more positive and constructive mindset.

Getting the Most Out of CBT

After you've pondered on all the questions above and have decided that CBT is the right choice for you, it's time to discuss how you can make the most out of it. Here are a few ways you can do that:

Embrace change

CBT is all about creating positive change in your life through your thoughts. Sometimes change can be hard — maybe even painful — but it's a crucial part of life. Trust in the process, even if you feel a bit of distress or discomfort. You have to understand that sometimes, things can get worse before they get better, just like how it always seems the darkest before dawn.

Set a time table for yourself

It's good to have goals and then set deadlines for yourself on when you want to achieve them. This gives you a sense of urgency and makes you more committed to getting better through CBT.

Be honest with yourself

It can be scary to think about your deepest fears and insecurities, but it can also deliver the best possible results CBT has to offer you. So no matter how painful it may be to think about what you're going through, you need to allow yourself to be completely honest and emotionally vulnerable in order for you to succeed in therapy.

Reflect on what happened

Everything you do in CBT has a purpose, so reflect on it. CBT helps you understand the dysfunctional thoughts, feelings, and behaviors you experience and redirect you towards a better, healthier way of life. Taking the time to ponder on what these problems are will give you a better idea on how to resolve them and enhance your therapeutic experience.

Integrate CBT into your life

Perhaps the best and most effective way to get the most out of CBT is by integrating it into your life. This ensures that, even after this book's 21-day step by step program with CBT is over, it can still create real and lasting change in your life.

You can do this by setting aside some time from your schedule to practice CBT techniques and methods on a regular basis or coming back to them every time you encounter a personal problem. Remember everything you learn here and apply it as often as you can to yourself, your life, and even as advice to others. Only by doing so will you be able to reap all the benefits and rewards of Cognitive-Behavioral Therapy.

Chapter 9: How to identify negative thought patterns

Identifying patterns of thought

CBT takes a systematic approach to helping you deal with negative thoughts and, so, have better control of your anxiety. The technique used is called cognitive restructuring or cognitive re-framing. It involves you challenging negative thoughts that make you feel anxious. There are three basic steps involved in the cognitive restructuring process. They are:

Identification – Your therapist works with you to identify maladaptive or irrational thinking patterns and beliefs. A person with anxiety issue typically considers situations to be more hazardous than they really are. You can identify these by paying closer attention to what you think about when feeling anxious.

Dispute – After identifying these negative thoughts, you are then encouraged to challenge them. You will be taught how to question the veracity of your thinking patterns. If you fear that something bad might happen in a situation, for instance, your therapist can teach how to realistically assess the probability of such happening.

Alteration – Cognitive restructuring also involves altering or replacing negative, fear-inducing thoughts. This should be easier after completing the first two steps successfully. Once you are able to prove that your anxious thoughts are irrational, your therapist helps you to replace them with positive, more realistic ones. This step may also involve the use of self-affirmations when in a situation that induces anxiety.

Mindfulness Meditation

Meditation is practice that allows an individual to attain mental and emotional clarity. This technique uses strategies like mindfulness, breathing exercises, and self-awareness. Meditation can be done in a lot of different ways.

With that being said, there are several known types of meditation, each catering to a specific aspect that can essentially promote a clearer mind and soul. Breath awareness meditation pays attention to mindful breathing. This helps the individual focus more on the way they breathe and disregards all the thoughts that enter their mind. It benefits the individual by minimizing anxiety, worry, greater concentration and a better emotional state.

There are also other types such as Zen Meditation, Transcendental Meditation and Loving-kindness Meditation that can ultimately help individuals arrive at a clearer mind set and better soul.

Focusing more on mindfulness meditation, this particular type of meditation is also recognized to be an effective technique in promoting cognitive behavioral therapy. It can be used as a tool in aiding problems within the cognitive and behavioral aspect. Mindfulness is a type of meditation that coaxes individuals to be aware of the things happening within the present time and become more vigilant of their surroundings. This entirely disregards the past and focuses on the events we have at hand. It dictates that the present surroundings are the only things that matters.

This unique type of meditation can be practiced anywhere, at any time of the day. As an illustration, when individuals are waiting for a long line to purchase something or waiting for the bus at the bus stop, they can easily take note of everything that is currently happening around them. They become more aware of the things that surround them such as the different people, sounds and smell. They perceive what their senses perceive.

Mindfulness can be found in a majority of the meditation techniques. It can be extremely helpful in focusing on different matters. Breath awareness meditation is one example of where mindfulness is also incorporated.

Mindfulness meditation is known to be a great treatment for a lot of psychological problems, ranging from depression to anxiety and PTSDs. The benefits of mindfulness meditation include lower fixation of unfavorable thoughts and emotions, better focus, sharper memory, reduced impulsive reactions and satisfaction in relationships. Mindfulness meditation can promote CBT because it also alters the way the brain works and how it processes information. It can reduce negative emotions, as what CBT also does, and boost positive ones to take their place. It lessens anxiety and helps us to change the manner we behave in certain situations to make us be better. Through mindfulness meditation, not only will the individual's mental health be enhanced but as well as their physical structure too.

Mindfulness pays closer attention to thoughts and emotions which are actually the 2 main and crucial aspects of CBT. Since it promotes a positive and desirable outcome for an individual's train of thought, it will most likely result to favorable emotions and better behavior.

Body Scan Meditation

The Body Scan exercise may be facilitated by a therapist who gives instructions on what to do. It can also be done without an instructor for as long as the person remembers what to do. This particular mindfulness exercise is best done in a place where a person can stay for half an hour to an hour without being disturbed.

It starts with the person lying on his/her back with palms facing up and feet slightly apart. Otherwise, this can be done as he/she sits on a chair with feet upon the floor. He/she is to keep still for the entire duration of this exercise and only moves deliberately and consciously when necessary.

The person then brings his/her attention to his breath and notices its rhythm and the sensations that accompany his/her inhalations and exhalations. While doing this, the person must not try to alter the way

249

he/she is breathing but simply hold a gentle awareness upon his/her breath.

The attention is then directed towards the body; in particular, what sensations are felt, the feel of clothes upon the skin, the hardness or softness of the floor or the chair, the temperature of the environment, and so on.

The focus is then brought into the body parts with unusual feelings, such as tingling, heaviness, lightness, soreness, tension. The person takes note of body areas that are hypersensitive or numb.

A body scan is usually done in a sequence to avoid missing areas on the body. The order may be as follows: the toes, the feet, the ankles, the lower legs, the knees, the thighs, the pelvic region, the abdomen, the chest, the back, the hands, the arms, the neck, the face, and the head. It may also be done in reverse order starting from the top of the head down to the tip of the toes.

Upon scanning the entire body, the person brings his/her awareness back into the room. It is best if he/she opens his/her eyes slowly to avoid disorientation.

Chapter 10: Goal Setting and Problem-Solving Techniques

Problem Solving is also another common and notable technique used in Cognitive Behavioral Therapy. In this method, individuals are taught on how to solve their issues, cope with the different problems they are faced with and try to regain better control over their lives. Problem solving uses a unique way in dealing with psychological problems. It directly deals with life's challenges and takes it head on. It immediately faces the problems with the use of cognitive and behavioral interventions.

This method teaches individuals how to have an active role when making decisions for an extremely difficult decision. As a result from repeated disappointments or chronic mood problems, some individuals may prefer to take the back seat and get a passive role during tough times. However, problem solving is here to teach individuals that they have to get more initiative and do whatever it takes to arrive at the goal they want.

This treatment gives one specific problem that may also apply to different situations in life wherein people can use that example problem and relate it with other real-life situations that may enable them to make better and more productive decisions all on their own. If an individual's problem solving skills are enhanced, it may lead to a surge of self-confidence and other positive impacts on one's life.

When it comes to problem solving, there are actually four different core items that individuals have to take note of. The primary component of problem solving is distinguishing the problem orientation. Different people have different approaches to various problems. All these people have their own technique on how to solve a problem and how the way they think in order to address it.

So, knowing how you approach a problem, how you act towards it and the methods you take in order to solve it is very crucial in problem solving. There are some people who are much more comfortable in using the submissive approach. In this way, they can get rid of the problem immediately and not have to deal with it anymore. On the other hand, there are also different individuals who are much more strong-willed and outspoken, but do not take the problem into much consideration. They immediately jump to conclusions and speak their mind without processing all the information or thinking about the consequences. This aggressive behavior is a product of a compulsive approach.

The second item is clearly pinpointing the root cause of your problem. Misdiagnosing your own problems is quite a common thing to do. However, you must not be blinded by the things you feel but rather look at the situation clearly and see what the main factor is. As an example, you are having anxiety and stress at work. Some people might blame themselves and think it's their fault because they feel these things when, in reality, it's actually their work environment that's making them feel that way. The real problem in this equation is not their stress and anxiety, but rather the things they experience at work and the amount of tasks they have to accomplish per day.

The next core component of problem solving is brainstorming. Individuals must find different solutions and alternatives to solve their problems. After performing the two steps mentioned earlier, this step is actually the easiest yet most crucial step of all. Individuals simply have to find a positive solution to solve their negative problems. However, if they miscalculate the situation and end up doing more damage than good, then it might cause negative results in the end. Take note of as many solutions as you can and slowly eliminate each one to determine the best solution for you.

The last and most important step of all is Taking Action. All of the things you've done in the past will only go to waste if you don't take action. This step will determine the viability and effectiveness of your problem solving skills. It implements all the things you've planned out from the first step and will ultimately decide if your problem is actually solved in the end, or simply gotten worse. Taking Action is the key component in actually solving the problem and doing something to make a difference. Through this last step, you can clearly show all the things you've been trying to do and the effort you've placed into getting positive results. Every little thing you've done in the prior steps will all lead to you taking action in your life and doing something you think is right and what's best for you.

Problem Solving connects in with CBT because it manages the way a person thinks and behaves towards a situation. Through problem solving, individuals can first assess the things they are currently thinking and finding positive ones to replace the negative ideas in order to have a positive impact. After that, it manages the way we behave towards the situation since the individuals are looking for the best solution to solve the problem. A person's rash behavior is canceled out because he/she must plan the things he/she must say and do to promote a better and positive result.

Assertiveness Training

Habit Reversal Training or HRT is one of the most used types of behavioral therapy in treating OCD. With the name itself "Habit Reversal", it reverses the habit formed by individuals that are typically performed in certain situations and help them to overcome the urge to do it. This is also helpful in treating different behaviors caused by a variety of conditions, like Tourette's syndrome.

HRT is seen to be highly effective in helping people with unwanted behaviors or habits, such as hair pulling, tics, repetitive behaviors or nail biting. When treating OCD, it is highly recommendable to use this type of behavioral therapy since it helps them get rid of the urge to follow the OCD and minimize or possibly stop their repetitive behavior. This training is made up of five different parts that can help individuals overcome their disorder. It starts with:

Awareness Training

If you want to minimize or put an end to your behavior, it is important to know it and accept it beforehand. How can you put an end to something if you are not aware about it? Same goes with this; you can't stop your behavior if you aren't even aware of its presence. Through awareness training, individuals can pay attention to their behavior in order to work a way in diminishing it. This step allows you to figure out when you typically perform this particular behavior, what are some triggers and signs before you actually do it. Awareness training helps individuals know and understand their behavior more deeply and find out some things they never knew before.

Identifying and strategizing

This step identifies the problem in your behavior and partly continues the work you've done in the first step. Once you've identified all the triggers and urges you have, it is time to strategize a new behavior or a way to combat your urge. This new behavior will replace the old one. It is important to practice this new behavior and be aware. Whenever you want to go back to the old behavior you have been so used to, you can try to do this instead. For example, if your typical behavior in response to nerve-racking situations is by biting your nails, the new behavior you'll have to do is to purse your lips instead.

Finding your own motivation and sticking with your plan

When doing something difficult, we tend to find a source of motivation to keep us doing or to remind us why we're here in the first place. Same goes with habit reversal therapy, there will be some instances where you'll question what you're doing or why you're even doing it in the first place. This is why you need to write down a list of all the reasons why you want to go through HRT and make this a source of your motivation. Find all the people you want to do this for and all the problems that you've had because of your unwanted behavior. After finding you motivation, it is important to stick with your HRT and try to comply with it until the very end.

Reducing and Relaxing

These unwanted behaviors tend to show up whenever a person's body is put under a great amount of stress. So, it is important to reduce your stress level and eliminate any triggers that may induce your tics. Relax your body more and give it enough time to rest. In this part, it is important to know different relaxation techniques. There are some that also coincide with the CBT techniques such as deep breathing exercises, progression muscle relaxation, mindfulness meditation and the like.

Testing and Training

After all the different processes you've went through, it's time to test out and practice your new skills and behavior and see how you respond to different situations. You may be placed in front of triggers and it is important to train yourself to get rid of the urge to go back to your old habits. This is the most crucial step of all because it displays all the work you've done in the past. Once you've practiced this new behavior enough, it will soon become an automatic response for you and successfully replacing the old behavior you once developed.

These steps can help individuals overcome their unwanted tics. With a little effort and concentration they can possibly get through and develop a new behavior. Here is a situation example for deeper understanding.

An individual has OCD and tends to bite their nails off whenever they're under stress. So, to overcome this unwanted behavior, they have to become aware of their habit and understand it. Afterwards, they need to find a different behavior to replace that, let's say pursing their lips. When this is done, they need to practice this behavior until they get used and more accustomed to it. HRT can be done on your own. However, it is still more advisable to seek professional help in order to fully eliminate your old behavior.

Relaxed Breath Techniques

You would have to find a comfortable space for yourself

A note here. You do not have to be in the traditional meditative pose, which is most often cast as sitting cross legged on the ground and having your back erect and eyes closed. In this situation, finding a comfortable space for yourself could easily just mean getting to a less occupied area on the bus or train, your own table in the office or even doing meditation whilst standing up. (It can be done, you just need practice)

Of course, for the absolute beginner, or for just about anyone who is easily distracted by all the hum drum that life has to offer, going to a quiet spot like your home, a park, by the sea or in the mountains would be doing yourself no harm if you were looking to derive maximum benefits from meditation. For me, I would recommend that you choose somewhere that is very easily accessible. You may know a perfect spot deep in the mountains, with picturesque views and cool, fresh air. Yet if

255

you were to only go there for one or two weeks per year tops, it really isn't some place for you to consider as the spot to do your daily meditation. Most folks would be doing it at home, or somewhere easily accessible from home.

You would want to try and ensure that it is weather proof, which means you don't have to cut short your session every time there is a rain cloud. Fresh air would be a relatively good alternative to the air conditioned air we are constantly exposed to these days. Minimize the number of bugs in your meditative space so as to cut down on the potential distractions. Try focusing while having a fly attempting to crawl up your nostril. You get the idea. Once you have the constant space settled, then we move on to the posture.

The meditative posture

To be fair, the classic cross legged sitting on the floor with your back erect and eyes closed position is really one where most meditation centers and courses would adopt. You can use that as the benchmark which you would strive to attain, but that does not have to be your starting point.

You can begin meditation by sitting comfortably on a chair, just do not slouch. You do not want to compress your stomach and intestinal areas because you might limit your air intake, which would then affect your breath and focus. You can also begin meditation by lying on your back. Some folks do it on their beds, but a word of caution. Most times, people find that they would drift off to sleep just because it is their bed. As the human body is so sensitive and conditioned to anchors and cues that by just being on the bed, the urge to sleep would automatically kick in. Meditation does not equate to sleeping. That much has to be made clear at this point. For folks who find it needful to lie down, it would be best done on a harder surface. Perhaps a wooden floor or a thin mattress lay on the ground. The firmness of the ground would reduce the tendency for the body to fall into sleep mode, though I personally would like to state here that sitting up would still be one of the better postures to be in so that you would find it easier to concentrate.

Focus on the Breath

256

Now with all the sundry duties settled, it is time to get down to the actual process of meditation. Your primary focus will be on your breath. You would be paying attention to your nostrils as you take in the breath, and again to your nostrils as you breathe out. Always breathe through your nose, which is another reason why sitting up is good because most folks would be able to do nose breathing whilst sitting up. You will pay attention to your nostrils expanding slightly, and the coolness of the air on the intake, and you will pay attention to your nostrils puffing out slightly and the hotness of the breath on the exhalation. All your attention and focus should be centered on your nostrils.

During this practice, thoughts as well as images would tend to come into this personal space which we are trying to create for ourselves. It is all well and easy to just give you a simple - ignore them, but it doesn't quite work that way does it? Our primary focus is our breath, so what should we do now those images and thoughts are dragging our attention away from the breath and onto them?

At the start, you can give those thoughts and images the attention that they crave. If you start thinking about what to eat later, or what movie to watch on the weekend, you can actually allow your consciousness to pay attention to them. Try to build up your awareness such that you seem to be looking at those thoughts with a sort of detachment. It is as if you are looking at someone else's thoughts instead. You give these thoughts the attention, but you try to build up that detachment where you look at these thoughts through the lens of a third party. Then you want to watch these thoughts as they spiral away after initially demanding your focus and attention. As they fade off, you will refocus your awareness and concentration on the breath.

This focus on and focus off the breath due to the interruption from our mental thoughts would be a pretty constant occurrence in the earlier stages of meditation. Some of the learned folks would compare your mind to a monkey, and your focus on the breath as a chain tied to a stout post, which is binding the monkey. At the initial stages, the mind or monkey would jump up and down, but after exhausting its energy, there would be periods it would just lie still. Those are the times where you find yourself being able to focus on the breath for a protracted period. Just to be clear, there is no hard and fast rule to what is termed as a protracted period. It all depends on every individual. For a person who has a hyperactive mind, having five or ten seconds of focus on the breath can be termed as a protracted period.

As the meditation practice grows, you will find that the monkey tends to disturb lesser. Even during the incidences of disturbance, you would tend to be able to make it go rest in a shorter amount of time than before. With the growth of your concentration on your breath, you will find that your sessions will start to stretch. From ten minutes to twenty. From half an hour to the full hour.

During the course of the session, your entire focus will still be on your breath. There is no need to bring in any thoughts or imagery which may be troubling you.

I will not be expounding any of the benefits that breath meditation will bring, but I would rather leave it to you in experiencing them. As a parting word, I can say personally a calmer approach to life seems to be something which I have experienced.

To a fulfilling meditative journey. Please start.

Chapter 11: Maintenance

You can think of cognitive restructuring as a more specific process that's used in CBT. When you're trying to change the way that you think about certain situations, the first thing you have to do is to identify what's wrong.

This means pointing out which factors in your life are causing the cycle of negative thinking to take place. Since it's called "cognitive" reconstruction, the focus is on getting rid of the thoughts that lead to negative feelings and behaviors.

This process is important for practitioners because it allows them to pinpoint an important item in our negative cycles: Automatic Thoughts.

Automatic Thoughts

You may be surprised to know this, but everyone has automatic thoughts. They're called such because they're our default ideas whenever something happens. Without prodding or influence from anyone else, we tend to think of certain ideas or statements when faced with certain situations.

These thoughts are "triggered" by various stimuli that we experience every day. From failures to promotions, we all have automatic thoughts. In the case of someone suffering from depression and anxiety disorder, their automatic thoughts are a good place to start for CBT. You can be sure that these people have negative automatic thoughts which immediately start bad cycles in their behavior.

A good example of this tendency is your personal reaction to failure. Take this short exercise to see if you have a healthy sense of automatic cognition.

Suppose you are a student and are preparing for a large exam that will constitute a large portion of your overall grade. Being the scrupulous person you are, you make every effort to prepare well.

You've studied and participated in joint review sessions with other students that shared your drive to pass. With all your preparation, it would be easy to assume that passing will be easy.

Suppose you were met with the opposite result despite your best efforts. What's the first thing you think of when you imagine such a scenario? Take a piece of paper and write down the first few emotions that flow through your mind. What are the thoughts that immediately take place? Interestingly, your automatic thoughts may not come in the form of single words. You could be spouting complete thoughts to yourself:

• Am I stupid?
• Was this really meant for me?
• Didn't I prepare enough?
• Is the school cheating on me?
• Should I have cheated?
• What did I leave out?
• Why did other people pass and I did not?

Do your answers fall along these lines? Again, take note that it's alright to be upset about bad experiences and results. That's a normal part of life. It's alright to question your methods and preparation. That's how most great work is done.

The problem here is the nature of your thoughts. Are they as black and white as you think? Are you really just stupid and incapable of passing the exam? Or was it just a matter of you skipping a few nights of review? Were you looking at different materials for study?

Are you even thinking about other possibilities during this time? Or are you stuck with just one central automatic thought?

Take a look at the things you've written down and be perfectly honest with yourself. Are you capable of branching out your thoughts into other possibilities or are you stuck with one general theme of understanding?

This is where CBT comes in. Reviewing your answers and sentiments is the beginning of therapy. You cannot fix a broken perspective on life when your automatic thoughts are already bad enough to begin with.

Thought Analysis

Although it's not enough to identify these thoughts, what's required is to analyze them. Not every automatic thought can induce depression and anxiety disorder. One of the first things you have to check is if these thoughts are reasonable.

When you (or the patient) finish writing down thoughts and sentiments, the next step is to evaluate these automatic thoughts.

The good thing about writing down your thoughts is that it helps you to immediately look at yourself from a 3rd-person perspective. This may take some practice.

Take, for instance, someone that immediately thinks their boss hates them just because their boss didn't greet them in the morning. It's a plausible assumption but not a certainty. To think of this as true would be unwise. To worry about it further without any evidence would be counter-productive.

How about a person that immediately blames themselves when something goes wrong? What about a basketball player that's starting to think they weren't meant for the sport just because he failed to stop the opponent from scoring the winning point? Although there are grounds for blame, is that enough to quit basketball altogether?

As someone practicing CBT, it's your responsibility to help the patient realize that their automatic thoughts may seem well-founded but they're emotionally-charged in the wrong direction.

Now, to accurately show the patient (or yourself) that your automatic thoughts need to change, there has to be some mental leg-work involved. This is where real-time analysis takes place.

Finding Evidence

This is where the CBT practitioner puts their logical mind to use. With your automatic thoughts written down, go through each item and review the situation. As you go about your enumerated items, question the validity of these claims by trying to find evidence.

What reason does my boss have to dislike me in the morning? Have I done something bad yesterday or today that they might be holding against me?

Did I fail that test out of stupidity? Couldn't it have just been a lack of proper planning? Did I review the wrong things? How well have I performed in other exams?

Complement your automatic thoughts with positive evidence; if there is any. The key here is being objective with your inquiry. The less emotion you bring to your investigation, the higher the integrity of your efforts.

Question your motives for coming up with these automatic thoughts. Are you being too hard on yourself? Are you trying to compensate for your lack of planning? By looking at things objectively, you separate fact from opinion and in the end, justify a logical conclusion.

If you're practicing on behalf of someone, it's very important that you do not force a new idea onto the patient. They have to come to your intended realizations on their own. Think of it as a gentle debate with a very stout member of the opposition. You're better off changing someone's mind if you can make them see that changing it was their idea in the first place.

This is where leading questions come in. As you go over their automatic thoughts, acknowledge them and place them in an objective arena where they are subject to scrutiny.

• "What makes you say that?"
• "Is that just a gut feeling?"
• "How many times has this happened?"
• "Are you 100% certain about this?"

These leading questions are meant to trigger curiosity and shift the paradigm into a more productive area. It is your duty as a practitioner to help the patient see the importance of retrospection and self-inspection.

The same thing should also be done for contradicting evidence, especially if you want to eliminate negative forms of automatic thinking.

Categorize your evidences as such, and weigh them out with the patient at the end of the activity. Is there more evidence pointing out the possibility that your boss hates you? There may be more evidence

262

pointing out the possibility that your boss just didn't notice you. Here, the next step comes in.

Finding the Full and Objective Perspective

Once you've lined up your evidences, both supporting and contradictory, the next thing to do is to put them all together into one mental image.

This image will become your unbiased guide to reprogramming your cognitions. This is where you (or your patient) come to the intended realization of the activity.

Your boss doesn't hate you. He just didn't hear you because he was on the phone. You're not stupid; you just didn't cover all the necessary review points.

With a full and objective perspective, you've already done half of what CBT needs to accomplish. You've already assisted yourself into creating a new perspective that will later on disrupt your current negative cycle.

But this alone is not enough. Here, careful monitoring and self-awareness is still important. As you view this unobstructed perspective, take personal note of the way you're feeling. If you're practicing on a patient, take a step back and remind the patient to write down what they're feeling as you look back on this new perspective.

Does it ease their anxiousness, knowing that there is a more logical perspective compared to their hasty automatic cognition's? Are they frustrated that they haven't seen this perspective before? You have to be careful not to make the patient (or yourself) become frustrated at how your approach was successful.

Cognitive Distortions

In line with identifying negative thoughts and changing them, it's important to know what kinds of automatic thoughts contribute to unrealistic perspectives and creates mental issues.

These are known as cognitive distortions. Understanding their various natures helps you point out what's causing irrational emotions and behaviors.

Filtering

This is one of the most common automatic thoughts. Here, one solely focuses on negative aspects of a situation, regardless of the nature of that situation.

Here, people tend to just concentrate their thoughts on one single, negative aspect and disregard everything else. A good example of this would be a perfectionist student that got one mistake during an exam.

Instead of focusing on the fact that they passed and garnered one of the highest scores on the exam, they will think they failed because they let that one mistake go past them. There, they will start questioning their ability to get a perfect score. From there, it's a downward negative spiral out of what should have been an impressive feat.

Polarized Thinking

With polarized cognition, people limit their perspective to two polar opposites. They think in terms of only good or bad, black or white. For them, there is no gray area in which special cases lie.

This is common in negative parenting habits. Children may sometimes be raised to think that they're either good or bad based on their life choices because their parents pummel that idea into their heads.

This method of thinking is also prevalent in certain forms of government, especially those with various parties that represent different interests. For certain parties, it's either a policy goes against them or it is for them.

Over-Generalizing

Individuals that over-generalize have the habit of taking one bad incident and using it to label them for every other instance of the same occasion.

A good example of this is a person that failed an interview for one specific job at a specific company. The positive way to take this event is to learn from your mistakes and attempt to apply with another company.

However, this could turn sour if you begin to generalize your worth as an employee based on just one interview. You tend to think that interviews are really not meant for you and you will forever be in search of a job offer.

Melodrama

Here, people are prone to blowing things out of proportion, attaching unreal values and influences that just make matters worse. This could happen in both directions.

This could either be a person that thinks their one mistake during a task will destroy all their efforts over the years. It could also be the same person thinking that their one mistake is too miniscule to ever have an effect on the bigger picture.

It's more of an issue of a skewed perception of things that leads to miscalculated choices and unrealistic expectations. Both lead to big disappointments which push you further into depression and anxiety disorder.

The Fallacy of Change

This distortion manifests itself in the manner of two untrue beliefs. The first one is the notion that you can manipulate everything and everyone around you to your liking.

With this notion in mind, people are more likely to connive, deceive, beg and even command other people around them as they see fit. They become aggressive and overbeating to the point that they no longer consider what is good for other people or how they even feel.

The second is the notion that by changing the way other people and things behave, they will become happy and comfortable. This makes a very dangerous combination that may lead to dire consequences.

Take, for instance, the case of an employee that thinks this way. If this person is unhappy with their job, their first notion will be to change the way other people behave around them, regardless of their position.

To do that, they will complain, perform poorly, gossip and even confront other people just to implement the changes they want. When the changes they expect do not happen, they feel hopeless or angry.

When that happens, they either withdraw or do something drastic to draw attention to them. This employee could end up resigning or making a bold action at work to disrupt everyone.

Extreme Personalization

People that suffer from this distortion are of the mind that almost everything is their fault, regardless of how accurate that notion may be. When something goes wrong, they are quick to look at their own actions and contributions and begin to doubt their worth. They question their own motives and effort and begin to feel useless.

Did I do enough? Was that my mistake? If I had done this, then maybe it wouldn't have happened. This was my entire fault. These are the things that these people think about when they brood over a large failure.

This could be an employee starting to think that their small, but precise work was the cause of a company shut-down. This employee would be prone to thinking that they weren't instrumental in trying to save the company and contributed to its downfall.

Blaming

This is the opposite of personalization. People that suffer from this distortion are more confident of themselves, too much to the point that they are quick to find fault in others.

Even if the failure is a personal matter, these people will find an irrelevant external factor on which to claim their comforts.

This could be a spoiled student that blames their parents for not teaching them proper studying habits which caused them to fail an exam. This could also be the employee that is quick to point fingers at the other departments for a fault that originated from their level.

Fallacies of Control

On another note, there are also those people that suffer from the habit of thinking that things are either always under their control or not. This fallacy can manifest itself in one of two ways as well.

This could be the employee that thinks a poorly-lit working environment is what's causing their lackluster work. It could also be that same employee thinking that their colleague made a mistake because they chose to trust that colleague in the first place.

The problem with this notion is that people stick to one side of the coin all the time. For some, they think that nothing's under their control; that includes their attendance, motivation and emotions.

On the other hand, there are also those that think that everything falls under their influence; this includes the actions of other people with their own minds.

Fallacies of Fairness

This one is very common in today's day and age. Many people believe that everything is fair and should be kept that way at all times. When someone else seems to get ahead in life, they will keep the idea that the same thing will happen to them very soon.

This, in turn, leads to unrealistic expectations that could end up in deep resentment when these expectations fail to materialize. These disappointments end up fortifying a sense of helplessness which then leads to depression.

People that suffer from this distortion do not believe that life can be unfair at times. For them, everything evens out immediately.

Emotional Reasoning

Again, another common misconception many people today are quick to make. It is most likely because of the direct link people have between feeling and thinking.

In the midst of feeling something, people tend to immediately use their emotions to reason out without drawing from logical conclusions. In short, these are people that say:

"I feel. Therefore, I am…"

For instance, you could be feeling like you're slow at the moment because of a lack of breakfast. This distortion will lead you to the false generalization that you are slow by nature.

It doesn't even have to be about feeling slow. Some other worse examples are feeling stupid, weak and even depressed and anxious.

Although it is true that our feelings sometimes get the better of us, it is important to understand that what you are feeling may or may not be entirely true about yourself as a person. Yes, you may be feeling sad, but you may not be depressed. Yes, you may be feeling anxious, but that may not necessarily mean that you're suffering from anxiety disorder.

On the same note, even positive feelings can be misconstrued into false realizations. You may be feeling smart at the moment, but that may not mean you're a natural genius.

Karma/Heaven's Fallacy

While believing in karma or heaven's wrath is more of a religious question, people tend to attach human time-restraints on when karma or heaven gets the job done. This is unreal and will definitely lead to disappointments and even more cognitive dissonance.

Regardless if karma is true or not, it is unwise to expect someone to get their fair share of karma. It is even more unwise to attach a time frame to this expectation. Even if karma was true, what methods do we have of measuring how long it would take for it to happen? You will tend to attach realistic premises to something intangible. That is a sure way to become resentful when things do not happen as expected.

Creating the Habit

Take note that this is just one event. This is one encounter. This roughly constitutes only one session if you're practicing. Again, CBT is not some overnight wonder. It's a long-established method that implants proper thinking habits.

Use this small triumph to develop a habit of mindfulness. Train yourself and your patient to take a step back and take out a sheet of paper to begin cognitive reconstruction.

As you progress through repetitions of this activity, you will begin to see how powerful this positive habit is when it comes to dealing with depression and anxiety disorder. The ultimate goal here for CBT is to train the patient to do these things automatically without engaging in previous thought patterns and behaviors.

Behavioral Activation

If it's possible for CBT to realign your thoughts with proper Cognitive Restructuring, the same thing can be done through a behavioral approach.

This is where Behavioral Activation comes in. In contrast to Cognitive Restructuring where unhelpful thoughts are identified and replaced,

Behavioral Activation takes a different route. It focuses on bringing life into activities normally deemed senseless and futile by those that suffer from depression and anxiety disorder.

The Initial Problem

Most inexperienced people would say that all a sad person has to do is to do something happy, which is in all honesty, a fair enough solution. You counteract negative thoughts and emotions with activities that foster a positive environment to balance everything out. If things were that easy, depression and anxiety disorder wouldn't be the well-known problems they are today.

The main issue with this approach is that a person suffering from depression and anxiety disorder experiences things differently compared to a mentally-healthy person. Take, for instance, a birthday party.

You would know these occasions to be joyous celebrations of a person's life. Here, people are surrounded by friends and relatives to wish someone a longer life and more happy years to follow. The premise that plenty of people love you and want you to live longer is enough to make anyone feel happy.

On top of the well-wishing, the activities such as the eating and other birthday-related activities make this event something to look forward to every year.

A depressed and anxious person doesn't perceive this to be the case. For them, a birthday is just another reason to get out of the house. They don't focus on what the birthday is. For them, it's just another useless social gathering.

It's not that they despise birthdays and other joyous occasions. These people are as far from hate as they are far from happiness. It's just that they don't feel anything at all, even when the situation or context pushes them towards a certain emotion.

It's because these people have fully grown into their cycle of apathy and hopelessness that they are unfazed by supposedly joyous events. They do not hate being there. In fact, they do not feel anything at all. It is all just a big mesh of people gathered in one place in their eyes.

This is why Behavioral Activation isn't just a simple immersion into positive activities. It's a sincere effort to add meaning to these events and showing that meaning to the patient so that they can once again learn to enjoy these things.

Following the basic model of CBT, once a person suffering from depression and anxiety disorder can learn to enjoy life events, it disrupts the negative cycle of behaviors and emotions and brings about a self-induced change.

Activating Pleasure

Behavioral Activation entails participation in valued activities. Take note that these aren't just your ordinary day-to-day activities. They are called valued activities because they still hold a special meaning to the person involved in them.

In order to get the most of these activities, a few steps are involved when engaging a patient in Behavioral Activation.

1. Identifying Mood Fluctuations

Although it was mentioned earlier that depressed people do not feel any emotional changes at all, their mood still peaks at certain points. Those peaks aren't very noticeable, though, but they're there. Humans are not robots, after all.

If you are practicing CBT on behalf of someone, then you should understand that it is your responsibility to identify and label those particular changes in mood. This is easier said than done.

What's required here is constant monitoring. Whether you're practicing on yourself or someone else, you should be able to constantly note changes in mood. The first thing you should do is to take note of the various things that you or the patient does on a daily basis.

This includes rudimentary courses of action, such as brushing your teeth and bathing. You'll be surprised to know that these things can still affect your mood if only by a miniscule amount.

Once you've laid out your day, create a scale on which to rate your mood during these activities. A simple scale of one to ten should do it. That amount should provide plenty of variety for the way you feel about certain activities during the day.

Now, don't be anxious to fill up your work just yet. Go throughout the day and literally ask yourself or your patient how your mood is during those activities. Stop and inspect yourself and be honest with your responses.

Here, you have to be very sensitive. The differences of your mood throughout the day may be very small; but they'll play an important role later on. Be sure to write down even the smallest differences. The more specific you are about what you feel, the better the method will work for you.

2. Review after a few Weeks

Yes, you read that right. This activity won't just take a full day. It takes about a few weeks to come up with a comprehensive understanding of your mood fluctuations.

Now, these differences may be small, but every great effort needs a small beginning. This will be yours.

Give yourself about two to three months. That should be enough time to garner a good scale of common entries.

Once that is done, group the activities that show you as being in a "better" mood. You can label these activities as positive activities to address them properly. It doesn't matter what kind of activities they are, as long as you're seen to have a slightly better mood while doing them.

On that same note, it is also important to group the activities that sink you further into depression. You can call them negative activities since that's what they do for your mood.

With this review, you now have a working tool that will help you constantly improve your move over the following weeks. This is where the hard work will truly begin.

3. Modify Your Daily Schedule

As common sense dictates, if it's doing you good, try to add more of it. This will also apply to your daily activities. Now that you know what improves your mood and what doesn't, it's time to put that information to good use.

This can be very difficult for someone going through depression and anxiety disorder. You may be of the impression that almost anything you do will not bear fruit. It takes a tremendous amount of willpower

271

and mental discipline to commit to something like that. You have to remember that this procedure is backed by research and science. Trust in the fact that it will work.

To bolster your confidence, draw strength from the fact that Behavioral Activation is often used as a standalone treatment for depression by most experts. It's that effective. It's that powerful.

Rely on the premise that small steps will take you where you need to go. It will take some time but you will get to a better mental state eventually. Remember the effort it took for you to monitor your mood over several weeks. That effort will not go to waste.

It doesn't matter if those activities are simple walks outside with the dog or washing dishes. As long as your research and monitoring showed that your mood is better during these times, it's vital that your drizzle them out over your day to keep you in a constant state of progress.

This will also take some planning. You may not be able to complete these activities at certain times during the day. This will require you to do some problem solving as you lay out the rest of your week.

If you're working alone and by yourself, it's best that you involve someone close to you so that they're aware of your schedule and help you adhere to your change of plans. Having someone to count on is a great way to keep yourself motivated as you grow through these lifestyle changes.

4. Look beyond Pleasure

You may find that your positive activities mostly consist of naturally pleasurable tasks, such as walking and playing certain games. Although it's inherently good for you to do more of these activities every day, you must not forget your responsibilities at home. You may be depressed, but you're not debilitated.

Try to look at your list of positive activities. Are some of them achievement-based? Does cleaning the house give you a small sense of accomplishment? What about giving the pets their bath?

Try to also include these kinds of activities in your day. You need a healthy balance between pleasure and accomplishment to fully give meaning to the things that you do.

When you aren't able to accomplish anything during the day, it doesn't help the process. You're likely to harbor thoughts of being useless at the end of the day, which will interfere with the general aim of the program.

5. Ignoring the need for Motivation

In most cases, people having difficulty motivating them will use a lack of motivation as an excuse not to engage in a certain activity. This sort of mentality is counterproductive and has no place in Behavioral Activation.

Here, motivation comes during and after planned activities. You mustn't wait for the motivation to come your way. It arrives as you complete your daily planned activities and after you've done them. In a way, they become their own reward.

This is another hurdle for someone that lacks motivation. It's hard to commit effort into something when you cannot muster the will to do so. For someone experiencing depression and anxiety disorder, that's even more difficult. This is why the next step is equally important.

6. Positive Conditioning

One good thing about Behavioral Activation is that it operates on sound psychological processes. One of these processes is positive conditioning.

When a certain activity is followed by a pleasurable reward, then it's easier to accomplish that act the next time because of the premise of a reward. The same principle can be applied to Behavioral Activation.

Make it a point to reward yourself or your patient after a successful completion of an activity. This works wonders for your subconscious mind. On top of the automatic motivation that comes with completing your daily tasks, the reward that comes after will make it easier to begin acting on the same task the following day.

Prepare yourself a nice snack or buy yourself something as a small reward. The form of the reward doesn't matter, as long as it is something pleasurable for you. It could be a grandiose gesture like a night out with drinks or a simple ice cream cone. It's more of a personal preference at this point.

273

On top of helping you perform the same thing over the following weeks, rewards also help build your positive emotions as you go about your daily activities.

Given a few weeks, you'll notice subtle changes in your demeanor as you go about your daily life. With constant adherence to your schedule, you'll suddenly regain a desire to go about your routine and find new meaning in the things that usually don't have any importance for you.

As you go about this process, though, it's important that you still maintain constant monitoring of yourself. Keep a journal with you and record the way you feel as you complete your activities. That way, you'll learn more about how these activities affect you and develop even better methods to improve your mood as you progress.

Conclusion

CBT is a practical therapy to deal with emotional challenges. Various kinds of CBT, like exposure therapy, might ask that you confront predicaments you would rather avert such as flying in airplanes when you harbor a fear of traveling. This also can result in temporary pressure or anxiety. The impact of CBT therapy in solving most of the disorders and mental issues mentioned in this book cannot be overemphasized as it has been proven to be more effective than other similar therapies.

CBT techniques may also be beneficial for just about everybody, for example, people without a kind of mental disease but who have chronic pressure, poor moods and habits they'd like to work with.

Be honest and open as success with this therapy is dependent on your willingness to share your thoughts, emotions, and experiences, and on being open to fresh insights and means of doing matters. If you're reluctant to discuss certain issues due to debilitating emotions, embarrassment or fears regarding your therapist's response, then allow your therapist to understand regarding your bookings.

CBT isn't the best way for all clients. Those who have significantly more chronic or recurring illness may need repeated interventions. Or they could need a change to tactics apart from CBT to tackle early life adventures along with personal, interpersonal, and identity troubles. And given that CBT can be quite a valuable device in treating emotional health disorders, including depression, post-traumatic stress disorder (PTSD) or an eating disorder. However, perhaps not everybody who benefits from CBT comes with a mental health state. It can be effective tools to assist anyone who learns how to manage difficult daily living conditions.

Manipulation

The Best Techniques for
Influencing People with
Persuasion, NLP, Dark Psychology
Analyze People, Use Mind Control

Daniel Peterson

Table of Contents

Introduction to Manipulation

Congratulations on purchasing your personal copy of Manipulation: The Complete Step-by-Step Guide on Persuasion, Manipulation, Mind Control, dark Psychology and NLP. Thank you for doing so. The following chapters will discuss some of the many ways you can manipulate the thoughts, beliefs, and behaviors of others and how you can recognize when that same manipulation is happening to you. You will discover how important our step-by-step guide is to identifying manipulative strategies and techniques that are being used to persuade you to do another's wished, and how quickly you can turn the tables and apply those same steps to achieve your desired outcome.

Manipulation is a topic that most people are going to turn their noses up at. They do not like the idea that comes with it, and they assume that they are above and beyond using these kinds of techniques. As we will discuss later on in this guidebook through, each of us uses manipulation in some form or another to get what we want, even though most of us are not going to do it at the expense of someone else in the process. To help us out with this we need to first take a look at manipulation and what it is all about. Manipulation is going to be the practice of using some indirect tactics to control the relationships, emotions, decisions, and even behavior over the target and how they react to things. This is often going to use a lot of different options that you are allowed to use including persuasion, mind control, deception, and more to get what they want.

Most people are going to use some form of manipulation at some point or another in their lives. For example, if you have ever had a day that wasn't going well or you weren't feeling that good, but you told someone who asked that you were doing "fine" then this is a form of manipulation. This is considered manipulation because it is going to control the perceptions and the reactions that the other person has concerning you. Even if you did it to avoid a confrontation, to avoid having someone pity you or some other reason it still changed these perceptions of you. Manipulation, at least the way that we often think about it, and the manipulation that is used in dark psychology, is going to have consequences that are often more insidious. This can sometimes include some form of emotional abuse, especially if the manipulator is in an intimate relationship with the other person. This is why a lot of us assume that all forms of manipulation are bad, but we will hold this opinion, even more, when we see that it harms the mental health, emotional health, and physical health of the other person who is the target.

While people who are the manipulators are going to do this to their target because they want to have some control over their own surroundings and environment, it is true that the urge to do the manipulation is going to stem from some anxiety and fear that is deep down. In any case, it is not going to be seen as a behavior that is all that healthy for either party. Engaging in manipulation is going to seem like a great idea to the one who is manipulating. It allows them to gain the control that they want, and they get to receive whatever they wanted in the process. However, when they use this tactic, it is not only going to cause some harm to the other person, the target, it is going to make it hard for the manipulator to connect with their own authentic self and get the benefits that come with that.

Chapter 1: Introduction to Advanced Manipulation

Now that we know a bit more about the importance of the analysis of your potential target of manipulation it is time to move to the second step of influencing other people. And this second step is going to be all about manipulation. Once you have taken a bit of time to successfully learn about your potential target, and you have been able to do a full analysis on the other person, it comes time for you to actually manipulate them. Manipulation is the part where you are going to start planting the seeds in the mind of the other person, your potential target so that you are able to get them to start agreeing with what you want them too. There are a variety of different tactics that you are able to use when it comes manipulating the target. When you are able to pick out the manipulation that includes a few different tactics, and that will allow you to gain the agreeance and acceptance of the subject that you are working with. You want to really rely on the analysis to make sure that you pick out the right technique that you want to use on your target.

Never try to work on the manipulation before you have a chance to do a good analysis. This is tempting to do for a lot of beginners. They assume that they can just jump right in and start using some of the techniques that they have learned along the way and that it will all be just fine. But this is a horrible way to get things started. If you don't do the analysis first, you will end up using the wrong kind of technique when it comes to manipulation, and you will waste time, find yourself exposed, and really lose out on the goal that you want. Even if you only have enough time to spend a few seconds or a few minutes on the analysis, like what may happen if you are in sales, you still need to take that time first. Using the wrong manipulation tactic on one of your targets, which is something that is likely to happen if you don't plan things out and think them through, is going to end badly for you and can make manipulating that target, and many others who are in your sphere of influence, really hard. If the target is able to figure out what you are trying to do, they will not be happy. Even if the manipulation is meant with no harm and would benefit both of you if the target feels that manipulation is there, then they are going to keep far away from you, and there will usually be some anger in the process. This all comes together to end with you having no chance of success with manipulating that target now or in the future. While we are spending our time in this guidebook talking about dark psychology and how to use manipulation, you have to make sure that you use that analysis above, and the persuasion that we will talk about below, in order to make it all work out well for you. Because of this, it is important to not only find the right manipulation technique to help you out, but you also need to learn more about what works for the other person and what may turn them off from talking to you in the first place. Only then will you be able to see manipulation actually benefit you.

Many people are going to have a pretty negative view when it comes to manipulation and how it is going to affect them. They assume that they have never used manipulation at all and that manipulation and the techniques that go with it have nothing to do with them at all. But think of it this way, have you ever tried to word a phrase or a request in a certain way in the hopes that the other person would help you out? Have you ever told a little white lie to get out of trouble, or to spare the feelings of the other person? If you are able to answer yes to any of these, then you have used manipulation. Most people are going to think about manipulation in the negative term, and we are going to show a few examples through this guidebook of techniques that are going to follow along with this as well. This kind of manipulation is just going to benefit the manipulator. It has no benefit for the one who is being used. They may get hurt physically, mentally, and emotionally along the way, and it doesn't really matter to the manipulator. In some cases, the manipulator wants their target to get hurt because it ensures that they are able to get more of what they want along the way.

However, the manipulation that we usually bring out on a regular basis is not going to be this bad. We often want to get something, but we will do it in a way that is going to be mutually beneficial to us and to our targets, or at least in a way that the target is going to not get hurt. When a cars salesperson tries to sell a car, they want the customer to find a good vehicle that they like. This makes the customer happy and makes the salesperson happy because they make some money. When you want someone to help you with a report, you are hoping to get some help, without any harm coming to the other person. This is the difference. It is all about intention. If the manipulator wants to get something regardless of how it is going to affect the other person, then this is seen as dark manipulation, something that is generally seen as a bad thing by most people. But if you are just hoping to get the manipulation to help you get what you want, and you don't want the other person to get harmed in the process, then this is going to be something that is not frowned upon quite as much by those around you. Manipulation is going to be something that is seen in a negative light, but you will find that there are times when we will be manipulative without really trying to cause some harm. But that doesn't mean that some form of manipulation wasn't used at some point or another. Learning when we have used manipulation and some of the different techniques that you are able to use to go along with this will make a difference in who you are able to manipulate, how you are able to manipulate them, and more. With that said it is important for you to remember what manipulation is. We spent a bit of time talking about this in the first section of this guidebook. But remember that with this part, we are working to plant a few seeds in their minds. This is meant to ensure that the target is going to start thinking about the things that you are saying, and will start to see why it is a good idea to agree with you. Even though you used a variety of tactics to make this happen the target is going to reach this through methods that make them feel they were the ones who came up with this decision on their own.

Chapter 2: Types of Manipulation

1. Positive Manipulation

We always think of positive reinforcement as a good thing, but malicious people can also use it to manipulate their victims. The fact is that we all use positive reinforcement in one form or another. Parents use it to get their kids to behave properly, teachers use it to make their students more interested in school, bosses use it to encourage productivity, and partners use it to modify each other's behavior in relationships. It is an integral part of our social interactions, but it only becomes a problem when it's detrimental of the person it's being used on. The answer is a thumping yes! Constructive manipulation can be used for transforming negative energy into a positive experience through physical, psychological and spiritual attributes of your personality. Imagine trying to manipulate a drug addict to give up drugs or a binge eater to start eating in a healthier fashion. Now that's not so bad, is it? You are resorting to positive or constructive manipulation to get someone to do what is good for them.

Positive or constructive manipulation has been occurring since ages. What do you think Jesus Christ, Martin Luther King or Mahatma Gandhi were doing when they drew people like magnets? They restored to spreading a highly positive energy through their own fine example and actions to lead others on the same path of equality, justice, humanity, and brotherhood. Would you call them manipulators? Not in a negative sense but they did positively influence or manipulate people through their hypnotic personalities, words, ideas, and living examples to learn important lessons of life. Think about this for a minute. There are several times in your life when you've felt compelled to reach out to someone that needs your assistance. Yet, for several reasons, he or she has turned down you straight-laced attempts for help. Is it bad then if you manipulate them to comply for their own good? Your motives can be hardly ascribed as selfish or self-fulfilling in such a scenario. The tactics you use can also be barely labeled as devious, wicked or crafty. We are all familiar with the term: "desperate times call for desperate measures." Sometimes approaching people to convince them about what is good for them in a straightforward manner falls flat. In such a scenario, when you've tried everything in the book to persuade them positively, the only communication tactics you may have to resort to may be the ones that are viewed as downright crafty or evil. The intent is precisely what distinguishes negative manipulation from constructive manipulation. In the latter, your intent isn't to twist the other person to suit your will. It is only a means to get past their stubborn, obstinate and illogical defense mechanisms. Let's take an example of how this works.

You have a childhood friend (let's call him Peter) you deeply care about. You grew up in the same neighborhood, went to the same school and your families have been thick too. You've learned through a mutual friend that Peter is about to sacked from work owing to deteriorating performance that can be traced back to him being abandoned by his partner for another man. Peter was planning an elaborate wedding ceremony with his ladylove when she ditched him a few days before the wedding and eloped with another man.

Peter felt betrayed, hurt and broken, which made into slip into a state of depression. This is now taking a toll on his professional life and affecting his performance at work. As a friend, you suggest that before anything more untoward and disastrous happens, Peter go and meet a counselor to seek some solution for his situation. Peter vehemently denies that anything at all is wrong with him and refuses to fix an appointment with a counselor. No amount of persuasion, cajoling or pleading works.

As a childhood friend, you are utterly concerned about his condition. What do you do next to bypass this obstinate approach by Peter? Overcome by absolute desperation, you speak on how a co-worker's son slipped into a coma for days before he got back to living a normal life following a near-fatal accident. You talk about how your co-worker was deeply affected, disturbed and depressed throughout the time his son was in a coma. The expressions, tone of your voice and words are carefully chosen to convey the right emotions. You then go on to state how his performance at work was an absolute disaster, and he was on the brink of losing his job.

Then you masterfully and carefully introduce how the co-worker agreed to meet a therapist on your suggestion, which changed things around for him completely. You begin to elaborate on how a combination of therapy, antidepressants, and a strong will led him to get back on his feet and become the awesome worker that he once was. Peter will be stirred by this emotional take of will over a challenging situation that was accomplished by seeking the help of a therapist. He will most likely be moved and inspired by the emotional account of an unlikely hero's tale of fighting all odds to emerge victoriously. Of course, you made up or fabricated that entire tale. None of your co-workers or even someone you ever knew had their child slip into a coma, following an accident. There was no depression and no looming fear of a layoff. You just devised that story as a means to manipulate Peter into seeking professional help for his deteriorating psychological condition. It can at best be seen as a way for bypassing a person's defenses or obstinate, where reason or rationale does not seem to work. Manipulation opens that tiny window of hope where you can get your loved ones to do what is good for them.

Well, there's no denying that the strategy you resorted to was manipulative, scheming, dishonest and may be deceptive. However, it was also an innovative, resourceful and creative way to get Peter to do what you wanted him to do for his own well-being. If it leads him to reevaluate or rethink about his own reluctance about seeing a therapist, it may be worth it. In this case, it can be hardly classified as immoral, unethical or unprincipled. You're manipulating your friend into thinking and believing something as someone who cares about him. Sure you may have taken the recourse of devious ways, but your intention was compassionate and unselfish. This is exactly what sets apart negative manipulation from constructive or well-intended manipulation. It is the intention that sets the tone for whether someone is using manipulation in a positive (caring, loving and compassionate) or negative (selfish, deceitful and self-fulfilling) manner.

Plenty of therapists use constructive manipulation for helping their clients transform their lives. Think back to all the instances where you've been slightly imaginative and shifted from a more conventional approach to promote someone else's welfare. You are doing this simply to boost your odds of reaching out to a person who seems shut off to a more straightforward, traditional approach that is linked to his or her own welfare. We use such techniques without even realizing them to minimize another person's resistance and bring about a positive behavioral change.

Sometimes, much like the world leaders, we discussed above, we use constructive manipulation to bring about a beneficial change at a social or human level. This change is good for everyone or the overall good of a family, workplace, community, nationality, race or humanity. Using manipulation to bring about a positive change isn't as devious, evil or crafty as manipulation is made out to be. When straightforward techniques do not work too well in getting people to respond, manipulation proves to be the last ditch attempt.

Much like any other tool or method, nothing is inherently good or bad. Its positivity and negativity lie in the manner in which it is used. C'mon now, even when you are training a puppy to "sit" by holding their favorite treat over their head, aren't you actually manipulating the creature to do what you want them to? Well yes, it is called training you may argue. But that's just clever wordplay or semantics. You are training your puppy, so it leads a more disciplined life that keeps it out of harm. In future, it will find a good home should you have to give it away if it is well trained. So, is manipulating the puppy in such a scenario dubious and evil? No, right?

If you've raised kids or currently fulfilling the herculean task of being a parent, you pretty well know what constructive manipulation is. We are constantly teaching them lessons we want them to believe in. We make up stories about angels, Santa Claus, witches and fairies to get them to do what we want them to for their own welfare. We all know eating vegetables or fruits will not give them superpowers, but sometimes that is the only way to get them to agree to eat it. Several times more subtle or gentle types of manipulation can be utilized for motivating or inspiring people to do things that are more beneficial or safer for them. These approaches can be used to transform a person's self-image. If you are manipulating someone to quit smoking or give up junk food, that isn't such an evil thing, is it? Think of manipulation as fire. It is a powerful, lethal tool that can be used to offer warmth as well as cause destruction. How you choose to use it is totally up to you. It's like that little matchstick you have in your hand. You can light the fireplace or a bunch of candles to keep you and your loved ones cozy and comfortable or you can misuse it to cause devastation.

2. Negative Manipulation

Negative reinforcement is a form of psychological manipulation which is used to make people feel obligated to act in certain ways in order to avoid certain levels of mental or physical pain or discomfort. In positive reinforcement, you get a reward for acting the way the manipulator wants you to act, and the desire for that reward is what modifies your behavior in the future. Negative reinforcement is, however, a bit more complicated than that. To understand the concept of negative reinforcement, you first have to understand how it's different from punishment. Both of them are popular manipulation techniques, but there is a subtle difference between them. Many people assume that they are the same thing, but they are not. In punishment, the manipulator adds something negative when you don't act a certain way. In negative reinforcement, the manipulator subtracts something negative when you act the way they want you to act. Reinforcement is meant to strengthen voluntary responses, while punishment is meant to weaken voluntary responses; the manipulator will choose one method or the other based on the kind of outcome that they desire in that particular situation.

While punishment is meant to stop a certain behavior from occurring again, reinforcement is meant to encourage the behavior to occur again. A manipulator would use punishment to stop you from doing something he doesn't want you to do. However, he will use negative reinforcement to force you to do (or to keep doing) something he wants. For example, nagging is more of a negative reinforcement technique than a punishment. When someone wants you to do something, they keep nagging you to do it, and the nagging (which is the negative stimulus) stops when you comply. So, negative reinforcement works on you because you want to put a stop to a negative stimulus that already exists, while punishment works because you want to keep something negative from happening. Every time someone does something negative to twist your arm to get you to take a certain course of action; that is negative reinforcement. When you are trying to break up with someone, and he/she cries very loudly about it in a public place, until you change your mind, they are using negative reinforcement to manipulate you (at that moment, you feel that the uncomfortable stares from strangers will only stop if you take the person back).

Sanctions are also a very common form of negative reinforcement. They are used by powerful nations to get other nations to bend to their will, but they can also be used in interpersonal relationships or at work in one form or another. A sanction is basically a threat of a future consequence if you fail to do something. Sanctions may be used in relationships for the common good or for malicious intentions; you have to assess the individual situation to tell if the use of sanctioning (or any other negative reinforcement technique) is malicious. Since childhood, most of us have experienced fear manipulation. Our parents manipulated and controlled us by physical discipline or emotional blackmail, and our teachers managed us by threats and humiliation. Unfortunately, our perspectives and beliefs weren't changed at all, only our behaviors—and those changed only temporarily. What many learned by the time they were teenagers is that they didn't want to be around parents and teachers, and the friends or peers whose realities were similar became our closest network with the greatest amount of influence over them. To illustrate this point, let's look at Raul. Raul entered the tenth-grade with a reputation for being a trouble-maker. He harassed all the girls in class, destroyed the classroom desks and books, and disrespected his teachers. When Raul tried his usual tactics with his English teacher, Miss Slater, she decided to call his father. Expecting that Raul's father would offer his support, she never dreamed he'd come down to the school and humiliate Raul in front of all his friends.

Unfortunately, Raul had to sit next to his father all day long as his father accompanied him to every class, pulling him by the ear from one room to another. Did it put the fear of God in him? I'm sure it did. Unfortunately, when the fear factor no longer held him hostage, Raul's behavior was even more disrespectful and threatening than before. He still harassed the girls in class, but now he warned them if they told he would meet them outside the classroom and make them sorry. What Raul's father had taught him was to manipulate through fear. Because Raul didn't experience positive manipulation, his reality was the same —act out and get all the attention you want. Since negative attention was all the attention Raul every experienced, he knew no better.

Not only did he continue to disrespect the girls in class, but he covertly sabotaged his teachers with practical jokes that were destructive and dangerous. He blew his nose and wiped the discharge between the pages of brand new textbooks. He keyed his teacher's car, and one day he sucked in the fumes from a butane lighter and blew them out as he lighted his breath. The fire was like a torch, catching the girl's hair on fire who sat in front of him. Instead of changing his behavior, practicing manipulation through fear hurt others and got him permanently expelled from school for the remainder of the year.

Comparing Negative Manipulation to Positive Manipulation Attempts

The next year Raul returned, along with his reputation for being a rebellious bully. By now, his reality was "get them before they get me" school of thought. The fear manipulation hadn't achieved any beneficial changes in Raul's behaviors or perspective, except to reinforce the negative. What made matters worse is he was now a year behind his classmates and in danger of becoming another dropout statistic.

Fortunately for Raul, he got more than he bargained for in one of his new teachers, Mr. Thompson. Mr. Thompson was obviously a teacher who realized how to move and empower his students through positive manipulation; thereby, helping them to create a new reality for themselves. Raul came into the classroom with the same old mean-spirited, sour attitude, but instead of a write-up, after the reprimand, after another write-up, what Raul experienced was a teacher who believed in teaching through the continuous power of healthy relationships. One day, both were in detention—Raul for disciplinary reasons from another hard-nosed teacher, and Mr. Thompson to act as supervisor for after-school detention. Mr. Thompson had a whole week of after-school detention time to build rapport with Raul. Mr. Thompson questioned Raul about his likes and dislikes, only to discover Raul's love for fast cars. Since Mr. Thompson's hobby was rebuilding an old muscle-car he had inherited from his great aunt, he decided to involve Raul in the process. He brought the car to school and stored it in the industrial arts building. Every day after school, Mr. Thompson and Raul would work on the car together.

Through his questions and rapport building, Mr. Thompson manipulated Raul to change his "get them before they get me" perspective on life. The improved behavior that began in Mr. Thompson's class soon spread to other aspects of Raul's life as well. As they finished the car, Mr. Thompson permitted Raul the privilege of taking dates out in his amazing muscle car. Girls had a new respect for Raul and his disrespectful attitude changed for them as well. Raul's mechanical talents surpassed that of Mr. Thompson, and he was often called to the house to assist him with needed repairs, strengthening their friendship and mutual respect.

Although it was a challenge to catch up, Raul passed that year with flying colors. As the years passed, he grew more confident and changed from rebellious to productive. His grades were good, and it was evident Raul had a real talent to repair anything mechanical. Toward the end of his senior year, Raul talked to Mr. Thompson about his inability to afford college and together they discussed other employment options. Graduation night, Raul had the biggest smile of any other student as he collected his diploma, knowing how hard he had worked and how many obstacles he had overcome with Mr. Thompson's help. His mother and father had since divorced, and Raul's mom and younger brother were the only ones who cheered him on that evening. He searched the crowd for Mr. Thompson's familiar cheery face but was disappointed when he failed to see him in the line of teachers wishing their students good luck in their future endeavors. It was difficult for Raul to hid his disappointment as he slowly led his mother and brother down the front steps and out to the parking lot. Raul felt so sorry for himself that he didn't see the bright red, 1965, convertible Mustang GTX at first until his mother touched his arm and spoke in a tearful voice. "Raul, I think Mr. Thompson has a surprise for you."

"I looked for him, but…"

"He's right there with your present."

There parked right in front of the steps was the car they had worked on for two years. It had a huge gold ribbon around it, with the words "Class of 1999" written on the window. Mr. Thompson was there to hand Raul the keys and wish him good luck in his future endeavors.

Chapter 3: Emotional Manipulation

This is not wholly distinct from the carrot and the stick but much of manipulating people involves emotional intelligence. There are a variety of ways in which people emotionally manipulate others. All of these, in some sense, work with the tools above to affect the actions of another. It might seem natural to conclude that the goal of emotional manipulation is to provoke irrational behavior – however, that's rarely the case. Emotional manipulation is much more likely to distort the truth, to the extent that someone's alters their path to achieve their goals, through a perceived change in reality. Examine an approach to emotional manipulation called the guilt trip. The guilt trip involves trying to make someone feel worse about an action they have taken (or an action they have failed to take, which amounts to the same thing i.e. sitting around and not tidying your room is an action).

By guilt tripping someone, you are attempting to affect their emotional reaction to their error. The return is for that person to feel indebted. You are altering their perception of a situation, so that they will either: correct their behavior at the next opportunity or make amends for their error.

Here is a breakdown of the mechanics:

• They are concerned about their loss of reputation. If they develop a reputation as someone who cannot or will not help others to achieve their goals, the result will be a loss of power. Solving the issue by making amends is a way to salvage their reputation.

• You are persuading them of the severity of their error. As previously mentioned, failing deception, this requires you to either offer genuine new information, such as a previously unknown negative impact of their error – perhaps a financial cost to yourself or another – or have enough of their trust that they believe your opinion of opinion of events to be valid, causing them to reassess their own.

• Naturally, you can use deception to fabricate the above – inventing a detail that changes their perspective. An example could be lying about an injury they caused to someone else unintentionally, playing up its severity. While you will be found out eventually, this might be an effective short term tactic to provoke a confession.

• The person who has committed the error is also affected by your power. If you have the ability to remedy the problem they have caused, they are likely to be submissive to your demands. Your power is the ability to help them achieve their goal of saving their reputation and naturally that increases, the greater they perceive their error to be. Guilt tripping is far from the only form of emotional manipulation. It is difficult to draw the line between ethical and unethical emotional manipulation. For example, what constitutes guilt tripping as opposed to simply expressing disappointment? They are essentially the same.

Fortunately, this book is avoiding these issues for now but you'll find more information on the ethics of manipulation in the next chapter. There are many terms for many different types of emotional manipulation. It is not necessary to memorize, or even learn, all of them. By understanding the mechanics of emotional manipulation, you can easily analyze and understand them as they arise. Here are a few examples:

• Intimidation – Provoking fear in a target, such that they may alter their strategy for achieving their goals. In particular, intimidation that carries a threat of violence can encourage a target to change their course of action in ensuring their own self-preservation (a fairly universal goal). Acting to appease their intimidator is a way for the target to survive, and becomes their future behavior.

Note that there is nothing irrational in the behavior of the target here. Emotional manipulation is not necessarily the provocation of irrational behavior. Bonus points if you recognized that this is hardly distinct from the "stick."

• Seduction – Manipulating a target by presenting them with an object of desire, and withholding it until the target performs an action. The object may be the seducer or some other asset, like money. Scam emails from Nigerian princes work by seducing the target with the prospect of easy money. Sexual seduction may include provoking irrational behavior, based on the promise of endorphins. An alternative way of viewing this is as a persuasion to manipulate the goals of others, prioritizing a sexual encounter above everything else. Seduction revolves around power, as it is presenting and persuading the ability to offer somebody what they want. Bonus points if you recognized that this is hardly distinct from the "carrot."

• Minimization – This is the effort to reduce someone's perspective of an issue, or error you have caused. It may involve any manipulation tools to reduce the magnitude of the issue.

It normally involves persuasion and deception, highlighting or fabricating facts to demonstrate the lack of importance. It can also involve rationalization, which is explaining the reasons for one's actions in an attempt to justify them.

Although this bears no direct relation to power, observe how differently people respond to this behavior from someone who has perceived power, compared to someone who is perceived to lack it.

• Blaming – Passing the blame for an error onto someone else is a way to preserve your power, by protecting your reputation, using either persuasion or deception.

Note how easy it becomes to break down familiar actions, like blaming, using these three tools.

As well as passing the blame, creating blame can also be a useful smokescreen. Blaming a victim is a way of persuading a victim that their reputation is under threat, in order to manipulate a vulnerable person. At this point, you may also recognize that blaming is closely linked to intimidation. There is damage or the threat of damage to someone's reputation, which can alter their actions by making them feel responsible or concerned that others will hold them responsible.

Chapter 4: Covert Manipulation Technique

Covert is when an attempt is made to communicate with the subject's unconscious mind without the subject knowing that he or she will be put through hypnosis. It comprises a string of technique such as conversational hypnosis or NLP (neuro-linguistic programming), body language and other powerful communication and interaction strategies. The primary objective of covert hypnosis is to gradually change an individual's behavior at a subconscious level to lead the subject into believing that they changed their mind on their own accord. You simply lead them into believing that they weren't influencer or manipulated by changed their mind on their own. When covert hypnosis is successfully performed, the subject isn't aware that he or she is being hypnotized. There is considerable debate about the fine line between conventional hypnotism and covert hypnotism. While standard hypnotism is about drawing the focus of the subject, covert hypnotism is primarily about relaxing the subject a bit or softening their stand by using deception, confusion, interruption and a series of other techniques. If you've watched the series "The Mentalist," you'll realize that covert hypnosis is used in a particular instance when a perpetrator tries to influence various characters and tries to murder her employer.

8 Proven Covert Hypnosis Techniques

Here are some forms of covert hypnosis techniques for beginners

1. Deception

Deception is one of the most commonly practiced covert hypnosis techniques to lead the subject into doing what you want without them knowing about your real intentions. For instance, you may want a close friend to give up addiction and resort to plain deception to lead them away from their addiction triggers or suggest something false without making them catch your true intentions of making them give up alcohol or drugs. As a practiced hypnotist, you create an illusion or sense of false reality to help the subject believe something you want them to. We have all been susceptible to deception at some point or the other. There is a tendency of believing fictional information without ever asking for details. Clairvoyants, psychics, and hypnotists used this method generously to create an illusion by gaining the explicit trust of the subject through clever rapport-building techniques.

2. Eye Contact Clues

People almost always display a particular body language type that reflects their deepest thoughts and feelings. Hackneyed as it sounds, "Eyes are truly windows to one's soul." Analyzing an individual's body language (especially their eyes) will award you with a good sense of how a particular word, action, sound, image or emotion is perceived by him or her. The subject is read based the direction's his or her eyes are darting in. Examine the subject's eyes thoroughly for cues. This technique is more complicated than it sounds and needs plenty of practice.

3. Misdirection

This covert hypnosis technique is widely used by magicians all over the world to manipulate their audience or create an illusion. Magicians sneakily use the power of misdirection to distract their audience's attention to another point of focus to perform a quick action that they wish to hide. For instance, if you are attempting to get the subject to do something by directly sowing the suggestion, they are more consciously aware of your intentions. However, if you are accomplishing the same goal, you distract their attention elsewhere and make the same suggestion worded in another context.

4. Sub modalities

There is great variance between the responses of different to the same information. This can be detected by the manipulator using several sub modalities (under various contexts) to generate the desired response. Look for voice tone, body language, facial expressions and eyes cues. When the use of certain words or actions creates positive submodalities, you can continue using them to invoke specific feelings or emotions.

5. Generalized Reading

Generalized or warm reading is a covert hypnosis technique based on making a generalized observations or statements that could be applicable for just about anyone that do not take into account unique observations or responses gained from the subject. Fortune tellers, psychic and clairvoyants use a lot of this technique to manipulate their clients into believing that the readings are unique to them, when in fact, these are general observations that can be applicable for just about any person.

For instance, "You are an ambitious person who also strives for happiness, contentment and inner peace. You've learned and evolved from your past experiences. You have overcome your past mistakes to look forward to new and exciting life ahead." You can ask any person to read this, and he or she will end up believing this was written only with him or her in mind. It leads the subject's mind to believe that it is about him or her since they are unique. Warm readings can be used as icebreakers to establish a rapport of trust with the subject (by making seemingly accurate statements) before they begin to talk. This gives you the advantage to build upon the all too accurate beginning statement.

6. Hot Reading

Hot reading differs from general or warm readings in a manner that you have some prior information about the subject (which he or she is completely unaware of), which completely amazes them. You've got to find a way to obtain important bits of information about a person without him or knowing about it, which can be tricky. The subject will then be led into believing that you have been blessed with supernatural or psychic abilities.

7. Cold Observations

While warm observations involve making generalized statements that can be applicable to everyone and hot observations are sneakily obtaining specific information about a person to use it to your advantage, cold observations are made based on your initial impression about a person by closely studying them. You then build upon the general statements by making more specific statements based on their responses. It is regularly used by mentalists, psychics, and spiritualists to form an illusion that can accurately read a person's mind or perform telepathy. Subjects are led into believing that they are indeed everything they are told they are by the manipulator. It comprises making vague statements after making a few first impression observations of an individual, which can easily be acquired after practicing a few people reading and analyzing skills. For example, you can simply say to your subject, "I have a feeling you are a self-assured and confident individual although you tend to hesitate at times based on past experiences." You wait for a response from the subject.

The subject can come up with a bunch of responses such as, "yes, you're right. I am generally confident and expressive but tend to be held back by past experiences" (which means they are generally confident people), "Oh yes, I do tend to reflect a lot on my past actions" (which means they are more shy and hesitant than self-assured and confident). Once they respond to a general statement, you can use their response to make more specific or direct statements about the person.

8. Ericksonian Hypnosis Theory

This technique comprises using stories, examples and anecdotes for eliminating the wall of resistance built by our subconscious mind. The hypnotizer or manipulator narrates a story, which ends with a moral that the manipulator desires to convey. The subject's subconscious mind builds a connection or deep relationship with different aspects of the story. You lead the subject into emotionally linking with the story that sounds similar to the situation they are in currently. This is s strategy for making indirect suggestions using a story to distract or divert the conscious mind, thus leaving the unconscious more receptive to suggestions.

Chapter 5: NLP Manipulation Techniques

NLP or Neuro Linguistic Programming is one of today's most widely used mind control, persuasion, manipulation and influencing techniques. It is applied by everyone from salespersons to political leaders to media bigwigs. The method was invented by John Grinder and Richard Bandler in the 70s, and its popularity spiraled in the world of marketing, public relations, advertising, sales and even personal/social relationships. People who master NLP are known to be equipped with the ability to trick people into doing whatever they want them to in several incredible ways. The duo Bandler and Grinder came up with a sort of new age version of hypnotherapy. While conventional hypnosis is dependent upon putting the subject or client into a state of trance, NLP isn't as heavily loaded. It is about layering or planting suggestions into the subject's unconscious mind through the clever use of language or semantics, without them knowing that you are using the technique.

Today the strategies of NLP and hypnotic writing are widely used in the internet marketing, social media and make money online scams. The sales copy of most get rich quick schemes is cleverly worded to manipulate the unsuspecting reader into taking the intended action. People trained in the art of NLP are experts in watching out for eye movements, pupil dilation, flush of the skin and other neurologically linked signals that reveal plenty about the person's thought process.

For instance, simply by observing a person an NLP trained person can determine what side of the brain is dominantly used by the individual. They can also identify what sense (sight, hearing, smell, etc.) is most powerful in the person. The manner in which the brain organizes, stores and uses information (can be determined through a person's eye movements) and when they are giving false information or making stories.

For example, an individual who is primarily focused on seeing will use words and phrases that hold visual metaphors such as, "Do you really see my point?" Similarly, a person is more focused on hearing with tend to use "Hear me" or "I hear you." This is the language that you should stick to as a manipulator trying to get them to do what you want. You'll score higher points with a visual person by using words such as "look at the situation in this way." It is all about wording your talks in a way that plays on their linguistic programming. By mirroring a person's body language and specific linguistic patterns, the manipulator is aiming to build a rapport. It is a psychological process where a person lets their guard down and arrives at the conclusion that the manipulator or NLPer is similar to them or like them. What the NLPer does is fakes certain social clues that lead a person to drop the defenses they build around themselves for other people (especially strangers). This makes them more open and receptive to any suggestions that the NLPer plans to embed in their mind.

NLP helps the manipulator train others into thinking and doing what they want. It is about influencing the subject's thoughts, feelings, and behavior in a way that is beneficial for the manipulator. Skilled manipulators know how to use the power of anchors (external influences) for sparking or triggering specific emotions in people. For instance, a song that is associated with the subject's first kiss can be used for triggering all emotions related to that moment.

Do not we all experience this in everyday life? Certain songs remind us of particular moments or phases in our life and hence become associated with the emotions we felt during those moments or phases. Each time we hear those songs, our subconscious experiences the same feelings and emotions. The song in this example acts as the emotional anchor to help induce feelings and emotions that you want in the other person.

Let's take another example. Each time a person buys coffee for you, you talk about something pleasant that happened in his or her life like his or her marriage or the birth of his child. If you talk about the birth of his or her child consistently every time the person buys you coffee, they will come to associate buying coffee for you with pleasant, positive emotions. It acts as a sort of anchor for his or her feelings. NLP is a complex discipline that cannot be acquired in a day. It needs hours and hours of practice with reading people's subconscious behavior, understanding their neurological programming and more. However, as beginner manipulator, you'd want to understand some popular techniques used by NLPers on their subjects.

Here are a few expert techniques NLPers use to manipulate people or control their minds.

1. They Observe Eye Movements

NLPers will always closely observe their subject's eye movements to determine what part of the brain is being used, and how the subject stores/uses information. They give the impression that they are keenly interested in what the other person is saying and actually care about knowing their thoughts when in reality they are simply analyzing how a person access information from different parts of his or her brain. Within a few minutes, practitioners of NLP can tell if a person is lying or telling the truth. The subject will almost end up believing that the manipulator has some psychic abilities or telepathic superpowers. NLPers carefully calibrate eye movements to know conclude which parts of a brain are most active in a person, and how they process information.

2. Use the Power of Touch

NLPers use the power of touch effectively to induce certain feelings and emotions in their subjects without the subject even realizing it. Let us say for instance that the subject is in a particular state of emotion such as happy, angry, upset, sad, etc., NLP practitioners will use touch (light tap on the subject's shoulder or touch their arm) and anchor that particular form of touch by linking it to a specific emotion. Each time you want to invoke that specific emotion in a person to fulfill your intent, simply use the particular touch that you did when the subject was experiencing the same emotion earlier.

3. Use Vague Words and Phrases

One of the fundamental methods of NLP is the generous use of vague verbiage for inducing a sort of hypnotic trance on the subject. NLPers believe that the more ambiguous and vague your language, the less likely is to your subject to opposing your ideas or disagree with you, thus making it easier to lead them into the trance state. You are basically limiting their ability to react to what you are saying. Did you notice how effectively former United States of America President Barrack Obama used this technique during the famous "change campaign?" It was a word wrought in complete ambiguity. Anyone could interpret it in a way they wanted.

4. Relaxed and Permissive Words

Expert NLP hypnotists never start by telling their subjects what they want them to do outright. The commands follow more permissive and relaxed issuances such as "please feel free to de-stress or relax" or "you can have this for as long as you like" or "you're welcome to test this product." The subject is sort of given a loose rope, and the impression that the NLPer really wants to relax and enjoy without restrictions. The language use is more relaxing and permissive. Skilled hypnotists realize that this is more effective when it comes to driving the subject into a state of trance over immediately commanding them into it. When you begin with, "please feel free to let your hair down and relax completely", they are likelier to go into a trance gradually.

5. Layered Language

Skilled NLPers will always use language that is deeply layered or has hidden meaning/connotations attached to it. They'll use widely believed facts and slowly slip in their agenda into to manipulate the subject's subconscious mind into thinking in a particular way. For example, food, sleep and going outdoors with me are the formula for a healthy life. On the surface of it, the subject's subconscious mind tends to agree with it because everyone has been conditioned to believe that food, sleep and getting fresh air is good for their health. They will tend to agree with it without giving it much thought. However, the layered message here is – going outdoors with me. And boy did you just get someone to agree to that on a subconscious level? This is an extremely subtle yet powerful NLP technique that is harnessed to the hilt by experienced NLP practitioners.

You also follow up one question with another to create what can be termed as a conditioning by association. For example, you ask someone, "How many fingers are there on the human hands?" followed quickly by "How many on ten hands?" The answer to the first will be ten, while the answer to the second question most likely will be 100. The first is, of course, right, while the second is wrong. The answer to the second is 50. As an NLPer, you are creating a trap for getting your subject to think the way you want to through careful conditioning through association. In NLP, you essentially build anchors or baselines that you can lead your subjects to whenever you want. It can come to anyone with a little bit of training and practice.

Talking about the power of association, it is widely used by advertisers to manipulate consumers into associating certain products with specific attributes and lifestyles. For instance, Coca-Cola always has these fancy advertisements about beautiful young people gulping glasses of bottles of the aerated beverage. They are hot (or cool if you please), rich, in gorgeous settings and look extremely cheerful. What are your impressions as you consume those images? That drinking Coca-Cola gives you access to the good life. The idea and associations are deeply installed and embedded in the subconscious mind and leads you to make a rather quick decision when it comes to purchasing.

6. Get them to Agree

If you can get your subjects to answer in the affirmative to several questions in a row, it will be tough for them to refuse your final request. NLPers know this only too well and use it liberally on their subjects to get them to do what they want. This is one of the many clever manipulation and persuasion strategies used by sales and marketing folks. They will launch into a series of questions, the answer of which will rarely ever be in negative. After getting consecutive positive replies from their subjects, they will go for the kill and lead them into making impulsive and emotionally driven decisions. The entire technique is designed for engineering spur of the moment decisions by switching off the subject's ability to make logical decisions.

For example, an insurance salesperson will ask his client questions such as

"Wouldn't you like to financially secure the future of your loved ones?" Yes. "Wouldn't you like to use a policy that offers hassle-free claims?" Yes. "Wouldn't you want to protect your family's dream for a low as $123/month?" Yes. "Wouldn't you like your children's education and future dreams taken care of even when you aren't around?" Yes. "Wouldn't you want coverage for the immediate family under one policy at a single rate?" Yes.

"Then you should not waste any more time because you never know what happens in the next moment. Sign up for the policy immediately while it is available for a low monthly premium for a limited period."

See how a person is led into making a decision using the power of affirmatives or getting someone to agree to a series of questions before finally getting them to agree to the main thing. This can be as effective

307

when you're asking someone out on a date. When a person replies in the affirmative to a series of mostly emotional questions posed by the NLPer, it is hard for the subject to refuse the final offer.

7. Use Gibberish

NLP practitioners resort to using a lot of gibberish mumbo-jumbo with the intention of attempting to program the subjects internal emotions and leading them into where the manipulator wants them to go. As an NLPer, you can't afford to be specific or explain precisely what you meant. You have to utilize trance invoking ambiguous language that throws the subject off gear and allows you to take complete control of their feelings and emotions. Phrases such as, "As you let go of this emotion slowly, you will see yourself transitioning into a state of alignment with the aura of your success." It does not make any sense in the logical scheme of things, but your subject is befuddled into doing exactly what you want him or her to. Since it cannot be comprehended immediately, they'll be less prone to rejecting it in a state of confusion. When you do not know what to do or can't think for yourself, you are more susceptible to blindly following the instructions of the person who is guiding or leading you.

Chapter 6: Dark Psychology

Dark Psychology is one of the arts of persuasion and mind control. Psychology refers to the study of the behaviors of human beings. It is the center of every human being's thinking, their deeds, and socialization. Therefore, Dark Psychology is basically the phenomenon through which human beings apply manipulation, persuasion, and mind control techniques to fulfill their intentions. In dark psychology, there is the 'Dark Psychology Triad' which is one of the easiest predictors of manipulator's behavior, collapsed relationships, and also being problematic. The Dark Psychology Triad includes:

• The psychopathy - They are friendly and always charming, impulsive, selfish, lack empathy, and are not remorseful.

• The narcissists - These kinds of people are filled with ego, grandiosity, and have no empathy or sympathy.

• The Machiavellians - These kinds of people use manipulation, persuasion, and mind control to exploit and lure people. In addition to this, they are always immoral.

No one in this world would wish to be a victim of manipulation even though it happens whether you are conscious or unconscious of it. In the case you fall under manipulation, it is not necessarily someone in the Dark Psychology Triad, but you will face persuasion on a daily basis. Manipulation tactics always manifest themselves in regular commercials, Internet advertisements, sales tactics, and in your workplaces. If you are a parent, you must have come across these tactics in your everyday life since children tend to experiment with tactics so that they can get what they want. Dark Psychology is used by people who you genuinely love or trust. In Dark Psychology, the manipulators use the following tactics:

• They flood their targets with love, compliments, and buttering up to acquire what they want.

• They lie too much, exaggerate things, tell untruths or even tell partially true stories.

• They deny their love to those they are targeting through withholding their attention.

• They give some choice routes that distract you from the choice you do not want them to make.

• They apply reverse Psychology, which involves doing something which motivates their victim to do the opposite, which turns out to be what they wanted.

• They use words assumed to have the same definition, but later tell you they meant something else throughout the conversation.

Dark Psychology aims at reminding you how easy it is to get manipulated. You should, therefore, assess your techniques in all areas of your life, workplace, leadership, intimate relationships, and parenting. The people who use these Dark Psychology tactics are aware of what they are doing and manipulate you intentionally to get what they want. Some end up using unethical ways in their manipulative techniques though they are never aware of it. Other people learned their manipulative techniques at very early ages. For instance, if you applied a particular behavior when you were a kid, and you got what you wanted, you are more likely to use the same technique every time you want something.

Others are trained or get to know these tactics just by happenstance. The training programs that can prepare you on the ideas and concepts of Dark Psychology and unethical persuasion techniques are mostly the sales and marketing programs. When doing sales or marketing, dark tactics are applied to either create a brand or sell a product which ends up benefiting the sales assistants rather than the customer's needs. You get convinced that using such dark tactics is okay as it helps the buyer. The following are the people who use Dark Psychology tactics the most:

• The Narcissists – Narcissistic people always have a high sense of self-worth. They want everyone to realize and recognize their superiority. They still want to be adored or worshipped. Therefore, they use dark tactics to manipulate, persuade, or control the minds of their targets.

• The Sociopaths – They are charming, bright, but impulsive. They lack emotions and are remorselessness hence end up using Dark Psychology tactics to mend relationships with people they can easily take advantage of.

• The Attorneys - Most of the attorneys emphasize on winning their cases such that they opt for dark manipulation tactics to acquire what they want.

• Political Figures – They are always using shady manipulation tactics while campaigning for people to elect them. They use dark psychological techniques to prove to the voters that they are the best and deserve the post they are fighting for.

• Salespeople – The salespeople are always focusing on the benefits rather than the customer's satisfaction. They use dark persuasion tactics to make the buyer buy their products.

• Leaders – They use dark manipulation tactics to have great efforts, submission, and higher performance from their dependents.

• Speakers – Various speakers, especially public speakers, practice dark persuasion tactics to influence their audience. This helps them sell more products, predominantly in the final stages.

• The Selfish – Anyone with a hidden agenda of self before others always uses dark manipulation tactics to get what they want first at someone's costs.

Most of Dark Psychology tactics seem to step even on your own toes. Speakers and salespeople are everyday users of these dark tactics. You should, therefore, note that, whether working, writing, talking, or making sales, you are neither supposed to use these dark tactics. Various people tend to admit that their professions require them to practice dark tactics, especially if their aim is maintaining the company's top positions or to avoid losing customers.

It is unfortunate because if they fail to exercise these tactics, there will be short-term sales as well as revenue that will ultimately lead to customers not trusting the company, poor business tactics, employees becoming disloyal, and less successful business results. This calls for you to know the difference between motivation and manipulation tactics that are good or dark. This can be achieved if you assess your intents. If a tactic benefits you alone, then it must be an ominous manipulation task.

How to Use Dark Psychology Techniques Ethically

At Place of work: The three personality characters of the Dark Triad can as well be used ethically at your place of work. It can be used in getting the top leadership positions. You can use your manipulative techniques to have interpersonal influence that can get you promoted easily in your workplace. Internet elves: Most of the people who troll others on the Internet mostly use dark psychology tactics. They are always antisocial, psychopaths, and aggressive. Everyday trolls indicate that people have bad lives behind the keyboards and such has been linked to bullying evident amongst the youths and young adults. As a coupling scheme: Most of the couples use dark triad tactics, primarily in their sex lives. Most people with these personalities steal bedmates from other people and have low self-esteem. Outward Look: At first sight, you can tell a person with dark triad personalities due to their appealing appearance. They concentrate more on their clothing and makeups, a look that could be put down if someone pulled off their clothing and wiped off the makeup. Most of those who concentrate on looks are the narcissists.

Chapter 7: Analysis Techniques

Now that you are clear on why analysis is used and why it is so essential to your manipulation practice, it is time for you to learn how you can actually analyze people! In this chapter, you are going to learn about three primary types of analysis, as well as when you can use them and how you can maintain your secrecy in the process. The three main strategies we are going to pay attention to are: body language (including facial expressions), profiling, and verbal cues. These three areas are the most important when it comes to analyzing someone prior to manipulation.

Body Language

There are two types of body language that you want to pay attention to when you are reading someone's physical expressions: their actual body language, and their facial expressions. Both of these will give you a large amount of insight as to what they are thinking and how they are feeling at any given time.

You want to begin by paying attention to someone's body language before you even begin talking to them. Get a sense of how they carry themselves, how they tend to move and express themselves when different types of things are said to them, and how their body language changes when different moods are experienced. Ideally, the longer you can comfortably observe someone from a distance, the better. This gives you a chance to get a stronger idea of who they are and what they are like before you enter a conversation with them. However, there are many times that you do not get a significantly long period of time to analyze someone before you begin your conversation. In these circumstances, it is beneficial to have already spent time practicing analyzing people and then use this practice to generate an idea of how your target is feeling and their personality in a short amount of time.

When you are reading someone's body language, start by getting a "baseline" of what they are normally like. Pay attention to their face, their arms and hands, and their feet. Also, if they are walking, notice their gait and how quickly or slowly they are walking. You also want to know how they are carrying themselves. Then, once you get a baseline, take a moment to pay attention to how their baseline changes with different stimulus. For example, when they are happy or when they are annoyed. You want to essentially get an idea of their three primary states that matter most to you: normal, positive, and negative. This will help you when it comes to conversing, as it will give you an idea of whether they are having a positive or negative reaction to what you are saying to them.

The benefit of body language is that virtually everyone has a similar type of body language expression. This is a form of communication that we unknowingly learn as we grow up, and because we all tend to communicate in the same way, our body language tends to work in the same way from person to person. For this reason, if you do not have a long time to observe or analyze someone first, you can use basic body language knowledge to generate an idea of what they are thinking and feeling, and about how they are feeling in response to various things you say or offer them. Now that you understand body language and how you should be reading it, let's start focusing on specific cues and readings that you can understand from someone when you are analyzing them. In the following sections we are going to explore three types of body language: the body language itself, walking or mobile body language, and facial expressions.

Body Language

Body language comes in two forms: basic cues, and complex cues. Basic cues are ones that you are likely already familiar with. They include ones such as stomping your feet or making fists with your hands when you are angry, slouching in your chair and resting your head in your hands when you are bored or upset about something, and other similar cues. You are likely already familiar with the majority of basic body language cues, so we are going to focus more on the in-depth cues here. Complex body language are things we unconsciously do any time we are feeling a certain way. These cues give on-lookers the ability to know exactly how we are feeling. Most people looking at us only know subconsciously and get a "feeling" about how we are feeling, or they may even overlook it entirely in favor of their own thoughts and feelings. As an experienced body language reader, however, you would be able to easily identify what these cues mean and how they relate to what the person is thinking at any given time.

314

Let's take a look at them, now. When you are reading body language, you typically want to start with getting an idea for a person's overall body language. This is how they tend to carry themselves when they are "at rest" in the conversation. It may vary from conversation to conversation depending on their pre-existing emotions at any given time, but in general you should notice that most people have a fairly neutral "starting" position. Knowing what someone tends to look like when they are in neutral allows you to recognize when they make changes and what these changes mean about how they are feeling and what they are thinking.

To read someone's complex body language, start by looking at their hands and arms. Where are they placed, and what are they doing? Are they near the body, or further away? In general, the further the hands are from the body, the more relaxed a person is feeling. This is true unless the hands are tucked in neatly but are completely relaxed and not tensing, fidgeting, or grasping at anything. If their hand is rested comfortably on their lap, for example, it would show that the person somewhat submissive and relaxed. If both of their hands were folded and rested in the center of their lap, it would show that they were completely submissive in the situation. When people touch their arms with opposing hands, this often signifies that they are feeling uncomfortable or uncertain in a situation and that they are trying to understand it at a greater level. If both hands are touching the opposing arms, however, this indicates that they are feeling shut down on some level. If the hands are relaxed on the opposing arms, the person is feeling defeated. If they are tense, the person is feeling agitated. Sometimes, hands may not be positioned on the body itself at all. Instead, they may be placed elsewhere. For example, on an object. The message then comes from whatever that object is and the tension of the grip on that object. For example, if they are lightly gripping their cup in front of them, they are relaxed but waiting for an appropriate moment to take a drink. If they are holding their purse or keys in their hand, they are ready to leave but are waiting for the right time to say that they are ready to go. If their hands never left their purse or keys, it means they were not intending to stay long and that they may be uncomfortable or untrusting in their surroundings. With hands, there are two things you are looking for: placement, and grip. If the hands are placed on an object, consider what that object means to them. If the object is something that the person would typically use if they stay around for a while, then the person is likely relaxed and well-engaged in their environment. If they are gripping anything such as their keys, their purse, their wallet, the door handle, or otherwise, this means that they are ready to go and do not want to be here any longer. The next place you want to look is at their legs and their feet. Unlike the hands, feet do not grip anything. For that reason, the biggest thing you can learn about someone from their feet comes from which direction the feet are pointing and what movements they are making, if any. Where the feet are pointing says a great deal about what the person is thinking and where they want to go. If, for example, they are pointed at the person in front of them and at the door, that means that they want to leave with that person. If both are pointed at the person, they are comfortable in the environment and completely tuned in to that single person. If they are pointing at multiple people in the conversation, they are engaged in a group conversation. If they are pointing at the bar, they want another drink. If both are pointing at the door, they really want to leave.

The feet may be making a variety of different movements, too. If they are still, this means that the person is either relaxed or focused. They are engaged in whatever is going on around them, and so they are not thinking about any movements. When they begin to move, however, they can signify a variety of things. For example, if a person is feeling anxious, they may rapidly move their feet back and forth. If the feet are only gently rocking back and forth, or if you are looking at a woman and she is slipping the back of her shoe on and off, it means that they are feeling some form of attraction for the person that they are talking to. If a person has their feet crossed at the ankles and they are bouncing them around, this may signify that they are bored and wish that they were somewhere else, or doing something else.

Pay attention to both the hands and the feet when you are reading someone's body language. Both will give you a clear identifying factor of how they are feeling and what they are thinking. The best way to get a full read on a person is to read what both parts of the body are telling you and then put it together as a full message. That way, you know exactly what the person is thinking and feeling.

Walking Cues

How people walk says a lot about how they are feeling in any given moment. In general, the faster they are walking, the less they are thinking. This doesn't necessarily mean that they aren't thinking about anything it all. Instead, it usually means that they are only thinking about one thing. For example, they may be late and they are thinking about what they are late for and so they are walking fast. Or, they may be angry and looking for the person they are upset with, and the only thing on their mind is that anger. Since the faster a person walks translates to less thoughts on a person's mind, the slower a person walks translates to more thoughts on a person's mind. Therefore, if you see someone walking about slowly, they are often thinking about a lot. They may be walking slowly with an inquisitive look on their face, as though they are pondering something large and looking for the answer while they walk. Or, they may be walking slowly with a somewhat dazed look on their face, thinking about anything that comes to their mind.

Aside from the speed of a person's walk, think about their posture, too. A person who walks with a tall, straight back and their head held high is one who is confident and sure of themselves. Someone who walks with their shoulders slumped down and their back shrugged forward and barely picks up their feet is someone who is feeling unconfident. If a person generally walks with a tall, straight posture, and you see them walking with a shrunken, slumped posture, this likely means that they are upset about something in the moment. If the opposite happens, then the person is likely happy and has experienced some form of achievement in the very recent past. In general, the taller and straighter someone's posture is when they are walking, the surer of themselves they are. This can go all the way up to them having their chin turned upwards as they look down their nose at people, meaning that they likely have a grandiose sense of self-worth. Likewise, the more shrunken and slumped their posture is, the less sure they are of themselves. This goes all the way down to being completely slumped and skulking along, showing that they are feeling really low and down on their luck.

317

Facial Expressions

There are three areas you want to pay attention to one someone's face when you are using it as a tool for analysis. These three areas include the mouth, cheeks, and eyebrows. These three parts of the face have the tendency to move the most when it comes to expressive looks, and therefore they will also tell you the most about what a person is thinking or feeling at any given time. Facial expressions change rapidly throughout conversations, so pay close attention to these. In general, an emotion will first be expressed on the face, then into the body. They say that if a negative emotion is already being expressed in the body, it's too late and you may have lost the trust and faith of your target when it comes to manipulation. You have to be very swift and confident to turn that emotion around and regain their attention and trust.

With the mouth, there are many things you can tell. For example, someone who's mouth is soft and relaxed is either bored or uninterested in what you are presently talking about. You are losing their attention, and fast. If their mouth is slightly pursed, this is usually the sign that the person is interested in what you are saying and that you have their focus. If the mouth is tightly pursed or even pushed out slightly, this would indicate that they are angry and trying to "bite their tongue" from what they want to say. Smiling typically indicates happiness, but smiling with soft eyes that do not feature crow's feet at the sides indicates that the smile may be out of nervousness or obligation. A true smile always results in the eyes crunching and expressing crow's feet at the sides. If someone's mouth is pulled down at the sides, it may indicate they are sad. However, if it is pulled down and tense in any way, it may instead indicate defensiveness or annoyance. The biggest thing to pay attention for in someone's cheeks is their tension. If someone's cheeks are tight and pulled back towards the ears, this typically indicates that the person is feeling fearful or nervous. If they are tight and pushed forward toward the mouth, this would mean that the person is feeling angry. If the person's cheeks are tight and pressed up toward the eyes, this would indicate that the person is feeling happy. If they are soft or seem to be drooping toward the floor, this would indicate that the person is feeling sad.

Lastly, the eyebrows are another expressive place on the face that you need to pay attention to. If a person's eyebrows are pulled down at the edges and turned upward slightly in the center, this would indicate that they are feeling sad or even pitiful. If they are furrowed, this would mean that they are focusing and trying to take everything in. However, if they furrow and their entire face tenses up, this would indicate that they are angry. Eyebrows that stay lightly raised for the entire conversation indicate that the person is interested in what you are talking about. However, eyebrows that quickly flicker up and then down indicate that a person is surprised by a piece of information. If they are fairly neutral and don't move, this means the person may be disinterested.

Profiling

Profiling is where you look at someone's surroundings to get a better idea of who they are. This can be easy in some cases, and harder in others. Let's take a look at the three main areas you want to pay attention to with profiling: who they are with, what they look like, and their environment.

Who Are They with?

Start with who the person is with. If the person is close with the person or people they have come in with, then the interactions you see between those two people will be more accurate to how that person feels when they are comfortable. It also allows you to look at the pair or group as a whole to get a feel for what they are like. For example, if they are all dressed in a country-esque theme, you can conclude that they may be more outdoorsy and do-it-yourself type people. However, if they are all dressed in business or business casual clothes, their preferences may lean more toward outsourcing things and getting the best of the best - already made for them. If they are with people they are not typically with, you will be able to tell as the interactions will be a little tenser between them. Although they may still be comfortable, especially if the person is confident, it may seem a little more professional than casual, even if they aren't together for anything business-related.

What Do They Look Like?

Pay attention specifically to what the person you are targeting looks like. Are they well-groomed? Do they look after themselves well? Or are they unkempt and looking somewhat messy? This can give you an idea of how they feel about themselves, and how they think others feel about them, too. If they are well-dressed and groomed, this would indicate that they are confident and care what other people think and want to be perceived well by others. If they are unkempt and not well groomed, it may indicate that they feel low on self-esteem and self-confidence and that they don't overly care about what other people think of them because they don't think that they are worth high praise in the first place. In addition, pay attention to what they are wearing. Their sense of style will tell you a lot about who they are. Bold, bright clothes that have fancy designs, for example, indicate that a person's personality would be bold, bright, and unique. If their clothes are boxy, unfitted, and dull, however, the person may lack individuality and not have a clear sense of who they are. Someone who dresses neatly and in neutral colors likely believes everything should be clean-cut and modern, and has a fairly similar clean-cut personality to match it.

What is Their Environment?

Lastly, pay attention to their environment. The places they spend the most of their time equate to the places they feel most comfortable in. If they're spending a lot of time at concerts and at friend's houses, this would clearly indicate that they are outgoing and into a party lifestyle. If they are regularly spending time at up-scale bars, high end fashion boutiques and galas, this would indicate that they are a part of "high society" and that they like things to be the best of the best. If you can, pay attention to their home, or how they keep their work space and car, too. If they keep them clean and organized, this indicates that the person is someone who has a clear frame of mind and works best in a clear and organized space. If they keep things messy and chaotic, it likely reflects on a disorganized frame of mind and an uncertainty about things. They are also less likely to be reliable than those who are more clean and organized.

Chapter 8: Manipulation Techniques

Everyone in the world has likely used manipulation at some points in their lives. This could have been through telling the most straightforward lies to get out of situations or by flirting with others to get what you want. In understanding the techniques used by manipulators in their work, you need to ask yourself the following question:

Who is at threat from a manipulator? To regulate their victims, the pullers of the strings (manipulators) use several tactics, but most importantly, they do this by targeting specific kinds of personalities. You are more likely to be a victim of manipulation if you have low self-esteem, if you are inexperienced, pleased easily, if you are not confident about yourself and if you lack assertive instincts.

What are the requirements for successful manipulation? Primarily, successful manipulation encompasses a manipulator. Manipulation is also likely to be achieved through covert hostile methods. For successful persuasion, a manipulator has to:

• Cover their violent purposes, deeds, and be friendly.
• Be aware of the psychological susceptibilities of the targeted person so as to conclude which strategies are likely to be the most effective.
• Have an adequate level of callousness to have no doubts about triggering injury to the victim if necessary.

The manipulators exploit different defenselessness habits that exist in the victim's character and such include:

• The naïveté of the targeted person - Based on naïveté, the targeted person experiences hardships to buy the notion that many human beings are always sneaky, deceitful, and hard-nosed. This means if you are the victim, you will be in denial that you are being victimized.
• If you are over-conscientiousness - This is where you find yourself ready to grant the exploiter the advantage of distrust. The manipulator ends up blaming you and supporting their side, which makes you trust them easily. If you are too honest, you end up thinking everyone else is reliable as well.

• Self-confidence - Controllers often check whether you are a self-doubting person and whether you lack self-assertiveness, and this makes you go into a defensive mode effortlessly. You end up not giving a second thought about errors.

• Over-intellectualization - This makes it hard for you to understand and therefore, you end up believing your manipulator's reasons for being hurtful.

• Your emotional reliance - If you have a submissive personality, you are more likely to be a victim of manipulation. The more you rely on your emotions, the more vulnerable you are to being manipulated.

• Loneliness - If you are a lonely person, you are likely to agree to take little proposals of social interaction. Some manipulators will propose being your companion, but at a price. This also involves being narcissistic whereby, you fall easily for any kind of unjustified flattery. Lonely people act without any consultations. Therefore, loneliness goes hand in hand with being impulsive.

• Materialistic - Having a get-rich-quick mindset makes you cheap prey for manipulators. This means you are greedy and want to get rich quickly, hence end up acting immorally for some sort of material exchange.

• The elderly are also at a higher risk of getting controlled easily because they are fatigued and not able to multitask. Likelihoods the elderly will have a thought that a manipulator might be a conman are very rare. Manipulators thus take advantage of them and commit elder abuse.

Techniques of Manipulation

Manipulators take time to explore and examine your characteristics and find out how vulnerable you are to exploitation. They tend to control their victims by playing with their psychological characters. Having read the points above, now you need to know what the tactics and techniques are manipulators use to control their victims. They include various methods, as discussed below.

Techniques of manipulation

Reinforcement: This can be either positive, negative, or intermittent forms of reinforcement.

1. Positive reinforcement: This involves the case where the manipulator uses praises, charms, crocodile tears, unnecessary apologizing, public acknowledgment, cash, presents, consideration, and facial languages like forced laughter or smiles.

2. Negative reinforcement: A manipulator removes you from a negative situation as a favor.

3. Intermittent reinforcement: This is also known as partial reinforcement. This creates an environment full of fear and doubts. It encourages the victim of manipulation to persist.

Punishment: The manipulator acts in a nagging manner. There is yelling, silent treatment, intimidating behavior, and threatening of the victim. Manipulators cry and tend to play the victim card, thus emotionally blackmailing the victim and can go further by swearing they are the innocent one.

Lying: it entails two ways; lying by commission and lying by omission.

1. Lying by commission - You will find it hard to tell when a manipulator is lying the moment they do it, and the truth won't reveal itself until it is too late. You should understand that some people are experts at lying and thus you should not give in easily to their tactics.

2. Lying by omission - This is a subtle way used to manipulate, and it entails telling lies, and at the same time, withholding significant amounts of the facts. It is also applied in propaganda.

Denial: Manipulators rarely admit they are wrong. Even when they have done something wrong, they will refuse to believe it. They are rational and always assert that their behavior is not harmful or they are not as bad as someone else has explained. They accompany every exploitation with phrases like, 'it was only a joke'.

Attention: This includes selective inattention and attention. In this case, manipulators deliberately refuse to listen or pay attention to anything that distracts them from their agendas. They always defend themselves with phrases like, 'I do not need to listen to that'.

Deviation: Controllers never answer any questions directly and always steer the discussion to another topic. If not so, the manipulator gives irrelevant or rogue answers to the direct questions asked.

Intimidation: In this case, the manipulator applies two methods of intimidation; covert intimidation and guilt trip. In underground extortion, the manipulators throw their targets onto the self-justifying side through the use of implied threats. A guilt trip is a technique where the manipulator tries to suggest to the meticulous prey that they no longer care and this makes the victim feel bad and they start doubting themselves, hence, they find themselves in a submissive position.

Use of Sarcasm: The manipulator shames the victim by using put-downs and sarcasm that makes the victim doubt themselves. Making the victim feel unworthy gives an entry for the manipulator to defer the victim. These shaming tactics may include fierce glances, unpleasant tones, rhetorical comments or questions, and subtle sarcasm. Some of the victims end up not daring to challenge the manipulator as it fosters a sagacity of meagerness to their targets. Belittling their Target: Manipulators use this technique to put their target on the self-justifying side, while at the same time, covering the belligerent aims of the persuader. The persuader then misleadingly blames their target in response to the victim's defensive mechanisms. This also involves the case where a manipulator plays the victim role by portraying themselves as victims of circumstances to gain sympathy, thereby, getting what they want. This technique aims at the caring and compassionate victims as they cannot stand seeing someone suffer, and thus, the manipulator takes that chance to get the victim's cooperation.

Feigning: Manipulator pretends that any harm caused was unintentional or they are being accused falsely. Manipulators often wear a surprised face, hence making the victim question their own sanity. Feigning also involves the case where the manipulator plays dumb and pretends they are totally unaware of what the victim is talking about. The victim starts doubting themselves while the manipulator continues to point out the main ideas they included just in case there is any doubt. This happens only if the manipulator had used cohorts in advance that helps them in backing up their stories.

Seduction: In this case, the manipulator uses praise or any form of flattery, which involves supporting the victim to gain their conviction. Manipulators can even start helping you to increase your loyalty, and it will be hard for you to suspect their ill intents. The manipulator can as well play the servant role where their actions will be justified by phrases such as, 'I am just doing my job' or 'I am in service to a certain authority figure.' In this case, the victim will give their trust and end up being manipulated.

Brandishing anger: The manipulator shows off how angry they are in order to intensify the victim's shock to get their submission. In the real sense, the manipulator is never angry, but they act like they are, especially when denied access to what they want. A manipulator can as well control their anger to avoid any confrontations or hide their intents. Manipulators often threaten the victims by saying they are going to report the cases to the police. Anger is a way of blackmailing the victim to avoid telling the truth, as it wards off any further inquiries. This makes the victim focus more on the anger of the manipulator rather than on the manipulation technique being used.

The Bandwagon effect: This is the case where the manipulator tends to comfort the victim by claiming that, whether right or wrong, many people have already done some things, and thus, the victim should do it anyway. The manipulator uses phrases like 'Many people like you...' This kind of manipulation is mainly applied to those under peer pressure conditions. Similar cases are when a manipulator tries to lure the victim into taking drugs or abusing other substances. The techniques discussed above are the tested and proven tactics that any manipulator will strive to use to get a strong control of their victims. Before a manipulator persuades their victims, there are those steps they have to follow to make sure they fully control their victim's minds.

Whatever the reasons for manipulating someone, you should always play your cards safely. That is why you should learn how to manage and control the thoughts of people, the strategies, and steps you need to use in various situations. There are three authentic manipulating skills you can learn quickly through the steps discussed below. If you want to manipulate others in an easy way, come on! Shed a fake tear and follow the following steps.

Effective Steps of Manipulation
Honing Your Persuasion Skills

1. Take an Acting Class: If you want to be a manipulator, you first need to learn how to master your emotions and make others interested in your forced feelings. Now, if you desire to look more distressed that you really are or even want to apply a variety of emotional techniques to get what you want, then take an acting class since it will improve your persuasion powers. When considering an acting class, you need to

note you should never tell people you are taking a drama class if you are learning how to persuade and control people's minds. This is because they may get suspicious over your skills rather than believing in you.

2. Taking a Debate Class: After you have taken acting classes and learned how to master your emotions when convincing others to get what you want, you need to take debate classes, which might also involve public speaking classes to learn more on organizing, presenting what you think and making you sound more convincing.

3. Pacing: In this step, you will learn how to establish similarities. You need to learn how to mirror your victim's body language, then see how effective you can control your tonal variations and other body languages. The gentle and manipulative technique is the best when persuading your employer or fellow employees to get them do something for you. In this case, you should NEVER be emotional since this is a professional setting.

4. Be Charismatic: Once you are charismatic, you will have the tendency to get what you want. In this step, you need to learn how to smile and light up a room. You should as well have approachable body gestures so your targeted people feel willing to talk to you. You should be flexible such that you can hold up a discussion with anyone despite their age, body size, or profession. The following are other techniques you should apply to be charismatic:

• Making others feel special by maintaining eye contact when talking to them, asking them how they feel and what are their interests. Show them how much you care about knowing them even if you know you do not mean it.

• Love yourself and what you do by exuding your confidence. Have faith in yourself so others can take you seriously and fall into your persuasion intent.

• Be confident even if what you are saying is true or false. When speaking, be glib as this makes your target fall into your purpose easily.

5. Learn from Other Manipulators: Since you are still an amateur, you need to learn more from the masters. Look for your friends or family members who are persuasion masters and take notes. This helps in getting new insights on how to persuade and influence people even if it means you end up being a manipulation victim. If you are interested in

the art of mind control, you might also find yourself manipulating one of the masters.

6. Read People: You should also learn to read people as everyone has a different emotional and psychological composition and should, therefore, be persuaded for various purposes. Before you apply your latest manipulation skills, take time to learn your target by understanding what makes them tick, then evaluate which approach suits them. The following are the most proven factors you will come across when getting to know more about people:

• The majority are vulnerable to emotional responses. They are emotional themselves as they can cry while or after watching a movie; they love pets and are sympathetic. This means in order for you to persuade them, you will have to play with their emotions until they empathize and sympathize with you and give in to your intents.

• Others were raised in authoritarian backgrounds, hence have a guilt reflex. Since they are used to getting punished for every little wrong deed, they grow up feeling guilty about anything they do. As a manipulator, make them feel guilty for not fulfilling your demands, and within no time, they will grant your wishes.

• Other people are amenable to rational approaches. They are always logical-minded, tend to read the news every day, and they always ask for facts before deciding on anything. In this case, you will need to apply your calm mind-controlling powers to influence these people rather than using your emotions.

Apply Different Persuasion and Manipulation Techniques

1. Always Start with Unreasonable Requests in order to Get More Reasonable Ones: This step is a time-tested technique for persuasion. As a manipulator, you should always start with unreasonable demands, and then wait for the victim to deny you, then follow it up with a more approachable request. It will be hard for them to reject you for the second time, as the second request will sound more appealing as compared to the first request.

2. Ask for a Rare Request before Your Real Request: This is another way of getting what you want as it entails requesting a strange thing that throws your target off guard, making them unable to deny you. Then ask for the more usual type of request, and the victim will not be

able to deny it since their mind has been trained to avoid these activities.

3. Stimulate Fear, Then Liberation: For successful persuasion, tell the person what they fear, and then relieve them of it, and with no doubt, they will be happy to grant your wish. It may sound mean, but you will get your results instantly.

4. Make your Target Feel Guilty: Making your target feel guilty is another step for a successful manipulation. You need to start by picking someone susceptible to feeling guilty. This should be followed by making them feel like they are bad for not granting your requests, no matter how absurd it is. The following can be the unchallenging victims who will fall into your persuasion technique:

• Parents - Manipulate your parents by making them feel guilty. Mention to them how you feel your life is full of sufferings since childhood because they are not granting your wishes.

• Friends - Remind them of all the good deeds you have done for them or else tell them how they usually let you down.

• Significant partner - Conclude your quarrels by saying 'Okay-furthermore I expected this.' This will make them feel guilty about letting you down several times.

5. Bribe: In this step, blackmailing is not necessary to get your wishes granted. Bribe your victim with an unappealing present. You can as well offer something you would have done anyway. First, you should figure out what your targeted person wants or lacks at the moment, then try giving it to them. Secondly, do not make it sound like you are bribing, but portray yourself like someone who is willing to help your victim in return for something you want.

6. Playing the Victim: Making yourself the victim is always a great manipulation technique. You should use this step sparingly and effectively to pierce your victim's heart and get what you want. You have to act like you are a wonderful person, philanthropic, and that you are always the victim of every evil on earth. Play dumb as it makes your victim believe you are honestly perplexed by why evil things always befall you. Saying 'It is okay- I'm used to this' makes your victim feel like someone who cannot help you wall you a number of times and this tactic will make you get what you want. Finally, always be pathetic.

'It is okay- I'm used to this'

7. Apply Logic: This step works better for the rational-minded people. Logica; acts as the most excellent persuader, more so when you carry along with come-oriented whys and wherefores on how what you are after would benefit both of you. While presenting your case, do it calmly and rationally to avoid losing your control. If you want to manipulate a rational person, NEVER be emotional. In this step, act like your request is the only option you have, and your victim will judge the case your way.

8. Never Break Character: When your friend, family member, or co-worker tries to manipulate you, pretend to be more upset than them. Look more hurt and tell them you are even amazed and you did not believe they could ever think that about you. This will make the victim feel guilty and sorry for you.

Manipulating Anyone in your Life
Getting everything you want

1. Your Friends: This is one of the final steps now that you have equipped yourself with the active manipulation steps. When it comes to your friends, it can be a bit harder since they know you well. But this does not mean you cannot manipulate them. You should never tell them you are trying to persuade them, as this might destroy your friendship. The following are the steps you should follow if it is in your friend's case:

• First, butter your friend(s) up. This is done by being friendly, doing small favors for them, and telling them how amazing they are to you, and this is done a week before you make a request for a straightforward indulgence. Do everything a friend is supposed to do without going overboard.

• Your friends should care for you, specifically when you are emotionally down, and this is a significant step to get what you want. This means your friends will do everything possible not to see you upset. Use the skills acquired in your acting class to make you look more emotional than you really are.

• Remind your friends of how amazing you have been to them and how you have sacrificed substantial space and time to save the friendship.

2. Your Significant Other: This is the simplest step. You have to turn your partner on and then ask what you want because, in this state, they can hardly deny you what you want. There are also some other ways to persuade your significant partner than this subtle route. Look sexy when making the request, and they will grant your wish based on how cute you look.

3. Your Boss: This step requires you to apply rational and logical approaches. You should NEVER show up at your employer's desk crying or manifesting your problems as the likely result for this is getting fired. You should instead be logical with your employer and back up your request with detailed explanations. Therefore, you should:
• Be a model employee a week before requesting a favor. This can be achieved through working late, keeping a smile always on your face, and even bringing pastries in the morning.
• Request the favor in an offhanded way. This entails requesting the support like it is no big deal. Rather than saying, 'I want to ask for something really important from you,' be casual as you request this or you might alert the employer about your intents.
• Manipulate the boss at the end of the day or during breaks. In the morning, employers are stressed about all the work they have to do for that day. Persuading your boss during these mentioned hours has the highest probabilities of being successful, as the boss will instead grant your wish rather than waste their time.

4. Your Teacher: This step works better if you combine professionalism with emotions. You need to:
• Be a role model to the other students by arriving to class early enough, reading ahead of the teacher and being active in class work.
• Appreciate your teacher by telling them how great they are in a composed manner. Tell them how much you love the subject and how much you enjoy their way of teaching.
• Talk of how much you are suffering at home as this will make the teacher feel awkward and sorry for you.
• While talking about your private life, wait until the teacher gets uncomfortable, and for instance, offers to give you an extension to rewrite an assignment. Let your tone trail off and start crying. You can as well opt for walking on your way home as the teacher would not be able to withstand this and will end up granting your wish.

5. Your parents: You have the right to maximum parental care and persuading your parents is also one of the easiest steps. If the parents love and support you, be a model son or daughter a while before making your request. Help out around the house as much as you can, then when you start persuading:
• Make your request in a reasonable way. Do not sit down and have a big talk about your request. Make it hard for your parents to say no to your request.
• State your claim while doing other household chores, such as folding the laundry. This reminds them of how good you are.
• Tell your parents about your friends, how their parents have granted the wishes of your friends and why your parents should feel okay too and grant the request.
• Make them feel guilty by talking on how you will get every detail of either a concert you missed or blame them for ruining your life by causing you not to have significant experiences in your life.
Having learned the steps for successful mind control, and how easily you can influence your friends, parents, boss, teachers or significant other, you should also know how effortless it is to manipulate someone hangs on the impressions you have of them. You should always be deceptive, use your emotions, and persuade using the waterworks approach in a public place, then finally use bribes where necessary.

Chapter 9: Persuading and Influencing People Using Manipulation

Human being as a social being is in constant communication for many reasons, giving information, getting information, asking for help, making promises, telling your feelings and thoughts, or trying to learn someone else's feelings and thoughts, and so on. Communication is established within a certain structure and order. At this point, one should look at the definition of communication: Inter-human communication; It's the process of transferring information, emotions, thoughts, attitudes and beliefs and forms of behavior from one person to another through a relationship between the source and the recipient for change. As can be seen in daily life, in many situations where communication takes place, people either try to convince someone about the accuracy of the information they give, either to change their behavior or to convince them of something else because persuasion is an important and common reason for communication. The famous philosopher Aristotle defines communication as all the appropriate meanings of persuasion".

The concept of persuasion is defined in the dictionary as follows: Convincing, convincing; deceit; "Based on this definition, it will not be wrong to consider persuasion as a form of communication that is realized to achieve the desired aims." Indeed, when we look carefully, it can be seen that the difference between daily communication and persuasion is to achieve the desired goal. Not every communication phenomenon that is established in daily life is intended for persuasion, asking someone's memory only aims to learn about the person's condition and health. However, rather than persuading a person on a particular issue, it should be dealt with to uncover the desired change in the person who is exposed in the final analysis, which should be established with a certain systematic structure.

In the meantime, an important issue should be included here. It is also the effects of communication and how they occur. The effects of communication are:

1. Change in the recipient's level of knowledge
2. Changes in the attitude of the recipient
3. A change in the receiver's opens behavior.

In the second stage, the attitude change that came into the agenda is also realized in three ways:
1. Strengthening or strengthening the existing attitude
2. Change of existing attitude
3. New attitude formation

The effects of communication are often expected to occur sequentially and usually do. It is possible to see the effect of communication to a large extent in the change that may occur in open behavior. This is where the difference between daily communication and persuasion comes up. Persuasive communication is the expected and desired changes in attitude and open behavioral changes that will occur after the information is given. The attitude change that is expected to occur is determined by some attitude measurement techniques (Likert scale, etc.) developed in cases where open behavioral change can't be observed clearly or if it's not possible for different reasons, for example, an individual's Facebook, and so on. If it is desired to learn the attitude towards social media, a questionnaire consisting of expressions reflecting this attitude can be prepared. These statements; it allows people to share, enjoy the time, etc. can. It is possible to say that a Likert-type scale was used to measure the attitudes of the respondents to measure attitudes.

The concept and process of persuasion is a subject that has been studied intensively. In general, the biggest factors contributing to the success and failure of communication emerge as convincing communication and its proper structuring. With good understanding and knowledge of persuasive techniques; an educator, an advertiser, or a politician, in other words, it is possible to evaluate anyone whose purpose is to change the thoughts and actions of others. It should not be ignored that some essential variables exist in persuasion. Each of the variables in persuasion must be identifiable, distinguishable, and measurable. Scientists working in this field, these variables fall under two headings. These are called "dependent variables" and "independent variables. Arguments are made or occur with the communication process. We know what these variables will be, how they will be formed, and

334

predict and produce their effects. Dependent variables, on the other hand, have to be done, and convincingly. We often hope to replace dependent variables with independent variables that we manage and control. Dependent and independent variables are called a convincing communication matrix.

The convincing communication matrix is a precise and complete data about all dependent and independent variables in human relationships throughout human life. Independent variables should be considered in many aspects and aspects of communication. However, dependent variables occur only when a person receives a persuasive message in terms of the information process. The main issue that needs to be emphasized about independent variables is the operation of the basic process of communication: "who, whom, what, through which channel and what kind of influences. The arguments that make up every convincing communication state appear in this case as "source, message, channel, receiver, and purpose. The dependent variables of the persuasive communication matrix are divided into six steps according to the characteristics of new behaviors, events, and phenomena in which the person is convinced. First, a convincing message must be presented. The second step is the participation of the target person in the communication, and this person needs to understand what is to be discussed. It's important that the recipient supports communication until the message is sent later and third. The fourth step is the understanding of the message, as well as the acceptance of the recipient or at least verbal adjustment. The fifth step is the most basic requirement. This step is the ability to accept until the effect can be measured. The sixth and last step or dependent variable is the ability of the target person to show the new behavior as open behavior. For example; depending on the main objective of the persuasion campaign, the purchase of a certain product, the selection of the candidate or leaving a harmful habit, etc. they are always concrete indicators of this last dependent variable. An analysis in the context of dependent and independent variables can help organize ideas about persuasion. The persuasion process is analyzed at all levels of communication.

These steps are as follows: Source of communication, form, content, and organization of communication, characteristics of the channel to which the message will be delivered, ability and characteristics of the intended recipient and intended behavior and attitude changes. Thus, under these five headings of communication, the efficiency of the persuasive communication process performed under the six steps of the dependent variables of persuasion is defined and evaluated. Examination of the persuasion process shows the importance of understanding and attention in a way. For example; when asked what kind of connection can be made between an intelligent buyer and persuasion, he will probably tell you that only a much smarter individual can convince that person. In other words, the more knowledgeable and intelligent person can only direct the person's point of view to another party. This point shows the variables of the connection between intelligence and persuasive communication. However, other points that should not be forgotten are the role and importance of attention and acceptance in the persuasion process.

Persuasion Techniques

The basis of persuasion is to direct the other person to the thought you desire and to make it normal in the basic belief and vision system. To simplify, it is to make the other person think the way you want. That's exactly what it means to convince. If the other person thinks the way you want, you can take the action that you want to take, that is, buying a product or consuming a product. Located below are techniques to persuade and convince some of the most effective techniques effectively. Persuasion techniques are not limited to these, but they are important for efficiency. You may encounter many other techniques of persuasion, such as rewarding, punishing, creating a positive or negative perception.

1. Creating Needs

One of the best methods of persuasion is to create a need or to reassure an old need. This question of need is related to self-protection and compatibility with basic emotions such as love. This technique is one of the biggest trumps of marketers in particular. They try to sell their products or services using this technique. The kind of approaches that express the purchase of a product to make one feel safe or loving is part of the need-building technique.

2. Touching Social Needs

The basis of the technique of touching social needs are factors such as being popular, having the prestige, or having the same status as others. The advertisements on television are the ideal examples. People who buy the products in these advertisements think that they will be like the person in the advertisement or they will be as prestigious. The main reason why persuasion techniques such as touching social needs are effective is related to television advertising. Many people watch television for at least 1-2 hours a day and encounter these advertisements.

3. Use of Meaningful and Positive Words

Sometimes it is necessary to use magic words to be convincing. These magic words are meaningful and positive words. Advertisers know these positive and meaningful words intimately. It is very important for them to be able to use them. The words "New," "Renewed," "All Natural," "Most Effective" are the most appropriate examples of these magic words. Using these words, advertisers try to promote their products and thus make the advertisements more convincing for the liking of the products.

4. Use of Foot Technique

This technique is frequently used in the context of persuasion techniques. Processing way is quite simple. You make a person do something very small first because you think you can't refuse it. Once the other person has done so, you will try to get him to do more, provided that he is consistent within himself. First, you sell a product to a person at a very low price. Then you get him to buy a product at higher prices. In the first step, you attract him to yourself, so you convince him to buy it. In the second step, you convince yourself to buy products at a higher price. Their acceptance of a small thing will help you to fulfill the next big demand from you. After refusing the small request from the other party, you feel a duty to make a big request from the same person. This is usually the case in human relations. For example, you agree when your neighbor comes and asks you if you can keep an eye on the shop for a few hours. If your neighbor comes to ask you to look at the shop all day, you will feel responsible and probably accept it. This means that the technique of putting a foot on the door is successfully applied.

5. Use of Orientation from Big to Small

The tendency to ask from big to small is the exact opposite of the technique of putting a foot on the door. The salesperson makes an unrealistic request from the other person. Naturally, this demand doesn't correspond. However, the salesperson makes a request that is smaller than the same person. People feel responsible for such approaches, and they accept the offer. Since the request is small, by accepting it, people have the idea that they will help the salespeople and the technique of moving from big to small requests works.

6. Use of Reciprocity

Reciprocity is a term for mutual progress of a business. When a person does you a kindness, you feel the need to do him a favor. This is one example of reciprocity. For example, if someone bought you a gift on your birthday, you would try to pay back that gesture. This is more of a psychological approach because people don't forget the person who does something for them and tries to respond. For marketers, the situation is slightly different from human relations. Reciprocity takes place here in the form of a marketer offering you an interim extra discount" or "extra promotion... You are very close to buying the product introduced by the marketer you think offers a special offer.

7. Making Limits for Interviews

Setting a limit for negotiations is to provide an approach that will affect future copyrights. This is particularly effective when negotiating prices. For example, if you are trying to negotiate a price to sell a service, it might make more sense to start by opening the price from a higher number. Opening from a low number is not the right method because you have weakened your stretching share.

Even if the limitation for negotiations is not always useful, it's particularly useful in terms of price negotiation. Say the first number and get on with the bargaining advantage.

8. Limitation Technique

Restriction technique is one of the most powerful methods to influence human psychology. You can see this mostly in places selling products. For example, if a store has a discount on a particular product, it may limit it to 500 products. This limitation can be a true limitation or a part of the limitation technique. So you think that you will not find the product at that price again and you agree to buy that product at the specified price. The restriction technique is particularly useful in new products. As soon as a new product goes on sale, you can convince people to buy it for a limited time or by selling a limited quantity of products with extra promotions or discounts. People who think that the product will not be sold again at a similar price may choose to buy the product you have chosen thanks to the success of your persuasion technique. Persuasion techniques are not limited to these. Different techniques can provide more successful results in various fields. However, most of the techniques that we may encounter in our daily lives consist of the methods here. If you want to be a marketer, if you are trying to sell a product or service, you need to have detailed information about these techniques if you want to make them available.

Difference between Persuasion and Manipulation

There are many similarities between Persuasion and Manipulation as the two words confuse non-English individuals: Natives too. There are many comparisons between the two concepts, and because of the overlap, people think these two can be used interchangeably. There are convincing good people, and there are good manipulators. Both try to make sense and encourage others to accept their views. However, although there are similarities in manipulation to making a cousin or persuasive sibling, there are differences to be emphasized.

Persuasion

Persuasion is a behavior from someone else directed in a specific direction. You've managed to convince when you try to explain a certain way of behavior logically and correctly, and others accept your opinion that they think is of mutual benefit. If you have good marks on your test and you asked your mother for an expensive gift, you are trying to convince her to buy you a gift. This persuasion is convincing because it sees the logic behind your request and buys gifts. The salesperson is persuaded to sell a product or service to customers as he tries to create the need for the product or service in the customer's mind.

Manipulation

Manipulation is the act of exploiting the instability of others and misleading them to accept your point of view. Manipulation is not mutually beneficial, only advantageous for the manipulator. At the subconscious level, people strive to control each other in an organization or a family. Instead of persuading them for their benefit, they try to manipulate them. Manipulation can also be for the good of the person, even as a child's mother says that instead of eating all of them from the cookie jar, they can get a cookie. This creates the possibility of illusion, and your child can easily accept for fear of losing the jar without a single cookie. You manipulated the child's behavior for his good. Manipulation can also be bad, and manipulation is bad because the manipulator aims to trick and benefit from it.

The distinction between persuasion and manipulation

• Manipulation, managing others to benefit flawlessly.
• Persuading a particular person to change his or her thinking logically and rationally by reasoning with himself or by presenting arguments
• Manipulators can achieve short-term success, but people know who is manipulated and who convinces them in the long run.
• Persuasion is the art of achieving what you want by creating changes in the behavior of others, but it is manipulation. However, the difference is your intention.
• A person with good communication skills but malicious intent is dangerous because he can be a good manipulator.

Popular Persuasion techniques:

Brainwashing
Influence in various ways to alienate man from his thought and worldview, to think and act in another direction. Man is a creature that thinks and is very wrong at the same time. Because no living thing is as open to human influences, both from its internal structure and from outside, it is not as influenced by human influences. Brainwashing is the exploitation of the human being's ability to be exposed to internal and external influences.

Brainwashing can be classified as being performed in a long and short term. Short-term brainwashing: This is a method of brainwashing using medical and psychological procedures. The essence of this method is the excitement of human beings by preparing tired, sleepless, drugged situations in which the said things are accepted without details, uncontrolled, it is to constantly influence it and put it into behavior that

340

does what is desired without discussion. The founder of this method is the Russian scholar Pavlov. Pavlov concentrated his work on conditional reflexes.

"Reflex" is the body's reaction to a natural warning. The spontaneous withdrawal of the hand's approach to fire is an example. Conditional reflexes are reflexes that are dependent on habit and gained over time. Pavlov used dogs as test subjects. Many times he gave the dogs meat just after a ringtone. In later experiments, it was observed that the dogs drooled with the ringing sound even though no meat was given. Pavlov has given dogs various conditional reflexes. In 1924 there was a major water disaster in Leningrad. Pavlov's dogs flooded the building. The dogs stayed for days at elevated water levels up to their noses. After rescuing, it was seen that dogs lost their conditional reflexes. It was this event that led Pavlov to the brainwashing method. He concluded that events such as extreme fear, excitement, and fatigue erased acquired conditional reflexes. The next experimental tools were people who were victims of the communist regime. Such methods were developed so that the mental angels of a human being were disrupted, their memories and imaginations were erased, and with the logic of making, a robot personality with other emotions was created. The first condition for this was to bring about the mental collapse of dogs in humans. This is a state that has long been seen in humans and is called mental collapse. Pavlov developed new methods for creating a mental collapse. Four conditions were needed to ensure this.

1. Fatigue: The first thing to do to brainwash is to tire. For this reason, one is prevented from sleeping during long circuits. For example, by keeping strong light on the face, both fatigue and sleep are provided.

2. Astonishment: When the mental activities are weakened and solved by the effect of this big fatigue, the poor person is rained for hours of questioning. His mind is so confused that the connection between truth and lies is completely lost.

3. Permanent pain: Wounds open on your body that will last for a long time. It is connected to the clamp or chain, and its movement is prevented.

4. Continuous fear: The ways to create feelings of tension or fear is resorted to. As a result of these applications, the exhaustion of the human reaches its limit and image dissolves. The out of control of the

mind has the following consequences: Person is deprived of referral and effort. Memory clutter: Memories, interpretation, and reasoning skills; old habits are completely lost. The sequence of events has been forgotten. The nerves between the dream and the truth have become dark and blurry.

Melancholy: The mind wriggles in the grip of an unknown problem. One wants to commit suicide. Increased ability to be instilled: By taking advantage of this weak and defenseless state of man, they instill memory into a false form through suggestion. The new ideas they want to be believed are placed in the patient's tired mind as a form of suggestion.

The brainwashing process is now complete. Such a method of brainwashing has been used by the communist states, especially Russia and China. As a result of the brainwashing of the American soldiers who were captured by the Chinese in the Korean War; "We have seen the facts now. We were servants to the imperialists. The goal of communism is to achieve world peace. The Chinese couldn't apply brainwash to Turkish soldiers who were captured during the Korean War. Psychologists have shown the strength of faith in the Turkish soldier, their unshakable discipline and commitment to each other.

Long-term brainwashing: This method is carried out by propaganda. Propaganda: Persuasion, persuasion, deception, arousing suspicion, and intellectual and spiritual oppression activity. It is a sensitive and special method which is applied by having a positive or negative influence on the ideas, opinions, thoughts, and feelings of individuals and society.

Propaganda means; satellites, sports, and art activities, the press, television, radio, and books, they are the communist countries that give the most important to the brainwashing of people with propaganda. Russia has allocated 1/4 of its national income to propaganda. The aim of the propaganda is the human's ideas, feelings, that is, the spiritual. The brainwashed men are the prisoners of the enemy with a stronger chain of captivity than the first and medieval slaves. A wicked man who has been brainwashed against his nation and state can't understand that he is the slave of the enemy until the end of his life because of the values to show that what he did was bad. The measurement of value is only determined by having national and spiritual feelings and owning them. The person who loses these values acts according to the desires of the enemy. This is a slave, or rather a robot. The robot follows orders, for a normal person, the order was given to him as, suggestion, faith, and decides through the filtering of national values and reason. The degeneration of the human brain instead of arms, deflating intelligence, and ensuring the nation's morale and spirit in the direction of dispersion will be directed.

Chapter 10: Mind Control Techniques

Mind control

The term mind control has many definitions and interpretations, but the crucial thing to note is that it doesn't involve any sort of magic or supernatural ability; it just requires a rudimentary understanding of human emotions and behavior. Mind control can involve brainwashing a person, reeducating them, reforming their thoughts, using coercive techniques to persuade them of certain things, or brain-sweeping. There are many forms of mind control, and we could fill an entire book discussing all those forms, but for our purposes, we will look at the concept in general terms. Mind control means a person is trying to get others to feel, think, or behave in a certain way, or to react and make decisions following a certain pattern. It could vary from a girl trying to get her boyfriend to develop certain habits, to a cult leader trying to convince his followers that he is God.

Mind control is based on one thing: information. We have the thoughts and beliefs that we do because we learned them. When we are subjected to new information on a deliberate and consistent basis, it's possible to alter our beliefs, thoughts, or even memories. The brain is hardwired to survive, and towards that end, it's very good at learning information that is crucial for our survival. When you receive certain information consistently, your brain will start to believe it even if you know it's not true. For example, even if you are the most rational person out there, if you go online and watch 100 videos about a certain conspiracy theory, you will start to believe it to some extent. That explains why people who seem smart can end up getting indoctrinated into cults or even terrorist groups.

Mind control also works more effectively when one is dependent on the person who is trying to control his/her mind. Even in relationships that are involuntary, the victim can start buying the perpetrator's world view if they have been dependent on the perpetrator for a long time. That explains phenomena such as Stockholm syndrome (where people who are kidnapped or held hostage start being affectionate towards their captors and empathizing with their causes). The worst thing you can do is assume that you are too smart for mind control to work on you. Under the right circumstances, anyone can be persuaded to abandon their world view and adopt someone else's. Mind games are covert tricks that are deliberately crafted in order to manipulate someone. Think of them as "handcrafted" psychological manipulation techniques. While other techniques are applied broadly, mind games are created to target very specific people. They work best when the victim trusts the perpetrator, and the perpetrator understands the victim's personality and behavior. Most of the psychological manipulation techniques we have discussed thus far can be used when crafting mind games. A person who understands you will tell you certain things or behave in certain ways around you because they are deliberately trying to get you to react in a certain way. It almost always involves feigning certain emotions.

People who play mind games use innocent sounding communication to elicit calculated reactions from you. Psychologists refer to such mind games as "conscious one-upmanship," and they have observed that they occur in all areas of life. Mind games occur in office politics, personal relationships, and even in international diplomacy. At work, someone could try to make you feel like you are not up to the task so that they can steal an opportunity from you. In a marriage, your partner could make certain seemingly innocent slights against you so that you feel like you have something to prove, and you take a certain course of action as a result. In dating, there are "pickup artists" who use different kinds of tricks to get you to lower your guard and let them in. Mind control is not the whole of the vague information you hear in gossip, accompanied by conspiracy theories. It is the product of secret experiments with systematic studies dating back to World War II, perhaps older. Of course, the 20th-century totalitarian regimes, who wanted to robotize their subjects, also played a major role in this. Therefore, the first thing to note is that developing technology facilitates the mind-control efforts of the oppressors every year. Like Telegram scourge that happens today… But mind control; it is something that can be done without technology with the support of psychology and orator. The most striking example of this in history; this is the work carried out by Goebbels, the Minister of Propaganda of the Nazis. Goebbels succeeded in engraving his name in gold letters in this lane, which was the disgrace of humanity.

Mind control; It is the name given to all the unethical activities of some power centers to manage people in line with their goals, to shape their ideas and control their lifestyles. While technological opportunities can be utilized in mind control, human psychology, propaganda knowledge, and social engineering are essential. Also, mind control; it is applied in a highly systematic, insidious way by people who have done as much research as required by a master or doctor. In other words, it is essential that people don't realize the engineering applied to them, so to be hypnotized. Therefore, it is challenging to recognize and resist. Also; every political and intellectual propaganda is not minded control. Mind control, as we mentioned above, is a different matter.

Effects of Mind Control on human

The effects of using mind control on human beings are seen in different ways. Some of them are as follows;
• "Memory loss and behavior disorders
• Change in direction, intensity and content of sound heard
• Speech deterioration by checking eyelids
• Severe heart palpitations
• Forcing accidents on the shoulders and arms during laborious work
• Jogging of the elbows and preventing work while doing something
• Pain and unnecessary movement of the legs, right and left swing and excessive stiffness
• Itching and blushing in hard-to-reach areas
• Contractions of large muscles in the back
• Checking hand gestures
• Reading thoughts or transmitting thoughts from outside
• Seeing moving imaginary images
• Keeping eyelids constantly open
• Continuous tinnitus
• Jaw and teeth shivering for no reason

Chapter 11: Manipulating Mass Opinion as a Public Speaker

Remember that earlier we talked about three different steps that have to come into play when it is time to work with influencing someone to do what we want. Whether we want them to finish a report for us, give us some extra tips, help us out with some work or with our kids so we can get a break, or even to sell them a product, we need to be able to use these three steps to help us get what we want from the target. First, you need to work on analyzing the other person. Depending on how long you plan to know this person and how much influence you plan to do, you will need to spend a bit of time doing an analysis to help you see success. Once the analysis is done and you have a good idea on what is going to work the best for your target, it is time to move on to manipulation or planting the seeds of what you want the target to do.

Once you have been able to work through some of the strategies that are presented in that chapter on your target, it is time to move on and learn a bit about how to work with persuasion to get what you really want. There are a number of steps that you are able to use in order to persuade your target. And you will find that a lot of these are easy, and maybe already done if you have gone through the two other steps and some of their techniques from earlier. When you are ready to start persuading someone to do what you want, make sure to follow some of the steps below to help you to get started! And overcome the trust issues that are there. One of the first things that we are going to work on is the idea of trust issues that could be there. It is possible that the person you choose for your target is someone you have just met. Or maybe you have known them for a long time and yet have had very little to do with them over the years. And now you want to come in and really get them persuaded to do something that they may not be that sure of on their own. There is bound to be some trust issues. It doesn't matter how good you are with manipulation. And it doesn't matter how likable of a person you are in the beginning. What does matter is how much the other person trusts you. And you need to be willing to work on building up that trust, and learning how to overcome any trust issues if you really want to make sure that you get the best results here.

The good news is that there are a few steps that you are able to follow in order to really work on some of these trust issues. Once those are resolved, you will find that it is easier than ever to really work with persuasion and to get what you want from anyone. So, let's take a look at some of the different steps that you can take as a manipulator when it comes to trying to build up that trust that you want.

First, you need to make sure that you learn how to study the actions of other people. Often times we are going to because of hurt because we believe that there is some promise there that has never been held as true or taken care of. And sometimes that thing has nothing to do with you but something in the past that your target is now dealing with. Watching the actions of the other person, and learning what trust issues may be there, and how you can fix them, can help them to open up and value you way more than before. One of the best things that you are able to do to build up some trust is to ask a lot of questions. You are never going to know what the other person is mad about or what causes them to have some trust issues if you have no idea why they are mad about something or why they have the trust issues. You need to ask a bunch of questions to figure this out sometimes.

This can be done no matter what kind of relationship you have with the other person or not. If you find that you are a salesperson who is trying to sell a product questions can help you to figure out why the person hasn't purchased the product in the past, what issues they may have gone through with purchasing this item or another one that is similar in the past, and what you would be able to do to make it better. Maybe the customer is nervous about purchasing a car because the last few were sold to them by someone they trusted, but these vehicles ended up being duds and costing way too much. You can take that information and then work on how to make it a bit better so that they trust you. Even if you are trying to build up a long term relationship with the target than you would as a salesperson, you will be able to use some of the manipulations and some of these questions in order to help you to do this. The more questions you ask the person about their past, about some of their friends, about what they are looking for in the future, and more, the more likely it is that you are going to be able to figure out what may have broken their trust in the past, and what you are able to do to increase that trust in the future.

You can also work on gathering information as much as possible. Your friend may not trust someone, but that isn't a sign that someone shouldn't be trusted. And maybe this is what is happening with you and your target. They have a friend who doesn't trust you for one reason or another (they may have never met you in the past either), and so they just don't trust you either. Knowing this information, and then talking to the more logical part of that person, rather than the emotional side that is listening to the friend, it going to make a big difference in what you are able to do to build up some of that trust. Go slowly. There are going to be some relationships that you are able to jump right into, even when you are working with a target of manipulation. But then there are some of those that need to go a little bit slower. There are those who have been hurt in the past or those who are just naturally wary of others around them, and they will want to be careful with anyone they are interacting with.

If you decide to jump into the mix too quickly, then you are going to scare them away and they will want to have nothing to do with you. But when you are really able and willing to just take things slow and let people get to know you (or at least the story of you that you want them to know), you will find that it is much easier for you to really gain their trust. Trying to get the target to blindly trust you is just going to make them clam up even more and this makes the situation so much worse. Instead, talk to them slowly and give them some time to determine if they want to be in this kind of relationship, whether it is a romantic one, a friendship, a working relationship or something else or not. If you take it slowly, it also gives you more time to really work with some of the other techniques that we have talked about, which can make a world of difference in how much success you are going to see here.

It is so important for you to gain some level of trust with your target. Even though persuasion and manipulation don't seem to go hand in hand with trust, it is impossible to persuade your target to do anything that you want them to do. Building up some form of trust, whether it is a short term trust that you do in the spur of the moment as you meet them at work or one that you build up over time because of the long relationship that you are going to be in.

Know what your purpose is

Before you ever try to persuade anyone to do what you want and before you use any of the other techniques that are found in this guidebook, you really need to make sure that you know what your purpose is. You don't want to do all of the work that is presented above, and then find out that it is not enough because you have no idea what your purpose is. This purpose is really going to drive all of the other things that you are going to focus on when it comes to working through this guidebook. We are going to focus on what we want to get the target to do. What actions are they able to take that will ensure we get what we want in the end?

If you are not able to answer that question, then it is hard to really have any idea of the steps that you need to take in order to make this happen. Think about what your purpose is here. Your main purpose is to get someone to do what you want so that you can reach your own goals. Sometimes this is going to be beneficial for both of you. This can be seen when the target comes in to purchase a car. You sell it which benefits them because they get a new vehicle, and you benefit because you made a sale and get to keep the money for your paycheck.

But with manipulation and persuasion, sometimes the result for the target is not going to be as positive. In fact, many dark manipulators are not going to care about how their actions are going to affect others. They just want to get the benefits that they need and feel that they deserve, and that is all that they are really going to care about at the time. This can be seen in manipulative relationships. The manipulator is going to woo someone into the relationship and will keep them there. The target is not going to receive much from this relationship, and often they are going to be harmed in the process and be emotionally, physically, and mentally drained by the end of it. But the manipulator doesn't care because they will feel like they got what they wanted for the length of the relationship. This is why we need to understand our purpose. If we don't understand why we are walking into the process of manipulation (to get what we want), it is possible that we will be turned around by emotions and not do what we set out to do. This could end with us not getting the sale, not getting the relationship, or not getting something else that we really wanted.

Be calm and confident

As a manipulator, you really need to learn how to keep your emotions in check as much as possible. This is going to be one of those things that often seems easier said than done, but it is definitely something that you need to be able to focus on as much as possible.

Think of it this way, if you say someone comes over to you who seemed to be a bit agitated, or they were snickering with an evil grin on their face how likely is it that you would give them the time of day? It is likely that you would turn away and want to have nothing to do with them at all because you would feel like something was up.

And this is exactly the same way that the target is going to feel if you are not careful about how you react to situations around them. You need to be willing to stand up for yourself, be calm, and be confident, in order to ensure that the target feels comfortable with you and to ensure that they are not going to feel like something is up before you even get a chance to speak with them.

First, we need to take a look at the steps to remaining calm around the target. You do not want to come up to them sweating, heavily breathing, bouncing around, and acting like you are nervous. Sure, it's +very possible that you do feel these things. But on the outside, it is going to look really suspicious and it is going to be really hard for you to build up any of that trust or that connection that you need with the other person at all. If you are able to come up to your target with a lot of confidence, and you are able to show them that you have no fear, and you are sure in yourself, in your message, and in what you have to say to them, then this issue is gone. Now, it is normal for you to feel a little bit antsy and anxious when you are first starting out. That is the beauty of practice when it comes to working with persuasion. Over time you will get a lot better. If you still find that the nerves are bothering you and you are not able to get them under control, you have a few steps at your disposal as well.

Before approaching the target, take a few slow and cleansing breaths in and out to let it all go. Count down or up from ten, and see if that is able to help clear your head, get the shaking to go down, and will help you to stay as calm and collected as possible. The next thing that we need to concentrate on is the idea of adding some confidence to your stance and to your life. Confidence is hard to do, but it is something that you are able to fake a bit in order to convince someone else that you possess a lot of confidence, even if it is not really there for you. If you are worried about how to do this, then some of the steps to make you appear more confident to everyone around you, even though you may be sweating bullets and feel like there is no confidence around you at all, includes:

1. Avoid your pockets: Those hands need to stay out of the pockets. Put them almost anywhere else, but do not let them get lodged into your pockets and out of site.

2. Do not fidget: When you are nervous it is easy to spend some of your time fidgeting and not able to sit still. This is a clear sign that you are tense, hiding something or worried. When you become more conscious about the fidgeting that you are doing, you will find that it is easier to make it stop, and confidence is going to follow.

3. Keep the eyes forward: Nervous people are going to glance all over the place except at the person they are talking to. We have already talked a bit about why this is a bad thing and the importance of eye contact, so make sure that your eyes are on the target, and not glancing all around the room in a nervous manner.

4. Stand up straight: Not only does slouching make you look bad and like you are unorganized, but it is also going to look bad when it comes to how much confidence you have in yourself. Make sure that when you meet with anyone, but especially with your target, you stand up nice and straight with your back up and your shoulders back. No matter how nervous you are, this kind of stance is going to really make a difference in how much confidence people have in you.

5. Take steps that are wider: Don't go crazy with this one. If you are short, your steps are not supposed to reach so far that you fall over or anything. But if you are taking steps that are quick and short, then it may feel like you are sneaking, creeping, or scurrying, and these are not words that are used when it comes to someone who is confident. Do a nice stance while you walk (based on your own height), and see what a difference it makes in the confidence you have.

6. Firm handshake: We have all had that one handshake that never seems like it is completed. You have to pretty much do all of the work of holding onto the hand, much less making sure the handshake gets

done. Don't be like this. Use a firm handshake that is going to impress all of those around you.

7. Proper grooming: You have to take care of yourself when it comes to showing others that you are really confident in yourself. Keep your hair nice and kept up on a regular basis, wear clothes that are meant to impress, brush your teeth, take a bath on a regular basis, and make sure that you wear some perfume or cologne that is a nice scent, but not too overpowering.

8. Smile There is nothing better to helping out with your confidence and making you appear better to others than smiling on a regular basis. When you are confident, you really have no reason to worry about anything. Try this little experiment for a moment. The next time that you are walking down the street or the hall at work, give someone a smile. Chances are pretty high that this person is going to smile back at you. This is because you show confidence and it helps to rub off on them as well. You can do this with your target as well when you are working on that confidence.

9. Don't have your arms crossed when you are socializing: When you cross your arms, it is showing that you are trying to protect something. This is an action that we are going to do when we are on guard, nervous, or cold. And none of these things are going to inspire a lot of confidence, are they? It is important to do something else with your hands. Put them casually by the side. Or, if this seems a bit off, you can consider using hand gestures to help get your point across while still having something to do with your hands.

10. Use contact when you want to show some appreciation: A pat on the back is something that is considered a lost art in our society. But it can not only sow some of your own confidence, but it is going to be a great way to feel closer and more connected to the target when you need. Be careful with this and only use it with those who are going to be comfortable with your actions.

As you can see, there are a number of things that you are able to do in order to make sure that your target is going to see you as calm and confident all of the time. You will be amazed at how the projection of these two character traits are going to get people to jump at the chance to do what you want, and they are easy things that you can learn without a ton of practice or hard work along the way.

Manipulate the body language that you are using.

The next thing on the list that you are able to work with is manipulating your own body language. Many people think that this is just something we can't do at all. We assume that because we often don't think about our body language, there is no way that we are able to manipulate it to do what we want it to. While it is true that a lot of body language can happen on its own, without us even thinking about it, this doesn't mean that we can't put some control with it. It is going to take some work, but it can be done.

First, we need to take a look at the different things that you are able to do to start adding in some manipulation to your body language. Start with the face. For the most part, you will want to make sure that you have a smile around your target. This is going to make them feel more comfortable around you, and can really open up the lines of communication that you both have. However, a true smile and a fake smile are completely different. The fake smile only pulls up the corners of the mouth, and many of us are able to spot this kind of smile and we won't form the connection with it like other options. A real smile is going to involve the whole face, from the mouth to the eyes and everywhere in between. Go in front of a mirror and see if you can tell the difference. Put on your fake smile, the one that you use when you want to be polite or you are trying to smile to someone you meet in the hallway. Now think of something that makes you really happy, something that can always get you to smile, and put that on your face. Notice a difference? Your goal is to get the second one to show up each time that you talk to your target.

Next, we need to work with the eyes. You are not going to keep the attention of your target if you are constantly looking away or trying to look at your watch or something else. This gives off the appearance that you are either trying to hide something from them or that you would rather be somewhere else. And neither of these are going to give a great opinion of you to the other person. You also don't want to stare the other person down because this is going to greatly intimidate them, and that isn't going to help you out at all either. Rather than doing this, your goal is to use some natural and easy eye contact to ensure that there is a level of comfort there. You will notice that when you are able to maintain eye contact, without staring the other person down like you

356

want to scare them, that it is much easier to get them to feel comfortable around you, and for you to make that connection that you want. Next is the hand gestures. You want to make sure that there are some being used in all of this. Keeping your arms stiff and right next to you is not going to work. But moving the arms around and making sure that they are used to talk about your point and in the right amount, can make a world of difference. Try to find a happy medium between arms crossed and arms that are flailing all over the place and about to hit someone else.

Your stance is important as well. You need to make sure that you have a good, straight posture the whole time. Slouching is not going to put you in the best light with the other person, and just doesn't give you the confidence that is needed to do well and leave a good first impression. While we are at it, work to make sure that your body is pointing in the right direction. To show the target that you are really interested in what they are saying and where this conversation is going, you want to make sure that your feet and body are turned towards them, and that you lean in a little bit to them as well. These are just a few of the things that you are able to do in order to manipulate your own body language when you are around the target. Adding these in can be as easy as you make it but the point is to make sure that every part of your body shows that you are interested in the target and that you want to make a connection. If any part of your body language goes against this, then it is going to mess with the message and can make the target feel like you are trying to hide something from them along the way as well.

Practice guilt trips

When it comes to manipulation, there is nothing that is used as often as the guilt trip. This is going to ensure that the manipulator is able to get what they want. And they are so successful with it because they can use the emotions of their target against them in the process. The manipulator, even when they are the ones in the wrong, are going to be able to use this kind of resource in order to get the target to acknowledge the fact that they (manipulator) did a lot of things wrong, or that they are the ones to blame. This takes any of the responsibility from the manipulator and places it all, unfairly, on the target.

So, how do we use the idea of a guilt trip to get what we want? First, you need to start bringing up the conversation of what went wrong and talk about how this person has done other similar things in the past. There is usually going to be some story that goes on with it and makes them feel bad. They may say, "You never have time for me anymore. Remember last week I needed help with something and you didn't have time. And now today I need help and you are too busy again."

This brings up the idea that the target is never there for the manipulator when the manipulator needs them. Never mind the fact that the target was maybe stuck in traffic and couldn't get home last week or they are horribly sick this week and that is why they can't help. It is all about what the manipulator wants and needs, and they are going to use that guilt trip to get it. In this step, the manipulator is going to make the situation seem so much worse than it is. They may sigh and act disappointed by the fact that this is now a type of behavior pattern that they expect, and that they don't really deserve to be treated this way all of the time either. It is most effective when the manipulator is able to surface matters that are comparable to whatever they want their target to admit to doing wrong, even so it can really be used to bring up anything that upsets you.

This whole process is going to really play on the feelings that the target has for the manipulator. The manipulator is going to take the time to let the target know that they now query how they do feel about them (manipulator). In other circumstances, this may be true, but in reality, the manipulator is just doing this in order to prey on the target and make them feel bad. The point here is to get the target to feel so bad that they want to prove how they care about you (the target) and they want to make it better. The manipulator may also spend some time reminding the target of all the sweet good things they have been doing for the (the target) in the past. They are going to put the supposedly bad actions of the target in light of all the good things that they have been able to do for the target over time. The grander the gesture that the manipulator is able to pull out, the better this is going to be. And often the action doesn't have to relate with the topic at hand, just as long as the manipulator comes out looking like they are on top.

Now, you have to remember that in many cases, the target is going to try and point the finger back at you. This is especially true if the situation is the fault of the manipulator, rather than of the target. But your job is to put as much, if not all, of the guilt on the other person, so you need to deflect any other efforts if any to actually make or turn the whole situation into something that is your fault. Even if you have done something in this situation that is wrong, you should not accept it at all. If anything, it is much better if you are able to turn it all around reflecting what your target did.

For example, maybe you really need your partner to apologize because they were texting someone else. They may try to turn this around and ask why you went through their phone in the first place. Instead of admitting that what you did was something wrong, you would turn the conversation back on them and tell the them "Well, it actually seems I had enough reason to suspect that something was not right, didn't I?

And finally, make sure that you are able to bring up the feelings or if you like emotions that bring about the guilt trip as much as possible. If the target is really fighting against this and they are resisting all of your attempts of this guilt trip, then it is time to resort to some of the drama. This is where stomping around, yelling, crying, and any other big emotion is going to come in. Sometimes this works because the other person is going to say anything and everything you want in order to get you to feel a bit better. Remember, the point of working with the guilt trip is to get the other person to take the blame and the responsibility of something that went wrong. It doesn't matter in manipulation if they are the ones to blame or not. Once they accept this blame, the manipulator has the control. The target is going to want to do something in order to get that trust back or to release the blame, and they will turn to the manipulator to figure out how to make this happen.

Play the victim

The next thing that you can work on is playing the victim to your target. This kind of tactic is always going to see you as the one who is downtrodden, the one who is not getting the attention that they deserve, and who is being treated unfairly all of the time. This is a tactic that is going to work the best on those who like to feel and take care of things based on their emotions. This is because their aim is to aid the manipulator, not realizing that most of the stories they are hearing from the manipulator are made up and not really true. When it comes to playing the victim, no one is going to be better at it then the manipulator. They know how to play the victim better than anyone else around them. They can make you feel guilty about almost anything that they want, without batting an eye about it either.

It always seems like the world is going down hard on the manipulator when they play the victim. Someone was unfair to them at work. The neighbor's dog was barking too much (Even though they brought the dog in at 9), and they were not able to sleep. They thought you were mad at them and this caused them a lot of anxiety. They found out that they were passed over for a promotion and it isn't fair, even though they never get their work done on time and have only been at the business a few months. It seems like the manipulator is able to complain about everything and anything under the sun. It is all out to get them, from other people, the word, and every situation that they encounter. It doesn't matter that they have done nothing to make the situation better and that often they have purposely tried to make it worse to guilt trip the target. And it doesn't matter if the target has had a bad day as well for some legitimate reason. No one has had it worse ever than the manipulator, and the target is expected to feel sad and guilty about that fact.

This is a technique that is going to play on the emotions of the target. The hope here is that the target, even if they had a bad day or aren't feeling the best either, will feel bad or sorry for the manipulator and what that person is going through. They will be there to provide some level of comfort, and maybe they will even try to make things easier in another way. They may get the manipulator that promotion, wait on them hand and foot at home, and to other things in the hopes of making things a little bit better for the manipulator. Of course, things are never going to get better. The world is always going to be out to get the manipulator in some manner or another. This is just how things work in this kind of relationship. If the manipulator started to say that things were getting better, then they would not get the love and attention that they wanted from the target, and they would lose that amount of control. And if you find that you are able to get the target to do what you want after these sessions of playing the victim, know that you have the control over them that you want.

Use the logic that you have to appeal to rational people

If you are working with a target who is really into the logic, and really into the idea of needing to know the facts and the figures before making the decision, then this is what you will need to focus on. It is not going to do you much good to bring out the emotions with this kind of target. It isn't that this kind of person isn't going to respond to emotions or that they don't have any emotions. But they are going to form a bigger connection with the facts and figures instead, and being able to point them in this direction is going to make a world of difference. When you want to be able to manipulate this kind of person, you want to make sure that you are able to bring in a lot of facts and figures to the mix. Show them, with studies, math numbers, and more, why this method is going to be the best one for them to work with. Let them see how it is going to benefit them by really saving money, how it is going to be good for so many reasons, and so on.

The more logic that you are able to add into the mix, the better this is going to work. You do not want to worry about the emotions or anything like that. If you are able to write up a report with all of the facts and figures, then this could serve you well. Don't worry if you can't, but it's the idea that you need to really think through the actions and the argument so that you can appeal to this kind of person as much as possible.

Inspire fear and then provide some relief to the person

Fear can be a powerful motivator to get someone to do what you want. But remember that it needs to be done with a certain amount of delicacy. You can't go through this process and start causing fear right after you have met the person. If you haven't done your analysis or worked with some of the manipulation techniques from the last section, then this is going to end really badly. The other person may become fearful of you and never come around you again, or they may decide that you are just going to use these tactics against you and walk away from the relationship.

You have to form some kind of connection with the target first. This will help to keep them around, to ensure that they stay with you, even when the fear is there. It takes some time, but it can make the target feel like they need to act and behave in a certain way in order to avoid the anger and the fear from you and to really keep things smooth.

Adding in the fear is something that is going to scare the target quite a bit. They don't want to be fearful of anything. They don't want to feel like something is wrong or like they are walking on eggshells. And if they have a good connection with their manipulator to start with, they are going to do whatever they can to avoid this feeling and get things back on track.

If you are able to inspire this fear in your target, and then offer them a path they can take to make things better, to make sure that you are happy (and in their minds, they are happy too), then the target is going to do what you want. They will learn what inspires the fear, and what inspires the relief, and they will start toeing the line and doing what they are told in the process.

As you can see, there are a lot of different methods that can be used when it comes to adding persuasion into your influence of other people. It takes some practice and it is not always as easy as it seems. But you will find that if you do all three of these sections together, and you take your time with them rather than rushing to the manipulation, they are going to start falling naturally into place as well.

Chapter 12: Dealing with Manipulation and Manipulating People

It is one thing to understand manipulation, and how it works and can wreak havoc on your life. Understanding all the different tricks and tactics that a manipulator can use against you. May make it seem like it is impossible to defend yourself against manipulation. But the truth is that by understanding in excellent detail how manipulators can use a wide array of tactics against you. You use their weapons against them, something they are not expecting. To understand a potential enemy and the tactics they might use is to beat them at their own game. Too often manipulators enter our lives because we find their companionship pleasing, we let them fill a need that they create. This need can come from many places, for some a broken home, for others a simple need for action. To not know yourself is the greatest asset a manipulator can use against you. They act like parasites burrowing their way into your life and sucking you dry, getting all that they can resource-wise and then leaving you.

The good news is that you can avoid having this happen to you if you don't let it. Too often we let people dictate how they can treat us by our actions. If we let someone convince us that we are weak and need them to succeed than is it their fault for us getting sucked into their web. Or is it perhaps our fault for convincing ourselves that this "relationship" is good for us. The truth of the matter is that manipulators like to prey on people who have been hurt before. Their charm, and glib cons us into thinking that they will help us with whatever issue we are dealing with. It may sound cold or blunt but by keeping your guard and check and not letting yourself get too close to someone upon meeting them you can quickly avert any potential mishaps or crisis that may come forward within that relationship.

I would also like you to consider that for some individuals their manipulation is pathologic, meaning that there is some underlying mental illness that is causing them to behave this way. These types of people are the most dangerous for the simple fact that they do not realize that they are doing anything wrong, Think of your sociopaths or bipolar. For others their tendencies for manipulation can be linked to a faulty maturation process, they think that it will always be their way or the highway. In the end, the motivations remain the same for all manipulators when boiled down and simplified, they want what they want, and they are going to get it by whatever means it takes.

Being confident is your first step in averting a manipulative attack, depending on the type of manipulation used you are going to want to be confident in different areas. The manipulation that a salesperson might use varies greatly than the type of manipulation a jaded lover would use on you, so knowing how to respond to each is paramount. For example, if you know a car is cheaper than someone is saying is be firm in your argument and do not let up ground. The same can be said if you suspect your partner of lying in a romantic relationship. By showing dominance in an encounter you say to the manipulator that you are not someone who will fall for their bait, you will not be their plaything. Moving on from just simply being confident and knowing your situation, there is de-escalation. Many manipulators when confronted about their behavior like to make the stakes of a situation seem higher than they are. With their end goal being that you will back off and drop the conflict out of fear.

Their goal is to scare you into submission, through whatever means required. Some will threaten suicide, some will threaten you directly, in the hopes you will back down. The trick here is to call their bluff and remain firm in your conviction that you know they are just trying to manipulate you.

Do not buy into their bluffs as once a manipulator realizes they can get away with something once they will do it again and again. As you set a precedent for them that manipulative behavior is okay. Calling a manipulators bluff in a high-tension scenario like this, in the beginning, may lead to them getting irater and more irrational. But if you are firm and stand your ground, they will quickly come to terms with the fact that they will not win here. The other component of de-escalation is not losing control of your own emotions, manipulators are very good at learning what buttons to press to set you off. Understand this when interacting with them, because if you just buy-in and get as angry and irrational as them then you are stooping to their level and letting them get what they want from you, which is usually attention. There are some simple calming techniques you can use when you feel your emotions brewing up. Take a slow deep breath and count to five in your head, you can also try peaceful imaging. Imagine yourself on a calm beach or somewhere pleasant to draw your mind away from the situation with the manipulator. Presenting yourself as calm shows a potential manipulator that you won't stoop to their level and are willing to not compromise your integrity. De-escalation tricks are pointless if you do not take active steps to change things from there, this can be as simple as trying to set firm boundaries. The way you do this is that you let someone know what your limits are what you won't put up with, for example, if someone lies to you and you catch them you are firm and consistent with the consequences of it. If establishing boundaries and trying to de-escalate the situation don't work, then it may perhaps be in your best interest to reduce the amount of contact you have with the manipulator.

Going low or no contact with a manipulator guarantees you that they cannot harm you. The problem with doing this is remaining firm in your conviction, it is very easy to tell someone that you are going to stop contacting them but doing it is much more challenging.

Once a manipulator feels you are pulling away, they will ramp up their scheming in the hopes they can entice you into staying with them. Simply put leave them to block their number and possible leave any friends you both shares. Manipulators love to use other people to do their bidding. This allows them to act through proxies and avoid arousing suspicion that they are the ones responsible for certain behaviors. You may find that the more challenging part of reducing contact with someone who is a manipulator is the obstacles you set yourself. Manipulators like to make you second guess yourself and doubt your instinct in the hopes that you will follow through with their intentions. This is why knowing certainly how you want to act is important. Take time to do your diligence before making any major decision pull back for a little bit and analyze all the facts at your disposal.

By taking a calm and measured approach to your decisions and actions you present an image of someone who is not weak. This more than anything will prevent you from becoming a victim of manipulators attacks. Because it represents the image that you are in control of their emotions and as a result can't have your own emotions used against you, as manipulators commonly try to get you to do. In closing know that you have a basic understanding of some of the methods manipulators use and how to defend yourself against them. You are now better able to understand where manipulation truly comes from and what drives people to use someone's own emotions against them. As a result of knowing how their weapons work you can utilize them in tricky situations in life, where they may prove incredibly useful. Because manipulation is so common in today's fast-paced world it is imperative for you to understand it if you want to get ahead. That is why I would like to discuss how psychological disorders play in manipulative behavior. Since these personality disorders present themselves as continues displays of abhorrent behavior it is easy to recognize them when you know the signs. The three most common disorders that make people prone to manipulative behavior are Antisocial Personality Disorder (APD), Narcissistic Personality Disorder (NPD), and Borderline Personality Disorder (BPD). Understanding the pathologies and behaviors characterized by these kinds of psychological disorders allows you to quickly weed out people who could potentially be manipulators. While it may seem cruel to avoid someone because they have a "disorder" when it comes to your wellbeing and security you can never be too careful.

To begin the conversation on disorders that make one manipulative I would like to start with the lesser-known Borderline Personality Disorder or BPD. BPD as a disorder is characterized by an intense pattern of instability in both interpersonal relationships and sense of self, this instability is accompanied by an extreme of abandonment, when combined with the general impulsiveness and mood swings BPD brings make for a perfect storm of destructive behavior. Since individuals with BPD have such an intense fear of abandonment they may lie and manipulate to keep you closer to them while at the same time getting angry at you for spending so much time with them. This splitting between their desires and fears is where the term borderline comes from, their emotions are always bordering on the edge. Ever so close to teetering off and having a nuclear meltdown but still so far away. Often people with borderline personality disorder present their symptoms in a chaotic or disorganized fashion, which reflects the fact that they are unsure of who they are themselves. It is not known what causes an individual to develop a borderline personality disorder, but it is theorized that growing up in an abusive home or experiencing severe trauma at a young age makes someone more likely to develop it. An individual with Borderline personality disorder may be able to lure you in with how they may appear to make themselves vulnerable.

They are prone to sharing intimate details with their life very early on in a relationship in the hope of establishing trust and moving the relationship along quickly.

This where the instability in relationships comes to play, a person with a borderline personality disorder will want to move a romance or relationship much quicker than it should be. Their reasoning for this is their fear of being abandoned, this fear drives their whole being to such an extent that they will burn all their bridges in the ill-guided hope of keeping you. One of the final characterizations of BPD is a repeated pattern of intense tantrums and meltdowns when people leave them, for lack of a better word when this fear of abandonment ends up coming true due to self-sabotage borderlines have a bad tendency to self-destruct and burn down everything in their path.

Your best defense against a borderline is leaving before you are too involved. If someone wants to move a relationship quickly in a direction you don't feel comfortable with then it is in your best interest to leave while you can and when you have not invested much emotion. Moving on from one of the least known disorders, I would like to discuss a disorder we have all heard of Narcissistic Personality Disorder or NPD.

NPD is characterized by extreme self-centeredness and an inability to comprehend and understand the consequences of their actions. Because of this inability to understand consequence narcissists tend to repeat the same self-destructive behavior over and over again. We have all heard this term used to describe someone. Few of us actually understand what narcissism truly looks like. We are quick to label any behavior we don't like as narcissism when in reality it is subtler than that. Narcissists are not the overt self-centered people the media likes to portray them as. A narcissist likes to utilize subtle tactics to get you to come in line with their way of thinking, as opposed to overt manipulation. By getting you to question your judgment they can replace your ideas with theirs. One of the main behaviors all narcissists follow is the inability to take responsibility for their actions.

They will pin the blame for their actions on others instead of realizing that they are the reason misfortune keeps befalling them. As a result of this inability to learn from past mistakes, the narcissist will often repeat the same behavior over and over again to try and meet the same goal. This is what makes them so dangerous, they are willing to go to extreme measures to get their goals. The largest danger from narcissists comes from what is called a narcissistic meltdown. When a narcissist feels cornered like an animal, they will meltdown and destroy everything in their path even if it means damaging themselves. This can take many different forms, for some narcissists, this means something as extreme as suicide or even murder. For others, they may trash a lover's house when asked to leave the relationship. In short, when a narcissist realizes their game is up, they tend to blow a lot of fuses in their heads.

It is hard to postulate what motivates a narcissist as to behave this way current psychological research, points to a poor sense of self. But the truth is it does not matter why they do something that matters is your ability to avoid it. Narcissistic manipulation mainly takes the form of what is called gaslighting. Which in simple terms is the act of getting you to question your judgment of a situation and get you to think that you're the one with the issues and not them? By getting you to question your own beliefs regarding their behavior a manipulator is then able to live rent-free in your head! This is extremely dangerous behavior because it allows for self-doubt to be reinforced and allows for the manipulator to instill dangerous thoughts and ideas into someone's head.

The main thing to look out for in someone who behaves like this is how they were in past relationships if you see a pattern of them avoiding any responsibility for their actions then run away immediately. Manipulators can accomplish gaslighting through a variety of ways the main method in which they try to manipulate you is by breaking you down over time, slowly wearing away at you with the same line of garbage over and over again till you are forced to believe it. Once a narcissist has convinced you of their positioning it is very difficult to

368

get a clear view, they obfuscate the truth and lie at every chance they have to try and get you on their side. They'll make you feel guilty for not going along with their behavior

The fact that this happens over a slow time is what makes it so damaging, it becomes difficult for you to realize that the behavior you are being presented with isn't normal, and usually by the time you have realized it is already too late. Narcissists are great at luring you back into their grips through very clever manipulation tricks, by subtly getting you to doubt yourself they slowly hook their tendrils into every aspect of your life until you feel powerless without them. The trick to getting past this kind of manipulation is just biting the bullet and running away. This can be hard to do because narcissists are very charming and good at convincing you, they will change. But the truth is a narcissist is never going to change their manipulative behavior is only going to get worse and continue. One of the narcissist's other dangerous weapons is to break down self-esteem in others. For instance, imagine you're an architecture and you are working on a new model for a house. Your manager gives you the rough blueprint, which you noticed there are a few areas that could use some improvements. You begin sketching your blueprint version and proceed to make a cardboard model of what they envisioned. A week later, your manager comes to see your progress, to which her face shows frustration. Raising her voice, she points out the different designs from hers, comments on how the rooms look too small and talk about how the deadline is in two weeks. Situations like these, where you are bombarded with criticism, figure out if what they're saying is constructive or destructive. Whichever one you decide it is, you want the person to get all their criticism out before trying to amend what you have done, since they will most likely ignore you while in such a state. Quietly take their words and wait until they're finished.

Afterward, explain whatever changes you made and your reasons for doing such a thing.

It is always good to know before being confronted if the change was worth it or not, so make sure to evaluate all your decisions. In any case, ask her to clarify her opinion. There is a good chance she will explain what she meant. However, if she were to dismiss your explanations and continue criticizing, at that point you can safely take her words for a grain of salt. And realize that the comments may not be reflective of what is truly going on in the situation. And instead, consider that what she is saying may simply be an attempt to manipulate you and get you to do something she wants.

Accepting that you are in a destructive relationship with a narcissist. Can be a difficult thing to do but once you start to look at all the signs together it ends up making sense. Someone who is going out of their way and lies and get you to believe things only through their worldview is not someone you want to be with. That is perhaps the saddest part of the manipulation. It doesn't tend to change and happens to only get worse as time moves on. Taking this examination of a relationship to the heart is required evil in the world we live in today. Perhaps arguably the most common form of manipulation in today's fast-paced society is the manipulation that salespeople will try and use on us. Most sales tactics play on simple human emotions such as need or desire, and very specific fears like a fear of missing out or not belonging. Advertisements target us so subtly that we do not realize we are being taken for a ride until we make a purchase that we do not need. By using fancy colors and enticing cinematic, advertisements can play on very primal parts of our brain and get us to do what they want.

Look at the newest advertisements for the iPhone, and how they show people who happy while using their fancy brand-new iPhone. Are they truly happy because of their new iPhone or is it perhaps the situations they are shown in?

The first step any successful advertisement has to take in getting you to buy its product is to convince you that you need it. How can they sell you something if you don't need it? Simple, they do so by creating these huge social media marketing campaigns in which they show thousands of people lining up to buy the newest and greatest fancy phone. They can convince you that if you want to be one of the cool kids that you should also buy into needing something you don't need at all, such as the new iPhone.

This manipulation works by playing on a psychological concept called "the fear of missing out". Your fear of not keeping up with the curve will entice you to buy the product even if it sets you back financially and even if you don't need it. You may have noticed how in lots of stores the kid's toys are all colorfully lit and have cool and interesting cut-outs designed to catch the attention of your little tyke. These bright colors and exciting stimuli fire up the reward centers of our brains and get us primed to make a purchase.

The other trick salespeople will try and utilize is the "fake sale".

You are probably wondering what I mean when I say fake sales, well simply put say an item has a sticker on it that says was 15 dollars now ten dollars, you will assume that is on sale and if you buy it now, you're getting a good deal. Well, the truth is much different than the reality you assume it to be the item is always marked as "on-sale". By marking playing on this fear of missing out, salespeople manipulate you on a very primal and basic level, as such it can be hard to avoid and defend against it.

Your best defense is knowing how much something is worth before you purchase it. Do your diligence and research prices of the item in question, shop around at different outlets to get an idea of what it is truly worth. This is especially important when purchasing a car, as the stereotypes about used car salespeople exist for a reason. They will tell you whatever you want to hear about a vehicle. Their main trick is trying to quickly get a read on you and discern your likes and dislikes once they do this, they can lure you into thinking they're your friend. And a friend will always give you the best deal, right? This is not always the case the people who are in this industry are in it because of the good people-pleasers they know what to say to people and how to get what they want from them. You can utilize some of these tricks in your own life, the main thing to remember when interacting with someone, is to make them feel validated and special. By doing this you get their trust, and from there, you can go far. Feeding into the fact that car sales are mostly a trick. There is also real estate where a realtor will try and convince you that something, you're going to invest in will only grow in value and you are missing out by not purchasing it.

They will try to woo you with stories about how great the local farmers market is and how their produce is so fresh, or how the schools in the area are so highly rated, but the truth is these things are usually just embellishments or flat out lies. One thing you may have noticed when looking at a potential house to buy is how the realtor may have baked cookies or how there will be premade candies or cakes. This is to get you to believe that the house is lived in and this also plays on strong

371

mnemonic cues, humans associate smells strongly with emotion, as a result, we are quick to dismiss logic, and we will just go with our heart and ignore the facts.

All manipulation shares this idea of selling us a fake good, the end goal is the only thing that differs. Now that I have gone over the many ways that manipulators behave and act. I would like to dedicate the rest of this chapter on in-depth ways to defend yourself against each form of manipulation. With an understanding of the very basic ways to defend against manipulation, you are now equipped with the prerequisite knowledge required to hopefully avoid manipulation. As well as what to do when manipulation becomes unavoidable.

Let's start with emotional manipulation. We already understand that emotional manipulation is the act of someone trying to dictate and control how you feel. But how do you nip that behavior in the bud, so you can end or even perhaps avoid it? Allow me to use a hypothetical situation between two arguing lovers, as a training exercise in how to defuse a manipulator, as well as what behaviors within this scenario constitute emotional manipulation.

A man and his girlfriend have recently moved in with each other after dating for around three months. What drew this woman to this man is how he always seems to say the right thing, and always makes her feel good. Yet she cannot seem to shake the feeling that at times his platitudes are perhaps disingenuous. She also has begun to realize that her boyfriend is starting to slack off and not contribute to the rent of their shared apartment. She decides that she will sit down with him one day and discuss that perhaps it is time for him to get a job as to allow them to both maintain their current living arrangement. So the following day she sits down her boyfriend and says " Honey, I know you love me very much, but since we have moved in together I feel like you have somewhat been taking advantage of me, in the sense that you are not paying your share of rent here, and if we want to stay in this nice apartment than we both need to carry our weight."

Right as she completes her sentence her supposedly loving boyfriend begins to fly off the handle in what can best be described as rage, "Well your parents pay for everything, why should I be expected to get a job and pay when you have never worked for anything ever in your life. You know you're never going to find someone who loves you as much

372

as me." Now before I dive further into this example allow me to provide some analysis of the behavior exhibited by the boyfriend, and why it is manipulative. In addition to how the girlfriend should appropriately respond to both de-escalate the situation and how she can avoid being manipulated further by him. To start first considering this, when most normal people are presented with an uncomfortable situation like this one where they perhaps could be in the wrong. Usually, their first reaction is to not fly into a rage. Most people will calmly listen to what is being presented to them and take it as such. In this case, we can see that the first thing the boyfriend did was get angry when presented with the possibility that he was in the wrong and as a result to try to deflect blame onto his girlfriend.

This projection took the form of him telling his girlfriend that he should not be asked to pay rent since she is already given money by her parents. This kind of behavior qualifies as manipulation because it sets up an unfair precedent for his convenience. He automatically assumes that since she is getting money for free then why should he be required to work and pay his fair share. The simple fact is that they both are in the apartment together and as a result both need to contribute equally if they want to stay together. By him getting irate at her and throwing abuse, he is trying to scare her into not pressing further with it, via the threat of ending the relationship.

For the girlfriend knowing how to react in this situation can seem to be very tricky, because on the one hand she loves her boyfriend and does not want him to leave her. On the other hand, thought him living rent-free in her apartment is just straight up unfair, so what should her course of action be? Well, the first step anyone should take when dealing with a manipulator, especially one who is prone to anger, is to keep their calm. If you can stay calm when presenting to a manipulator how their behavior is damaging than in a way you prevent further manipulation. From here the next step would be for her to make her boundaries very firm with her boyfriend. Saying something like this "If you are going to blow up at me when I try talking to you then there will be no relationship, and I am more than happy to just kick you out right now, with or without rent being paid."

The most important thing to remember when laying out firm boundaries is to follow up with them.

So, in this situation, she has laid out that if her boyfriend continues getting irate with her and being rude than she will just cut him off now. Here is where the problem lies, manipulators are excellent at getting someone to come back to them. In our example, it is very likely that even if she breaks it off with her boyfriend that he will come back and say to her. "Sorry honey I did not mean to blow up at you". Basically, telling her everything she wants to hear, and then when another incident between the two occurs he will promptly repeat the same behavior. That is why when dealing with a manipulator you must keep these boundaries firm and not falter or even give them an inch because they will take a mile. Now that we have gone over how to deal with manipulation in relationships. I would like to dive deeply into how the media uses manipulation to get us to purchase things, or even sway our opinion and how we can protect against it.

Take the mainstream news in the United States for example. Instead of reporting on simply just the news and happening events around the world. Certain news outlets will be composed of nothing but talking heads and editorials giving their opinion on everything. In a sense, they are trying to get you to think the way they want, whether this is out of malice or simple incompetence is up for debate. But the crux of the issue is that when a news story is reported today, it is no longer simply just "news" it is filled with many different people's opinions. And depending on the political leaning of the news outlet they may not report on other things. Another more damaging example of this kind of manipulation can be seen in social media such as Instagram and Facebook. And that is in the realm of the influencer, someone who is paid to present a false lifestyle and show off how certain products, whatever they may behave helped them attain it.

This form of manipulation preys on a common psychological trope and that is called the fear of missing out. When we see these people living super blessed lives and how they have everything one could want. We start feeling bad for ourselves and as a result, will go out and buy these products in the vain attempt that they will help us live the same kind of blessed life. The truth is that all sales try to get us to assume that our lives will be better with whatever product their pitching. Now that we know this how you can better equip yourself so that you do not fall victim to frivolous purchases of things you do not need. The first step in avoiding this type of manipulation is to take a glance back and realize, that what people post on social media is what they want you to see. In the same mindset that often what manipulators tell you is what they want you to hear. With that knowledge, you can better keep yourself from being swayed if you look at it like this. The second thing to understand is that if you do happen to decide to go and purchase the products, do research on them do not go and just buy something because it has Kylie Jenner's name stamped on it with a bunch of fabulous claims.

Always remember the truism that extraordinary claims require extraordinary facts. From there you can truly make an informed decision if you want to purchase something or not.   If you have concluded that what someone is posting is a pure promotion or the product is harmful than drop that social media then and there, you're better off not following it, that will be your final solution if all else fails. Jumping back to media manipulation I would like to also talk about how advertisements try to use the same trick as social media influencers in getting us to purchase things that perhaps we do not need. I mentioned earlier in the book how whenever a new iPhone comes around apple the company that makes the iPhone will run a whole bunch of ads showing people from all walks of life in very happy scenarios with their fancy little iPhone. These ads are created this way to drive home the point that you can attain more happiness if you buy these items.

This feeds in on our desire to be like others and to also feed into our fear of missing out. This form of manipulation is also seen when we go to supermarkets with colorful ads and things that draw our attention from what matters. So, your best defense against these forms of manipulation is to research something before you buy it.

Too often than not we get convinced to buy something on emotional impulse and then try to justify it later. This is how we get manipulated we let our emotions override our logic and as a result, make incredibly poor decisions. To defend against this when shopping or trying to buy something always have an idea of what it is your buying and do not allow yourself to be swayed by mass advertising as if you do that you will be setting yourself up for a whole world of hurt and loss. Moving on from how salespeople try to manipulate you I would like to move

375

back to emotional manipulation and how to defend against it. With some people, they will try to manipulate you within the confines of a romance while others such as friends or family. Will manipulate you within the confines of that already preexisting relationship. Simply put it can be easier for your friends and family to manipulate you because they do not have the issue of trying to get you in a relationship with them.

Manipulation in relationships are common places to spot them, yet the most unspoken relationship that manipulation persists is between family members. In most cases, relatives won't speak up against one another because since they're related by blood, they emotionally feel that it would be wrong to speak against them. Imagine this scenario; your cousin and his two children asked to move into your house, which you allow them to willingly. After some months go by, you notice that he has stopped paying rent, doesn't buy his groceries or utensils rather he uses your ingredients and your silverware.

You are being used.

So, you decide logically to bring up the fact that he is not carrying his weight in your house. So, you say "Hey cousin Tommy, I know you and your family have been hit by hard times, but if you are going to live within my home. Then you need to get a job and help contribute to bills and you know just carry your own". Keep in mind that when you brought this fact up to your cousin you said it very calmly and reasonably. If your cousin responds with "oh it's hard, working long hours at my job and school supplies for my kids. You understand right?" Your cousin's response indicates that your cousin has no incentive to pay any amount of money to you and they will continue leeching off you. By saying "you understand, right?" they are manipulating you to feel guilty for them and let them continue to abuse you and take advantage of you.

No – I what I understand is that you are not paying your expenses!

Make it clear that they will have to pay rent and if you want to compromise, they will be allowed to eat your food. If not, he will have to buy their own.

Conclusion

Throughout this book, we have discussed all of the things that are important to remember to avoid being manipulated, and to include positive persuasion in the way that you interact with others. It isn't something that is going to be achieved overnight, but with more and more practice, you can remember that you have what it takes to get the things that you desire most. The biggest mistake that some will make after learning of these methods is to use them to only their advantage and take from others rather than spreading the happiness and satisfaction received through influence. It is a lot easier to negatively manipulate someone than to positively persuade them. Sometimes, persuasion means building trust. Manipulation can simply mean instilling fear. While manipulation might be easier, it is going to cause a lot more difficult things in the end that you will have to clean up afterwards!

Remember that this process starts with really understanding someone's personality. There are common types of manipulators out there and you might be able to sense this personality trait in another person right away. Similarly, you will also recognize that there are hidden qualities that won't always emerge at first. Remember to recognize that not all manipulative behaviors presented by an individual indicates that she is a malicious person. Having manipulative parents or long-term partners can rub off on our behavior, so we might sometimes say and do things that aren't meant to be manipulative but can come off that way. Always look at intention when determining if someone is really being manipulative or not.

Also, don't forget that body language can play a huge role in how someone will be perceived. You can start to see persuasive body language in others more often than you did before as soon as you become aware of what this kind of body language looks like. Ensure you are aware of your own body language as well so as not to be manipulated by others.

At the end of the day, manipulation is generally a way for a person to get the things that they desire most. We all have basic human needs and

377

instincts that drive our behavior. If we are not careful with how we go about getting these things, we can hurt others. The more equipped we are with the skills needed for positive influence, the easier it will be to achieve our deepest desires in a healthy way that benefits many.

To continue to grow your level of influence, remember that it starts with small moments of persuasion. Don't tell people what to do, encourage them from personal experience and stories learned from others. Don't try and trick someone into doing the things they don't want to do. Be honest with reward and consequence so that they can properly make the decision for themselves.

Always ensure that you are reflecting on your own behavior to make sure that you aren't going about things in the wrong way. With becoming influential, there is a certain level of confidence that comes along as well. If you are not careful, that confidence will drive you too far ahead of others, and you can get lost in what you perceive to be best for everyone. The better you can reflect and ensure you have the right intention, the easier it will be for others to be legitimately inspired by you. While it might be hard to do the right thing in times where what is easiest will also benefit you the most, remember to be empathetic towards others. Though it might be challenging, you will still ultimately get the things you desire most when you are doing so in a fair and rewarding way.

NLP

The Essential Guide for Beginners
Explaining the Secrets on Mind
Control, Manipulation, Dark
Psychology, Persuasion, and How
to Reprogram Yourself

Daniel Peterson

381

Table of Contents

Introduction

Downloading this book is the first step you can take toward understanding dark psychology techniques, neuro-linguistics programming, manipulation, and persuasion, among other techniques, used by different people across the world. If you are tired of being manipulated and used or would like to help a loved one who is in a manipulative relationship, this book is designed for you. Also, if you want to understand how NLP can be used for love, relationships, and success, the book has very important information.

However, the first step is always the easiest; you need to take the information herein to heart. You may apply it immediately or in the future. The sooner you start to apply the tips, the better it is for you.

The following chapters will discuss manipulation techniques involving neuro-linguistic programming and everything that you need to know when it comes to NLP and using it to get what you want.

However, there is a lot of good that can come with the effective usage of NLP. NLP is something that helps you to learn more about the people around you.

There are so many great benefits that can come from using NLP in your own life. It allows you to learn how to work with other people, how to read what other people are thinking and meaning, and ensures that you are able to get more of what you want and need out of life. When you are ready to learn more about NLP, especially dark NLP, and how to use it in your own life, make sure to check out this guidebook to help you get started.

Every technique introduced in this book will build on information that has been previously discussed so that learning each new concept will feel like a natural progression and will not be confusing or difficult to understand. By the time you have reached the end of this book, you will have gained a solid understanding of the concepts and techniques that make up dark psychology and manipulation using NLP, and you will be ready to try out these techniques in the real world on any target that you choose.

Without further ado, let's get started!

Chapter 1: What is NLP

Neuro-linguistic programming is termed to be a gentle yet so powerful technique that can affect significantly both your personal and professional life and ultimately improve your living standard. It makes you develop plans that can be realized, and it ensures you accomplish them.

There are a few principles with NLP. The first principle is the saying "the map is not reality." What this means is personal perception being your truth. To further explain, our perceptions are our own realities, but these are individual and differ from person to person. What someone else may see as reality may not be the same in your opinion. What we see, or perceive, is our reality regardless of what others think. This is because we all perceive and process things differently. The most important thing here is that we represent what we perceive well within ourselves and our realities are useful for us. Or as the saying goes, "be true to thine self."

Another principle is that you must know your outcome. This is extremely important. It needs to be well thought out, useful and must comply with the following criteria. It must be stated positively in that you need to focus on what you want not what you don't want. Know which senses will cue to you know when you have been successful. These senses are sight, hearing, smell, touch, and taste. They must be acquired under appropriate conditions. They must be achievable, so you need to make sure that you will have access to the appropriate resources when needed. They must be ecological as previously mentioned in this chapter. This means the outcome needs to be, or should be, balanced. The outcome needs to be worthwhile. Lastly, you need to be ready to take the needed action and not procrastinate.

The next principles are sensory acuity and behavioral flexibility. We have looked at these also, but they need to be mentioned here. This is our ability to read the cues sent by others in their body language and other non-verbal cues. We then need to be ready to change our tactics accordingly. If what we are doing isn't working, try some other tactic. This requires more than knowledge of the process. It requires absolute attention to the other person and the ability to immediately change direction while doing it all correctly.

The last one is the physiology of excellence. This is your current state at that given time. You need to be relaxed and comfortable. If, for some reason, you are not in this state, its best to wait until you are. For instance, if you are too cold, you can use anchors to change this in order to make yourself feel relaxed.

There are some techniques with NLP that we will now discuss. The first is the calibration. This is both internal and external but, for our purposes, we are going to look at external. This is relating to, what is known as, sensory acuity. What this means is the ability of perception with others. Through their appearance, we are able to understand what they are most likely thinking or feeling at that particular point.

The second technique is anchoring. This can be seen as synonymous with the association. Anchoring is matching a sound or touch with some particular state. The ability to anchor another person can be done openly or covertly. There are some negative effects of anchoring.

Lastly, there is mapping across. Usually, this is done with the use of sub-modalities. What are these? These are the finer details of our internal experiences. Here is an example. You think of someone that you are particularly fond of and, after thinking about them, you picture them in a pleasant fashion. The overall picture of that person is modality. The way in which you are picturing that person in your mind is the sub-modality. Obviously, this isn't limited to people or things. The possibilities are endless. Again, mastery of this can prove to be extremely beneficial. Sub-modalities can be kinesthetic, auditory, visual, and so on.

If you want to become successful using NLP, you will need to practice. This is a never-ending process of constant learning and skill acquirement. Remember, this isn't only to persuade others but can also be very beneficial for our own mental health. Having suggested this, let's look at some techniques which have been proven to work well with NLP and persuasion.

The get an understanding of dark NLP on a theoretical level, you first need to have a good understanding of the ideas that come with NLP, and what it is based on. NLP began when two people developed a set of ideas that looked into human behavior and how it could be influenced.

Their ideas soon became known as neuro-linguistic programming, more commonly known as NLP. While the techniques that went with NLP were first unknown, they started to get more exposure through the years. Many people know about NLP and what it is all about, but very people really know how to apply the techniques.

NLP comes with three main areas, looking at the way that ideas are filtered. These three areas include learning, subjectivity, and consciousness. NLP is going to teach that there isn't an absolute or objective understanding of the world around us, and instead, each person is going to work to form their own picture of the world. This picture is going to vary from one person to another and each one is going to consist of data that comes in through the five senses, and the language that the person attaches to this data.

NLP is going to see people as behaving in ways that go with the three key aspects, mainly the why, the how, and the what. The what is going to focus on the external behavior and the physiology a person exhibits in a given situation. Then the how is going to deal with some of the thinking patterns that the person has internally and are going to govern their own patterns of decision making. And then the why is going to deal with the supporting beliefs, values, and assumptions that point a person in one direction instead of another one.

If you are supposed to fully understand the three aspects that are part of NLP, then you will be able to effectively model the complete reality of someone else's behavior. It is important to note that it is the internal process that is being copied, and this is going to be what will lead to the external behavior, rather than just crudely mimicking the external behavior on its own. Without both the internal and external parts, the behavior that you are trying to work with is going to look pretty phony and insincere.

Advocates of NLP are going to beyond just passively accepting these factors, the ones that are going to compromise the behavior of the person. Instead, it advocates that there needs to be an active exploration of it and how it is going to be able to manipulate the variables at hand. When this happens, there is a better understanding of the relationship between each and which ones are going to be the most essential to achieve the desired results.

Now, you will find that there is a big contrast between the NLP model of understanding behavior and the traditional way of looking at behavior. Traditionally, we are going to start taking on a new behavior by learning one piece of a skill at a time, and then all of these little parts are going to add up and form a new behavior. When we are looking at NLP, you will find that it goes the other way. the person is going to be presented with all of the components of the behavior at once, and then they will start to subtract out the different parts until they are able to have just the essential aspects.

This is a process that is going to simplify behaviors and then reducing them to only their crucial aspects is similar to the business process which aims to map out a series of steps and identify which are essential and which are not. When we are looking at this sense, the process of refining behaviors with the help of applying NLP, and this is a way for you to ensure personal efficiency.

As we go through on this guidebook and learn more about dark NLP, it is important to understand that no one has an identity that is fixed. Each person is able to be influenced, and with all of the different influences in our lives, it is common to see them change on a regular basis. For some people, changing their beliefs is going to be easier to adopt than it is for some of the others. It can be upsetting because it often means that we don't have all the control in life that we wish we did. But it can also be a bit liberating because it means that each of us has the freedom necessary to reinvent ourselves at any stage of life that we choose. We are never too young or too old, we can go through and make the changes that we want in our lives.

Here it is also important that we learn how to embrace the fact that what we consider as conventional morality is just an illusion, and people are actually willing to perform a variety of acts that will go against what is seen as moral in their culture if there is some benefit to them for doing this. It doesn't matter what the morals are and how closely the person may have said they were going to follow the morals in the past. The fact remains that if they think it is going to benefit them to act in a different manner, they will.

The next thing that we need to understand is that morality is actually something that is relative, and there isn't a standard that exists. Although we are able to see some prohibitions that are common through any different cultures, there isn't going to be a universal standard of morality out there. indeed, these similarities can be explained that they are in accordance with the theory of evolution from Darwin. This states that if something is found to be useful when it comes to the survival of the species, then it is going to be incorporated into the moral norms for that time.

In many cases, dark NLP is going to encourage you, or even open up the mind, to the idea of operating in a way that is different than what you have been taught at church or through other forms of social influence.

There is a lot of things that dark NLP is going to go against. Mainly, you must have a willingness to see that acting your own self-interest is not something that has to be immoral. In fact, over time you will find that the idea of morals is fluid and ever-changing, and this means that it is not a good thing to base your decisions on. This is why many of those who practice dark NLP will choose to base their decisions just on self-interest, rather than worrying so much about morality. This is the best way to consistently guarantee that the outcome you get for your choices is going to work in your own favor.

How to see the world with dark NLP

The first key to understanding that the user of dark NLP needs to reach is that it doesn't matter as much about what you say or do, what matters is the result that you are able to get out of this process. This means that the process is going to be very tactical and results oriented. The dark NLP way of viewing the world is going to present the user with either an opportunity or threat. Some people, upon hearing that they should focus only on the result, will protest that they need to actually work and put their focus on doing things in the right manner. But then there are other people who will find this idea comfortable and they are happy to use any means that are necessary in order to reach that goal.

No matter what your initial reaction is to this thought process, it is important that you learn how to come to the realization that it is always more important to get to the end result that you want, and this needs to come above any of the other considerations that you have.

So, with that in mind, what are some of the ways in which you can put the idea of focusing only on the results, and less on the methods that you use to get there, to practice. We can see this apparent in the professional world. Imagine that you are one of the managers for a company, and you have one employee, in particular, you need to motivate to do more work and to keep up with their job a little bit better.

When you look at this through the view of dark NLP, the only thing that is going to matter is that you are able to get through to your employee and see their motivation increase. This can sometimes conflict with some of the other ideas that are out there about motivation, and some of these will state out how you should talk to the employee and more. But dark NLP isn't going to worry as much about that because it is going to teach the manager that they need to say and do whatever it takes to get the outcome that they want. With dark NLP, the result, and not the journey, is the only thing that is going to matter.

The second attitude to work with when it comes to dark NLP is that you must remember that everything in the world is going to be subjective. Even is two or three people use the same kinds of words in their speech, they could associate different meanings with them in their mind. So, what is this going to mean practically? It is important that you never assume that when someone talks, you automatically know what they mean when they are using a specific word unless there is some evidence of that meaning.

It is also a requirement that you understand how two people could be at the same event or situation but they will have different meanings or different things that they see as important in that event. For example, you could talk to a couple who are about to get married. For the one partner, they are going to be taking the time to participate in a very important religious event. But for the other partner, they may feel that they are just doing something because it is a tradition that is seen as mandatory. Always remember that people are going to work to assign their own meaning to some events.

So, how can dark NLP work with this idea? First, this is going to show that users who are effective with dark NLP are going to be able to influence the way that others around them perceive the situation around them. Let's look at an example of this from management. You are a manager who needs to get the workers to take on some extra hours to ensure that the project gets done by their deadline. In the minds of the workers, it is going to feel that they are being exploited.

But, if the manager has some experience with dark NLP though, they will be able to tie in all of this extra work to the values of the workers. This gives the workers a better chance to take on the hours, and they are less likely to feel guilty or upset about it.

Another thing that this kind of NLP is going to emphasize is the fact that the language people are going to use will not be an absolute representation of what that person is feeling or thinking. You have to spend some time learning about the person and see how they do with their words and how they assign meaning to words, and then you can use this to your advantage.

You Have the Advantage, Learn How to Exploit That

With any new thing that you are trying to do and the techniques that you are going to learn from that, there is going to be a kind of learning curve along the way. you will be able to look at some insight into some of the typical stages of progress that occur when someone is learning dark NLP for the first time. Each of the different stages of progress will clearly be described out to you, and then you will have the advice that is needed in order to progress to the ultimate aim of dark NLP, which is to become a constant predator.

To start with is the first stage of dark NLP. This first stage is often known as a tentative form of exploration. During this stage, someone who has heard about the dark NLP and some of the unique ways that it is able to change your perspective on life and the world will begin to consider its ideas, and then can weigh these new ideas against some of their own perceptions of the world.

When you reach to this point, it is possible for the person not to agree with the ideas of dark NLP, they may agree with some of the parts but not all of them, or they may decide that they agree completely with the ideas that come with dark NLP. These individuals are merely judging them in light of the experience that they personally have. To help the individual go beyond this kind of phase, it is advised that you actively seek to apply your understanding of dark NLP to the world around you.

After you have spent a little bit of time looking at dark NLP and some of the basics that come with it, and you have had some time to see whether the ideas are a good match with your own personally views of reality, you may agree that there is at least the potential of dark NLP to be useful. This is the stage of the process that is often known as cautious acceptance. It is during this time that you will start using the lens of dark NLP, but it still takes some conscious effort to look at the world in that manner. You may even start to question your own understanding of morality when you are in this part.

The next thing that you want to work on is figuring out how to push beyond the cautious acceptance. You are able to do this by making a conscious effort to put some of the techniques of dark NLP to the motion. You will want to specifically pay attention to any of the techniques that are related to influencing yourself, as well as others, as fast as you can. You will find that through more experience and practice, and for seeing personal success, using a technique, you will find that it is easier to accept these techniques in your life.

Following the cautious acceptance that we talked about above, you will then need to progress to a new level of using dark NLP that is going to be known as casual competence. When you are at this stage, you will stop having to put in so much effort to use the dark NLP techniques. You will start to naturally think in terms of dark NLP concepts, and over time, it is going to require progressively less effort on your part. You may even find that you are able to use the ideas of dark NLP to take control over your own life and to make sure that you are able to influence others near you, without even having to think about it.

The biggest distinction that comes with this is that once you reach this stage, it is going to show that you are to a new level of progress. You will know it has happened when you realize that you have gained some influence over others, and when you realize this, there isn't a level of guilt that comes with it.

To make sure that you are able to get the most out of this stage, it is important to begin to put it into practice, and to make sure that you track down the patterns that you see with your success. You may find that at this stage of your progress, you are going to benefit from keeping a journal so that you are able to keep track of the different routines that you do, and what happens to work well for your success. You stand the best chance of moving past this particular stage if you can learn how to identify the difference between those times when you are successful, and the times you are not.

We can then move on to the level that is beyond casual competence. These are all going to involve a good mastery of Dark NLP, one that can take a long time to reach and succeed at. There are no longer so many levels that are distinct when it comes to progress as there are gradual degrees of improvement. Signs that someone has gotten to this stage of dark NLP is going to include many things such as the ability to read the power balance no matter what situation you are in, the ability to mirror the other person without even thinking about it, and even how to influence the other person with some deep and artificial rapport, without all the effort.

The mastery that you have of dark NLP is going to be reliant on how willing you are to absorb some of the concepts and techniques that are described in this guidebook. To make this happen, you need to be willing and able to take some big actions in your life to get the right influence with dark NLP. You also need to be willing to figure out what patterns are going to lead you to success, and then use this to reach the next level of your mastery in the shortest space of time as possible.

As you are looking through your feelings and your emotions, you will come to a part that your mind is going to automatically think in terms of the concepts that are important to dark NLP. Once this happens, you will be able to interact with someone in a way that is going to force some rapport with them before exploiting them for your own needs. This means that you have gotten to the ultimate goal that comes with dark NLP, which means that you are now a constant predator.

Neuro-linguistic programming manipulation techniques

Visual squash

Visual squash is one of the most popular NLP technique of all time. It assists an individual in the road to acknowledging how each part constitutes a whole. What you should keep in mind about this particular technique is that every piece is integrated to a level that is relatively higher than what has been previously decided based on what the limits are. This is done until a unified state is achieved. There is also a tendency that this process would pile up until every level of logic that is deemed as the unconscious is attained. Every part is described in relation to its ability to function well and its relationship with its corresponding parts. Nevertheless, experts have commented as to how visual squash is a productive and efficacious tactic in settling conflicts among the different parts. As soon as there is unity among these parts, you will have a high chance of producing success.

The main idea of visual squash is rooted in the process of reconditioning a former emotion or thought into something much more positive. There is a high chance that this former emotion or thought used a negative pattern, which can be seen as an obstacle to achieving your ultimate goal. Thus, the sooner you are able to decondition, the sooner you can recondition, and the sooner you can achieve success. Decondition entails the removal of your old perspective. Recondition, on the other hand, is the act of replacing these old perspectives into positive emotions.

Collapsing anchors

Do remember that anchors are defined as either positive or negative. The main point of all of these is to eliminate negative thoughts. In relation to manipulation, you can use this NLP technique to manipulate yourself into getting rid of your bad habits. The same goes for when you want another person to do your bidding. The entire process is the same. The difference would lie in the thought pattern that you would want the other person to acknowledge or get rid of. Part of this entire process is the collapsing of the negative anchors. As explained, anchors are established by associating to a particular state, and it brings about a certain state that you desire to accomplish at the same time you are attempting to realize its actual success. On another note, keep in mind that negative anchors have the potential to tamper with your positive state allowing you to feel uncertain about specific things, especially if it has been originally affiliated with a negative experience. Thus, there is a need for you to learn how to successfully collapse these anchors so that you are better able to remove any association with this negativity.

Personal history change

Another neuro-linguistic programming technique is the means to change one's personal history. If the previous point talked about the elimination of a bad emotion, thought, or habit in an individual, personal history change focuses on the alteration of certain events and experiences in one's life. If you can learn this technique, you can very well manipulate yourself and others to reconsider an option that they do not initially acknowledge due to a particular memory. However, we are getting ahead of ourselves; let us start with identifying this change in personal history. What is it? Well, as you may know, our experiences play an essential role in our decision-making process. There are specific memories that compel us to make a certain decision in life, most of which may not be even beneficial for you in the future. Some experiences generate fear and, as we result, may hinder us in taking opportunities that are yet to come. Furthermore, it is possible that you may not have possessed the necessary information, or you may have been hurt before, which led to a faulty foundation in your overall behavioral pattern.

Change personal history, which is referred to by most experts as CPH, is a technique typically discussed under neuro-linguistic programming. CPH is when a person redirects all of the influences that are negative and that tend to play an essential role in your current decision-making processes still. By accurately assessing the situation and identifying certain impacts, an individual can easily face past adversaries and scenarios with a renewed sense of hope that they will experience success once all of this is over. When you recall certain memories or instances from the past, you are forced to dig up stored information from your mind. These memories are usually placed in your unconscious mind. Nevertheless, the act of sharing something that happened in your current situation only brings about the information gathered by your five basic senses. In NLP, this is how past and present experiences are distinguished. The act of drawing back something from memory is a common feeling in most people. They are affected by the notion that they can no longer change something that has already happened. Memories and experiences from the past tend to haunt any individual even when there are present experiences that continue to be incorrectly interpreted. These are wrongly interpreted because they are caught up with using a past traumatic situation repeatedly when trying to make decisions for the present or the future. What one should know is that through CPH, you can easily relive the same situation; the only difference here is that you no longer have to suffer the same fate because this time, you will act differently.

Belief change

To make it more cohesive, let us try to define what belief is. This is your understanding of the world. In the first few chapters, we have established how an individual uses their own five basic senses to collect facts about the external world. Moreover, how they interpret the gathered information is a crucial element in how their personality is formed. Nevertheless, it is possible to change this developed persona by changing one's reaction via changing two states. Here, you link an initial state to an alternative one that is its exact opposite. Then, you collapse all emotions and thoughts associated with the initial state. In CPH, you are taught how that every decision you make is probably affected by experience or memory. To make every memory conducive for success, you change how you react to a particular memory. You do not necessarily change what has happened in the past, but you alter how you feel about what has happened in the past. This goes the same for your set of beliefs.

Since a belief is an individual's understanding of the world, it is possible that a belief of one person may not truly exist, or it may depend on how one interprets it. Belief is subjective. Nevertheless, an essential element aids you in responding to a certain situation. Some principles discuss how an individual goes about their decision-making process. Your behavior will always be dictated by your belief, and your belief may have been dictated by your experience. In turn, a pasty experience is how we interpret that data gathered by our five basic senses. Nevertheless, whatever your belief may be, it can be either beneficial or detrimental to your overall success. Thus, you have to eliminate any bad behavior that may trigger useless generalizations.

Calibration

With calibration, you put into good use the communication skills that you have learned in the earlier chapters of this book. Even without having other people tell you their message through words, you can pretty much read into what they are trying to convey via body language. Furthermore, body language is much more accurate as compared to actual words. With practice, you will develop an instinct or feeling of what their true intentions are, what their beliefs are, and how they comprehend their memories or experiences to affect their daily lives. With all of these in mind, you re much more equipped to act accordingly depending on the situation. Furthermore, you will even predict what the other person's reaction will be. Calibration is an NLP technique that utilizes your ability to relate to other people and decide on that critical moment what you should do.

When manipulating another person, you should be able to calibrate their state of mind even without the other person telling you anything about their current state. Assess and calibrate their state in different periods.

If you need help with your calibrating skills, start with the visualizing exercises in the previous chapters. Moreover, try to master the ability to read body language, especially facial expressions. Then, you can start feeding them with incomplete and ambiguous statements and see how they would react to these triggers. Always pay attention to non-verbal cues as this is much more accurate and loyal to what the other person is thinking. While it is advisable to use all five basic senses in gathering information about the person being manipulated, your eyes would serve as the most important sense. Focus on acquiring objective data and try to become an effective, intuitive communicator. Depending on what you want the other person to do or believe, you need to be able to utilize the right resources to convince them that what you are providing them will be much more beneficial for them as compared to what they have in their current state. Remember, successful manipulation is something that is not traced back to the manipulator. You must make the other person believe that they make their decisions independently, which is why ambiguity also plays an important role in manipulation.

What is neuro-linguistic programming for?

When all has been stated and done, have you ask yourself what NLP is for? Even though this book focuses on the use of NLP for dark psychology and the manipulation of others, it is also essential to define NLP as a toolbox of skills, thoughts, and attitudes in itself. If you want to understand the true essence of manipulation, then there is also a need to understand the purpose of NLP because this phenomenon will be at the center of this book's discussion. With that considered, here are a few of NLP's purposes:

NLP helps you with your communication process

Neuro-linguistic programming is a crucial element in the improvement of one's communication process; thus, it also plays a vital role in reading other people. The communication process is improved through NLP because you will be forced to redefine your emotions and thoughts so that you are better able to communicate them. When you become verbally competent, you will be able to have a much stronger influence on other people.

NLP paves the way to success

Whatever issue you may be facing right now, whether it is personal, professional, or romantic, NLP enables you to change how you perceive your current situation. With NLP, you can alter how you interpret the information from the external world gathered by your senses. You will be able to identify your priorities in life and see a deeper meaning to these things. NLP is the ability to shift your perspective into something that will benefit you in the end.

NLP unifies your body, mind, and feelings

At times when you find yourself unable to fulfill or put into action your goals and dreams, this could mean that your body, mind, and feelings toward a specific purpose are not in harmony. NLP focuses on one's ability to interpret the world that we live in. Your senses gather information about the external world, and your body, mind, and feelings may not agree with what is being collected. To state an example: you have been accepted into three universities, which we will identify as the desires of your body, mind, and feelings.

Chapter 2: Understanding How You Think

Ever heard the expression, "You are what you think". When you think negative thoughts about yourself, you are participating in a sort of self-loathing self-fulfilling prophecy. If you are always telling yourself that you are lazy and worthless, you encourage yourself to do types of behaviors that you consider worthless or lazy. You start to think about yourself as the worst version of yourself. This is something that needs to be battled against. Positive thinking is much better for your overall health. Positive thinking will improve hour mood and attention span and even your physical health.

Positive thinking means that you are shifting from the perspective of bleakness and gloominess and starting to acknowledge the beautiful things that you do experience often times, it is o that there aren't beautiful experiences in our lives, but rather than we are not accessing the experiences that are right in front of us. Positive thinking means shifting just a little, fro "ugh, its dark out today and I don't want to go to work" to "its dark out today, but I am going to do my best at work and maybe take a nap afterward." It is not all sunshine and rainbows. The positive thing should be realistic and attainable.

Confidence will be greatly strengthened when you get into positive thinking. Confidence is something that is difficult to measure and difficult to grow. It comes from deep down in the spirit, and it knows that one can be kept safe and sound by his or her own will. Confidence comes from self-security. If there are a bunch of things that you hold in shame, like past experiences, or other sources of embarrassment, you will not find it easy to have confidence. To have confidence, you must let all that stuff go and admit to yourself that you are a person who is worthy of being listened to, hear, and understood, and then communicate yourself that way.

The best and most classic way to be confident is to be yourself and to own it. If you are a tall person, love that you are tall and share it with the world. If you are a short person, own it and love your shortness. There are all kinds of body traits and all kinds of people who love people with your body traits. Whatever mental or physical traits you might have insecurities about, you just have to give up on those anxieties and let go. This will better you in the long run. Motivation is extremely important to address for people with depression. Depression in large part very dependent on motivation. The lack of motivation is what drives depression, and often times this turns into a cycle of lack of motivation and negative feelings. Motivation is a nebulous concept, but we can pretty much say with confidence that when your body is healthier, you are generally more motivated. When you are spending all of your time on addiction or in unhealthy habits, you are feeding this cycle and your motivation will be cut short. This is unfortunate, but it happens.

A big part of positive thinking is learning to self-talk about good things and also to separate yourself from the bad thoughts. You can just let yourself know that thoughts are not real. You don't have to disprove thoughts, you can just say that they are mean or unnecessary and do away with them. Lots of people out there pace way too much value on their thoughts, their tiny little thoughts, and their content, and they spend all of their time "strategically" thinking, as to bring out some kind of satisfaction. But the satisfaction never comes.

What is helpful for this situation is to learn how to tell yourself declarations. You are not your thoughts. Your thoughts only exist in your head. Sometimes they are correct, or true, and sometimes they are not. It doesn't matter. In either case, they do not make you up. You are not a good person or a bad person for what you think.

The Subconscious mind in Psychology

What do we mean by the conscious mind? It is the part of the mind, which is thinking, feeling, and expressing itself at the moment. It is the conscious source of material that is easily accessible. The top of the iceberg is the smallest part of the iceberg, however, and if you dive deeper, you can see that most of the iceberg exists underwater.

The subconscious mind is made up of all the memories and associations that you have, and all the experiences with different people that you have.

The subconscious is responsible for the sexual drives, which we have. It is governed by the pleasure principle, which basically states that we are driven by pleasure and that pleasure is the ultimate motivator. This

403

is why advertising works so well when it engages ideas of sexual motivation and other forms of pleasure. The old saying "sex sells" is ever prescient to this day. Think about the phenomenon of sexual attraction. You might understand consciously that you are married, and happily so, but you will still find yourself wanting to engage in sexual conduct with others, even though you have agreed with your partner to not do so. This is the very essence of the id. It is always present, lurking, and it is the most animalistic pressure. In fact, sexuality is often part of Dark Persuasion tactics. A leader is often very attractive in physicality. This is part of charisma and it is a very effective way to engage in someone's subconscious drives.

Sexuality and other base drives are an important part of dark Persuasion. Since the dawn of time, humans have been subject to manipulation due to sexual urges. Sex and drugs have always been a way to control and manipulate a population.

What's going on it there?

Memory is a tricky thing. If two people witness an event, they will both have different accounts of that event. One person might remember it as a situation in which they were victimized. Another person might think of it as an event that was fair to all parties involved. Memory can fade and come back within a lifetime. Think about the earliest memory that you have. Undoubtedly, it will be one of your childhood. Is it a pleasant memory, or an unpleasant one? Sometimes the unpleasant memories are what stick out the most.

This will be something you can lean on to identify instances when you are being manipulated or persuaded, brainwashed or deceived. You can tap into this mysterious system of the subconscious, you will be able to defend yourself. This is no easy task, and it takes a lot of trial and error and it takes experience.

Managing Your Mind

Allow yourself to believe the unbelievable

In order to change your habits or way of thinking, you must fight back against the impulse to believe that nothing can ever change. This is one thing that often gets people stuck; it is the belief that the way they are now will be the way they are forever. Banish this thought, for it will only leave you undeveloped and will keep you away from self-realization.

Give yourself permission to be successful

Many people have in their subconscious the belief that they can never be as successful as they want. Some people have complexes from growing up poor that tell them that they will never have enough money and that they should always act as though having enough money will never be an option for them. We keep ourselves unsuccessful, as well in other ways. Some people think that they can't be creative, or they can't do a certain type of job. You just have to switch this thinking, and when you find these thoughts arising from your subconscious, you can tell yourself consciously that you are capable; you are able to be successful.

Resist others' projections

We are all subject to the projection of others. Projection is when a person has beliefs or feelings about themselves, and they think that all other people are like them. They start to think that everyone around them is actually matching them in some sort of characteristic or habit. People will put you in a box, and expect you to act a certain way. You must allow yourself to totally reject their thoughts about you. Resist their attempts to put you in a box.

Give yourself some positive reinforcement

The very essence of resisting Dark Persuasion is being able to understand the dark forces at work and giving yourself the opposite information. Being able to understand Dark Psychology means that you will have to engage in the darkness just a little bit. However, once you do this, you will have to balance out your energy with some positive thinking as well. If you are able to give yourself positive messages to balance out the negative darkness, you will find that you are able to overcome all manipulation and deception.

Be real about your success

Don't be humble. Of course, being humble is a virtue, but only up to a point. Being humble will eventually lead to your downfall. You need to stand with Machiavelli on this point, and let yourself be able to praise yourself wholeheartedly. Individualism is one of the main tenets of Western culture, and this means embracing yourself, your needs, and your way of living. Celebrate yourself. Tell yourself that you are the one who deserves success. Be real about what you have already accomplished – chances are; you have accomplished a lot.

Envision your future

Be bold about your future. If you are always envisioning a future that is full of pain and suffering, you will probably be working toward making that real. If you are able to create a future vision for yourself that is one of success and domination, you will be much closer to creating that in reality.

Point out your own weaknesses so that you can work on them

Your subconscious will play tricks on you. Sometimes, it will make you think that you are perfect and have no flaws, when in fact, this is not the case. Most people have one or two areas that they can work on. If you are able to point these out to yourself, you will find that you are able to morph more closely towards self-realization.

Embrace gratitude

Embracing gratitude is all about fostering a healthy self-image, which will help you on your path to self-realization. Some people have damaged their subconscious, and they get bitter and weakened because of past failures. You must learn to resist this urge, and you must find gratitude in the world. This will make your defenses stronger and it will teach you that there are things that are worthy of your pursuit of happiness.

Identify what you want, and get it

Stop messing around and keeping yourself from getting what you want. If you don't know how to get it, then try to learn how to get it. If your goal is a certain career path, then ask someone if you can be his or her apprentice. If it is something you can learn on your own, do your research and start to learn how you can achieve this goal on your own. Read books, the internet, and ask other people about how they have achieved what you want to achieve.

Get rid of your attachment to the "how"

The "how" is not important. The "how" is what keeps you from getting what you want and need. This is where judgment comes in. The subconscious will sometimes push you towards judgment, and you will find that if you have a voice that pushes you towards judgment, this will start to create a space between what you want and where you are. You should work to reduce this space as much as possible.

Chapter 3: Fundamentals of Reading People

Analyzing and speed-reading people are the ultimate weapons for understanding people and helping them cope with their inner feelings and emotions. People who can identify other people's inner feelings are people who are gifted and can do wonders. It will help one better one's relationships, professional performance, and social skills.

To analyze human behavior, one has to look into their values, lifestyle, what they are thinking, beliefs, and all other aspects that affect him or her directly or indirectly. Behavior analysts tend to analyze people with behavioral problems so that they can study the changes that the environment has on them.

Analyzing people's behavior leads to a deeper understanding of a person's personality provided that they are armed with sufficient knowledge about psychology. When trying to analyze human behavior, never analyze one item without analyzing the rest of the details. When someone is afraid of cats, don't assume that the person encountered an unpleasant ordeal with a cat and that it is the reason that they are afraid of them. You have to look at all possible aspects of her life that could have resulted in her having that fear. Maybe the fear of cats could have been brought on by the fact that they fear.

Communication has always played a critical role in human interaction. Furthermore, experts have also claimed that communication is mainly non-verbal. Without the necessary internal and external resources used for interpreting body language, the individual will most likely miss the message. Thus, reading people, which takes a massive part in the communication process, should be given utmost importance.

If you genuinely want to understand this book and fully utilize your ability to manipulate people, you must learn how to read people through verbal and non-verbal ways and identify their Secondary Gain. Once you have identified this as an external resource utilizing your internal resources, you are better able to achieve your desired outcomes. Keep in mind that comprehending the patterns of human behavior and learning body language allows you to view past the façade most people put on. Behind an individual's perfect smile, there ought to be some form of sadness, and reading people using the concepts discussed in this book will allow you to see past through individuals' projection of themselves. Furthermore, by using the underlying concepts of neuro-linguistic programming, you can better gauge the entire process of communication between individuals without being misled by what society deems as merely polite gestures.

In reading people, you must know what they truly feel without relying much on what they actually because, in reality, each one of us lies. Thus, verbal communication cannot guarantee the truth. Without the truth, reading people is a waste of time. You read people so that you can learn about the truth. It is essential that you find out what they are really thinking, what their true thoughts are, and how they feel about a particular situation. If you know the truth, it would be easy for you to understand that person; thus, it would also be easy for you to handle them accordingly and manipulate them.

On another note, it is important to remember that reading people is not possible if you are clinging on to past grudges or biased judgment. You have to let go of all of these misconceptions and prejudices about people before you can genuinely interpret body language as these biases only distort the truth. As a result, you may acquire false assumptions about someone, which will jeopardize your entire process of manipulation. If you want to influence other people's actions, you need to know their true desires. To do this, you need to learn the patterns of human behavior and the secrets of body language.

How to read what is in the other person's eyes

If it is true that the eyes are the windows to the soul, then this is definitely something that you need to consider when trying to use NLP on another person. To begin reading the eye movements of another person, it is important to ask a series of questions and make a mental note of the direction of the eye movement as they answer. Start by asking the person something that is factual, one that you know they are going to answer in a truthful manner. You could ask their name or the date of their birth. Pay attention to where they look. This lets you know which direction they are going when they are telling the truth. Then, if they go in a different direction, they will most likely be telling you a lie.

Finally, you should ask a question that you are hoping to get a lie out of the other person. So, if you know that this person is pretty insecure about the salary that they make, ask them if they make a figure that is a bit higher than what you are sure they make. There is a high chance that they are going to agree with you because they won't want to reveal the lower amount that they are insecure about. The movement that the eyes are going to make, as well as the tone that is in that person's voice, will help you to detect if there is something that they are lying about in the future.

Chapter 4: Fundamentals of Body Language

In this section, we will talk about understanding everything there is to learn about body language cues. This is crucial as manipulation heavily relies upon these non-verbal cues. Manipulation is defined as an act of altering the environments to adhere to the characteristics that you want. Thus, to change these environments, you must be able to know the truth first. From here, you employ questionable tricks, such as misdirection, temptation, and distraction, to get what you want.

Functions of non-verbal communication

To read people, you have to rely on both verbal and non-verbal communication. Verbal communication is as direct as it is. However, no one can guarantee that people are always saying the truth every time. With that in mind, those who wish to manipulate and influence people to do specific actions must rely on non-verbal cues to learn more about the other person.

Complementing

Complementing is done to add credibility, as well as support what has been said. If you are to look at non-verbal communication as something genuine, then the message is strengthened. However, if it were fake, you would doubt the authenticity of the word. When you are happy, a real and genuine smile will complement the actual message that you are satisfied. If you say that you are happy, yet you are not, there is doubt placed upon your confession of being happy.

Regulating

One can regulate communication using non-verbal language. Whenever you are conversing with someone, you cannot keep telling the other person that it is their time to speak whenever you are done with what you have to say. Through non-verbal language, a person is already able to tell when it is their time to speak.

Substituting

As the name suggests, substituting allows non-verbal language to take over verbal communication. There is a variety of non-verbal language that is obvious. Whenever someone you do not like is invading your space, you take a step back to say in a non-verbal way that you do not like the fact that they are too close, no words necessary. Even one's facial expressions are clearly non-verbal language that is easily picked up by another person.

Accenting

Another function of non-verbal language includes accenting. This is used to emphasize your verbal message. A great example would be to hold someone's hands when delivering bad news. When you are disciplining a child, you touch their shoulder as a means to reassure them that you still care for them in spite of the anger you feel at that moment.

Basic body language cues

Most of the time, people would interpret non-verbal cues without ever knowing they are doing it. For example: if you are talking to someone and they suddenly changed their facial expressions, you will be able to pick up on that using your senses. As a result, you will be more careful with what you say next. Depending on what you want to attain, you can read the other person's body language to confirm their true emotions.

Now, in mastering neuro-linguistic programming as a means to manipulate people, you need to start with the basics, and that is reading some of the most common body language cues.

Eyes

Those who have studied NLP would agree to the adage that the eyes are the windows to the soul. You can read another person's true emotions by observing how their eyes move or how fast they blink. Even though the eyes are relatively small as compared to the other body parts, the eyes can create numerous expressions that can reveal the entire truth.

Let us start with telling whether or not a person's way of blinking is normal. You have to assess whether they are blinking too fast or too slow. If someone is anxious about something, they tend to blink fast. Moreover, rapid blinking also indicates that they are telling a lie. On another note, if the person is blinking slowly, it shows that they are trying to control their eye movement. You can assume that they are hiding something or trying to suppress an emotion.

How the eyes move also shows how engaged the other person is in the conversation. Those who show interest in the conversation would rarely break eye contact. If an individual frequently breaks eye contact, they may be distracted or bored. Moreover, it can also mean that they are naturally submissive or may be nervous about conversing with other people. Whenever you are talking to someone whom you are trying to decipher, pay attention to how they glance at certain objects in the room. Anyone who barely maintains eye contact and always glances at their watch or at the door is secretly saying that they wish to end the conversation and leave.

The size of the pupils can also reveal how much a person is interested in the conversation. Now, determining whether or not the other person has dilated pupil can be a bit of a challenge even under the right conditions. Moreover, you have to consider that a dilated pupil may have been affected by light. These are the things you have to consider when trying to decide if a person is genuinely interested. The good news is that you are always allowed to test this out. Remember, the dilation or contraction of one's pupil is automatic, so you have to have a keen eye. Next time you are conversing with someone who appears to be bored, immediately switch the topic into something you know elicits interest from the other person and observe the change in their pupils.

Voice

If we are talking about body language, then it is crucial that we discuss the use of vocalic. It is important to note that vocalic is different from the words that pass a message. Vocalic is all about how people communicate with their voice; this includes the way you open your mouth, the tone of your voice, how loud or soft you are when you are talking, and more. If you pay close attention to another person's vocalic, you will notice certain differences in what they are saying and what their voice is revealing. It is important to note that an individual's voice can change depending on the person they are speaking to, the gender of that person, their level of attractiveness, their social ranking, or even their age. Notice how the voice you use when you speak to your friends is quite different from the voice you use when you speak to your supervisor from work. Moreover, notice how your tone changes when you are talking with someone you like or someone you find attractive.

Even those who are not experts in voices can easily distinguish the vocalic of an individual. Human beings are made to understand paralanguage long before they could also formulate the needed words to communicate. Animals, such as dogs, use paralanguage to respond to their masters' commands. They may not necessarily understand the words, but they are able to understand what the message is through the vocalic of their masters. If you can understand the paralinguistic elements of verbal communication, then you can pretty much manipulate the conversation, and thus, shape the other person. Of course, you also need to master how you would react when conversing with someone. You need to know your strengths and weaknesses and be aware of your vocal strengths. This level of awareness will let you influence others because reading their vocalic gives you the ability to analyze them and their true intentions. Thus, you would like to know how to handle them regardless of what the situation is.

There are six types of vocalic that you should be familiar with – rate, volume, tone, pitch, vocal signature, and rhythm. The rate of speech pertains to how slow or fast the person speaks. With this, you will be able to tell people's emotional state, credibility, and even their intelligence. If you are talking with someone and they answer almost immediately, it goes to show that they are very much assured in what they have to say. On another note, hesitation is a sign that the person is hiding something or is lying about something. They needed the time to form the lies in their head. It is important to note that these rules do not apply in public speaking because the speaker would want to be slow as it means they want to emphasize certain things. If a public speaker talks fast, it may indicate nervousness.

Volume pertains to the audibility of the person's voice. By carefully listening to the vocality of the speaker, you will be able to tell their speech's level of intensity through the volume of their voice. One of the most common myths when it comes to the volume of the voice is that a soft voice always represents humility; this is not always the case. A soft voice can very much radiate intensity, especially when combined with the right tone and facial expression. In fact, a soft voice that has a compelling intensity can be very daunting and may sound threatening. Thus, when considering the volume of the voice, you also need to take into account their tone. The tone helps you assess the emotions behind the speaker's words.

Furthermore, the pitch pertains to either the highness or lowness of the tone of the voice. The low-pitched voice most often represents authority and credibility. The high-pitched voice sounds like a small child. If you want to possess vocal power, it is best to practice yourself speaking in a low-pitched voice. The last type of vocalic is rhythm. Rhythmical paces exist in various languages because of the accents. Much like the rest of the vocalic types, rhythm also affects how individuals interact with one another.

Chapter 5: Manipulating the Mind Through NPL

The first step that you need to use in order to gain a level of influence over someone is to figure out what their secret blueprint is that makes them who they are as a person. There are going to be several aspects of a person you need to understand in order to gain control over them that you want. This blueprint is going to show you their doubts, hopes, fears, and the things that they like and dislikes about themselves. You will now be shown how to figure out all of these aspects of a person's blueprint and how to take action based on this information to increase the amount of influence you have over the other person.

To help you understand more about the fears that someone has, there are two main methods that work the best for that. These can either be used on their own or in conjunction. The first method that we can take a look at is the passive method. This method is just going to involve you simply paying close attention to the other person, listening to how they talk, and what they talk about, in order to determine the things that worry them the most.

You will find that different people are more or less obvious in the way that they reveal this aspect of themselves. Some people talk about things and clearly state they are worried by them, while others are not really all that explicit about it, and instead they are going to use some hints at it with the general demeanor and tone of voice that they use when it is time to discuss certain issues.

The second method that you can use is a more active method. For this one, you can listen for a bit, and then try to lead the other person to the responses that you are looking for. For example, you could causally lead the conversation over to the topic of health with a particular person. Depending on how willing the other person is to talking about the topic, their tone of voice, and how physically comfortable they are with it, you will be able to figure out how much that particular person worries about health. You can use it for any topic in order to gauge the fear that the person has on that issue.

Uncovering the hopes of another person is often going to be easier than determining the fears that they have. This is because you will find that people are more willing to disclose their hopes rather than their fears. Many people like to give away what they aspire to in life by disclosing their aims for the future. Even some of the aspects that seem trivial amount a person, such as the purchases that they choose to make, can indicate the way that they are going to see themselves, and how they like to be seen by others.

If you are looking to encourage others to open up about their hopes is to start talking about some of the hopes that you have. This can help make it so that the other person feels more candid. A manipulative and dark NLP spin that you can use is to disclose some of your hopes, ones that aren't sincere, that are specifically intended to increase the comfort level towards a certain topic. For example, if you tell the other person that you have some money worries, even though you don't have those money worries. This makes the target feel that money worries is acceptable to talk about, and they will then open up to you.

There are a lot of things that you can use when it comes to how you can use this same idea to manipulate the other person. You can use the things that the person likes and dislikes about life, they could lower the self-esteem of the other person by insulting them in a subtle way, and can play the fears against them. You can look at their dreams, their hopes, the things they are afraid of and more. You are able to observe the other person to determine what makes them tick and how you can best manipulate them.

NLP, manipulation, and mind control

Can NLP help you avoid negative manipulation and mind control? Yes, NLP can help anyone to fight manipulators. Often, we move along life on autopilot-responding to life in an extensively automatic way. This leaves us vulnerable to manipulation because we hardly analyze situations critically and make strong decisions. When living life on autopilot, we tend to follow what other people are doing (social proof) and also allow other people to influence our choices. Sometimes go through life drive by those subconscious programs which we have learned and practiced for years – some of them we practice since childhood.

Some self-development advocates and personal change ambassadors can fail to explain to us how we can avoid the specific tools we should apply to improve our lives. On the other hand, NLP lays out the tools you need to implement that change. It informs you that you are responsible for your actions, reactions, and responses to the situations in life. NLP allows you to get behind the steering wheel and take charge of your life instead of having another person drive you around.

NLP is practiced more because of its practicality – The tools are functional, and a wide range of challenges can be addressed through NLP. Some of the issues include;

Developing better relationships,

• Becoming more healthy
• Overcoming phobias and fears such as fear of public speaking,
• Improving communication
• Being more successful and impactful in your career and family life.

Success in any field of life, be it career, sport, family, requires excellence. Neurolinguistic programming is a roadmap for this excellence. Although other factors like luck and innate ability play a role in the success of an individual, the majority of NLP tools must be applied. Success is a predictable result of behaving and thinking in a certain way.

Mind control, hypnosis, and brainwashing are all closely linked together as concepts, but it is important to keep in mind their differences so that you know which one is the best technique to use in whatever situation you might find yourself in.

Mind control is perhaps the most subtle out of the three concepts, but it is also easily the broadest as well. Mind control refers to any series of words, actions, or behaviors that you can speak or perform in order to take command of another person's mental processes and dominate them. Ideally, when you perform mind control techniques, your target should not be aware of what you are doing, both before they have been mind-controlled and afterward. Your target should not be able to trace mind control back to you. Instead, you should be able to use mind control techniques without being detected, which is made easier when you model your mind control techniques on concepts from NLP, the

Dark Triad, and the principles of persuasion and deception. In addition, mind control is not a permanent procedure. While you can certainly perform mind control techniques on a particular target more than once, they will not remain mind-controlled by you for a very long time. There are ways to extend the amount of time that your target is mind-controlled, but they will never remain mind-controlled for incredibly long periods of time. Out of the three concepts, mind control is the easiest to pull off successfully and requires the fewest amounts of resources for you to use.

Mind control can be best thought of as an influence system significantly disrupting the individual on a very core level. The techniques used in mind control affect the identity of a person, which is, his beliefs, values, preferences, practices, behaviors, decisions, and relationships, among others, creating a new pseudo-personality or pseudo-identity. You see, Mind control can be used for the benefit of the victim, for instance, to help a drug addict overcome his/her addiction. However, in this case, we are concentrating on the unethical and inherently bad practices.

There are some important distinctions you need to make. Firstly, Mind control is subtle, and that means, the affected individual will hardly notice the changes and the extent of influence directed to him/her. Note, this insidious process can have devastating effects because it entraps and causes harm to the victim. Because of the subtle nature of the influence, victims think they are still in charge of their decisions while in fact, there are other people making decisions for them. Furthermore, mind control does not happen overnight; that is why it is referred to as a process. It takes time – The amount of time taken depends on the techniques used, the intended results, the duration of exposure, the ability of the manipulator to influence, and personal factors. Nowadays, some manipulators are so skilled that they achieve their results in a few hours. Though there is no physical force used by manipulators in mind control, social and psychological forces and pressures are put to play.

"Mind Reading" Other People

You will also find that the choice of language that the other person chooses to use is going to be a really powerful indicator of what drives them, as well as how they see the world. For example, there are those who are going to show that they agree with you by saying something like "that feels right" "I know what you mean" or "I hear you". Their choice of language is going to show how they perceive the world, and whether that is through their logic, touch, or sight. When you know what the perception is for that person, you can then draw upon that and explain ideas you wish them to disagree with in a language that isn't in alignment with that system.

You will also find that by listening to the other person, they are going to start disclosing words that have a special level of meaning or some significance for them. For example, you may find that when the person is talking about someone they have a lot of admiration for, they may use the word brilliant. And this word is only going to show up when their emotions are heightened. This is a good sign that the word has some kind of significance to that person. You can then use this information to your advantage and deploy the word in some of the statements that you make in order to trigger an agreement from the other person. Make sure that it is used sparingly though. If you overuse it, this is going to seem obvious and can come across as an unnatural thing.

Often the choice of words that the person chooses to go with is going to change when their internal state is different. The more that you are around the other person, the easier it will be to figure out what words are used for each different internal voice of that person. This is useful because you are then able to modify your own choice of words and behavior to ensure that it is compatible with that person's world view at that time.

The power of mirroring someone else

The first thing that you can do to make sure that you are able to take control of someone physically, as well as with their inner state is to really take note of their body language. You need to always take a constant amount of notice of the people you interact with, and the way that they will move, hold themselves, their expressions, where their feet are positions, and how they move their hands, the smaller the detail, the better.

Once you have a good idea of the body language that the person likes to use, you are then able to mimic them as well. You don't want to do this too much, but using it a little bit is going to make a big difference in how the other person is able to react to you. If you use the same tone of voice, if you can move your hands in a similar way, and if you can copy some of the little habits that they have, they are instantly going to feel a new connection with you.

There are a few ways that you can double check to see if you have built up the amount and type of rapport that you want with your target. Of course, the main method to look at is through physical leading, which we will talk about a bit more in a moment. Some of the things that are going to become apparent after you have been able to mirror the other person effectively is that the target is going to find it easier to open up and talk with you. They are going to have an emotional tone that is warmer, and they may disclose more information. They may even agree with your opinions more because they feel that connection with you.

Using leading and pacing to take control

One of the most effective ways that you can check whether your mirroring efforts have worked and if they created a sense of connection is to see if you can physically take control of the interaction with your target. But how are you supposed to be able to do this?

The first stage of the process is to spend a period of time mirroring someone. You want to copy, in a subtle manner, any changes in the body language of that target so that they feel comfortable and like the two of you are on the same page. Then, after you do this for some time, you can make a little change in your own body language. You could make it as simple as moving where your right hand is. if you are successful, you will find that your target is going to start copying the body language that you did.

When someone starts to copy the changes that you are showing in your own body languages, this means that they have fallen deep into the rapport that you have set up, and they are ready to be led by you. This means that it is the prime time for you to get them to agree with what you are saying, or to get them to carry out any other kind of manipulation that you want.

If you find that you try out this step to lead the interaction, and the other person doesn't start to copy you, this doesn't mean that all is lost at this point. It may mean that you tried to move ahead too quickly, and you just need to mirror them a bit longer. It can sometimes take a bit longer with some people compared to others, and you need to just give it the time that is needed. Eventually, you are going to have enough of this rapport going on in the subconscious that they will start to follow your lead.

The key to being able to lead someone effectively in this manner is to start out by making some small leads before gradually working your way up to make some of the bigger changes that are needed with your body language. For example, you could start out with a rather small change of moving the position of just the hand. Then build up to moving the entire arm. And then move both arms, or do some other bold movement at this time.

The greater the mirroring level that the target shows, the greater the rapport that you have built up with them. And once you have reached this level, it means that you are now able to influence them on the corresponding event that you would like.

Truthfully, there are good decisions and bad decisions in life. In fact, there are some decisions we never make. Most of the situations that need decision-making skills have a number of choices to pick from. And these options are the cause of conflict. We are often torn between choices, hoping that we pick the best one. However, making the decision does not always solve the conflict, especially if things do not turn out the way we had hoped. Decision making means rejecting some possibly positive choices for others. And there is pressure to make the best choice and relieve the conflict. It is not always easy, but there are things you can do to improve the process.

To take control of our success and entire life, and to avoid manipulation, know what you stand for and use that as a guide. Do not be swayed by every bit of information people give you. Making personal decisions is very important, especially when you make mistakes. Technically, the secret to success is good decisions. To make good decisions, you need experience, and experience comes from bad decisions and failures. So, making mistakes should not scare you, if anything, it will improve your intuition.

Chapter 6: Making Comfortable Connections

Learning to apply psychology to friends, coworkers, and lovers is primarily a matter of boundaries. Each person might have different interests in their possible angle of manipulation. Each of us plays different roles in our lives. In one role, we are called to be a family member. This might refer to your given or born family, or it might refer to your chosen family. "Chosen family" refers to the people you include in your life to the closest degree. This might include friends or other people to which you have chosen to be closest. Coworkers include people who we are often required to be around. Some lucky people get to choose who they work with, but most of us are required to work with people at random. Friends are a category of people who we choose to spend our time with, mostly doing enjoyable activities. Lastly, lovers include those with whom we choose to be romantic.

For the first category, friends, we must establish the types of boundaries which we want to have when dealing with friends. Friendships should be the type of relationships that bolster your health as an overall person. Friends are people you choose to spend time with, and hopefully, you don't choose to spend time with people who are not good for you. Often, there is a mix of positives and negatives in a friendship. You might have a friend who is annoying sometimes, but at other times, you have great fun and close connection with. It is all about maintaining that balance. Friendships can become toxic if a person is using someone else, being selfish, or not establishing a connection. Friendships should be a place of solace and connection, but you also have the right to challenge friends. You have the right to push them to be better, and you should be able to tolerate them calling you out on your negative qualities, as well. Friendships are all about balance. A good friendship is a partnership that includes connection and positive energy.

Coworkers are a little trickier because these are not people we choose. They are mostly people we are assigned to spend time with. Some people have trouble separating their work life and their friend life, and they will have trouble acting professionally around people they like. They might try to make things too personal at work, and they will not be able to create the type of relationship that is appropriate for work conditions. A person must have a solid support system outside of the workplace in order to have a balanced work life. Having a good relationship with coworkers means that you are able to be pleasant and nice and effective in the workplace, while not asking too much of people about the intimate details of their lives. Sometimes, we have coworkers who we don't like at all. In this situation, you can let go of the possibility of being friends at all. This is okay! You can't be friends with everyone. Coworkers who we don't like are a great opportunity to grow as a person. This is a challenge for you. Will you be able to work effectively with this person, even if you don't like them? This will include the challenge of detachment. You have to tell yourself that even if this person is someone with which you don't want to spend time, you have to. This gives you the requirements to work with. In the workplace, you must learn to accommodate Frank's rigidity and bad mood. Now, this goes both ways, and Frank must learn to be at least partially pleasant so that he is able to have a job and work with people. However, if you learn to work with people that you don't like, you will have learned a great skill. Some boundary issues in this context with our example character Frank might be that you learn not to try to engage Frank in conversation outside of work matters. When you are with him, it's all about work. Adjustments like this have to be made. You have to just know that you are only going to get so far in the conversation and go from there. You must just learn to say, "This person is this way, and there is no changing that."

Now, there are often other challenges in the workplace. Sometimes, people are too friendly. These are times in which you must learn to remind yourself of the purpose of the day: to get work done effectively. You can learn to draw boundaries in this arena as well. These might include cutting a conversation short and learning how to "cut people off" as they start to ramble. These boundaries might also include not sharing information about yourself. You must learn that this is okay! It doesn't mean that you are shutting yourself off from the world. It just means that you have a good sense of boundaries.

Family is yet another category of people with whom we must figure out our relationships. In some cases, a relationship with family members is not possible or necessary. This happens in cases where people are separated from their family for whatever reason. For people who grew up with abusive parents, it can be healthy to cut out traditional family members and grow a new chosen family outside of them. However, for many people, family connections are deep and important. It connects us to our humanity and reminds us of where we come from. Parents should help nurture and grow their children, and we should be grateful for this if our parents did a good job. At a certain point in development, we are able to relate to our parents as simply people rather than a mom and dad. There are some boundaries in this area too. Some people have parents who are very expecting and controlling and might feel the need to draw boundaries where the parents are and aren't allowed to see or comment on their lives. This goes for other family members as well, like siblings and extended families. Again, it is all about striking a balance.

Once you have firmly established the different roles for people in your life, you can start analyzing whether or not the relationships are equitable. You might find that someone has set up the relationship to be more beneficial for them than for you. You might find that you are manipulating someone else!

Now that we have taken the time to understand ourselves through the principles of NLP to understand and leverage your own outcomes, drives, and values, you will be shown how to extend this kind of self-mastery and use it to take control over others. You will learn the right techniques that are going to make it easier to understand what makes a person act in a certain way, and then you can learn how to influence them through your words and actions.

One thing to keep in mind is that you should make sure that there is some caution with the techniques that you are using. They are going to be really powerful techniques, and the power that you can gain with this can't be overstated. Let's take a look at some of the steps that you can do in order to take control of others with the help of NLP.

Chapter 7: Using NLP to Avoid Manipulation

There are many reasons why people manipulate others. Some of the main reasons include power, greed, and lust. These negative aspects drive so much of people's behaviors. Look at the history of the world, and you will see the extent to which people were willing to sacrifice others for selfish gains. Over the years, there have been stories of schemes and manipulation at work which continue to date.

Most of the people who end up being victims of manipulators fall into the trap because they do not realize they are pretending. The best manipulators are aware of their hidden agendas, but they act so well that you cannot see the wolf in sheep's clothing residing within them. And there are many pretenders in the world today. And more cunning manipulators.

All this comes down to two questions; do you want to be the manipulator or the person that protects self and others from the wolves? These are choices which you have to make consciously. Every person who understands NLP must make this decision. In reality, you need to know how the manipulator and the victim function in order to choose a side.

Basically, NLP is not designed to facilitate negative manipulation, although a lot of people use it for selfish gains. Some people will use this wonderful technique to do more harm than good. How then can we use NLP to protect ourselves from manipulation?

Reasons we allow ourselves to be manipulated

The only time when manipulation is considered successful is the time when you allow it to control your emotions and thoughts. Thus, you must start to distinguish what is going on in you that allows you to be easily manipulated by other people. The three most basic reasons we let ourselves to be manipulated are as follows:

Fear

This emotion comes in numerous structures. We, as human beings, tend to fear losing a relationship; we may fear the disapprobation of other people; we dread to make somebody discontent with our actions. We additionally dread the dangers and outcomes of the manipulator's actions. Imagine a scenario in which they really prevail at doing what they threaten.

Guilt

Today, we are clouded by the idea and responsibility that we should dependably prioritize the needs and wants of other people rather than our own. At times when people would talk about the right to fulfill their own needs and wants, manipulators frequently abuse us and endeavor to allow us to feel like we are accomplishing something immoral in the event that we do not generally put their needs and wants in front of our own. Those individuals who are skilled at these manipulative tactics would tend to define love as the act of fulfilling their needs and wants as part of your obligation. Hence, in the event that we have an opinion that goes against their beliefs, we are manipulated into thinking that we are heartless; at this point, they would make us feel very regretful of our existence and would use guilt to manipulate us.

Being too nice

We appreciate being a provider, fulfilling individuals, and dealing with the needs of other people. We discover fulfillment. Moreover, our confidence would regularly originate from doing what we can for other people. In any case, at times when there is lack of an unmistakable feeling of these and fair limitations, skilled manipulators are able to detect this in people who are easy targets of this phenomenon, and will use certain tactics to further their own selfish gains.

What you need to do to avoid manipulation

Establish a clear sense of self

There is a need to know your identity, what your needs and wants are, what your emotions are, and what you are fond of and not fond of. You must learn to accept these and not become apologetic, as these are the things that make you. At times, we dread that in the event of speaking up, we are viewed by others as egotistical and called out for being selfish. Nevertheless, knowing your identity or what you really need in life is not at all an act of selfishness. Self-centeredness is demanding that you always get what you want or that other has always put your needs and wants first. Similarly, when another person calls you out for not following their orders or fulfilling their needs and wants, they are the ones being selfish, not you.

You should always be sensitive of people who are trying to copy your body language

When you are talking to somebody and you notice it as if they are sitting precisely as you or are trying to imitate the way you are talking, you should test them by trying to make some moves and seeing if they are going to make the same move.

Move your eyes in unpredictable and random patterns

The NLP person always pays attention to the movement of the eye of their client to determine how they store and utilize information in their mind. You may think that they are interested in what you are saying, but they are just trying to create a rapport. After studying your eye movements, they will be able to determine when you are trying to make something up or lying, figure out which part of your mind you are using when talking.

Avoid being touched by just anyone

We have already discussed how an NLP person can bring back a previous state like the state of hunger. For instance, you may be having a conversation with a person and are in a much heightened emotional state, like you are outraged, and that person holds your hand.

Educate yourself

Knowledge is power, and power is the game. To avoid manipulation, you need to learn the techniques used by the victimizers. This knowledge will help you to identify a person who is using NLP selfishly. For instance, when you see a person trying to 'anchor,' it will be easier to tell whether the intentions are good or bad. Undoubtedly, if you want to win against a force that is going against you, it is important to get educated in its ways. We cannot emphasize this enough. The skilled manipulator achieves so much because he/she knows that people can be tuned into doing things contrary to their intentions in many ways. You also need to know these ways.

Understand people

The game of power can only be mastered by someone who has developed the ability to analyze and understands people. A manipulator does not see things as either good or bad. Instead, he/she looks at situations as circumstances and events. This ability to retract emotions from a situation gives the manipulator an advantage over us. We normally cloud our minds with judgments as we label events and circumstances as either good or bad. A person using NLP is interested in 'the what and the how' of people getting motivated. That knowledge allows the person to either control or defend people.

Stay away from manipulators

To detect a manipulator, observe how they act in front of different people and in different scenes. Agreeably, we all have different behaviors for different life situations. There is a face for facing mom at home and the principal at school. However, a manipulator normally dwells on the two extremes. That is, he/she treats one person with extreme politeness while treating the other with absolute contempt and rudeness. At one moment, a manipulator might act helpless while at the other, he/she is very aggressive. If you observe such character in a person, it is better to keep a distance. You might be the next victim. Avoid engaging such people unless you have to.

Most of the people with manipulative characters have some deep-seated causes, and it is not upon you to change them.

Avoid self-blame and manipulation

Since the agenda of the manipulator is to look for, spot, and exploit your weaknesses, you will feel inadequate when around them. Do not blame yourself for not meeting the needs of a manipulator. These people are selfish, and probably, nothing can satisfy them. They will manipulate you to feel bad about yourself and look for ways to crush your self-esteem. With lowered self-esteem, you are more likely to surrender your rights and power.

Put the focus on the manipulator

When conversing with a manipulator, you will notice that the attention is on you. How so? A manipulator tries to avoid the spotlight so that he/she cannot be found out. Inevitably, a manipulative person will come to you and ask for a favor/ request/demand. He/she might make a very good offer to make you go out of your way and meet their needs.

If you notice that the manipulator is making an unreasonable demand or solicitation, it is important to put him/her under the spotlight and ask a few probing questions. This might help the manipulator to recognize the unreasonableness of the situation.

Take advantage of the time

Mostly, a manipulator will expect you to give a straight answer right away after asking for a favor. Their intention is to maximize pressure over you and control your situation. To avoid this manipulator, avoid closing the deal immediately. Leverage time to your advantage, create a distance between the two of you. Exercise power by simply saying, "I'll think about it." Those words are very powerful between a salesperson and a customer, or between an eager pursuer and romantic prospect. Take this time to evaluate the request, its pros, and cons. Do you want to negotiate some better terms? Would you rather say no in this particular situation?

Diplomatic but firm "NO"

The art of communication is very important in life. You need to be able to say no in a firm and respectful way. Effective articulation of rejection will allow you to stand your ground and at the same time, keep the relationship. Remember that you have the right to say 'no' (Fundamental human rights). You also have the right to set your own goals, and priorities and walk away if you must. Do not feel guilty for saying no to unreasonable manipulators. They are not guilty of manipulating you either.

Use safety measures while confronting bullies

A psychological manipulator also may also become a bully once he/she harms a person. Remember that bullies pick on people they perceive as weak. If you keep complying and staying passive, you make yourself a viable target, and the manipulator will keep attacking you. Many manipulators and bullies are insecure and cowards on the inside. They use the manipulative techniques and bullying to intimidate a target. Once the victim begins to show a backbone, (standing up for his/her rights), the manipulator will often back down. Bullies can be brought down in schoolyards, offices, and domestic environments.

Set consequences

When a manipulator insists on infringing your rights even after you have asked them to stop, it is time to deploy consequences. Let a bully know that their actions have consequences, and you are not a walkover.

Consequences are some of the tools that one can use to stand down a psychological manipulator. Effectively analyzed, consequences make the manipulator shift from violation of rights to respect. Identify and set your standards and let bullies know that overstepping them can lead to drastic results.

Understand that language

Basically, most of our choices, actions, and fulfillment depend on how we perceive things. For example, what you will have for dinner will depend on perception. If you perceive that fast food might lead to held to health problems, then you are likely to go home and make your own meal. Whether you will visit the gym today will depend on your perception, how you will vote is a result of your perception.

Be always cautious about permissive language

You should always be aware of this kind of freedom. This was mostly by NLP hypnotists the likes of Erickson. They discovered that in order to manipulate someone, you have to let them permit you to do so. You can command your client, like "Go into a trance." That is not possible, right? But they will tell you, "You may relax as much you like," and through this, they can control you however they want.

Be a keen listener

If you are not aware, you may find yourself agreeing to whatever is being said. To avoid being manipulated, always understand what is being said before giving out feedback. But as you were too quick to answer, you just agreed blindly, and a skilled NLP person can easily use this technique to manipulate you.

Avoid agreeing to everything

When you find yourself in a situation where it is like you are being led to make some quick decisions about something and you are feeling as if you are being steered, you just leave that situation. You should never allow yourself to make any decision, especially financial ones, in the spur of a moment. This technique is mostly used by salespeople specifically to direct your impulse to buy their commodities. When you feel that, leave it and use your mind.

You should always trust your intuition

It can be termed as the ability to understand something using instincts. You may be around a person, but your gut communicates that you should try to figure out a way to get rid of that person even if it means fleeing or requesting that person to show some respect and not use NLP techniques when you are around.

Say "no" despite the other person's disapproval

The ability to say "no" despite somebody's objection is a solid demonstration. Individuals who can do this are present in reality. Because in reality, there is no way that we can accommodate all of their needs and wants. When this happens, they will become baffled, even disappointed. However, keep in mind that what they are feeling is part of human nature. Most of these individuals would then forgive and forget.

Tolerate the other person's negative affect

We can demonstrate compassion for people's pity, hurt, or even annoyance when accommodating them without having the need to back down and reverse our decision. Keep in mind, a solid relationship is described by common minding, shared genuineness, and shared regard. In the event that you are involved with somebody who uses manipulation and unhealthy control consistently, begin to see little propensities that may not be clear to you at first. As you are more grounded, you are better ready to endure how the other individual's negative impact on you is only bringing you down. Thus, this turns into a positive development that liberates you from their manipulative grasps.

Understand the Motive

When you can detect that you are being manipulated or persuaded, the first step is to examine what the motivation is for the manipulator. What is it that you have that they want? This could be many things, and one of the most common is money. When you are presented with a situation where you are being persuaded to do something, you should first examine the possibility of monetary gain. If it is a business that is soliciting you for time or patronage, ask yourself if you need those services, and ask if your life is better off with or without those services. If it is a charitable organization, do some research into whether they do what they say and if they should be trusted?

Machiavellianism as Defense Mechanism

You should ask yourself if whatever is being presented puts you further away from your personal goals or closer to your personal goals. This will allow you to evaluate who is the winner of each situation. Remember, you should be focused on yourself in this mindset. This is not the mindset of helping people, although there are obviously many situations in which it is better to not adopt a Machiavellian mindset. If you are in a situation where you need to provide support for other people, or if you are in a situation in which you already trust the person you are encountering, the Machiavellian mindset is not appropriate. However, when you are trying to defend yourself from manipulative people or people who do not have your best interests in mind, you can lean on this mindset to help put up defenses.

The Machiavellian mindset is, at its core, selfishness. Most people think of selfishness as a negative thing. However, you should rethink this. Selfishness is a very necessary human trait. It is not something that you should employ all the time, by any means, but you should be able to use selfishness when it appropriate. After all, in a situation where you are being challenged with dark persuasion, it is you against them. It is a fight or be killed. So, in order to defend yourself, you must become selfish. Your foe in this battle does not deserve help or kindness. You are the one who deserves help and kindness from yourself. Do not give them an inch. Ask yourself what is best for you at that moment, whether it lets the other person down or not. Some people are so wired against this, that it becomes a challenge for them. Some people are so wired towards being a helper and a giver that standing up for themselves is very foreign and it is very different for them. You might find that this is true for you, and you will have to switch over from a mindset of a helper and pushover into someone who is self-interested and wants to help themselves.

These strategies are often used, by marketing companies, governmental units, and in interpersonal relationships, to manipulate you and make you act a certain way. NLP can help you resist these attempts.

NLP is a way of working that will help you to realize your way of thinking about the world, and engage with that to make changes. Remember, the map is different from the world. The world remains the same, but each person has a different map of it. NLP is all about finding how you present yourself with your map of the world.

For example, people develop different coping strategies based on what they have experienced in the past and how they got through it. There can be many ways of coping; some are what is called "adaptive" and some are what is called "maladaptive". Some are a mix of adaptive and maladaptive methods. Adaptive methods of coping are when a person finds ways to get through challenges that are healthy and propel the person closer to their authentic self. Maladaptive coping mechanisms are coping strategies, which draw people away from their authentic self and are more unhealthy ways to get by. One example of an adaptive coping mechanism is creating a support structure. Let's say that a person has a good job, and then suddenly, they are laid off. This presents a challenge to the person: they must find a new job where they can get paid and do work which fits them. An example of an adaptive coping mechanism would be if this person reaches out to friends, family, and acquaintances for help. This is a strategy that the person has employed that will help them to build connections. An example of a maladaptive coping mechanism would be if this person depends on drugs to get them through this difficult time. The reason that this is maladaptive is that it will help them in the short term, by taking away the feelings of sadness or frustration that comes along with the situation. However, they start to build a dependence on drugs for treating their feelings, and eventually, they will have to find other ways to cope, as the drug use becomes unsustainable.

Chapter 8: Spotting Insecurity

The tactics of Dark NLP and Dark Psychology are used around us every day. From car dealerships to governmental organizations, to interpersonal relationships, dark NLP tactics are something you always have to look out for. So how do you protect yourself from being persuaded against your will? It takes some self-knowledge and exploration, but you'll be able to unmask the dark persuader if you give it some thought. Awareness is a huge part of the journey.

First, you should try to learn about your responses in certain situations. The car dealership is a great example of this. When you go into a sales situation, you should recount your goals before entering and try to center yourself. Then, as you enter into the battle of the sales situation, you should try to recognize your responses to the situation as challenges come up.

The dealer might try to tell you what you want. This is a common method of dark persuasion for people who are trying to sell you something. The salesperson will tell you, sometimes quite literally, that you want something that they have, even if it is something that you don't need or want. When someone tells you this, what is your response? Are you able to tell them no, I don't want that? How are you able to get away from their advances?

It takes some strength of personality to pull this off, after all, persuasive people can be very difficult to go against the grain with. When the dealer tells you that they have a car that you have to have, and they start to pressure you, try to see how you feel in your body at that moment. Are you feeling grounded? If not, try and remember that you have two feet on the floor and you are there in space, standing somewhere. You are not floating above the ground. You are strong and planted in your position.

Another way to maintain grounded ness is to relax. Don't let someone get all up in your face and make you feel uncomfortable. You should remember that whatever you are doing is your right and your place to be doing. You have earned it, and you have the power. When you allow your body to get uncomfortable and for stress to manifest in your body, you allow yourself to become ungrounded and un-centered, and this will lead you a lack of strength. People who are weak are more easily persuaded.

Intuition is key here. Sometimes, it may be difficult to tell who is using dark NLP techniques, whether it is for their goals or some other overarching goal of an organization, or whatever. Intuition is key to being able to detect when these techniques are being used against you. Let's say you start a new job. It is a sales job, and you are taken to a group interview where you are asked to convince the manager that you are good for the job. Group interviews, well, they aren't the best sign, but you are looking for a job right now and need the money, and you decide, whatever, you will go have a look. You do well in the group interview and you are selected as one of the people who will be joining the team. You start the training process and you notice that something is off. When you are participating in the training, you are shown videos and told how to operate in the company. You start to notice that some of the videos tend to denigrate the people who are being trained. You notice that people go along with it, and agree that this job is very honorable and that they should be ashamed of their past. The management then goes on to try and convince you that this job is one of the only jobs that are out there and that this is the only job you'll be able to get, so you better not quit. Then, you are started to be told how wonderful the benefits are, and that you might be able to make a fortune at this job if you work hard. You should pay attention to your intuition in this situation because it should be warning you about every single one of these persuasion tactics.

Your intuition will be able to recognize these as malevolent because we have a natural sense of self-protection as humans. Evolutionarily, we have become accustomed to trying to protect ourselves in the wild.

Learning to tune into intuition might be a difficult task, but you will get there eventually. Think about times in the past when you were able to detect someone lying. Maybe you saw a little smile in the corner of their mouth, or maybe the story just didn't add up. Whatever it was that allowed you to get some insight into their condition, that's what intuition is. Intuition is letting yourself trust yourself to see into someone else's soul. We all have that capacity, and in fact, we all have the capacity to read peoples' minds. It is just something that people rarely recognize and even less often learn to develop and embrace.

Spot the tricks used by manipulators

As soon as you have realized how knowledge of certain truths about yourself can enlighten you to notice manipulative tactics by other people, you will start to divulge from what you are to what a manipulator can do. With that in mind, if you wish to overcome manipulation, you need to be wary of the basic tactics used by manipulators. Once you have a firm grasp as to what you want and what you do not want, you can go head-to-head with a manipulator and even counter some of their most-used techniques. Nevertheless, always keep in mind that as soon as you realize that you are being manipulated, the manipulator loses. It is simply a matter of whether or not you wish to turn the tables and become the manipulator yourself.

Accusing your rival of what he is blaming you for

This is often referred to as the act of pointing to another person's wrongdoing. When enduring an onslaught and experiencing difficulty regarding safeguarding themselves, manipulators tend to reverse the situation. They blame their rival for committing the exact things that they are being blamed for. **"You state that I don't love you! I think it is you who does not cherish me!"**

Appealing to power

Numerous individuals are in wonderment of those in power or authority, or those who have status. What's more intriguing is that there are various images to which individuals experience extraordinary dedication. Remember, those who are easily manipulated admire those who are in power. Moreover, those who are in power are aware of their ability to control others by never criticizing them. Instead, they use complex misleading tactics to maneuver their thoughts and alter their decision-making process.

Rabble-rousers that effectively control individuals realize that the vast majority are promptly deceived along with these statements. As a result, they collaborate themselves with those in power. This entails the need to look for experts and other educated individuals that will support their perspectives or, at least, not criticize them.

Appealing to encounter

442

Gifted manipulators and con artists, as well as politicians, would often state that they already have experienced or encountered certain situations in their life, which makes them someone who is in power, which can be associated with the previous point. Nevertheless, this appeal to experience provides them with an image of someone who is capable; this may be used to attack their opponent's lack of experience, even though they themselves have experiences that are limited. You can easily identify this manipulation tactic at times when someone is trying to distort their capabilities about a particular subject.

Appealing to fear

People have fears. The unscrupulous manipulators realize a reality that individuals will, in general, respond crudely when any of these feelings of dread are enacted. Subsequently, they speak to themselves as being able to ensure individuals against these dangers, even when they are not capable of doing so. This is the same for when we talked about giving the target a glimpse of how their most desired outcome is achievable, without really providing it to them. Nonetheless, there are politicians and legislators who frequently utilize this methodology to ensure that individuals line up behind administrative experts and do what the legislature – that is, the thing that the government officials – need.

Appealing to sympathy

Manipulators are able to depict themselves and their circumstance to the public in a means to make them feel frustrated about their current situation.

Consider the understudy who, when gone up against the fact that she has not gotten her work done, whimpers, and says, "You don't see how hard my life is. Utilization of this ploy empowers the manipulator to occupy consideration from those individuals who may be going through the same thing. Nevertheless, appealing to sympathy is a tactic that most politicians would use to redirect the attention of the public to matters that do not affect their demise.

Appealing to well-known interests

Manipulators and tricksters are always mindful as to how they introduce themselves as persons who possess the right qualities and perspectives among the group of spectators, particularly, the sacred beliefs of the crowd. Everybody has a few partialities, and a great many people feel contempt toward a person or thing. Experts manipulators tend to stir up contempt and prejudices among the crowd.

They suggest that they concur with the group of spectators. They go about as though they have shared ideologies. They attempt to persuade the group of spectators that their enemy does not regard sacred the ideologies that they hold sacred.

Appealing to confidence

This technique is firmly identified with the past points; yet, it stresses what appears to have breezed through the trial of time. Individuals are regularly oppressed by the social traditions and standards of their way of life, just as social conventions. What is conventional to most tend to appear as if it is the correct decision? It is important to note that manipulators infer how they regard sacred the ideologies and beliefs that the group of spectators is familiar with. These individuals suggest that their enemy aims to obliterate the customs, as well as social conventions. Moreover, they do not stress over whether or not these conventions hurt guiltless individuals. They make the presence of being autonomous in the crowd's perspectives; yet, it would typically be the exact opposite thing. There is a realization that individuals are generally suspicious of the individuals who conflict with present social standards and built up conventions. They realize enough to stay away from these. As a result, there is a kind of restriction on how social traditions are unwittingly and carelessly bound.

Creating a false dilemma

A genuine problem happens when we are compelled to pick between two similarly unsuitable choices. A false dilemma happens when we are convinced that we have just two, similarly inadmissible decisions, when we truly have multiple potential outcomes accessible to us. Think about the accompanying case: **"Either we will lose the war on terrorism, or we should surrender a portion of our traditional freedoms and rights."**

Individuals are frequently prepared to acknowledge a false dilemma since few are agreeable with the complex qualifications. Clearing absolutes is actually a part of their manipulative tactics. There is a need to have clear and basic decisions.

Hedging what you state

Manipulators frequently hole up behind words, declining to submit themselves or give straightforward replies or answers. This enables them to withdraw at times of need. Whenever they are found forgetting data significant to the current situation, they would think of some other reason for not being able to come up with said information. At the end of the day, when forced, they may be able to give in; however, to be an excellent manipulator, you should renege on your missteps, conceal your mistakes, and gate keep what you state at whatever point conceivable.

Oversimplifying the issue

Since most people are uncomfortable at comprehending profound or unobtrusive contentions, there are those who are fond of oversimplifying the issue to further their potential benefit. **"I couldn't care less what the measurements inform us concerning the purported abuse of detainees; the main problem is whether we will be tough on crime. Spare your compassion toward the criminals' victims, not for the actual criminals."** The reality being overlooked is that the maltreatment of criminals is a crime in itself. Tragically, individuals with an over-simple mindset could not care less about criminal conduct that victimizes criminals.

Raising only complaints

Your adversary is giving valid justifications to acknowledge a contention; however, the truth of the matter is that your mind is made up and nothing can change it. Gifted manipulators would react with objections after objections. As their rivals answer one protest after another, they would proceed again to object and object. The implicit mentality of the manipulator is that **"regardless of what my rival says, I will continue to object because nothing else will convince me otherwise."**

Shifting the burden of proof

This act alludes to when an individual has the obligation to demonstrate some of his declarations. A good example would be the instance that happened inside a court. The examiner possesses the obligation to prove guilt past distrust. Furthermore, the defense should not claim the responsibility of having to prove innocence. Those who are capable of manipulating others do not have the need to assume the weight of evidence for what they attest to. Along these lines, they harness the right tool in shifting the burden of proof to their rivals.

Talking in vague generalities and statements

It is difficult to refute individuals when they cannot be bound. So, as opposed to concentrating on specifics, those who are capable of manipulating others tend to speak in the most unclear phrases that they can pull off. We have already talked about how certain statements and generalities can put another person in a daze, which makes it easier for them to be manipulated. This misrepresentation is well known with politicians. For instance, **"Overlook what the cowardly liberals say. It's the right time to be tough, to be hard on criminals, to punish terrorists, and be tough on those who disparage our nation."** Manipulators ensure they do not utilize particulars that may make individuals question what they are doing in the first place.

Telling enormous falsehoods and big lies

Majority of the people are liars, even about the little things; yet, there is still a reluctance to say things other than the truth. In any case, these individuals realize that in the event that you insist on a lit long enough, numerous individuals will trust you – particularly, on the off chance that you have the tools of mass media to broadcast a particular lie.

Every gifted manipulator is centered around what you can get individuals to accept, not on what is valid or false. They realize that the human personality does not normally look for reality; it looks for solace, security, individual affirmation, and personal stake.

Actually, individuals regularly would prefer not to know the reality, particularly, certainties that are agonizing, that uncover their logical inconsistencies and irregularities, and that uncover what they hate about themselves or even their nation.

There are so many manipulators that are exceptionally gifted in telling huge lies and, in this manner, causing those lies to appear valid.

Know your wants and fundamental human rights

The first and most important guideline when dealing with a manipulative person is to understand your rights and recognize when you are being manipulated. As long as you do not violate the rights of others when defending yours, you have every right to stand up for

446

yourself. However, if you harm others in the process of defending your rights, then you may have to forfeit them.

The fundamental human rights mark the boundaries of our lives. Of course, there are people in life who do not acknowledge and respect the rights of others. In particular, psychological manipulators want to interfere with your basic rights so they can control and use you for their selfish purposes. The good news is, you have the moral authority and power to declare and take control of your life. After all, you are in charge of your life.

overstepping them can lead to drastic results.

Chapter 9: Communication Models

Most of what we communicate to another person is done through tone and body language. Most of us have heard of this before. However, with just a little common sense, one can see how this works. Take for instance someone who is being standoffish to you during a conversation. What would that person's posture be? More than likely, he or she will be standing a bit taller and will have his or her arms crossed. There will also be a distinct gaze and possibly the look of not wanting to be there talking with you. Parents, if you have teenagers you know exactly what this looks like. You will see the rolling of the eyes, tapping of the toes, and the sporadic checking of the time on a watch or phone. Even though your teenager hasn't said "okay dad but I'm tired of listening to you and I've got to go," you knew that was the case. Why is this? It's because getting that point across didn't require a single word. It simply took a posture and a slight attitude.

The neuro-linguistic programming theory states that every aspect of the world that we live in is one or a blend of five key strategies. In older versions of NLP, experts have only discussed three of these fundamental strategies. However, over the past decade, psychologists have added two more.

Memory

We have talked about how we use our senses to gather data from the external world. Well, our memories come into play when we are processing these inputs. Notice how you tend to access certain experiences when you are trying to determine whether or not an act is good, neutral, or evil. Moreover, this is the same process utilized when you are learning from a mistake or relishing in the memory of your past achievements. You may be unconscious toward this process, but each and every one of us is always retrieving information from our memory so that we can use it in our decision-making and critical thinking.

Belief

As soon as you process these memories, you establish your own set of interpretations and beliefs. By looking at your experiences, you begin to allow yourself to believe in a higher state that is achievable. With this, you try to aim for something higher. Moreover, you also allow yourself to believe in concepts that will aid your journey in achieving something higher than your current state.

Motivation

The concept of motivation is a combination of memory, belief, and decision. You see, memory is accessed by the individual so that reality is set. Then, you start to compare this set reality to a higher state. You decide which of the options available to you can lead you this higher state. With all of these combined, you feel motivated to achieve your goals. Motivation is typically different from each individual as it would depend on one's belief and experience.

Decision

As soon as you realize that there is a higher state that can be achieved, you start to notice the options that are available to you, and you begin to evaluate which of these can help you achieve your goals. You undergo an assessment of what you have experienced in the past, your current situation, and your possible future. After which, you identify how each option can lead you to success. These will serve as your guide on the road to achieving your ideal future.

Learning

The strategy of learning incorporates memory, decision, and motivation so that you are much more efficient in achieving your goals. Memory is accessed so that you are much more knowledgeable as to how you can handle the current tasks. Moreover, your past decisions allow you to assess all of your successes and failures. As a result, you'll be inclined to make wiser decisions in the future. Motivation, on the other hand, will prevent you from making the same mistakes.

Anchoring

When it comes to anchoring, you are actually connecting memories to a stimulus. This stimulus, which is referred to by some as an anchor, becomes a set off to the initial reaction. Do note that a particular anchor does not necessarily have any rational connection to the initial reaction. However, the utilization of these anchors will allow you to stimulate reactions that can change your behavioral patterns toward a condition. The stimuli of sound, sight, smell, taste, and touch are used in neuro-linguistic programming to bring about a particular mindset. This situation can be a memory that you wish to access so that you can change your perspective in life into something more positive. As soon as the stimulus is initialized, it elicits a certain mindset with specific emotions and thoughts. This is why hearing an old song makes you feel nostalgic about your childhood.

In NLP, anchoring becomes useful because you are given a chance to associate certain triggers that you wish to achieve. You are given the power to establish an anchor, as well as create a stimulus and induce a state of mind that is essential for you to achieve success. For example: when someone you love gives you a memento, such as a locket, then this locket becomes the trigger. Moreover, your memories with that person become a state of mind. These two are closely tied together that at times when you look at the particular object, you immediately think about the individual who handed it to you, a resourceful state. These anchors can be either visual, kinesthetic, or auditory. You can utilize these as tools to create a mental image that is easily retrievable from your memory so that you are better able to facilitate a response. This tactic improves an individual's critical and subjective point of view of the environment.

You may ask how all of these are essential to dark psychology and the power of manipulation. Well, we have already discussed that in order to manipulate someone, you need to be able to read them first. If you want to read people, then you would need to have a keen eye as to what their anchors are. Aside from paying attention to how their body reacts to certain things, knowledge of these anchors can actually facilitate in the gathering of information on the one being manipulated.

Trans-derivational search

This kind of search, which is also known as TDS, is a phrase utilized at times when an individual attempt to search for the meaning of ambiguous statements. It is a fundamental human tendency to look for the missing pieces of data from our experiences and memory to provide significance to these incomplete statements. There is a present state of confusion experienced by the individual during the time when the search is being executed; this actually allows you to experience a trance-like feeling. Neuro-linguistic programming experts can easily put their patients into a trance-like condition or state of hypnosis because of this. You have a better chance of manipulating another person by taking advantage of the window at which they are experiencing TDS.

Chaining states

A great example of an NLP technique is when your chain states together. This is where you redefine your current emotional state into something more applicable to achieving success and learning. This can also be considered as a great manipulation technique for when you want to get rid of a bad habit. If a person has a habit of doubting themselves, there are certain methods that can be utilized so that the individual is encouraged to change their mindset and attitude; thus, paving the way to a completely new perspective of the world. By chaining states, you get to enhance one's perspective, whether it is for yourself or another person, as part of the human race. You will find yourself opening more to the idea of executing new things. You will also take on more risks and feel braver to face challenges that may come your way. The term used by psychologists is that you "chain" from one state of mind to something much more conducive to success or learning.

Metamodel

Bandler and Grinder also developed NLP's metamodel. This aims to create a broader dimension of one's perspective of the world. The metamodel typically includes certain questions that allow you to illustrate a limitless perspective of your own on an event, item, or a person. This uses language; however, you may or may not be fully aware of all the things being communicated. The process of deletion, generalization, and distortions are heavily involved in the grammar usage and semantics of the metamodel.

When you are communicating something to another person, you do not necessarily have to provide them with all of the details. You can delete ideas or terms without altering the overall thought and message of your story. There is also the possibility of leaving the mind wondering, confused, much like the basis of TDS, because of an incomplete statement and unspecified details.

Meta programs

When talking about the different strategies of NLP, it is crucial that we talk about metaprograms. These are what you follow through your model so that it would lead to a particular outcome. Metaprograms aid in your decision-making process for various situations based on what you have learned in communicating with other people, reading other people through their body language, and assessing their behavioral patterns. As soon as you have gained the necessary information and subjective experience to achieve your goal of manipulating people, these metaprograms will be the one to encourage you to act on these. Remember, how you act in certain situations is affected by the information you have gathered using your five basic senses and your experiences. Moreover, how you act in these current situations will probably be similar to how your reactions may be concerning other situations that are yet to come. As a result, an approach based on strategy or a behavioral pattern will be developed in you as a person.

Keep in mind that Meta programs in neuro-linguistic programming pose certain benefits. It helps you define your behavioral patterns and that of other individuals; it enhances your communication abilities, and it increases your understanding of the world. In turn, you are better able to handle various situations that may come your way. Furthermore, you are now more capable of relating with other individuals and grabbing every opportunity that may come your way. Of course, you are also much more equipped in manipulating other people. All of these can significantly aid you in your road to success. Do note that this is not a universal pattern, and it differs with every individual. Do not think of

452

this as the incorporation of a particular pattern inside you so that you are more successful in life, because it is not. It is more of the development of your way of thinking and acting so that you can bring out your best qualities and utilize them to help you achieve success.

Chapter 10: Generating Genuine Understanding

We all want to create relationships with ease. No one wants to feel lonely or unable to fit in with others. According to researches, success is mostly based on the relationships one creates. People who are able to initiate and maintain good, mutual, and productive relationships with others are more likely to succeed compared to those who do not maintain rapport.

Building good relationships do not come naturally to everyone. However, with NLP tools and perspectives, this skill can be learned and developed.

In any relationship, communication is inevitable. Basically, communication does not stop. Even when a couple fights and the two people give each other silent treatment, communication is still going on - they are telling each other about the stress, anger, and manipulation quietly.

If a frustrated teenager chooses to eat dinner in his/her room behind closed doors, He/she is communicating something to himself and the family. Even in the most neural situations, people still communicate through body language and movement of the eyes.

Simply, understanding that communication is continuously taking place can make a huge difference in most relationships. Since much of our communication is indirect, unconscious and nonverbal, knowing the messages we pass through body language and eye contact can help us to become more conscious of the things, we say and do to others. Human beings send out signals to each other all the time and becoming more aware of how we pass the message is the first step to better relationships.

Once we acknowledge that our perception is not the only reality, then it becomes easier to understand and communicate with others. We cannot see the world in the same way because everyone has a different model and map, leading to different behaviors. Such an understanding can help you to deal with different people, including the manipulators.

The first habit of highly successful people is to understand then seek to be understood. In today's world, most of us are in a rush; therefore, have no time to understand others before responding. Many of us listen to reply rather than to receive the message. NLP informs us that our personal map of the world is not a territory that requires protection. We can benefit more from understanding the maps of other people rather than staying in our own cocoons.

The people with good communication skills, high levels of understanding, and flexible behavior are more likely to control situations compared to the rigid ones. Even in the wild, animals, and plants that adapt to the changes in the environment very fast are more likely to survive longer than others. Businesses that accommodate the changes in the economy and social environments are more successful than those opposing them. The same applies to individuals.

Basically, a person who understands the maps believes, and practices of others can switch between them and reach a wider variety of people. He/she will also be able to establish good and lasting relationships. Anyone who becomes rigid to one way of doing things and thinking will gradually be left become irrelevant as the world changes.

Strong relationships are formed on communication. Without communication, people will not know how to handle others. For instance, if a person is doing something which you do not like and you fail to tell him/her so, he/she will probably do the same things without realizing they are affecting you. However, if you express yourself in a respectful manner, the person will avoid hurting you. A manipulator needs to be addressed firmly and effectively in order to deter him/her.

The true meaning of communication is found in the response it produces and the results we get. In most cases, we blame others for failing to understand us. However, NLP teaches us that we are responsible for passing the message, and if the other person does not understand, we need to change our method of communication. Again, all this is about flexibility – being able to understand others and adopting their ways. To pass the message across, you sometimes have to communicate in terms of the other person, by first understanding his/her world, and getting to know the map. You need to put your perspective aside for a while and assess things from the other side.

NLP encourages us to take responsibility and helps us to understand that people operate from one of the two perspectives – cause and effect. When a person is operating 'at cause,' he/she sees that the control is in his/her hand and that it is possible to change or improve the situation. On the other hand, a person operating 'at effect,' blames other people for the current circumstances. When 'at effect,' we blame others for our failures. When ta effect, we take the responsibility and strive to improve the situation.

In all the perspectives, the truth is that we are in control of our circumstances – making the decision on where we should work. If a relationship is not working out the way you hoped, there are high chances of blaming the other person. In fact, a majority of us will want the other person to be put to task for our failures. The ideal plan should be to assess your own behavior and identify things that need to be changed within you. When operating 'at cause,' you are more likely to improve your circumstances than when at effect. NLP will help you to act from at cause through seeking to understand the perspective of the other person and listening to them with the intention of helping.

NLP helps us to build better relationships by making us understand that people are not their behavior. Technically, all of us are doing the best we can with what we have. The resources we have at our disposal are major determinants of our behaviors. If we had more or fewer resources and a different perspective, we would behave differently. Such an understanding can help you build a better relationship and deal with manipulators.

Do not label people based on their current behavior, may be given a different circumstance, and they would act better or worse. Maybe that manipulator had a very rough childhood, thus making him/her feel the need to be tougher than everyone else. Maybe the mind controller is feeling weak and afraid on the inside and is looking for ways to act have control. Note, however, that you do not have to allow people to manipulate you just because you are feeling empathic. Even though that empathy is pushing you to help such people, do not make yourself a victim – Protect yourself first. After all, you cannot offer what you do not have.

Behaviors change all the time as we grow and learn. What we consider as bad relationships can be turned around using NLP, once we learn how to be proactive and take control.

Chapter 11: Spotting Romantic Interest

One darker area where NLP can be applied is with influence. While the majority of people who use NLP are going to use it to help enhance their success in the dating world, there are those who have devoted themselves to learning some darker applications when it comes to what you can do with the process of NLP. These are generally not accepted as part of the social norms and morals, but they can ensure that the predator is able to get what they want.

Patterns Seduction

Patterns can be one of the techniques of dark NLP that can be used to seduce. A series of patterns gained notoriety when you are in the community of seduction, and they are now known as the banned patterns. The reason that these patterns earned their name is because they are seen as too amoral and too dark for most in the community to accept.

Since these patterns are going to have a good deal of notoriety with them, they are going to be sought out in some way or another by the community. But they are still going to be hard to find. These patterns are going to be presented in this section so that you can see how the good NLP and the dark NLP are similar, and how they are going to be different.

One of the patterns that fall into dark NLP is going to be called the shadow and the rising sun. This is one that is often put with the seduction community because it is going to draw upon some of the ideas that are found in the Jungian psychology, where it is going to work to unlock some of the dark sides of women, the hidden parts that come with her personality. This one is going to be achieved by the seducer talking about the idea of contrasts. They are focusing on talking just about imagery that contrasts, in order to show off the idea of darkness as light and dark, day and night, and yin and yang.

The seducer is going to take this even further by talking about how each person has their own dark side and how this is the idea of a rising sun that still casts a shadow with it. The seducer can then invite their target to step into their own dark side and to start accepting and viewing the world with this new lens. This is going to help put the target into a state of more susceptibility, where they may be willing to act in a way that they wouldn't do in other circumstances.

Another kind of technique that can be used is going to be done along with the above technique, but some things are going to be changed around. This one is known as the hospital pattern. With this pattern, the seducer is going to work to fluctuate the emotional state of the target between extremes, either extreme pleasure or extreme pain, and it is going to rapidly change between the two at regular intervals.

This rapid change of emotional states, which will go between the extremes multiple times, is going to help to make it so that the target feels unstable with their emotions, which makes them more susceptible to the influence. When the target reaches this new susceptible state, the seducer would then be able to anchor the perception of the target in any manner that they wish. They will usually make sure that the feelings of the target are going to be turned to feel immense pleasure with the seducer, which allows the seducer to trigger these kinds of feelings on demand.

Another dark usage of NLP is going to be with a pattern interrupt. This is when the seducer will use some of their dark NP in order to stop the actions of the target, and they want to reduce the defense mechanisms and rationality of their target as much as possible.

For example, if the target is talking to their seducer and they begin to list off some of the logical reasons why it doesn't make sense to be with the seducer any longer, when the seducer is going to try and distract them a bit and get their mind on something else entirely. They may say something like "what is your favorite color?" This stops the thought process of the target and can stop their defense mechanisms at the same time.

NLP has on occasion been used in more of a dark way to make it so that the target begins to question which memories they have that are real, and which ones may have been fabricated along the way. there are techniques out there that are going to put the target into a state of relaxation so they float between being awake and being asleep. This works for the seducer because the target is going to be highly suggestible during that time.

Both of the above can be used by the seducer in order to disrupt the feelings of identity that the target has. This causes the target to question the different values and beliefs that they have about who they are. This is sometimes what is used as the first step in brainwashing when you want to make sure that the target is a blank slate and that you are able to fill it in with what you want.

Hypnotic Seduction

The first thing that has to happen if you would like to use the ideas of dark NLP in a romantic way is to start eliminating some of the limiting beliefs you may have had in the past about this subject. There are a few limiting beliefs that often keep showing up, and they are going to make it harder for you to have the romantic seduction that you are looking for.

The most common of these limiting beliefs is that if you use the ideas of dark NLP to seduce someone, it is somehow seen as wrong or immoral. There are two sources for this particular limiting belief. The first is that the view of seduction needs to happen in a particular way, and the second issue is that there is really a big misunderstanding of exactly what the dark NLP seduction is going to entail.

We often believe that seduction needs to look a certain way because we have seen it in that manner through books and movies, rather than experiencing it firsthand. This can make us believe that things that make the best move scenes are going to be the ones that represent the process of one person becoming attracted to another. And if there is anything that goes against this in our lives, or in the lives of others, then it is going to mean that we reject it when something goes against our conceptions.

There are also those who are against the idea of the hypnotic seduction because they think that it takes the choice away from the other person, and they think that this kind of seduction is going to force the target into doing something that they don't want to do. However, this is not the truth.

With hypnotic seduction, we are basically learning how to connect better with someone, to connect with them on a deeper level than we could with other techniques, and we learn how to trigger some good emotions when the other person thinks about you. The target is going to

460

have all of the freedom of choice that they want, and they will not be forced into the situation. But you are just using your own influence your chances by your ability to give the other person a good experience and connect with you far faster than what you can with some of the other techniques.

And then there is the issue that some people are going to be really worried that they are not able to understand, or that they won't be able to actually use, some of the techniques that are needed to use the dark NLP for romantic things. This objection sounds logical, but it is going to be used as a type of mask of something deeper, such as having a fear of connecting to some of the other people in your life, or some other personal insecurity. You can overcome these and learn how to use dark NLP to help you to do well with personal romance, but you have to take the steps first to make this happen.

Mind Control with NPL for Love and Relationships
Is it love or manipulation?
There is a lot of information about relationships and love today. Social media, websites, counselors, and every other person who feel they know about love are willing to offer advice. Majority of us will listen to any advice about love. This is because love brings hope, and the world needs more of it. We hope that someone out there loves us, be it a parent, a close friend, or a partner. We look for ways to find lasting love and making it stay. The thought of an empowering and sustainable love brings us hope.

The thought of true love is enchanting and easy, but so many of us fall for the wrong people. A large number of people have fallen in love and not received the same. It was the hope for a better tomorrow that keeps people in the wrong manipulative relationships. How can you tell the difference between true love and manipulation?

True love is clear while manipulation is confusing
A healthy relationship has nothing withheld. The partners put everything on the table, and they feel comfortable and clear in its dynamics. Healthy relationships have love because the people involved have room to build each other. In manipulative relationships, there is no room for love because everything is chaotic. You cannot grow in this

461

relationship because problems pill up, and the manipulator is not willing to sort them.

Healthy love offers freedom, while manipulation involves control

Love is not an excuse to limit each other's space. In fact, for love to exist, there has to be space for every person to think rationally. The relationship should not limit freedom, especially freedom of thought. The only way a relationship can survive is if everyone can think and communicate without limitation. Healthy love allows the partners to be happy outside the relationship and to follow their personal desires. True love is not over-possessive.

Manipulative relationships cut out freedom. The partners become socially isolated and will do very little to explore their passions outside the relationship. Unhealthy relationships have very few friends and will limit their activities because of manipulation. Normally, the manipulative partner crushes the freedom of the other. Once a relationship becomes isolated to this extent, the two people become co-dependent and toxic to each other.

True love disagrees but manipulation fights

As the saying goes, all couples fight. When a couple has healthy love, they are able to move on even after disagreements. When a relationship is healthy, differences in opinions are not taken as the sign of the end; neither are the sources of blame. Different people have different opinions, and being in a relationship does not mean that you agree on everything. Healthy love will encourage this and even take it as an opportunity to grow. Healthy people allow others to have differing opinions.

However, manipulative relationships stand for my way or the highway. The partners do not agree to disagree; rather, they take every fight personally and destroy the relationship. Every difference in opinion is seen as an offense and a belittlement to the relationship. In unhealthy relationships, the disagreements escalate into horrible silent treatments and full-blown arguments until one of the partners (normally the passive one) succumbs and apologizes for the conflict or changes the plan altogether to fit the needs of the manipulator.

Healthy love will compliment while manipulation will insult

True love is very empowering. Each partner looks for the good in the other, becomes proud of it, and acknowledges it emotionally and verbally. Healthy love is supportive, communicative, and nurturing. The partners encourage each other to live their dreams. They pull each other up when there is some sort of failure. Healthy love wants the best and highest life experiences for everyone.

In manipulative relationships, the partners (especially the manipulative one) do not seem to enjoy the success and independence of the other. In fact, they somehow relish the moments of failure of their partners and will often tell the other "I told you so" when things go wrong. A manipulative partner will fear the independence of the spouse. Therefore, he/she will withhold emotional support. Behind these relationships is a lot of emotional violence. The intention of the manipulator is to keep their partner down so that he/she does not become strong enough to leave and be happier.

Healthy love is based on relationship while manipulation is based on agenda

In most cases, it is hard to differentiate between manipulation and love. That is why many of us stay in manipulative relationships thinking that it is love. Manipulation is agenda oriented, while true love is healthy and is rooted in relationship. In a healthy relationship, partners are not all about having power and control over each other –

There are openness and flexibility. No one needs to force the other into anything because the level of trust allows everyone to choose, be real and also vulnerable.

On the other hand, manipulative relationships are about power. Unhealthy love does not leave room for vulnerability because it is an opportunity for hurting one another. This love is bent to one side – the agenda of one person is more important than the other. In these relationships, the concept of love is measured by how much one person is willing to give to the other. Manipulative partners are not in a relationship to love; rather, they want to be loved. They convince the victim to do things for them then claim it represents love.

Healthy love is full of honesty wile manipulative relationships are hypocritical

When people are in a healthy relationship, they possess the integrity to stay honest with each other. They will tell each other the truth even though it hurts. Healthy love involves empathy; thus, active listening occurs – defenses are brought down, leaving room for truth and understanding. Feedback is given and received with a level of understanding and respect. Healthy love will inspire the spouses to become better for each other and maintain the relationship.

On the other hand, a manipulative relationship involves one person placing rigid rules upon the other. Interestingly, the manipulative partner does not live by the same rules he/she sets. When the manipulator is confronted, he/she becomes defensive and deflects all the problems to the partner.

Chapter 12: Creatively Collaborating and Resolving Conflicts

Let's look at a technique called "conflict integration." This is for conflict resolution. This is a good technique to do away with things such as bad habits, procrastination, and indecisiveness along with other conflicts. It also can create harmony within your mind. This technique is also intended for use with yourself and not others. Here is how to carry out NLP conflict integration. As with the others, first we need to identify the part creating unwanted behaviors. Then identify a part which is working in opposition. Bluntly speaking, identify the good and the bad parts. Then you need to create mental images of both. You can use anything which can metaphorically represent a part. Place your attention on one of the parts then move to the other. Ask each about their intentions. Remember this is metaphorically speaking. After this, identify the resources that each part has at its disposal. Here, you must merge both parts, the good and the bad, together as one. Then you create a third part and this is both of the other parts combined. You must absorb the third part in deeply then follow this by a few moments of relaxing and taking everything in. The last thing to do is look at your future decisions and consider how you are going to approach them differently now that you have created the third part which should allow you to approach it in a better fashion.

One common reason why people are bullied and manipulated is, they hunger for adoration and attention. Maybe there is a kind of attention you craved for as a child, but no one offered it to you. Or, maybe you are lacking that adoration from one of your current important relationships. If the manipulator detects this, he/she will take advantage and flatter you, saying how wonderful, different, and special you are. He/she will further claim that you have been really kind and helpful and thus deserves better. Because you have a void that needs to be filled with that attention, you blindly believe in whatever they say. In fact, you might take the credit while thinking, "I am special because I care and help others selflessly." Now, that state sets a stage for you to be played. Somehow you will be easily manipulated because you feel the need to help the person and not let him/her down or you want to feel good about yourself.

On a deeper psychological level, maybe the reason you are allowing people to manipulate you is that you do not know what it is like to be manipulated. That urge to feel wanted and valued can make you look for ways to make people need you. Consequently, you become vulncrable to manipulative people who will take advantage of you. You think that being available gives you power over a relationship. Well, it won't. And gradually, you realize that although the attention and feeling of being needed are good, you do not want people to use you. Then you will look for ways to get out of the manipulative relationships.

You can be manipulated for a long time before you realize it and choose to defend yourself. When you realize that what you considered as love is royal exploitation, your feelings can shift from benevolence and kindness to ultimate, hurt, anger, frustration, and resentment. Interestingly, you might realize that some of the people around you had tried to warn you. Once you start feeling those dark and hostile emotions towards the manipulators, it stirs a conflict because all along you have been kind, benevolent, and caring. Then you might feel guilty for having negative feelings towards a person you considered good towards you. As a result, you might do more in an attempt to cover up for your shame.

Now, before we start to dive more into the idea of NLP and how it is used, we first need to explore the idea of self-mastery. If you don't have a good mastery of yourself before jumping into all of this, then there is no hope that you will be able to master the thoughts, feelings, and emotions of another person. We are going to take a look at the importance of self-mastery, what this means, and how you can learn to control yourself so that it is much easier to start controlling other people with NLP.

You might also be a victim of manipulation because a person you considered close to you, such as a spouse asked for a favor, and you said no. Maybe the person went ahead and told you how pathetic hopeless and unlovable you are therefore you look for ways to prove them wrong. Maybe you felt guilty for letting the person down. Therefore, you are looking for ways to cover for it even though every one of your instincts has informed you that it's time to choose a stand. In fact, you might end up doing more for the person than before.

If you have any kind of relationship with a manipulator and are looking for a way to put it to an end, the first step is to learn how to say "No." Practice in front of a mirror if you must. Regardless of the situation, you need to defend yourself. Say "no" and when the manipulator asks for a reason, just reply "because I do not want to do that." Be warned, however, that the manipulator will look for ways to get to you. He/she might say things to make you feel guilty for turning them down and not explaining. Remember that you do not have to explain yourself. If a manipulator threatens by saying they will hurt themselves, say "I hope you will not do that." If he/she threatens you, tell them that they need to leave, or you will involve authority. However, do not bluff when you state your boundaries, mean it.

Know your outcomes

The first key that we need to take a look at when it comes to mastering ourselves is to know what you want, no matter what the situation is about. If you have no idea what you are aiming for, it is impossible to know which strategy is going to be the best, and which one you should pursue. Always go into a situation with a good and clear objective in mind. Realize that any kind of objective, even if it is not perfect, is going to be better than having no objective in place at all. You do have the option to adjust your goals and refine them as you go, but at least start out with some kind of goal in mind.

It is important that you make the intended outcome, also known as your target, as specific and clear as possible. You will be able to do this as you go along and learn what works for you. But you never want to make the goals too vague, even in the beginning, because then it is impossible to measure these goals, and how can you assess how far you have come. Make sure that when you are picking your goals, you go with something that is definitive, which you can measure the progress for, and which has an ending that is clear.

Know your drives

Knowing what outcome, you want to get out of the situation is a good first step when you are trying to work on self-mastery. But it isn't the last step. Without taking the time to know your deepest drives and the things that motivate you to take some massive actions right here and now, it is impossible for you to reach your outcome in an effective way. To start with, you should sit down and write out anything that comes to your mind when you are thinking about the things that motivate you. Don't question yourself or make any judgments during this time; just spend some time writing down anything that comes to your mind. When you are done and can't come up with anything new to put here, then you can put down the pen and stop writing. Now there is a list of different ideas and topics in front of you. Go through and rank each one based on which one gives you the most motivated, what gives you the second motivation, and so down.

You can then list out the three top motivators, the ones that you feel the most motivation from and you want to concentrate your energy on now. You should write these out on their own piece of paper, going in order from the highest to the lowest. You can then link these three drives back to the outcome that we talked about before. You can then start to see how your goal is going to relate back to those drives. And overall, this is going to ensure that you have the right motivation tied back to the goals, and you are more likely to work hard to reach those goals.

Know your values

At this point, you have now gone through and established your intended outcome, and then linked it back to one of the main things that will motivate your lie. This is very powerful, but to make sure that you can really increase your self-mastery to a new level, you will need to establish your values and then link them back to the intended outcome as well.

There is no point in us taking the time to suggest which values you would like to consider because this is a very personal topic. Just think about the things in life that are going to matter the most to you. And then write down the values that are going to be unable to help you keep those things. Once you have been able to establish all of the major values, take some time to rank them from the most powerful to the lead powerful, just like we did with the drives earlier. Once you have your top three values figured out, you can write them down on their own pieces of paper.

Just like what we did with the drivers earlier, you will want to go through and link your values into not only your outcome but also to your drives. You want to ensure that all of these factors are going to be in alignment, to ensure that you are focused on a deep and a subconscious level to achieve your own outcome. This may take a bit more time to accomplish, but it really does some wonders when it comes to ensuring that all of your motivations are going to reinforce each other, and keeps you away from isolating each one.

Your motivation can be temporary, but your habits are not

To make sure that you are able to achieve your intended outcome, you must make sure that you fully understand your values and drives. To motivate yourself about the outcome that you want, you must think about all of the ways that you are going to feel once you have been able to achieve that goal. For example, if your goal is to get that big promotion at work, imagine how you are going to feel, and what will change in your life, once you actually get for that promotion.

Once you have a clear idea of what your goal is and what achieving that goal is going to mean for you, you will find that it is much easier to stay motivated and to control yourself in order to reach that goal. However, motivation is easier to attain that it is to keep around for a long time. That's way, once you have your motivation, you should use it to help you build up the proper habits that are needed to support the outcome. If you don't make that effort now, you will end u falling into patterns that don't support your values and your influence in life.

It isn't enough for you to just establish some habits, and have motivations in place, but they are done in isolation. It is so important that you are able to link them together. You can do this by ensuring you link the motivation to the habits that you want to carry out on a regular basis. You may find that the anchoring technique from NLP can work for this. For this one, you would trigger your state of motivation by envisioning the good feelings that are triggered when you achieve the goal. You would then use a repeated physical gesture, such as touching your wrist when you carry out the routine habit.

Using this gesture is going to link the feeling of motivation to your physical gesture. You can then trigger this motivation just by doing the physical trigger. It is that easy. Once you have had the time to create these habits, you are going to keep going through and following through with them, even when you have lost out on some of the motivation. There are going to be days that are tough and days when your motivation is going to be very low. But if you develop the habits early on, you will continue to work towards your goals, and you will achieve them, even when things aren't as easy as they once were.

One of the hardest things to work on when it is time to start working with NLP is to learn how to master yourself. Once you have mastered how to handle all of the goals and dreams of your own, then you will have more control over dealing with control over others.

Conclusion

Thank for making it through to the end of this book. Anyone is able to learn how to work with NLP. It is not a secret that is just meant for some. The problem is that too many people are held back by not understanding what NLP is all about and they may decide that their morals don't allow for this kind of behavior. Because of this, they are going to shy away from even hearing about NLP, despite all of the benefits that this can bring to them.

This puts you at a distinct advantage over the others. You will be able to utilize the skills that we discussed in this guidebook to your own advantage, using the skills and some of the other options that we talked about, in order to make sure that you get what you want from those who are in your life. And since most people aren't expecting this to occur to them, you are going to end up being the winner in the long run. When you are ready to learn a little bit more about NLP, especially when it comes to dark NLP make sure to use this guidebook to make sure that you get started on the right track.

If you find the techniques that work best for you, then you will be more comfortable with manipulation as a whole, and you can work your way up to taking bigger risks and facing greater challenges. As long as you take the time to develop your newfound abilities and use them as responsibly as you can, then you will be guaranteed at least some level of success in your life. You are already a powerful and skilled manipulator, and frequent practice and occasional review sessions will help you develop into a master of dark psychology, manipulation, and influence.

Persuasion Techniques

Learn to Influence People through Manipulation, NLP, and Body Language. Understand Human Behavior and Mind Control

Daniel Peterson

Table of Contents

Introduction

Persuasion is an essential part of human communication and is a powerful tool when used in the right way. In this book, you learn many of the same secrets used by those who have successfully built up an influence on the people in their lives. While the art of persuasion has been a key tool in the lives of marketers and business people of all sorts, you learn that persuasion is a tool we can all use to our advantage. Whether you're a business owner trying to boost your bottom line or you're a mother trying to convince her children to eat their vegetables, persuasion is how you will accomplish your goals.

All of us want to have influence over people and get them to do what we want. Our motives may be evil or benign, that doesn't matter. The fact is that every day you face situations that make you wish you could get people to do what you want them to do. You may want to convince your boss to give you that raise, get your children to listen to you, win an argument, sell something, or get people to vote for you. You can do it the easy way by trying to cajole them or present your side of the argument and take the chance that they'll say no. Or you can do it the easier way by being persuasive, using subconscious techniques, and basically manipulating people into doing or saying what you want.

The purpose of this book is to go the latter way and teach you to understand people, comprehend what motivates them, and use that to your advantage.

You must carefully choose which detail to exemplify depending on whom you're speaking to. These are just a few examples of personalizing the message depending on the receiver. The principal goes beyond the business world to other facets of life. You should now be in a position to do the same depending on your situation.

People respond better to something they can see as opposed to plain words. Give the listeners time to process the information, then communicate again.

To make others see your point of view, you have to communicate with conviction. Make your listener see that there is a limited time. This is a strategy mostly used in marketing.

There is no doubt that having this skill and perfecting it can bring you vast advantages. But how does one acquire such an ability? Can you learn to be persuasive? Well, these are the exact questions we are going to answer in this e-book. The short answer is yes, persuasion is a skill you can acquire and yes, I'm going to teach you how. As for the benefits it can bring you...you'll learn that, too.

After learning the techniques in this book and the basic neuroscience behind it, you'll be better prepared to get the things you want when you want them. It may be surprising to know that we all need to use the art of persuasion in some aspect of our lives. In fact, while you may have purchased this book in an effort to boost your business or to advance your life in some way, the reality is that you're already used persuasion tactics to get where you are now.

The challenge in exercising this skill has little to do with mastering other types of arts but it has to do with understanding some of the basic fundamentals of the mind. We all have the ability but it is actually knowing how to recognize it and use it to our best advantage that will help us to achieve our goals. We hope that through the pages of this book, you will be able to bring to them up to the surface and put those techniques you already know out in plain view where you can analyze them and make them more tangible thus unlocking your hidden potential. The more you know about them the more comfortable you'll be with using them and the more advantages you'll get in applying them in your daily life.

Anyone can learn the fine art of persuasion, and even go further into the controversial territories of influence and mind control...you just need to go through the process, step by step and learn how. Luckily, this guide is here to help you out and teach you everything you need to know, with explanations, specific techniques and practical applications of your persuasive powers. Don't wait one minute longer to put your skill into practice. Start learning how to improve your persuasive skills now. Good luck!

Chapter 1: Meaning of Being Persuasive

The ability to persuade is a neutral power, if you want to completely master the art of persuasion, you need to understand the idea of neutrality. Keep in mind that the rules and capabilities of persuasion are neither good nor evil. Similar to nuclear technology, which can be utilized to generate electricity or create an atomic bomb, the power to influence others can be used to establish cooperation or to force submission. Whether the result is positive or negative depends on the individual using these principles and how he uses them.

Some people want to succeed regardless of the costs. They are willing to use all possible tricks and abuse the principles of persuasion.

In addition, they often use violence, temptation, blackmail, bribery, and guilds to get what they want.

On the other hand, if used appropriately, persuasion can help in promoting the growth of an entire community. By using persuasion, we can forge peace agreements between warring countries, initiate fund-raising programs, and convince drivers to follow traffic rules.

Persuasion requires adaptation. To become a successful persuader, you can't just imitate what others are doing. You need to have a concrete plan that you can use for the situations that you will be facing. Also, you should not simply memorize all the techniques written on this book. You need to have a clear idea as to which specific tools or techniques should be used for any given scenario. In order to acquire this skill, you need to proactively observe, examine, learn, and apply the principles of proper persuasion.

Successful persuasion has long-lasting effects. Effective persuasion is great since it offers enduring effects, but it entails detailed study and solid commitment on the speaker's part. You need to devote time and effort if you want to make sure that your statements have a lasting influence.

Although short-term persuasion tactics may seem to be ideal since they require minimal effort, you will be wasting more time and effort in the long run since your listeners will easily forget about your statements.

In the end, you will have to repeat the process of persuading your audience to make them believe what you are saying.

Have you ever noticed that there are entire jobs and industries centered around persuasion in our society? Think about car salesmen and their slick presentation on their newest model of vehicle. Or about lawyers and the clever way they need to present the facts in order to sway the jury and the judge. Even the most basic sermon in church relies on the preacher's ability to persuade his congregation. These aren't things we really think about that often, but now that I point it out, you can't stop thinking about it.

Going even further, there are industries whose sole purpose is to persuade. Take motivational speaking or the advertising industry – these people's job is to tap into your innermost thoughts and desires and use them to convince you to do something they want. It's more than a little unnerving that someone else – a stranger, at that – can have this much influence over you. It's almost like mind control, which we're going to talk more about in a following chapter.

What makes a person convincing? Why are they persuasive, and you aren't? This is the answer we're going to pursue in this e-book, but I'm telling you now, there is no single, short answer to that question.

What makes this persuasive influence so difficult to pin down and elusive is precisely this almost mosaic quality it has. It's the result, the perfect merger of several important aspects that you wouldn't normally attribute to such an influence. But hidden away, unbeknownst to the average person, the owner of this skill is a powerful person, in a powerful position, who benefits from most – or all – of these different qualities that make them who they are.

These aspects of their being don't only affect them, but affect us, as well. That's the fascination around it. It's all psychological, it's an overwhelming and sometimes unintentional psychological influence on the people around them.

Confidence

Confidence is the absolute most important aspect when it comes to persuasion. There's no doubt it's been scientifically proven that it's easier to persuade people when you're confident. That's because it's just assumed you're an authority on the topic and they'll listen to you, because they have no knowledge or experience, but you seem to have both.

It's also crucial to understand that humans are doubtful creatures. We're not very confident and we don't really believe in our own abilities or even experience, so when someone comes along and appears to be confident and to know more, we follow them like a herd of dim sheep.

It is precisely this confidence along with other traits that you will have to acquire in order to succeed in your persuasive endeavors and I aim to have taught you how to do it by the time this book ends. Slowly, but surely, you will become accustomed to becoming the confident one people look up to, instead of just another person who used to be dazzled by self-assured people.

If you've ever wondered what makes people convincing and how do become like them, then this is your answer, my friend. Some people have this innate ability to persuade, but that doesn't mean they have to have the advantage. You too can learn this with a bit of interest and effort.

On the outside, you're this dazzling, confident creature that can persuade anyone into anything because you've mastered all the important contributing factors: confidence, eye contact, body language, manner of speaking, tone, facial expressions, as well as your general demeanor.

Eye contact

Eye contact is good, but not really? Not at all. Eye contact is welcome and powerful, as long as it's employed at the right time and in the right manner. When you're trying to convince someone, making eye contact at key moments in your speech will strengthen your points, make you seem sincere and attract attention. Making eye contact the whole time will only make people nervous and on edge.

Body language

Make yourself look vulnerable. Make them laugh. Are they turned away from you? Attract their attention. One of the most important lessons in persuasion is to not only concentrate on yourself and what you're doing or saying, but also on your audience.

Manner of speaking

It'll come as no surprise that the way you speak can influence the opinion of those who listen to you, as well as the level of persuasion you are able to enact. Confidence is, again, key. But this time, it won't be displayed physically, but verbally.

Referring repeatedly to yourself will make the experience seem personal and will make you seem sincere, while referring to your audience gives them the ability to relate to what you're saying; it makes it seem more personal to them. The trick is to get them emotionally involved and you're in.

Facial expressions

Creating the impression that you mean what you say involves your face, because it will be the very first to betray you or, on the contrary, help you enforce your message. A serious, focused facial expression will give you much-needed gravity to convince an audience, while a happy, annoyed, or bored face will cause the audience to dismiss you.

But the ultimate way to exude authority and confidence is to just seem very relaxed. Why? Because if you're relaxed, then surely you're not worried about anything. You're not nervous. You're comfortable, you don't feel out of place. On the contrary: you own the place, that is what you're trying to convey.

There has to be an ease in the way you talk and you can never let your audience see it on your face that you're thinking, concentrating, panicking, **etc.** Most of all, you need to seem in control, from head to toe – relaxed face muscles, inviting eyes, and no scrunching or grimacing!

General demeanor

In other words, read the room. What's the atmosphere like? What kind of energy can you sense? Are people tired? Is there an upbeat feeling you can identify? Is there a sadness that overwhelms the space? Match your energy accordingly.

But if you act sympathetic and match their mood, they'll be able to relate and will be more open to listening to you. Perhaps it can seem almost manipulative to some people, but this is something all people employ in the persuasion business, from lawyers to salespeople to your local priest.

Persuasion is motivation

People don't buy **needs**; they buy **wants.** If you want to persuade them, you have to motivate them to act accordingly to their deep desires and wants. They will do it, and they will rationally justify their actions later. Usually, the one thing that separates a successful persuasive person from everyone else is the power of influence. The following are some of the tactics that have great potential in helping you to increase your persuasive powers. These tactics are not plucked out of thin air; they have been proven through psychological research.

The very best way to persuade your audience, especially if they are definitely not agreeing with you, is to speed up your pace of talking. Listen to someone who is talking fast; don't you find it distracting? Can you actually hear or pick out any flaws in the argument? Thought not. The opposite is also true; when you are talking with an audience that is definitely on your side, slow down your speech, let them hear exactly what you are saying and give them the time they need to agree with you a little bit more.

Talking with confidence is also a great way to boost your persuasive power. In fact, it has been proven beyond a doubt that confidence is even better than accuracy when it comes to earning trust from other people. Most people prefer to take advice and learn from someone who is confident, even going so far as to forgive and forget about a poor track record in someone who exudes confidence. Unfortunately, in a competitive situation, this can result in some people who offer advice, who want people to follow them, exaggerating just how confident they really are.

Swearing can actually persuade your audience

Just light swearing of course. If you go overboard and litter your words with profanity, you will lose all of your credibility and any respect your audience may have had for you. Recently, researchers gathered 88 participants and split them into three groups.

Get them to agree with you about something

When you attempt to sell something, be it a service, a product, or an idea, come up with a statement or a view that your audience can definitely agree with and get it out there in the open right from the start, even if it has nothing to do with the idea you are selling.

Chapter 2: Helping People

We are indeed human at the end of the day. It is because of this very reason that we get to dwell allot on the opinion of others in everything that we do. We always desire and adore getting validation from others so that we can subconsciously decide whether or not we shall be depressed in this age of the millennial, the norm has become to just brag about their wealth on social media. A lot of these bragging are often than not the truth. This ultimately leads to one having a loose relationship with reality. Self-deception of this type can dig deep into the human spicy, that a victim of these may one day wake up and realize that their perfect world is only existent within their maids. Depression will closely follow suit. The first step to attempting to defend yourself from persuasion and manipulation is confronting the situation and taking the stance of breaking off any illusions you may have. You will not be able to proceed normally with your life. You have to be wary of the fact that you are in control of your own choices. Then make the conscious choice of seeing things for what they are. That deal, which seems too good to be true, could actually be just that... too good to be true. The other thing you should follow is to definitely trust your instincts. There are times that a lie has been told to you in the most skilled way imaginable, that you will end up believing. But you can feel an imbalance on some instinctive level between what should be, what is, and then what is being projected onto you. There may be no physical signs to show that hey, something is wrong, but you feel something is wrong. The next important thing when you ask questions is to listen to the responses. This may sound somewhat unbelievable because you'll listen to the answers. The truth is that our self-disappointment can make us choose the answers we receive. We tell ourselves that we listen, but we only pay attention to the answers we want to hear rather than to the answers we receive. You may have broken the illusions around you, but some of you are still clinging to the comfort of those illusions. The pain of confronting the situation would prevent you from listening to the real answers to your questions. Actual listening requires a certain sense of detachment, but this time around not from reality. You have to get rid of your emotions. Your detachment from our emotions would lead you to the next step, which would logically process the new information. It can complicate situations more than they already are to act irrationally. It makes your exit strategy so much difficult to let all the emotions simmer and spring to the surface. When you face the truth, the irrational part of you may want you to let it all go hell. Your rightly justified anger can inspire you to take steps to calm your emotions in the short term. But you may come to regret these actions in the long term. I'm not saying that you should deny your emotions; I'm not saying that you do not act on these emotions. First deal with the situations and later deal with your emotions.

Act quickly

It's great that you have come to terms with the reality of things. But defense against these dark manipulative tactics entail so much more. While attempting to defend you from the claws of these manipulators, is often intense and exhilarating at first. This intensity of these emotions may cause one to slowly slide into denial. The more you delay in taking any action is usually what accelerates the onset of this denial, and when it happens, there are high chances that you might relapse and end up getting trapped in the same web. This can be avoided by taking action immediately you realize that someone is trying to manipulate you. This can present itself in the simplest of ways like when informing a close friend of some reality of the particular situation may be all that's needed so set in motion a series of events that will eventually lead to your freedom. You should know that the fabric of illusion is made from tougher material than glass after making the choice to act. The illusion could work its way back into your heart with your emotions in high gear by using fragments of your emotions to fix it. When a liar is caught in a lie, he or she may attempt to recruit others to enforce that lie when they feel that they are no longer holding you. A deceptive partner with whom you have recently broken things off would at this point try to use the other mutual relationships in your life to change your mind. If you want to get out of this unscathed, you will need both your logic and instincts. Although the truth of the situation is that when you discover that you've been lied to consistently, you become emotionally scarred, so the issue of leaving the situation unscathed becomes silent. Priority should be given, however, to take the route that allows you to leave this toxic situation without harming yourself further. You're all over the place emotionally. Rage, anger, hurt, and deception is the iceberg's tip. But logically, you need to think. Keep your head above the water and warn yourself.

Get help fast

When you're trapped by other people's manipulations, confusion is one of the emotions you'd experience. This helps cloud your rational thinking and leaves you feeling helpless. You might even question the reality of what you are facing at this point. It would lead to denial if you continue to entertain these doubts. You're probably going to want to conclude you've got the whole situation wrong. That you misunderstood some things and came to the wrong conclusion. Such thinking would drive back to the manipulator's arms. Resist the urge to give in by receiving a second opinion. People go to another doctor in a health crisis to get a second opinion. This is to remove any iota of doubt about the first diagnosis that you may have and to affirm the best treatment course for you.

Similarly, getting another person's opinion can help you discern the truth of the situation and what might be your next steps. Just remember, it's better to go to someone who has proved countless times they're interested in your best. The next step is to confront the perpetrator if you have the help you need.

Trust your instincts

You need to be open to the idea of trusting yourself and trusting others to be able to trust your instinct. Your failure to trust others would just make you paranoid, and it's not your instincts that kick when you're paranoid. It's the fear of you. Fear tends to turn every molehill into a hill. You must let go of your fear, embrace confidence, and let that lead in your new relationships. You are better able to hear the voice inside without the roadblocks put up by fear in your mind. Finally, your priorities need to be re-evaluated. If your mind is at the forefront of money and material possessions, you may not be able to see the past. Any interaction you have with people would be interpreted as people trying to take advantage of you, and if you dwell on that frequently enough, it will soon become your reality. You know how you attract into your life what you think of. If you're constantly thinking about material wealth, you're only going to attract people who think like you. Using this as a guide, look at all your relationships with this new hindsight; the old, the new, and the perspective. Don't enter a relationship that expects to be played. Be open when you approach them, whether it's a business relationship, a romantic relationship or even a regular acquaintance. You can get the right feedback about them from your intuition. Do not step into this thinking, too, that your gut will tell you to run in the opposite direction when you meet suspect people.

Chapter 3: Setting Up Ethical Foundations

These techniques will help you in setting up ethical boundaries when persuading others. The effects of persuasion are the result of their own psychological response to you and their own perception of you. It's not your fault they look at you and think "Wow, this person sounds like they know what they're talking about!", but you certainly "help" them arrive to that conclusion.

Keeping that in mind, here are some techniques that can help you:

Persuade Yourself First

In honing your persuasion skills start by convincing yourself that you are capable of applying the strategies in the areas where you need them. We've already learned that we go into every situation with a preconceived belief in its success or failure. Listen to your inner voice and figure out if it's sending you positive or negative message about your abilities. Be honest and recognize the areas where you need improvement. If your inner critic is telling you that you "in over your head" or that you're weak in a certain area you need to take active steps to prove it wrong. When you identify a weakness, start working on improving that area and keep doing it until you begin to believe it.

Start with Your Own Inner Feelings and Emotions

Take active steps to boost your self-esteem. If you have any doubts about your abilities, you need to address them first. These doubts are rarely the result of things that are happening today but are the consequences of a lifetime of negative experiences. Your self-esteem issues may be the result of a neglected childhood, a poor economic situation, or limitations in your social life. It may take some soul-searching but once you recognize the root cause of any social problems you may have it will become easier to convince yourself that you are able to influence other people.

Appeal to people's emotions

You have no idea how much we've got to lose because we're emotional creatures. But other people's downfall is your gain because of course this weakness can be exploited. Anything that elicits a strong emotional reaction, be it sadness, happiness, love, pity, **etc.** is incredibly attractive to people. We just love emotional highs, even when that emotion isn't positive, which is why people watch horror movies and go on rollercoasters.

Take care of the thinking

Do you ever have those moments when you're so tired, that all you want is to sit there and watch something stupid, so you don't have to think? That may be empty, wasted time, but it has value for you, because it allows you to just relax and stop thinking.
It's no surprise that people like it when others come along and offer to do all the thinking for them. However, that's dangerous, because someone might take advantage of that and purposefully, deliberately, and systematically put ideas into their head. Someone like you.

Use an anchor

This technique is based on comparison; specifically, creating the illusion of a positive comparison. Say you're trying to convince your friend to go on vacation to a certain resort, but you know they might be resistant to the idea because they think it's too expensive. In an effort to persuade them, you might tell your friend that these tickets would be double the price at any other time during the year, but now they're just **insert their preferred price here**.

Ask for something outrageous

You know that method every teenager has used at least at some point, when they have bad news? Give the parents some really horrible piece of news and then just go "I'm kidding", so by the time you tell them the real thing, they'll just be relieved? Well, if you've ever done that, congratulations, you were employing a psychological persuasion technique and you didn't even know it!

Ask for something small

Now, this one is similar to the technique before, but the other way around. Instead of asking for something huge in order to then ask for something small, go in asking for something small that anyone is likely to say yes to, and then use that as an opportunity to get your foot in the door to ask for something else, usually a bigger favor.

With a lot of these "tame" persuasion techniques, you've probably never even realized people are trying to convince you, but once you learn about them, it's like you can't "unsee" it. People pull this move all the time when they want to get something out of you but they can't ask for a bold favor right away.

Now you know what they're doing and you can do it right back to them. The reason why this works is that people feel bad, especially if you're in a pinch and no one else can help you. People feel a social obligation towards other people to help, so you've got to shamelessly exploit that and get them to do favors for you.

Use the hive-mind in your favor

One of the great things about being human is that we're social animals, and thus, we live in communities. We need society in order to survive and thrive and we're known to help each other out and build each other up. There are unwritten social rules we're not allowed to break, and you can spin that to your advantage.

Do favors for people

Now, this one is a little sneaky, but based on a fair principle. If you want someone to do something for you, then first, do something for them. It makes sense, right? You don't just ask for things without offering anything in return, because that's unfair and possibly, a little rude. You're putting someone out and asking them to go out of their way for you. But if you do something for them first, then the whole game changes.

Make use of authority

People like it when they don't have to think for themselves, because then they don't have to make an effort or accept responsibility for their actions. It's easier to just follow a self-proclaimed leader and "let Jesus take the wheel", as they say. Plus, remember what I said about people being insecure and lacking confidence in their abilities? If they perceive that someone is better than them in some way, they are more likely to listen to them or change their mind about what they think. You know how in school you used to copy off your desk mate's test? When you're unprepared, you feel like everyone else in the world must know more than you.

Use words of agreement

Most of the time, it should be so subtle, the other person doesn't even realize you're putting ideas into their head. You can frame it as a suggestion "Don't you think this would look amazing on you?", or even ask for agreement "Don't you agree that what Melissa said was so rude?". They won't notice it's you pushing these ideas and they'll never figure you out for suggesting things on purpose.

Drop hints constantly and repeat the same ideas

Repeat something enough times, and it sticks. Most likely, the person won't even know where the idea is coming from, it's like a subliminal message. All they know is that it's very familiar, it's coming up more and more often, and they can't stop thinking about it. Surely, it must be important or otherwise worthy of thinking about, right?

Demonstrate Your Knowledge or Skill

Use respectful terms when speaking to others. Even if you don't address a person's role directly, elevating your expertise above everyone else's could come off as boastful and demeaning to others. Keep your tone respectful and focus on building the other person up without diminishing your role in the situation. Keep in mind their underlying issue that you are trying to address. If the concern is fairness or justice, use that to your advantage but if they are concerned about teamwork or cooperation you should use that as well.

Maximize/Minimize the Situation

This basically means that you want to minimize the risks and maximize the possibilities for gain in each situation. Keep steering the conversation towards the more positive aspects of your argument and away from the negatives. The more you can keep their focus on the positive side of things the more relaxed they're going to be. When they bring up a negative point, don't ignore it or gloss over it but don't dwell on it either. Keep gently steering them back to the more positive side of things and keep them emotionally engaged throughout.

Trigger the Motivators

Every choice we make is because of these different motivators so by developing strategies to move them in a certain direction, you could overcome the challenge. Once you've identified what is moving the individual in a particular direction, you can use words that will tap into that motivator and possibly seal the deal.

Think Positive

Like minds think alike. People have a natural tendency to follow the vibe one sets. If you tend to focus on the negative, then chances are those are the areas your listener will focus on too. However, if you develop the skill of painting lovely pictures with your words, you tap into their subconscious and they will follow your lead. The more positive the picture is the more attractive your message will be. The right words will generate a feeling of warmth and establish a mental bond that your listener will be drawn to on a subconscious level.

Give Assurances

If you fail to make the strong emotional connection as soon as possible and provide them with a solution to their problem you could very well lose them. However, if you are able to provide certain assurances within the realm of possibilities you get them to lower their guard. Your message must be relevant to what means the most to them and gives them a promise of an improved condition in the life in some way. Only these kinds of words will have the power to influence people in ways that matter.

Life in general is full of uncertainty so any time you can offer assurances your message becomes very appealing. Showing them how they can benefit from what you have to offer can be one of the most powerful messages you can send. The more you reinforce that kind of thinking the more open they will be to your persuasive tactics.

You May Need to Change Your Belief System

Your words can be a powerful tool for good or for bad depending on how you use them and hopefully you will be able to use these strategies for the betterment of not just yourself but those who have the good fortune to interact with you but all of this starts with your initial practice. Simply by changing your viewpoint and your attitude about a lot of things you'll see how persuasion does have the power to change lives.

Chapter 4: Persuasion Not Manipulation

Persuasion Versus Manipulation

After reading all of this information on intentional persuasion, you may say, "That sounds like manipulation to me." And that's true. Manipulation and persuasion share much (if not all) of the same techniques.

When we discuss manipulation and persuasion, it usually comes down to a difference of **intent.** For instance, is the person who is persuading you to do something that will benefit both you and them? If so, that's the classic win-win scenario, and we could say that persuasion was used to help you come to the right decision.

But what if the same person gets you to do something that benefits him, but leaves you worse off? That would be characterized as manipulation, and that type of persuasion happens all of the time, too. You may have done it yourself without really realizing it, and not felt too good about it afterward.

Persuasion can be used for all kinds of purposes, both good and evil. People can manipulate you into giving them your money, your time, your faith, your talent, and provide you with nothing in return. Or they can persuade you into giving of all of these things, and leave you better off in the end. And sometimes, the lines aren't so clearly drawn.

What I will attempt to show you in this book is just how persuasion happens in various parts of your everyday life, how persuasion can be used to help you get what you want, and how to recognize persuasion techniques that are used on you. Ultimately, everyone makes their own decisions. By being aware of persuasion techniques, you can more successfully analyze your motivations and make sure that what you are doing benefits both you and others.

Persuasion works through a communication of new information, which proposes to re-examine personal values and convictions in a different light. The person thus enters in a gradual process of changes in their inner and outer attitudes. It is precisely there that the paradox of influence lies. The determinations and restrictions of a free will are not being imposed from the outside. They have rather just been proposed. It is a person who is being influenced that is imposing them on himself. The efficiency of persuasion thus depends on the ability to reach to the core of the other person's free will.

Numerous human actions are performed automatically, in a conventional manner. In many cases, it has been proven to be the most efficient way to act, in other cases it was a necessity. No matter what the reasons may be, the fact remains that these behavioral patterns make us easily fall under the influence of persuasive or manipulative individuals. There are particular weapons or tactics of influence that can be taught in order to obtain what one wants. It could be sufficient to do no more than pronouncing the correct word in a right manner. An act as simple as that can trigger an automatic reaction we have planned to obtain.

Too many people confuse manipulation and persuasion, and you must learn that they are completely different. Manipulation is the act of coercing a person to do something that they do not want to do through the use of force. Persuasion, on the other hand, is an art. It is the art of getting a person to do something that benefits you, but it's also of great benefit to them and is in their own best interests. We persuade people every day, and it is not difficult to recognize a self-interest behind our effort to make others do or believe the thing we suggest them. A new conviction produced in others is not only serving them but is also in our best interest. Without this self-interest, there is no persuasion. But there is also a clear distinction between self-interest in persuasion and a self-interest in manipulation. Manipulation brings forth a change by artful or unfair means and serves only one's purpose. What one wants, one obtains no matter what.

A person that is trying to be persuasive sincerely believes to be working work in the best interest of others. A persuader is concerned only with his benefits and can convince others to do something that is not good for them or what is even harmful. Persuasion also includes certain truthfulness and transparency of the process, which are absent or obscured in manipulation. The difference is equally visible in a net benefit or impact on another person.

Persuasion aims a will of another person. It's all about making others want to do what one wants them to do. The way of persuasion is therefore rather simple: to get others do what one wants, one has to arouse their want. And there is no need to invent new needs. Nature has endowed us with a sufficient number of them. In the most of the cases, it suffices to stimulate the existing need and another person will spontaneously go along the path we have traced for them. So it is useful to learn something about human needs.

There are basic needs such as food, drink, air, sleep, health, sex. Then comes the need for possessions, expressed in money and all that money can buy. Of great importance are also our emotional and intellectual needs with their aspects of growth and maturity, of social and personal impacts, of the pleasure and happiness they bring. Our spiritual need can make a big difference in our life, especially the one concerning belief in the life hereafter. Then there are highly esteemed needs like those for well-being, gratification or fulfillment. And at the end, there is one particular and crucial need: a feeling of importance, a desire to be great, the need to feel acknowledged.

Persuasion is a theme of dark psychology that can be said to share quite a bit of similarity to manipulation. There are a number of reasons why we adopt persuasion into our everyday lives, but the main one would have to be to get people with different ideas on the same page. In company, for instance, the persuasion method will be used to alter the attitude of a person towards an item, concept, or a particular event that is taking place. Either written or spoken phrases will be used during the process to express the other person's thinking, emotions, or data. Another common instance you can use persuasion is to fulfil a private benefit. This would include either advocacy for trial when providing a pitch for sales or during an election campaign. Although none of these are deemed to be good or evil, they are still used to affect the listener to behave or believe in some manner.

One understanding of persuasion is that it utilizes one's private or positional resources to alter other people's attitudes or behaviors. There are also several distinct kinds of persuasion recognized; the process of altering views or attitudes by appealing to reason and logic is known as systematic persuasion; the process of altering views and attitudes by appealing to feelings or practices is known as heuristic persuasion. Persuasion is a type of mind control that is constantly being used in society. You may attempt to convince them to believe the same way you do when you speak to someone about politics. You are persuaded to vote a certain way when you listen to a political campaign. This form of mind control is so prevalent that most people don't even know it's happening at all to them. The problem will arise when someone takes the time to convince you to believe ideals and values that do not suit your own value system. There are many distinct types of persuasion available. Not all of them have a bad intention, but they will all work to get the subject to change their minds about something.

Dark persuasion has no moral motivation whatsoever. The motivation is rather amoral and sometimes largely immoral. If beneficial conviction is understandable as assisting individuals to help themselves, dark persuasion can be seen as a mechanism by which individuals behave against their own self-interest. Sometimes people make it reluctantly, knowing that they may not make the best choice, but are keen to stop the continuous persuasion efforts. On other occasions, the best dark persuaders can make someone think they act wisely when they actually do just the opposite.

So, what are the primary reasons for these dark persuaders? It depends on the type of person who persuades. Some people try to convince others to serve their own interests. Others do pure harm by the sole malicious intent. They may not profit from persuading anyone, but they do it anyhow, solely in order to bring pain to their victims. Others just appreciate the feeling of control provided by dark persuasion.

The result of dark persuasion is also different from positive persuasion. Positive persuasion usually results in one of three scenarios: benefit of the persuaded, benefit for the persuader and the persuaded or mutual benefit for the persuaded individual and a third party. All these results have a positive result for the person to be convinced. Sometimes other people benefit, sometimes they don't. However, there is no situation where only the persuader benefits.

Dark persuasion has a very distinct set of results. The persuader always advantages either immediately or by his distorted need for control and impact. The persuaded individual is against their own self-interest and is not persuaded. Finally, not only do the most qualified dark persuaders' damage their victims, but they also damage others. Take a dark persuader who tells somebody to commit suicide so they can take advantage of an insurance policy. The persuader not only won financially, but also the victim lost his life and hurt everyone who knew or cared for them.

Who are these individuals who often tend to use dark persuasion? The main characteristic of a dark persuader is either indifference or an inability to be concerned about the impact of persuasion on others. They are either completely narcissistic and regard their own requirements to be far more essential than the requirements of others or they are sociopathic and unable to even understand the notion of the feelings of others. In a partnership, you often discover dark persuasion.

Elements of persuasion

The first element of this theme is that persuasion is often symbolic. What this means is that persuasion utilizes words, sound as well as images so as to get the message across to the specific victim. The logic behind this is quite simple really. For one individual to be able to persuade another into acting in a particular way, they will need to show them why they should act in said way and not vice versa.

The second key is that persuasion will be used deliberately to affect how others act or think. This one is quite obvious; you don't use persuasion to get them to change if you don't deliberately try to affect others. In order to get the topic to believe the same way they do, the persuader will attempt distinct strategies. This could be as easy as having a discussion with them or presenting proof supporting their point of perspective. On the other hand, to change the mind of the subject, it could involve much more and include more deceptive forms.

The distinctive thing about persuasion is that it enables some type of free will for the topic. In this way, the topic is permitted to create its own decision. For the most part, they don't have to go for it, no matter how hard somebody tries to persuade them of something. The subject might hear about the best car to buy a thousand commercials, but if they don't like that brand or don't need a new vehicle at that time, they won't go out and buy it.

Examples of persuasion can be found everywhere, including when you talk to individuals you know, on the Internet, on radio and television. It is also feasible to deliver persuasive messages by nonverbal and verbal means; although when verbal methods are used it is much more efficient

The ability to influence someone during a conversation and make a decision is necessary in order to become one of the most important people in the world today. This ability is useful in business negotiations, and in everyday life.

In general, the impact on people is not so obvious. The basic idea is that people's behavior is often guided by their subconscious simple desires. And to achieve your goals, you need to understand the simple desires of people, and then make your interlocutor passionately wish for something.

It should be noted that in order to influence people you should NOT try to impose or force them to make a hasty decision. It may seem incredible, but the person that wants to reach a mutually beneficial cooperation becomes a huge advantage compared to those that are trying to impose something on others. If you are willing to put yourself in the shoes of another person from whom you want to get something and understand his/her thoughts, then you do not have to worry about your relationship with the person.

The secret lies in the ability to help the self-affirmation of the interlocutor. It is necessary to make sure that your companion looks decent in his own eyes. First things first, there are six basic principles that will absolutely affect any of your interlocutors.

To achieve their goals, people often use the influence of psychology, which helps to manipulate man. Even in ancient times it can be seen that priests ruled the people, instilling in them that religion is harsh, and everyone will be punished if they cannot follow the established rules and practices. Psychological influence strongly acts on the subconscious, causing the victim being influenced to be led by a skilled manipulator.

If you want to succeed and learn how to manage people, these words of the great American entrepreneur should be your credo. You will grow your personality only when you are in close cooperation with the community. From childhood we develop the basic patterns of behavior and outlook, produced by the long historical, biological and mental development of humankind.

In order to have influence and control over another person, it is required that you know their personality and behavioral traits. Most importantly, learn how to use this knowledge to master the specific methods and techniques of influence and control the behavior of the other, on the basis of his outlook, character, personality type and other important psychological features.

If you want to learn how to manage people, secret techniques in this article will let you know not only the theoretical aspect of the question but also allow the use of this knowledge in real life.

To help people to look beyond the limits of consciousness, professionals use a variety of methods and techniques. One of the most effective of these is hypnosis. This method of direct influence on the psyche, whose essence consists of the introduction of human narrowed state of consciousness, makes it is easy to control someone else's suggestion and management.

Persuasion may involve the use of powerful symbolic words such as freedom, justice, and equality, nonverbal visual signs such as the holy cross, and the flag, and familiar images. Symbols are the tools of the persuader to drive the attitudes and mold opinions.

Although persuasion involves a conscious attempt to influence the person in question, there is a thin line separating it from manipulation. In fact, a persuader may never succeed in the first place if the persuadee denies to give in to the ideas proposed by the persuader. The persuader just provides the arguments for communication and proposes a particular idea.

One thing that remains true in both cases is that persuasion will not just form attitudes but will bring about a change. It involves molding and the reinforcement of attitudes, change of perspectives, and shaping up of new habits.

Persuasion rather requires a free choice to work. The persuader must induce and implant the message conveyed in a manner without being forceful or aggressive; that the persuadee starts thinking in a similar fashion. Then only the persuasion lasts for long. To sum up, persuasion is not about forcing someone to do what you want them to do but making them want what you want them to do.

Chapter 5: Developing a Growth Mindset

Emotions of happiness may compel you to buy an energy drink or cola. Similarly, negative emotions such as fear or pain may compel you to buy a medicine or a mattress that relieves you from that pain.

A persuader may present the persuadee with logical pieces of evidence, reasonably acceptable facts, and statistics to support an argument.

Advertisers often use this approach to back their products with technical details and straight facts to influence and induce a faith among their consumers thereby motivating the consumers to buy their products. You must have seen that print on your energy bar stating the number of calories it will provide as an instant energy alternative. Or the list of nutritive supplements shown on a pack of chocolate milk powder. All of such advertisements are examples of logos at work.

It's a normal human tendency that one believes a person who is more reliable, credible, and honest. The same applies to companies and their products. A brand with a higher credibility is more likely to be picked up over the other.

Often backed with statistical data from reliable experts, the persuader tries to induce a sense of reliability and belief that you can completely put your trust in them.

A persuader can do this by various means such as verbal and nonverbal cues, emotional expressions, psychological connections, and strong statements. Once the attention is attained, the persuader must create a need for the persuadee to keep them engaged.

The target must feel an urge to keep listening to the persuader. This is often accomplished by raising a common interest or an aspect that the persuadee cares about. Once the persuadee is connected, the persuader offers solutions that can satisfy the persuadee.

A sense of satisfaction and receivable benefits are the factors that drive a persuadee to get persuaded. The persuader draws a picture visualizing the transmitted idea or message for the listener. Imagination and visualization help in drawing the complete attention of the persuadee to buy the transmitted idea. Once an idea is accepted, the persuader provides the action steps to be followed to accomplish what's being promised.

Persuasion is Unavoidable

Persuasion is delivered from one person to another through a **medium**; directly in one-on-one communication, in-person in speeches and lectures, or through one of the many digital communication methods available today.

It used to be that people were only influenced through direct communication, one person to another. Then the printing press allowed for mass persuasion by allowing ideas to be spread to many more people at the same time. The advent of radio broadcasting furthered that reach, and then television added visual communication to the sound of the radio. Today, the Internet has amplified the one-to-many reach of broadcast communications into a one-to-many-to-one, always-on deluge of information and data available all times of the day or night. That much contact means that we can be exposed to persuasion of all types 24 hours a day, seven days a week.

Because of this, everyone needs to be much more sophisticated about the messages they receive, and the persuasion they allow those messages to have over them. Advertising began using persuasion techniques even before the advertisers realized what they were doing. But now, pure persuasion is everywhere, and it's much harder to hide away from it all. Unless you're going to hide under a rock or lock yourself away in a mountain bunker, messages are going to get to you. But if you learn how to read the techniques, you can learn to make more independent decisions, and compete for what you want on an equal playing field.

Persuasion Can Be Learned

Personal persuasion is often called charisma, and it's been common to talk about charisma as some innate talent. People are born with it, or they aren't. But now that we've done more research into what makes those people charismatic, we've found that persuasive ability not only can be learned but we can apply it on a mass scale in many types of one-to-many communications.

Because persuasion consists of techniques, it can be learned. You can learn it, you can practice it, and you can recognize its effects in the messages and communications you receive. Persuasion isn't wrong in and of itself, and learning persuasion techniques that you can use on yourself can help you to improve your well-being and achieve your goals.

Why you're not persuasive and how that's affecting your life

Like in any other aspect of life, some people were blessed, while others got the short end of the stick. Confidence and the ability to persuade doesn't come naturally to everyone, which is why the world is pretty much divided into two broad categories: born salesmen and the people who buy what they're selling.

You hesitate too much

Confident people aren't ones to hesitate; about anything. They are self-assured and everything they do is deliberate – what they say, how they say it, the way they look, and even the way they walk. Their decisions are clear and there is no room for doubt. They know what they're doing and why they're doing it and more than anything, they are absolutely sure that they're right. Any other option doesn't even exist.

Even if you're not yet as convincing as you could be, take some cues from self-assured people you know. Don't agonize over decisions and don't pick your words. Don't hem and haw over different options and choices; you know what you want. Or at least, you can pretend for now. People will listen to you if you seem to know what you're doing. Not so much, if you're hesitating.

You're not focused enough

You'll notice that really persuasive people have a clear direction or intent, whether they're talking or doing something. They're focused. If you, half-listen to a motivational speaker, it'll seem like they're just talking nonsense and waffling.

You're not relaxed enough

You need to change your outlook a little bit and build up some self-confidence. Trust me, it will start showing on your face, in your voice, and in the way you carry yourself.

You're not an effective leader

Have you ever run for student body president or something? Did you ever win? No offense or anything, but I'm guessing not. It's not your fault, you just didn't have the persuasive skills you needed to make a good politician. Maybe you don't even want to be one, but that ability to influence and lead people comes in handy.

As it stands, you will miss out on leadership positions again and again, because in order to advance in your career, you need to have underlings, but no one will take you seriously unless you start working on influencing people to see the 'you' you want them to see.

You never get dates

Think back – who in your group of friends is always the one to score dates? Is it the one who's all shy and asks quietly? Or is it the smooth talker who's super confident and could sell ice to Eskimos? No, don't answer that; we know it's the latter. The question is, do you want to be in their shoes? Cause right now, I think you probably strongly identify with the former type.

There's certainly nothing wrong with being reserved, but if you want to make a bold move and ask someone what – man or woman – you need to know how to ask in order to get a positive response. Persuasive skills basically do the job for you, but you wouldn't know anything about that, would you?

Chapter 6: Psychology and Humans

Human behavior

While the study of human behavior is vast and would take at least one whole book to grasp the entire concept, there are various smaller concepts around human behavior that you should understand to understand human psychology as a whole. Human behavior is believed to be erratic or unpredictable by many, but the reality is that there are actually many ways that you can understand and even begin to predict human behavior. The trick is not to look at behaviors themselves, but to look at the many variables that are factored into human behavior.

Beliefs

A person's beliefs heavily influence the way they act. People often formulate strong beliefs on how people should and should not act or behave in various situations, which generally lead to their behaviors. Beliefs can be formulated personally, often by their experiences with others and how they felt about them. They can also be borrowed or adopted by others in a person's life, such as family members, religious groups, or even their culture or society itself.

Values

A person's values will also shape how they tend to behave. Their values, sometimes known as morals or even their moral compass, will also determine how a person behaves in various situations. Most often, people will behave in a way that honors their values. For example, if they value financial freedom and money, they will likely be very diligent about paying off their debt quickly and making smart choices with their finances. If they value fun and enjoyment, however, they may be more likely to spend their money and increase their debt, in favor of having fun experiences.

Lifestyle

A person's lifestyle is a reflection of their past behavior, preferred behavior, and likely behavior. When you look at someone's lifestyle, you can often generate a prediction of what they are likely to behave like in various settings. For example, a fitness-buff would be likely to wake up and engage in some form of exercise and prefer healthy eating to excessive unhealthy food intake. Alternatively, someone who is passionate about food may eat a wider range of things, including those that are healthy and not healthy. They may also put less intention or attention toward exercise and fitness, therefore making them more likely to choose relaxing and pleasurable options over energetic and productive ones.

There are many other variables that are factored into human behavior, such as their way of thinking, their perspective, their personality, and other psychological things. When you are looking to influence someone based on their behavior, however, the top three things you want to focus on are their beliefs, their values, and their lifestyle. These will help you understand who they are, what they prefer, what they are willing and not willing to do, and what they are likely to choose based on their history of past choices and chosen lifestyle.

Persuasion is easy once you learn how, so take your time and focus on really mastering these steps so that you can rely on them in the future. It is also important that you do not skip to these steps before you have fully mastered analyzing people. Persuasion will not be nearly as effective if you have not fully analyzed the person you are trying to manipulate, so it is mandatory that you take your time and master that part first. Then, mastering manipulation will become infinitely easier. You will likely find that it takes you minimal timing to really grasp the concept and make use of these tactics if you have already successfully analyzed your subject!

If you feel that you are ready, read on how humans use psychology to persuade people out there!

Encourage Them to Say No

If you want to ask someone for something, such as for a sale or for something big, you often want to start by asking something that you know they will say no to, first. You do this by encouraging the person to say no to you through a tactic such as asking for something outrageous or unreasonable first, then asking for what you actually want second. You want to deliver it as somewhat of a two-part option, leading them to believe there is no third option. By manipulating your phrasing to sound like the person only has two choices and both are ones you have picked for them, you ultimately get to decide which of the two the person is going to respond to. Since you have intentionally made one outrageous or unusual, or simply one that they would most likely say no to, they are more likely to say yes to the one you actually want them to agree with.

Establish Similarity

People are attracted to people that they have similarities to. By creating the illusion that you have plenty in common with someone, you give the idea that you are the same. Through that, you are able to establish trust and chemistry. This will lead to the person liking you a lot more, even if they don't already know you. Once they feel this way toward you, they are far more likely to agree with you and want to do the things that you suggest. This is because they feel like you know them and that they can trust you to suggest things that would ultimately be to their benefit or favor.

Inspire Fear, Then Provide Relief

One very popular and highly effective way of manipulating people is to use fear. Whether someone is emotionally driven or logically driven, they are going to be easily moved and manipulated by fear. The trick with fear is to inspire fear in someone and then provide a solution for relief. This is a great tactic for selling stuff, spreading information (such as through the media), and for getting your way with virtually anything else.

This tactic works in an extremely simple two-step manner: cause the other person to fear something, and then give them a solution that inspires relief. In order to make the most of this tactic, you first want to have a general idea of what you can use to inspire fear. In other words, you will need to properly analyze the person so that you are clear on what they would actually be afraid of. Then, you can use this to create fear naturally. Once you have, you want the solution you are offering to be the form of relief.

Use Guilt, Play the Victim

By using guilt, you can make people feel as though they are obligated to comply or agree with you. Because you are able to point out a genuine reason as to why they "owe" you, they feel as though they have to fulfill that obligation. People do not like to feel indebted, and using guilt is a great way to make them feel as though they have to help you or do what you have asked. This is how they can make sure that they don't "mess up again", or "take advantage" after all!

Use Logic to Appeal to Rational People

People who are logically-driven are also emotionally-driven, as you know, but they also require you to cater to their logical side if you are going to actually get anywhere with them. This is not as hard as it sounds, but it does take some practice.

Using logic to appeal to rational people mostly works through providing a lot of factual evidence and statistics that back up what you are trying to "sell" or "solve". This can work in many different ways, but ultimately you want to infuse as many facts as you can. You want to make it seem as though you know all of the facts that are required in order for someone to make the decision so that they don't go and look for the facts themselves.

Bribe Them

Bribery is a phenomenal tool. It works on getting children to complete their chores, and it works on adults when you need it to as well. You can easily use bribery in a number of different situations to help get what you want. In some cases, bribery will be obvious. In others, it may not be quite so obvious. You will want to choose how obvious you make it depending on the situation. If you need to hide your bribery, you can word your sentence differently. For example, say you are trying to sell an expensive product to someone. You start by putting the product in their hands and getting them to interact with it.

Overcome Their Trust Issues

People are always going to have trust issues. One of the best ways to persuade someone is to learn how you can overcome someone's trust issues so that they trust you. While this can sometimes take weeks or even years for some people, master manipulators are great at earning trust in a matter of seconds. It works through being charismatic, staying confident, and holding authority in your conversation. When you are able to lead the conversation, be friendly and open to the person you are talking to, and really get them to warm up to you, it becomes a lot easier for you to persuade them to work in your favor. This is the very first part of persuasion that you should practice every single time, no matter what drives them, what the solution is, or what you want to gain from the experience.

Know Your Product (Or Purpose)

When you are trying to manipulate people, you are going to have to overcome objections. They are going to ask questions, have concerns, and want to make sure that you aren't just trying to pull their leg. Even if you are, it is important that it doesn't look like you are. Having a clear understanding of your product or your purpose is a great way to ensure that you can provide answers and explanations for any objections in a moment, without missing a beat. When you have to stop and think about why someone should agree with you, you ultimately give them several moments to think about why they should not agree with you. The faster you answer with your reasoning, the more likely they are going to agree with you. This shows that you are educated, you have a purpose, and you know everything that is needed to about either the product or the purpose behind what you are asking for.

Stay Calm and Confident

In addition to being able to appeal to someone's need to trust you and to being charismatic and authoritative in a conversation, you also need to know how you can stay calm and confident. There are going to be many times where you feel nervous, or like you want to break your character and express emotions other than calmness and confidence. If you do, however, you are not going to be able to persuade people. Instead, you need to emanate calmness and confidence the entire time.

This is the same during informative parts of the conversation as well. When they are asking questions, give the answers with clarity and confidence. Be extremely assertive as to why they need what you are offering, and never waiver. When they ask about a certain feature, explain what that feature does with complete confidence, even if you aren't completely sure that you understand it yourself. The more you can remain confident, the easier it is for you to keep people confident in you and what you are talking about. Then, they will be more likely to agree with you and take what you are offering.

Chapter 7: Dealing with Social Interaction

To learn how to manipulate people, you must know how it feels to be on both sides. After all, you need to understand the feelings and emotions experienced by each side. This section of the learning process will be much more efficient!

Psychology of influence is very simple and obvious. The secret lies in the ability to analyze your own and others' behavior.

Just focus on the moral side of the issue. If you are ashamed to receive from people that are important to you, you do not accept selfish purposes - better close and do not hurt their highly moral consciousness of the information received. This article is for those that want to live and have fun!

Here are some ways to interact and control people - they will certainly be useful to you!

Care and love

Almost all the methods of influence are based on the rule of mutual exchange. This is very common and well known in the psychology of the impact of the concept, the essence of which consists in bringing the person a sense of duty, and it is done on an unconscious level. There is no single hundred-percent method because there is an infinite number of modifications that could "boomerang".

Always know that there may be something fishy when someone starts to care about you for no apparent reason. Be careful not to accumulate a sense of duty - with a light heart, let rejection. This way of manipulating people is quite effective and widespread. You can become a generous man once in a while and ask what the person wants.

Repetition - the mother of learning!

Repetition - the basis of zombies. A simple example is what you see every day on television advertising very tasty seasoning for soup. Take a walk around the store with your wife and you will not notice how to buy it. However, why? Because you have already seen the ad a thousand times - and it has long been stuck in your subconscious. Still you think about learning how to manipulate people? Be watchful -

repetition can be easily linked to care, which is quite a powerful weapon. And you will not notice until you become a very good investor or loan shark for a not-very-good person.

Mind Reading

How do you learn to read the thoughts of other people using this energy? We all remember the famous expression that says that thought is material. That is, the human thinking process is a flow of energy and part of the information field. In this world, there are hundreds of examples where people in different parts of the world had seen the same dream about a great event that later took place shortly. This also explains the so-called prophetic dreams. Our task is to learn to control our mind and gain the ability to capture from the general stream of thought of a particular interlocutor.

Agree with your loved one regarding what he/she will intently think about any event you're also a part of, and which you once experienced with him. At the same time your partner should not talk about the event he/she is thinking about. Also, he/she should sit comfortably in a chair and not be distracted by extraneous noise. You must stay close.

Use Body Language Instead of a thousand words

In today's world, body language and facial expression are important but not compared to how important verbal communication is. Therefore, a great importance is attached to their interpretation. The use of a variety of gestures and facial expressions when communicating is called "nonverbal communication." It involves distinct movements, which are gestures used by man with the help of various items.

Understanding nonverbal communication when communicating allows you to "read" your opponent, understand how the other person took heard, and know what his opinion is even before it is made public. With expertise in the field of human subconscious, you can just adjust their behavior to achieve the desired outcome when dealing with other people.

The key communicative gestures and facial expressions, as a person, do not vary a lot in different countries. Someone that is happy – smiling; someone in grief – frowning. A man in a fit of rage and anger, too, has his own distinctive facial expression. A very clear example of universally valid, universally accepted gesture is a shrug. It is very clear for all people and means misunderstanding.

Nonverbal signs perfectly reflect the position of a person in the society, the level of education and occupation. Given the above, it is important to know and use the sign language so you can always put yourself at a greater advantage.

Chapter 8: How does a Human Mind Work

The brain is one of the most fascinating organs in the human body. While we are a far cry from understanding everything about it over the last century or so we have come to learn a lot. In fact, neuroscience has become a hot topic on university campuses, science research, and a load of other programs across the board.

No matter where you live, you've been advised on the right foods to eat, the right vitamins to take, and the right practices to do in order to maximize your ability to exercise your brain and get it to its peak performance. So, it just makes sense that we try to understand what's happening in the brain during a decision making process when we're trying to influence people to follow us in some form or fashion.

Before you can begin to hone your skills in persuasiveness, you need to know the steps the brain takes in the decision making process. One cannot begin to persuade a person to change his mind on any topic without understanding this fundamental aspect of the mind.

Every day, we each make thousands of decisions that can vary from very small and insignificant choices to life altering ones. The brain is the organ that makes decision making possible. For years, researchers have been trying to decide just how the brain filters through the millions of bits of information it receives every day to narrow a decision down to one single point.

The decision making process in the brain functions in a manner very similar to what happens in court every day. When a choice needs to be made the evidence is put forward. The brain collects visual cues, sounds, and other sensory data and "logs" it into its sensory circuits. Other cells in the brain then take on the role of jurors and weigh each piece of evidence presented. Once enough evidence is presented a decision is made.

The area of the brain where these decisions are made are not always the same. Depending on the type of sensory input the brain receives a different section of the brain may be involved.

After careful analysis, researchers have determined that there are actually two separate networks at work in the brain when it comes to making choices. The first determines that actual value of the object or condition in question and the potential reward while the second works out the actual behavior expected of the individual.

It seems obvious that the process of making decisions is part of our natural makeup. We do this instinctively without much forethought. In fact, many of our decisions are made without us being aware of it. We instantly turn our head in the direction of sound, our eyes scan for things to set our gaze upon, and smells automatically draw our focus. Through research, we've come to learn that this process is performed in different parts of the brain's frontal lobe. This is the area that is responsible for planning and/or reasoning on both abstract and concrete ideas.

Depending on the region of the brain, decisions can be made based on a number of rapid and complex calculations performed in the neurons. This is key to helping us to understand the science behind persuasion. If a decision goes wrong in someone's mind, the orbitofrontal cortex lights up. This area is located at the front of the brain and sits right behind the eyes and forces us to alter our behavior. In cases, where this area of the brain is damaged (drug addicts, accidents, lack of sleep, etc.) the inability to weigh the rewards of decisions and adjustments in certain situations is impaired.

Your subconscious mind is a gigantic memory bank with an unlimited capacity. It stores all the little and big information related to everything that happens to you. Your subconscious mind is in charge of storing and retrieving data and ensuring you respond in an appropriate manner. Your subconscious makes everything you do and say fit a pattern consistent with your master program and your self-concept.

Your subconscious is also subjective and does not reason or think independently. It obeys commands given by the conscious mind. The conscious mind works as a gardener that plants seeds in your subconscious mind, which serves as a garden wherein the planted seeds germinate and then grow.

Your conscious mind directs your subconscious to behave a certain way and your subconscious merely obeys it. While your conscious mind does command your subconscious, the subconscious mind holds all the power because it stores all data. Hence, to persuade and convince someone, you have to appeal to the person's subconscious mind.

Your conscious mind communicates using concrete thoughts and logic. Conversely, your subconscious mind communicates via feelings, emotions, and intuition. To persuade your husband to buy you a new car, using facts, figures, and logical data will not help you connect with him nor will it persuade him.

Instead, you should target his subconscious mind and use emotions and sentiments. You can do this by telling him how amazing he is and how you are glad he prioritizes; then, you will indirectly bring up the topic of purchasing a new car.

Similarly, if you want your boss to give you a raise, you will use the emotional element to convince him/her. You will focus on how much value you bring to the company instead of using logic to make your case that you deserve a raise. This tactic will help you easily accomplish your goal since humans are creatures of emotions.

Human Beings Are Creatures of Emotion

Emotions create action, movement, and energy. A logic driven conversation may seem boring, but by adding the right amount of emotions to it, you can instantly spice it up and effectively get your message across.

However, if your conversation is devoid of logic, it may not appeal to intelligent listeners. This is why it is important to maintain balance between emotions and logic: so you can appeal to all sorts of audience, those whose sway lies in emotion, and those whose sway is reason. This skill is what this book shall teach you.

Everyone has in their mind something called the **critical faculty**. The critical faculty acts kind of like a computer firewall; it filters ideas based on logic and reasoning. It is designed to protect us from harmful or incorrect information by allowing us to choose which information we would like to accept and which information is not good for us and should be rejected. However, it is also the biggest obstacle we face when trying to persuade someone, help them to see past their limitations, or guide them towards a new point of view.

In persuasion, the goal is to communicate with someone's subconscious mind without any objections, and get past this critical faculty. To bypass that person's critical thinking, you must add subtlety to your speech.

In order to get someone to see things our way, we don't want to have a battle of wits or try to prove someone as being factually wrong; in fact, quite the opposite. Doing this will not help you persuade people. Rather, it will cause people to dislike you. Instead, we want to use suggestions and triggers to access their subconscious directly, in order to guide them gently to our point of view.

To sway people without hurting their feelings, you have to add subtlety to your speech, which is where emotions come in. Imagine you are working with a team on a project and you notice a good way to direct the project. However, you fear your idea may displease the group leader because it contradicts with the group leader's idea.

Here, to prove your point, you could reason with the group leader but you fear this strategy may alienate you from the group. However, since you feel your idea has a greater chance of success, you decide to use emotions to persuade the group leader.

You gently approach the group leader and compliment him or her on the good job he or she is doing directing the team. This instantly cheers the group leader who ends up liking you. Then, you cleverly enforce the need to work in the company's and project's best interests.

Once the group leader agrees to your notion, you steer the conversation towards your idea by stating you read it somewhere. By appealing to the leader's emotions, you gently direct his or her attention towards your idea without offending him or her.

As you can see, subtlety and emotions help you sway people. In this book, we will uncover many strategies that help you tap into people's subconscious and influence them in the most effective way possible.

Chapter 9: Influence and Its Long Term Advantages

Influence is a step above just basic persuasion, as it's a bit stronger, more forceful, and more powerful. Influence is when someone trusts you enough to follow your advice, words, and general steering. Generally, it's easier to influence someone you're close with and know well, because you're more likely to develop this kind of relationship based on blind trust. In addition, they're more susceptible to the techniques you apply.

It's good to know that this isn't for absolute beginners, you need to have played this game for a while and know some tricks in order to be able to influence someone. While it uses similar principles to persuasion, this is a bit more advanced.

Influence Through Seduction

The whole point of seduction is to make someone want you. The motive is usually to cause someone to become sexually attracted to you. Seduction is one of the most powerful persuasion techniques because you are persuading someone to give their entire selves to you. There are multiple seduction tips and techniques that you can use. No matter who you are or who the person is who you are trying to seduce, these methods will work. What is ideal about them is that they do not require much preparation, so you can really start using them right now.

Choose the Right Person

You can seduce anyone, but you will put in less effort when you choose wisely. Look for a person who tends to be shy and reserved. They tend to be more vulnerable and in need of a person's attention. When you start giving them attention, it is easy to seduce them to take it to the next level.

Send Mixed Signals

This is a seduction technique that is as old as time. People feel challenged when they are getting mixed signals. A challenge automatically makes a person more interested in winning the prize, which in this case is you.

Create a Need

Make it to where the person you are trying to seduce feels like they need you. You can make this need purely sexual or make it deeper than that. When you create a need, it creates feeling of discontent and anxiety, both of which are more likely to make a person keep pursuing you.

False Sense of Security

When a person feels secure with you, this automatically creates a bond. This makes it easier to persuade them to give you what you want. This security is false, but by the time they figure this out, you will have what you have wanted.

Make Yourself Desirable

People do not like to lose. They do not like seeing other people with a person they are interested in. Once you hook someone, force them to see you with other people who also are interested in you. This creates an uneasiness that forces them to make their move because they will fear that they will lose you.

Create Temptation

No one likes to be tempted to something and then not be able to have it. This is true for everything from food, to career to romantic relationships. When you tempt the person, but then stop them once they are on the edge, this essentially drives them crazy. When a person is in this frame of mind, you can pretty much get whatever it is that you want.

Utilize Suspense

You want to give them some attention, but not your full attention. Just like when you create temptation, this is going to put them into a hyper-competitive state. You are going to be the only person that they think about. Their thoughts of you are going to filter into all elements of their lives. This is what you want, because at this stage, you have full control.

Be Mysterious

People love mystery. It draws them in and they want to do everything that they can to solve it. When you create mystery, you will naturally seduce those that become curious. The key is to give some information but hold back the juiciest details. Now, the mystery can be about anything really. However, avoid talking about an ex since this can have the opposite effect on someone you are trying to seduce. Other ways to add mystery include good eye contact, putting the attention back on them when they ask questions, smiling a lot and always speaking in a neutral tone.

Subtly Make Yourself Stand Out

You do not want it to be obvious that you are trying to get their attention. Instead, you want it to seem like you stand out just because of who you are. For example, women can wear red lipstick because this is not uncommon, but it still makes you stand out. Men can have the same effect with a bright or patterned tie. The key is to choose one small element that will make you stand out against the crowd that is relatively natural.

Utilize Scents

Did you know that the scent of a person can be all that it takes to attract another person? Now, all people have their own preferred scents, so it is a good idea to get to know a bit about the person and their preferences before you use this technique. Scent has a subconscious type of influence. It gives people information about another person without them even realizing it, so it is one of the subtlest and effective ways to up your seduction progress.

Be Mindful of Your Assets

Physical attraction is obviously a major element when it comes to seduction. However, you do not want to show off all of the goods because this can have a negative effect. For example, men with strong arms might wear a short-sleeved shirt. This way the person they are trying to seduce can see this asset without it being too obvious that they are trying to show off. Women might wear a form-fitting dress that hits below the knee and covers the chest well. In this case, you are covered, but the person you are trying to seduce can still see your full figure.

Confuse Them

One time you see them, give them all of your attention, but the next, only give them partial attention. This confusion ups their thinking of you and it makes you more mysterious and desirable. Just make sure that there is a good balance here or else you might actually turn the other person off.

Be Bold

Once you are ready to go in for the kill, you want to be bold. You have already hooked them at this point and they are yours to do with as you please. So, there is no reason to wait for them to make a move. Just grab the moment and make it known what you want.

Ways to Positively Influence Others

The world is actually shrinking as, at the touch of a button, the click of a mouse, we can keep up with and keep in contact with even the most remote parts of our globe, and we can learn from other cultures as easily as we learn from our own. No matter which part of the world we come from, we are not so different. We all have the same needs, as does any stranger that we meet. The same thing can also be said about the people that we work with.

It doesn't matter where you work, and it doesn't matter what you do for a living. We all have one thing in common – a large part of our waking hours are spent in our workplaces, some of us in jobs that we like and some in jobs that we hate.

If you are the latter, if you are working at a place or doing a job that you simply don't like, you can make your life much more bearable by persuading people to be on your side. You might even find that you quite enjoy going to work after all.

Here are ways that you can positively influence other people in your workplace and make life so much easier to bear:

Be Grateful

Or at least get into the habit of being grateful. Before you leave home every morning, look around at what you have and say the words "thank you." Be thankful that you have a home, maybe a car, food on the table and a family to share it with. Once you learn to appreciate what you have, your purpose will become much clearer – to bring home the money to pay for it all, the money that the job you hate pays you every week or month. As the day goes on and you face challenges that seem insurmountable, reflect on your gratefulness. It will make you happier, and it will make it easier for you to carry on.

Be Happy

Happiness truly is contagious, and there are, in all truthfulness, more than a billion reason to be happy. We weren't put on the earth to be miserable, so find a reason to be happy. Rejoice in the sky, the sun, the rain that gives life. Talk to your colleagues, the people who help you through each day at work; smile at those who don't help you. If you are alive and healthy, then you are doing okay. If you are happy others will be happy too.

Keep on Smiling

Even if you don't feel like it. There is an old expression, "fake it until you make it" and it has never been truer, especially when things go wrong. No matter what is happening, no matter how bad you feel - smile, and you will feel better. If the boss is on your back, your co-workers are not pulling their weight, your computer crashed and wiped out everything you did, just smile. There is actually a scientific reason for it: smiling helps to release endorphins in the blood, and these are not called happy hormones for nothing. Smiling also eases tension, not just in you but in those around you as well. People will notice, they will begin smiling, and the tension will ease. You and you alone will have persuaded everyone that everything is ok, with just a smile. A powerful way to smile is to look up at the ceiling while opening your arms and your chest. This simple move will increase your testosterone level and will boost your mood.

Always Say Your Pleases and Thank You

Good manners get you a long way and help to build up better relationships. This isn't just about the workplace, this works anywhere you go, to a restaurant, the movies, the grocery store. Be polite and show manners and people will do what they can to help you. In the workplace, your colleagues will more be likely to help you out if you are polite and treat them with the respect and courtesy you expect from them. Good manners show that you care so make it a habit of treating others as you want to be treated.

Steer Clear of the Gossip

At any given moment of the day, something will be happening in your workplace that gives people a reason to talk, to gossip about someone else behind their back. It is human nature to talk about things that happen, but the nature of gossip is that it often becomes distorted, purely for entertainment value. Gossip is demoralizing to the subject, and it can also be classed as bullying if it turns malicious. If you happen to be in a place where people are gossiping, and they try to draw you in, just smile at them and then walk away. Show them you will not become involved and avoid the negativity. Not only does it keep you stabilized, but it will also stop you from, wrongly, judging the victim and will also gain you respect from others.

Be Diplomatic

Everywhere you go, there will be people who say or do things that cause irritation. The real key is to stay objective and to stay calm. Losing your temper, or choosing to be angry as your very first reaction will do nothing more than providing the fire with a much-needed fuel source to keep on irritating you. Allow it to happen, and your colleagues will lose all respect for you. It doesn't matter how hard it is not to respond, when people say things that are hurtful or simply irritating, do not respond. Remain in control, remain calm, and you will be left alone. If you can muster one, smile at them and then continue with what you were doing. And if you do have to say something, keep your voice soft and be kind to them. It is your anger that they want, and

531

if you don't give it, they have nothing. You, on the other hand, will gain the respect of your colleagues. Always be non-reactive.

Do Your Very Best All of the Time

Your bosses and any colleagues who are influential will respect you more if you always do the very best that you can. Even if you are at odds with people, doing your best, putting in your effort, will result in milestones being reached and deadline met. People may not like you for one reason or another, but they can still respect you for being someone they can depend on, someone who remains focused. You will also have a better sense of self-worth and purpose. It may result in a raise or promotion, or it could just mean that you are in a better position to influence others in the future.

Always Be Honest

Honesty is always the very best policy, and when you add diplomacy into the mix, you have the makings of a great communicator, a true leader. When you are trying to talk to others about your ideas, keep to the facts; don't throw in a lot of technical jargon and don't try to be too smart – it will backfire on you. Never exaggerate your claim, and never embellish them as people can see through that and your chances of persuading them round to your way of thinking will be gone. It isn't always the contents of the message that work; it is the way the message is conveyed.

Respect Other Cultures

The world is multicultural and, no matter where you live and work, you will come across people of different ethnicities and different cultures. Get to know them, get to know their traditions, beliefs, food choices and develop respect for them. Each different ultra has something that we can all learn from, and it is our moral duty to show them respect. Walk away from racist conversations; if you stay, if you join in, you are no better than they are. Having that kind of name does not help you to be able to influence others, and everyone will lose a little of their respect for you. No matter where you go, no matter which nationalities you come across there will be good people and bad. Focus your energies on the good in all of us, and you will find that people are more prepared to cooperate with you, to follow where you want to lead them. These may not seem like ways to persuade people but think about everything I have said carefully. By being nice to others, showing respect and remaining calm and dependable, you are turning yourself into someone that others will trust in, that they will want to follow. This is an essential part of powerful leadership.

Chapter 10: Benefits of Being Persuasive

Charities

Charities use persuasive speech in every aspect of their business. Their goals are to motivate people to volunteer, make donations, and to speak out against and for all sorts of causes, often without any form of compensation. The success of a charity will depend largely on how effective they are in connecting with their audience emotionally and moving them to take action. To do this you need to influence people's opinions.

Teaching

A large part of teaching is influencing your students in some way or another. Whether you're teaching pre-school or at the university level, getting students to grasp your lessons and apply them in their lives will require you to have some pretty good persuasive arguments. A good teacher knows how to guide people's behavior so you need to know how people respond to others and use that to your advantage.

Marketing

If you are in any type of business, your ability to attract and keep customers will be directly affected by how persuasive you can be. Any business can get off to a good start with supportive friends and family members but to give your business any kind of staying power, you'll have to convince complete strangers to trust in you and the products or services you offer.

Management

Another crucial aspect of your business is the ability manage employees and get them to follow your directions. Part of being a good manager is being able to influence another person's behavior. But the skill is not limited to business but can also be used when interacting with family members, in social circles, and a wide range of other areas of one's life. Anytime you need to motivate someone to follow your directions, you'll need persuasive speaking.

For Help

Whether you're in need of someone to bag your groceries at the supermarket or you want that landlord to choose you over a hundred other tenants, it is the power of influence that will move them to do so. It is one thing to ask someone to do something for you and another entirely to persuade them to do it. Knowing how to make a request so people are likely to respond can get you the help you need.

Chapter 11: Overcoming Negative Persuasion

Simple Strategies You Can Adopt to Protect Yourself against negative persuasion

Whether you consider yourself highly vulnerable or resistant to manipulation, it always helps to be safe rather than sorry. Luckily, it is possible to keep the narcissists, psychopaths, and high Machs at a safe distance in your life. How so?

Psychopaths are present in our workplaces, in business transactions, in our personal relationships and even in our families. Sometimes, you just cannot avoid a psychopath by virtue of the nature of the relationship that exists between the two of you. For instance, it might be impossible to ignore or avoid your psychopathic boss because you need to do your job, get paid and advance in your career, or at least pay your bills. If your boss is a psychopath, you just have to deal with him somehow. You might, for instance, have to figure out a way of keeping your interactions to a bare minimum at most. However, if you ever have the choice to not deal with a psychopath, grab it and run. For instance, if you are starting to get to know a new person with the intention of dating them and start to realize some tendencies that match the psychopath criteria, run and do not look back. You do not need to stick around something or someone that is not good for you.

Do not fall into the trap of thinking you can change a psychopath, sociopath, or narcissist into being a better person. Not only is this not your job, but it is also virtually impossible. For starters, the things that make people dark and manipulative are so deeply embedded in their psyche that they cannot just be removed and replaced with sugar and spice at will. Secondly, change is a personal choice that is made by an individual. A person that changes does so because they want to change and not because another person asked them to. Last but not least, if you are dealing with a psychopath and thinking that you can change them, you are essentially waging war against biology and genetics. Who do you think is going to win?

536

Pay attention to actions more than you do words. Predators are very good with their words because words are their most powerful tools. Instead of focusing on what a person says, look at what they do. Did they fulfill the promise they made to you about doing a particular thing? Do they treat everyone as well as they want to make it sound? A simple way to check whether a person's actions match their words is by utilizing something that is referred to as the rule of threes.

Here's how it works: if a person seems to tell a lie or makes a promise that they do not keep on one occasion, you may be dealing with a simple misunderstanding. If this happens a second time, there is likely to be a serious mistake that requires addressing. However, if there is a third occasion, then you are probably dealing with a liar. Lies are often the first sign of manipulative behavior. If you are able to identify this recurring pattern in your relationship or interaction, then you know you have yourself a situation on your hands. How you decide to handle this situation will mean the difference between freeing yourself from the jaws and drama of a persuader or staying on for the most overwhelming ride of your life.

Whenever possible, let the psychopath win but not at your expense. The personalities that love to win are often aggressive and will go to great lengths to ensure that they trump all their competitors. If you ever find yourself facing a psychopath on a negotiation table, always go for the suggestion that guarantees a win for the both of you. This is an effective means of ensuring that you do not expend all your energy trying to fight off a psychopath who is trying to finish you.

When dealing with people, be they saints or sinners, always listen to what your gut has to say. Scientists who have tried to explain gut instinct say that it is the body's reaction to an intra-species predator. This makes a whole lot of sense when you consider how sometimes you'll feel uneasy around someone you do not know only to later find out that that person was not a good person. Do not let your gut instinct go ignored when it is working so hard to prevent you from making a mistake. In many instances, psychopaths assume roles such as mentor, boss, supervisor, church leader, guardian, or even parent. While these roles are indeed noble, your gut feeling might be screaming that the church leader is not as trustworthy as he might want to make you

537

believe. If this is the case, always give priority to the gut feeling. What your gut says is always a better bet than what you think you know.

Do not allow yourself to get drawn into the games that psychopaths, sociopaths, narcissists, and other dark personalities play. Sure, you've read this book and are feeling particularly confident about your knowledge on the dark triad personalities. At the back of your mind, you believe that you have what it takes to take on a psychopath and win. What you do not know is that while you have just read this book, a psychopath has had his whole life to practice on his victims. Do not be drawn into their manipulations. It is not your job to entertain the psychopath. Your number one job when dealing with a psychopath is to protect yourself against their tricks.

Learn to Analyze People

Analyzing people successfully is ultimately the first step to being able to easily spot negative manipulators. By knowing exactly who is trying to persuade you a you can choose your defense techniques wisely.

Rather than going in blind, you analyze people. This gives you the best opportunity to choose the next "vehicle" to get you to where you want to go. By paying attention to things such as their body language, their facial expressions, what they say (and what they don't say), and other important elements of said person, you develop an idea of who they are and what they care about. Then, you can use this to manipulate them to do virtually anything you want them to do.

When you are analyzing a person, you are looking for three things in particular: what drives them (emotions or logic), what their personality is like, and what they care about specifically. When you know what drives them, you know what strategies to use to manipulate them. When you know their personality, you know how you can persuade them effectively. And when you know what they are about, you know what "ammunition" you can use to really get into their mind or heart and start doing a number on them. This will give you specific topics, subjects, or content that you can use to get them to actually care about what your cause is and to agree with you or comply with what you are asking.

Analyzing people can take a few seconds, such as in a sales deal, or it can take several weeks, such as in a major deal or when you are trying to get something particularly large out of someone. The better you get, the faster you will be at analyzing a person. Certain things will require you to have more information than others, therefore certain things will always take you a fair amount of time before you can confidently say that you know enough about the person to manipulate them effectively. Take your time and learn to analyze people properly so that you can rely on this skill when it comes to the overall persuasion process.

Chapter 12: Practice Methods

For some people, the art of persuasion comes easily. You can watch them talk to almost anyone, and it seems like they will always get the response that they want from the other person. On the other hand, there are those people who may have the best message in the world who couldn't convince anyone, even their closest friends, to do something. No matter where you fall in either of these groups though, with a little bit of practice and hard work, you will be able to learn how to use persuasion to your advantage.

In terms of the process of using persuasion, there will usually be three parts that you need to follow including:

• The communicator, or the medium used as the source of persuasion

• The persuasive nature of the appeal

• The audience or the target person that the appeal is going to be sent too.

Each of these elements needs to be accounted for before you try to use persuasion on a higher level. It is always a good practice to look around you and check to see how many instances of persuasion are going on in your daily life. Some of these are going to be overt, but many of them are going to be pretty subtle. This can be great training for persuasion because you will be able to employ the same kind of tactics.

Methods of Persuasion

Below is a brief discussion of methods you can use to persuade someone to take up your ideas:

Questions

The questioning method is used to grasp the attention of your audience. When asked a question in a discussion, people begin to think about the appropriate answer to the question, and they also wonder the reason you asked them that particular question. However, you ought to be careful and to only ask questions that will add to your discussion because undoubtedly, your audience's minds will waver as they think of the right response to give. To get the right results, ensure that the questions you ask are short, simple, and logical. Let the questions inspire deeper thinking rather than taking away the audience's attention from your discussion.

Repetition

Repetition serves to incite and improve your brain's retention power. Once something is repeated to you, the odds of it getting stuck to your memory increase. Ensure that the sentences you speak highlight the keywords you want your audience to remember, and make an effort to repeat the most significant sentences or words. Place them strategically, and where possible, have your audience repeat them out loud, or put them down on paper.

Use Simulations

This is an excellent method for convincing strangers because you have not related before, and you cannot say anything about their mental abilities. You cannot also predict how they will react to certain statements, especially when discussing controversial issues. Using simulations creates an analogy by taking out the names of real places, people, and other things that could distract the listener and take his mind away from the subject.

Refute the Opinions of Others

Refuting can be difficult for many people, especially for those who hate or fear confrontations. It is also challenging because it requires a person to pay close attention to the opinions the other person has expressed, break it into smaller ideas, and then go about disapproving every one of them. Once you have knocked all of them down, now present your opinion and show how it is the better opinion. It is crucial that you rely on logic and reason throughout this process and present compelling facts that the other person knows about. That way, the other person will see the logic in your ideas and take them up.

Usage of force

The first method we shall talk about is the usage of force. The Persuader may decide to use some degree of force in order to successfully persuade the victim into thinking in some specific type of way. This is, however, dependant on the situation at that particular moment. This is however seen to be deployed in instances where, both the ideas of the persuader and the victim do not seem to match up, the type of conversation they are having don't seem to bear fruit or where the subject seems to be irritated or frustrated with the turn the conversation has taken. This may be classified as a scare tactic by most since it gives the victim minimal time to think in a logical manner of the events that seem to be transpiring as opposed to when the victim is of a normal state of mind.

Weapons of influence

Another method of persuasion that can be used is by using the weapons of influence that are available. We shall the weapons of influence below:

Scarcity

This is a weapon of influence that many people tend to be a bit familiar with but is often underestimated due to the basic definition of scarcity. If for one reason or another a particular idea or product has a limited time for which is available, it is most likely that a higher price will be attached to it.as human beings we are usually obsessed with chasing after that which we cannot get. When this issue of scarcity surfaces, it will play out depending on the context it is used under. What this means is that it may prove to be advantageous in certain scenarios more than in others. There are two main reasons why this tactic is likely to be successful. The first one is when products are usually a bit too hard to find. These goods will likely have a higher value attached to them. People attribute the high price to the fact that they are rare to find. The second reason is usually when something is not available as it normally has been. This makes the victim begin to have the feeling that they will miss out on the chance of a lifetime. Once both of these have happened, the victim will begin to assign the service that is scarce a higher value simply since it is going to become a bit hard to acquire.

Liking

This weapon will entail the manipulative individual who will be motivated to work hard in making the victim like them. The reason for this is because once the victim likes this manipulative individual, there is usually more likely to say yes to them if ever they make any request. There are mainly two main factors that will contribute to how well the victim will like the manipulator.

Subliminal messaging

This is a type of message or affirmation that is presented either visually or auditorily that is sent in a way that is below what is considered to be normal for human visual or auditory perception. For example, a record might be playing on repeat, but you cannot really hear it with your conscious mind. However, deep in your subconscious, you are hearing it and fully registering everything that it is saying. In most cases, the messages used are meant to control you in some way or suggest that you do something.

For example, subliminal messages are commonly used in today's world to promote smoking cessation or weight loss. In general, you listen to recorded tapes with a specific message when you are sleeping. Your unconscious mind gets the message, but you never really hear it as your conscious self. Either way, research shows that it can be an effective tool to change your smoking or eating behaviors. You can use a similar technique to aid in changing how people think to make them more vulnerable to the types of persuasion that you prefer to use.

How to Persuade

Whenever you have a valid point of disagreement, nothing should keep you from expressing your opinion. However, if you need to be heard, go about it with some form of decorum so that you know what to say, how to say it, and when to say it. Here are a few guidelines to help you through it:

Choose Your Battles

You cannot afford to go fighting or to argue with people everywhere. That would wreck your social life and even deny your inner peace. Instead, choose to ignore the trivial issues and only focus on the things that matter. When you do this, even those around you will respect you. You have very limited social capital-how much of it are you willing to risk on conflicts because you insist on speaking your mind all the time?

Always think before you engage with others, and weigh the situation to see whether the issue at hand is worth your attention. Most of the time, it does not.

Give It Some Thought

When you have thought about the issue and felt that you need to speak up, be silent and rethink your position. Are you sure that you want to take that position on the matter? Is that the right thing to do? Are there any supporting facts?

Having these thoughts will keep you from jumping on to a topic with minimal information and embarrassing yourself. Giving your ideas a second thought will also ensure that you have all the facts straight, and where needed, you may even change your mind. You could also realize that the issue in question is not worth your time, and you may give up on the issue entirely.

Avoid Being So Emotional

It is risky to get into an argument or confrontation when you are overly anxious, angry or resentful; doing it will get you spewing venom you would regret. Your counterparts will also be provoked to become harsh and unreasonable, and in the end, you will have prompted the situation to escalate to a massive issue while it could have been resolved rationally. If a situation aggravates or excites you too much, take a step back, take some deep breaths, relax and stay calm so that you can address people respectfully.

Ensure That You Are Not Making Things Worse

Sometimes you want to find a solution to a problem by putting your views across, but you end up making things worse. It happens to us all. However, the frequency of this happening will lower if you purpose to engage only in conversations and arguments that will lead to something productive. Stay away from idle talk that is meant to bring people down.

Do Not Insist on Your Way All the Time

Some people go by the erroneous 'my way or the highway' philosophy. Thinking that you are always right, but others are wrong is a sign of pride. Only a person who is so full of himself, a narcissist, will think that he is always right and cannot make mistakes.

Instead, you should pass your views as opinions to be considered rather than as the final decisions. Doing this will more likely produce a favorable response from your audience compared to imposing your will on them. The moment you force the other party to take a defensive position, know that you blew it already.

Let the Facts Lead

Your opinion is an opinion like that of any other individual, and it is based on your intuition and the information you have so far. Others around you could also have influenced your stand on any particular issue. For these reasons, opinions are quite subjective. Therefore, while you need to speak confidently about what you think, ensure that you stick to the merits of your position, and back them up with data and statistics.

Allow the Other Side a Chance

Your opinion, even when it is right, does not have to carry the day. There could be bits about the other side's view that could build on your ideas. Therefore, as you argue out your point, come up with creative ways to incorporate the other party's opinions too. Give support to their ideas and way of reasoning, and you will see that they will start to be friendlier and accommodating of your opinions too.

Chapter 13: Influencing Methods

Brainwashing

During brainwashing practice, the subject will be persuaded by a combination of different tactics to change their beliefs about something. During this process, there is not only one approach that can be used, so it can be difficult to put the practice in a clean little box. The subject will mostly be separated from all the things they know. From there they will be broken down into an emotional state that makes them vulnerable prior to the introduction of new concepts. As this new information is absorbed by the subject, they will be rewarded for expressing thoughts and thoughts that go with these new thoughts. The rewarding is what is going to be used to reinforce the on-going brainwashing.

The brainwashing process is accompanied by many steps. It's not something that's just going to happen to you as you go down the street and talk to someone you've just met. First of all, one of the main requirements that come with successful brainwashing is to keep the subject isolated. If the subject can be around other people and influences, they will learn how to think as an individual and there will be no brainwashing at all.

For the most part, when someone is just trying to persuade them from a new point of view, those who undergo brainwashing did so. For instance, if you're in an argument with a friend and they're convincing you their ideas make sense, you've been through brainwashing technically. It may not be evil, of course, and you could logically think about it all, but you were still convinced to change the beliefs you had before. It is very rare for someone to undergo true brainwashing where they will be replaced by their entire value system. It will usually occur in the process of coming to a new point of view, irrespective of whether or not the tactics used were forcible.

Hypnosis

Hypnosis is when a person enters a state of mind in which a person finds himself or herself vulnerable to the suggestions of a hypnotist.

Hypnosis is not new to us because many people have seen it in movies, cartoons or actually been to magic shows or performances where participants are told to do usual acts and they do it. One thing is for sure that, some people do believe that hypnosis actually exist and would do anything to avoid being a victim while others believe that its fiction.

Neuro-Linguistic Programming (NLP)

NLP is not as closed off as you may think since it is such a wide raging discipline that its mostly difficult to encompass all its branches and applications in our short definition. Using this enigmatic theme usually results in the altering or full elimination of existing behaviors if by any chance we are not satisfied by them to a more acceptable set of behaviors.

Neuron-linguistic programing is not usually based on the notion of new-age mantras or hanging some herbal trees in your room so as to be more notches with your inner self. This theme of dark psychology is usually based on some solid psychological principle. It is a rapid form of psychological therapy which is capable of addressing the myriad of problems that we are doomed to face in our day to day lives such as depression, some form of phobias or any form of negative habits we may have.

Body language cue

When you try to know more about your goal and how they view the world, body language is going to be so crucial. Too many times we get caught in the words that someone else tells us and we won't concentrate on the other indications they also give us. There is so much that can be disclosed by these body language clues, and it makes a large difference how effective you are in understanding and working with your goals.

Body language will refer to some of the nonverbal signals we use to interact with others. These nonverbal signals will take up much of the interaction we communicate every day. From the movement of our body to our facial expressions and everything in between, things we don't say can still share a ton of information during the process.

Deception

Deception is a theme that usually resonates within the spectrum of dark psychology. It has throughout the years been defined as any particular act that is used by a particular manipulative individual in order to instil certain beliefs within the victim that are usually false in nature or only those possessing partial truths.it is usually placed in the same category as deceit, mystification and suffrage. Deception is not usually an easy theme to understand since it involves a lot of different things like for example distractions, propaganda camouflage and concealment. The persuader is often able to easily control the subject's mind since the victim is often led to placing immense trust in this particular manipulative individual. The victims often believe in whatever the persuader will say, and might even be basing future plans and shaping their world base on the things that the persuader is feeding their subconscious mind. This strong element of trust towards the persuader can quickly fade away once the victim realizes what is going on. It is because of this very reason that a certain level of skill is needed for deployment of this theme, since only then will a persuader be able to skilfully change the focus of suspicion towards him and onto the victim's paranoia.

In most cases, deception will often present itself in relationship settings and can lead the victim to have dominant feelings of distrust and betrayal between the partners in the relationship. This usually happens because deception is a theme that violates most of the rules of most relationships, together with having a negative influence on the expectations that come with the relationship.

Mind games

When a person plays "mind games" on us, it is attributed to being innocent. Many people have come across this at some point in their life. Take an example when someone is planning a surprise party and doesn't want the other person to know and he does this by playing mind tricks in order not to give away what the surprise actually is. This is merely considered innocent and silly. Dark psychology mind games are not in any way innocent. Mind games in dark psychology are attributed to the hypnotist toying with the will power and sanity of his victim. This differs from other dark psychological manipulation in the sense that the persuader is playing with his victim for his own pleasure and enjoyment and is not invested in what the outcome will be. His interest in the victim would be to test the victim so to speak. Mind games are used by a hypnotist when other forms of suggestions to the victim are not effective and may decide to use mind games which are rather less obvious to the audience. The persuader may decide to use mind games to his own pleasure and amusement. Mind games are very effective in reducing the assuredness and psychological strength of the victim. The victim is eluded into thinking that he still has control. Manipulators are able to satisfy their twisted amusement when playing mind games. Such dark psychological manipulators do not see their victims as equal human beings and instead chooses to see the victim as a 'toy' and a person who can be manipulated and therefore, watch with amusement when victims do what they tell them to. Sometimes, a dark persuader will have known mind games all his life and knows no other forms of dark psychology manipulation. These manipulators can be dangerous because they know not of any other option and therefore no need of changing and being more humane.

Chapter 14: Specific Strategies and Tactics

There are tactics that can be utilized so as to make persuasion more successful. All victims are usually presented with different forms of persuasion on a daily basis. A food manufacturing plant will work on getting their victims to purchase a new product, while a movie company will focus on persuading their victims to watch their latest movie projects. These techniques of persuasion will be discussed below:

Create a need

This is one of the techniques that are often deployed by the persuader so as to be able to get the victim to change their way of thinking. This creates a need or rather appeals to a need that is already pre-existing within the victim. If it is executed in a skilled way, the victim will be eating out of the persuader's palm in no time. What this means is that the persuader will need to tap into the fundamental needs of their victim like for example their need for self-actualization. This technique will in most casework so well for the persuader because the victim is actually going to need these things. Food for example is usually something that we as humans need in order to survive and prolonged lack will pause as a big problem. If the agent can convince the subject that their store is the best, or if they can get more food or shelter by switching their beliefs, there is a higher chance of success.

Utilizing illustrative and words

The choice of words one chooses to use comes a long way in the success of using persuasion. There are many ways in which you can phrase sentences when actually talking about one thing. Saying the right words in the right way is what will make all the difference when attempting to use persuasion.

Tricks used by mass media and advertising

The media use two main methods which they use to persuade the masses. First is through the use of images, as well as the use of sounds.

Media persuasion by use of images

Our sighs and visual processing areas of the brain are very powerful. Just think about it for a minute, have you ever thought of a person without ending up picturing how they look? It is because of this that makes imagery and visual manipulation a preferred method by the media. Companies will often include split-second images of their product or individual inserted into an advertisement that seems quite innocent on the face value. This usually a form of subliminal persuasion. These split-second images that are usually assumed for the most part usually end up taking some form of control of the victim, which persuades them to purchase that particular service.

Media persuasion by the use of sound

Sound is yet another trick that is used by media in the persuasion of unsuspecting victims. Some people usually underestimate the powers that exist within the sound. But answer me this, how many times have you heard a song somewhere only to have it loops through your mind continuously? Songs usually have an influence on us even though we are not aware of it despite knowing you are listening to it. This is what the media tend to exploit in their quest for persuasion of the masses.

Persuade Only Those Who Can Be Persuaded

We can all be influenced at one time or another, provided the timing and the context is right. However, for some people, it can take a lot of persuading. Take a look at the politicians and their campaigns - they focus their money and their time almost exclusively on the small percentage of voters who are responsible for determining the outcome of an election. The very first step to successful persuasion is to identify and focus on the people who can, at that moment in time, be persuaded to follow you and your point of view. By doing this, a certain percentage of others - those who can't be persuaded at that moment in time - will be influenced later on to change their course.

Get Your Timing and Content Right

The timing is what dictates what we are looking for from other people and from life. Often, when we marry, it is to someone very different to whom we may have been dating in our younger years, simply because what we want at any given time is subject to change.

Uninterested People Cannot Be Persuaded

You simply can't convince people to do something if they genuinely are not interested in what you have to say. In general, the human race is concerned primarily with their own individual selves and most of their time is spent thinking about three things – health, love, and money. The very first step to persuading someone is to learn to talk to that person about themselves. Appeal to their self-interest and you have their attention. Continue to do it, and you will hold their attention for long enough to persuade them.

Be Persistent but not Overbearing

Take a wander back through history and look at the vast numbers of figures who have persuaded people through persistence, in both message and endeavor.

Be Sincere in Your Compliments

Whether we admit it or not, compliments do have a positive effect on us, and we are much more likely to place our trust in a person who is sincere and who makes us feel good. Try it – be sincere when you compliment a person, pay them compliments for something that they honestly wouldn't expect it to. Compliment them on something they had to work for: it can be something as simple as their clothing choice. Don't compliment them on their beauty or on other things they were born with. It's quite easy once you learn how to do it, and it costs nothing. The rewards will speak for themselves.

Set Your Expectations

One of the biggest parts to persuasion is learning to manage the expectations of others when it comes to placing trust in you and your judgment.

Never Assume

This is a bad mistake to make: to assume what people are looking for. Instead, offer them your value. Take the sales world; often products and services are held back because it is assumed that people simply don't have the money to purchase them, or they have no interest in them. Be bold, get out there and say what you have to offer, say what you can do for them and leave the choice to them. Be persistent, and it will pay off.

Make Things Scarce

Virtually everything has a value these days, on a relative scale. We need the bare necessities to survive, so they have a far higher value than something we don't need. Often we want something because someone else has it. If you want to persuade people to want what you are offering, it may not be enough to point out the benefits of things or services we are offering. It could be much more effective if we would tell people about its uniqueness and what they could lose. That would create a scarcity feeling, and the less there is, the more people want it. The logic of scarcity is very simple: when something becomes scarce, people want it more.

Create a Sense of Urgency

If a person doesn't have any real motivation to want something now, they aren't likely to want it later on down the line either. It's down to you to persuade them that time is running out; persuade them now or lose them forever.

Images are Important

Most people respond better to something they can see. Quite simply if they can see it, then it's real; if you just talk about it, then it might not even exist. Images are potent, and pictures really do speak a thousand words. You don't actually have to use images, just learn how to paint that image in a person's mind.

Build Up a Rapport

The human race is a funny thing. We tend to like those who are more like us, and this often goes way beyond the conscious into the unconscious. By "copying" or matching your behaviors, regarding cadence, body language, patterns of language, **etc.** you will find that it is easier to build up a rapport with them and easier to persuade them to your way of thinking.

553

Real-Life Examples of Influence

Persuasion in Sales

Persuasion in sales has been going on for as long as people have been selling things. There are so many tactics and systems and efforts geared toward making the sale that it may be one of the most intensely studied one-on-one interactions ever studied. In this section, we'll talk about a few of the Principles of Persuasion can be effectively used to make sales and increase business.

Originally, merchants would give people a free sample of a product, hoping that they would like it enough to want more. Getting people to purchase your product to complete their 'inner story' is as simple as getting them to associate ownership of your product with being the type of person they want to be.

Persuasion in Marketing

Marketing has now become a sophisticated endeavor that encompasses strategy and behavior studies at many top universities and management consultancies. For our purposes, we'll be including advertising in our marketing mix as well, as they are often close cousins when it comes to persuasion.

Persuasion in Customer Service

Many business owners think of customer service as a necessary evil, a headache, a pain point. But customer service can be an asset, a chance to lock in future business, and an opportunity to earn positive word of mouth. One way to make sure that customer service interactions go in a positive direction is through using some of the principles and tools of persuasion in all of your dealings with customers, not just when you are trying to get them to buy.

Many times, we need the customer to participate in a solution to a customer service problem. We might need them to send back an item for exchange, or send a picture of a broken part or damaged box.

One idea is to make the process as customer-centered as possible. If your customers feel that you are doing everything you can for them, they are more likely to return the good feeling in cooperation or recommendations to others. Offer a call-back option instead of making people wait on hold, email shipping documents and labels for returns, or give your customers no-wait appointments for help at your location. Showing that you take their time seriously will help you earn their help in return.

Persuasion in Negotiation

Both negotiation and persuasion share some similarities. In both, you as the persuader or negotiator have a goal to bring someone around to your way of thinking. Where the similarities end may be more in the communication mode used with each. With persuasion, the communication direction is mostly one-way. You come up with your best argument for your position, and you present it in the most effective way possible. You don't get a status report until you reach the end.

With negotiation, on the other hand, both sides are trying to persuade the other, so the communication mode is more two-way. Each party may present part of an argument, only to have part of the other side's argument then presented. Because of this, negotiation tends to be more reactionary out of necessity. It requires the ability to change directions, and adapt our presentation to address the input from the other side.

Persuasion in Relationships and Sex

Persuasion in close personal relationships can be a tricky business. Nobody likes to be manipulated or be in a relationship where they are not treated as an equal. It's important to focus on respect for the other person you are trying to persuade if you want them to stay in your life. Using persuasion in these areas require that you focus on benefiting the other person while still getting what you want.

We're not suggesting some magical spell that you'll be able to cast over the focus of your attraction that will make them override their own feelings. And we're not talking about mental reprogramming by force. But it never hurts to throw the odds in your favor when it comes to asking for that first coffee. Trying to make sure you do what you can during that first meeting so that he or she is more likely to see you again is not a bad thing. Don't use persuasion to hide your 'true self' from the other person either, because that will show through eventually, and you might both end up miserable. Call these tips a way to put yourself in the best light.

Once you do get a date with that special someone, the same types of subtle mimicry we talked about before can work to your advantage here, too. Adopting a similar sitting posture, for instance, or even some of the same language cues can make you seem more likable. Once people are together for a long time, they start to have these patterns without even thinking about it. You may find you pick up these traits naturally by carefully listening and watching the person you're with.

Chapter 15: Influence Authority and Its Possibility

Persuasion is an art which can be mixed in with science to formulate effective techniques. It's about using proven methodologies to get the exact results you want. Tips and pointers can only get you so far. Many expert persuaders have spent years formulating techniques that work for them. By sticking to their formulas, they're able to achieve everything from credibility to consistency. Not to mention, knowing they're using effective techniques allows them to instill confidence in their words.

That said, there is no one key for all. As a novice persuader, you will be able to experience firsthand how some formulas do not work for some people. If you're more of a down to earth person, making your audience picture the sky, will not be effective for you. You need to find your own voice and formula. However, using pre-made proven formulas is a good starting point to see what can work for you and what you should probably avoid doing.

Protection against Various Ways of Influencing Liking

Liking can be provoked by the uncountable variety of words, deeds, gestures or attitudes and even by their absence. It would be of little use to analyze each one of them or to try to detect the major principles of manipulation through the rule of liking. We will rather detect what is common in all these tricky ways that make us like another person and then we will try to find the best solution to keep us on guard and to prevent us making imprudent choices.

The mysterious force of liking lies in its unconsciousness. We are drawn towards an attractive person whether we think of it or not. And there is very little we can do about it. The goodness, the beauty, the charm or the smile disarm us, and we easily fall under the influence of other persons. How then to neutralize the unwanted effects of liking? In certain occasions, a caution or vigilance can prevent us from falling under the influence of manipulators. In another occasion, a bit of awareness leading to recognition could be of great help. But in a majority of cases, it would be advisable to develop a bit different tactics.

The good attracts a man. A brief analysis of the circumstances can help us realize if we like the other person trying to influence us more than we should. We should sincerely sense what is going on within us and, in the light of that feeling, clearly distinguish the person whom we like from the things he or she are offering us. We will then be able to freely take decisions according to the objective value of things, without linking it to the feeling of liking the other person has produced in us.

Neutralizing the Impact of Authority

The power of the influence of authority often lies in its element of surprise. We are so habituated to the presence of authority that we are not attentive enough in the situations when it is used to manipulate us. That's why it is necessary to be cautious about the presence and the influence of authority.

Even if a person is using a symbol of power, that does not mean that he is really an expert. A psychologist who is charging his clients for therapy at an extremely high price is not necessarily a very good one. It would, therefore, be of great use to inform ourselves about the competencies of another person. Before we submit to them trustfully, we should find out if they have sufficient knowledge and skills.

There are few more things to distinguish here besides one being a real authority or not. The first one is to realize whether a particular authority is relevant or irrelevant. The second one is to understand that to be an expert and to be an honest person are two different things. Many experts are just selling their products and the information they are telling us could easily be only in theirs best interest. We need to examine the trustworthiness even of the real experts and not make our choices before we have judged that what they are telling us is adequate to the facts.

Precautions against Pressures of Scarcity

Scarcity works according to the similar mechanism as other tactics do: it hinders our capacity to think and arouses our need. When something we desire becomes less available, we become physically agitated, our yearning increases and our thoughts become focused on only one thing: how to obtain the object you want.

Such a situation of emotional agitation can help us become aware of what is going on. The first thing to do is to calm ourselves in order to approach the situation with a clear reason. We can look for the tactics of manipulation if we can detect any of them. This more rational approach will help us see what is going on in a more objective light.

The second thing we could do is ask ourselves about the real value of the rare thing we want. Since with scarcity, all our attention is focused on the quantity of the thing, we should draw out attention also to the quality. Is the fact that it is scarce the main reason why we want it so much? Is it truly more valuable and of better quality than some other object that is not scarce? If the main reason why we want to possess the scarce thing is simply the joy of owning it, we are free to go. But if in reality, we are in need of a useful object of high quality, then we should rectify our desire, aroused under the influence of the pressure of scarcity. It will eventually bring us more pleasure if a thing is of good quality and suits our needs and wants than if it is something we only like because it is scarce.

Handling the Difficult Folks

Bosses tend to be a difficult target to persuade in many instances. They're the authority figure in the relationship and schmoozing them to your opinion requires work. Likewise, you can have difficult customers who have grievances you need to tackle. In such cases, it's vital to know a few extra measures you'll need to take to persuade such individuals.

The key here is to direct your opinion in a way so as not to cause a conflict. Often times you'll have to give a little critique to individuals who are not so receptive to your ideas. If you point out their negativity, you'll only reinforce it. But without pointing it out, your idea won't be listened or accepted. So what's the solution?

Simply tell a story and take the person you are trying to persuade out of the situation. Talking in a third person perspective helps to be more objective and logical. That said, this technique can easily be seen as a critique, and if used without proper skill, you're risking being shunned completely.

A second method you can use is to use your words wisely. Instead of verbalizing how bad a person's action is, you focus on how to make it better. For instance, you see someone litter around you. Next, it's important to always be accessible. Persuasion needs to be built, so being accessible to people who can reach out with questions and queries about your proposed ideas is important. It also helps to remind them of what you have proposed and subtly acts as its own form of persuasion. You don't need to verbally do anything until prompted, simply exist in front of the person you wish to persuade.

Common Perceptions of Authority

Speed Reading People

Before you can persuade other people, or understand how they may be trying to persuade you, it's essential to get a lay of the land. In one-on-one communication, this means learning how to read people effectively. Learning some of the basics of reading body language can help you see where other people are coming from, even if they don't tell you directly. Mastering the non-verbal cues, you are giving out can also help you communicate your message better.

If you're looking for what body language may be saying, what parts of the body should we be looking at? Body language experts say that hands and feet are both talking more than you may realize. For instance, stress and concern can often be shown through the hands clenching or fidgeting. People may relieve their stress in conversations by stroking their neck with a finger. Steepled hands, with fingertips together in a praying gesture, can show confidence in what a person is talking about, or their situation.

The bottom line, look for anxiety and nervousness in the hands, feet, and legs. They are often much more accurate in conveying context than facial tells.

Recognizing What You Don't Know

Experts in reading people agree on one thing. There is no foolproof way to read a person 100 percent accurately from non-verbal cues alone. Many people like to think they can read a person's face, for

561

instance. But former profiler Navarro says that facial expressions are some of the body language signals that are easier to fake.

It's important to try and process the entire situation and look for the holes before deciding someone you've just met. 'Trusting your gut' can only get you so far. Ask yourself what you really **know** about someone. When you try and piece together what the other person has said, are there any glaring deficiencies in what they've said. For instance, do they want to talk about anything but their job? If so, is there something that they are asking you to do that would benefit them professionally? If they are quite fervent about a cause that they are trying to get you to involve yourself with, have they mentioned their motivations? And do those motivations seem to match the person you see in front of you?

While there is no reason to be unnecessarily suspicious of everyone you meet, obvious holes in a person's story are red flags that need further exploration. Curiosity may keep you out of trouble if you can fill in a person's entire story with a few well-placed questions.

Recognizing Deception

In addition to body language, you should be looking beyond a person's words to look for their underlying motives. If you feel that you are being overtly manipulated, then you probably are. Experts in communication say that people who are trying to better themselves at your expense will generally make you feel uneasy.

An uneasy feeling may be hard to put your finger on, but here are a couple of specific warning signs to watch for in a possibly troubling exchange.

First, they seem always to keep circling back to the same thing. Single-mindedness about something another person wants you to do is a sure sign that they need this more than you do. Keep an eye out for conversations that seem to push you over and over again in a direction you don't want to go. Single-minded focus without regard to your wants shows a lack of empathy and selfishness, sure signs that a person will be looking out for themselves first.

The second indicator of possible ulterior motives is that obvious use of persuasive tactics. That's one of the purposes of this book, to make you consciously aware of these techniques. Use what you learn in this book to look for persuasive efforts by people you meet. If they are using these techniques in a way that doesn't seem genuine or honest, then they are probably after something you don't see. For example, you may have had a salesman who wants to talk more about your hobbies and kids than about what he is trying to sell you. Why doesn't he want to talk about his product?

An extreme opposite of this can be an indicator of trouble as well. If you are conspicuously missing from the conversation and all the other person wants to talk about is himself, this could mean that he is not really concerned about what happens to you at all. Being self-centered is a prerequisite for someone who wants to take advantage of you.

Sincerity, Care, and Getting What You Want

Persuasion is truly a type of art. You have to nudge hard enough to make progress, but not so hard that you appear aggressive. Once you advance your persuasion skills, you will be able to strike this balance every time without intense effort. To put it simply, with practice, you will naturally be a more persuasive person.

There are several techniques that you can use to persuade others. You simply need to analyze the situation and decide which one is going to work for getting what you want. Knowing these techniques makes it much easier to put them into action.

Only Deal with Issues You Can Control

The serenity prayer talks about getting the grace to control the things you can and leaving out the things you cannot. That is how you ought to simplify your life; do not result to moving mountains that you cannot even shake. Let the things that you cannot control be, but for what you can change, do all that you can to ensure a positive change.

When in a difficult situation, come up with a list of factors you can control and alongside it, write all the elements you cannot control. Focus all your attention on the things you can change, and those that are not on this list, do not give even an ounce of your attention. They will iron themselves out later, hopefully. Even if they don't, what can you do about it? Nothing.

See How You Have Come a Long Way

Sometimes, our focus is on the things that are yet to come, so much that we forget the mighty long way you have come. You have already overcome so much in life. You have gone through many difficult times, and none of them broke your back. You are still standing strong, and you can afford to give yourself some credit for all the effort you have put. Pat yourself on the back for all that you have overcome, and see that in time, you will also be happy you overcame your current predicament.

Have A Support System

One of the best things you can do for yourself is to surround yourself with the right people. They will provide support and help when the times get tough. Ensure that they are people who are honest, caring, compassionate, loving, patient, and forgiving.

Your support system will offer a helping hand, love you through your mistakes, offer you useful advice, and celebrate with you when you have overcome. If you surround yourself with people who are part of the problem, you are setting yourself up for disappointment, hurt, losses and sorrow for the long-term.

Persuasion Tips for Everyday Use

If you are looking to influence people, it is not enough to simply understand the principles underlying persuasion. You must also master the simple yet effective ways that you can put these principles to use in everyday life.

If you are a persuasive person, you will have a much easier time in life and will often achieve your intended results without having to jump through hoops. Some of the tips to being more persuasive can be implemented instantly while others will require a bit of practice.

Appear confident

Confidence does not come naturally to all of us. Some people seem to have an easier time being confident while others struggle quite a bit. Whether you are naturally confident or not, you must ensure that you appear confident to others at all times. If you are insecure about how you look or your abilities in a particular subject, nobody else needs to know this. Do not give your insecurities a platform on which to shine. Instead, practice faking it until you make it.

There are people in this world who do not know a whole lot of things and yet have managed to get scores of people to support them and their ideas. Reason? They are the epitome of confidence. They walk into rooms as if they own them. They speak authoritatively even when they are uncertain of what they talk about. Confidence says you know what you are talking about. People allow themselves to believe the people who know what they are talking about.

Be subtle with your approach

Even when they allow themselves to be persuaded into doing something, most people like to think that it was their idea to do something in the first place. Nobody wants to believe that they allowed a particular idea to be shoved down their throat. For success in persuasion, you must be subtle in your approach. Instead of introducing a certain topic full-on, consider starting with an anecdote. If you are looking to get someone to buy into an investment, start by mentioning how you and your friends went for a cruise last weekend after receiving your payout from Investment X. Do not even try to sell them that investment. Instead, get the other person thinking about how they could also have gone for the cruise had they invested in the particular investment vehicle. In short, entice people without being too obvious with your temptation.

Be flexible with your methods

The methods of persuasion are not set in stone. Different people respond to different things. Also, the same person will respond differently to different methods depending on the time and occasion. You must know when to switch gears accordingly. Sometimes you will need to work with the principle of liking and other times you will need to base your method on the principle of authority. Reading social cues will allow you to determine which methods to use.

Timing is everything

If you want to convince someone to buy a house, you'll have more success if you catch them when they are shopping for houses. This holds true for most things. If you want your crush to go from crush to partner, you will have an easier time if you talk to them when they are looking for a relationship. To master the art of persuasion, you must also master the art of knowing when the timing is right. If not, you will fall into the trap of harassing people to agree to things that they have no interest in. Nobody likes a person that is constantly pestering them into doing things, especially at the weirdest of times.

Being interesting is a plus

Most persuasive people are not boring. Nobody pays much attention to boring people. Boring people are not fun to talk to. They are not engaging, and they are definitely not memorable. If you want to win at persuasion, you must be an interesting person. The good news is that there are countless ways of being interesting. You just need to identify something unique about yourself and amplify it for the world to see. It could be a skill or a hobby that you are really good at. It might also be your sense of humor or the way you dress. Perhaps, you might even want to share your unique view of the world with your audience. Whatever it is that you opt for, make sure that it helps people remember you long after the conversation ends.

Listen more than you talk

You might think that being persuasive means doing a whole lot of talking, but this could not be further from the truth. In order to influence people, you must train yourself to be a good listener. Listening skills serve two purposes. First, as long as people are talking and you are listening, then it means you are gathering crucial information that you can use to your advantage. Second, people like a good listener. Why? Because people love talking about themselves. Keep your mouth shut and your ears open and you will be well on your way to increasing your likeability quotient.

Chapter 16: Putting Persuasion and Influence Together

Influence and Mind Control in Society

You see mind control every day and you have even fallen victim to it. The majority of it is used in advertising and marketing. For example, you see a television commercial that really captures your attention. The product is not one you absolutely need, but the commercial captured your mind and essentially told you on a subconscious level that you need the product. So, you go and buy it. You had no idea your mind was being controlled. In fact, you probably did not realize it until reading this section right now.

When you master undetectable mind control, you will essentially be marketing yourself. The end result will not be others buying you but giving you what you want.

There are several techniques that you will use when you are working to control the minds of others. All of these are relatively simple to implement once you have gained control over your own mind. The following are effective undetectable mind control techniques to learn:

• **Think for them:** When you need something from someone, do not give them a chance to think it over. Tell them what they are thinking and what they are going to do. People are naturally busy and if you ask them to consider something, they are likely to either forget or not give it enough thought to give you your desired outcome. When you help them not have to think, they view it as you helping them, making them more likely to give you what you want.

• **Ask for an inch:** When you are assessing how easy a person is to control, you want to take baby steps so that they never catch on to what you are doing. So, start with small things first, such as asking them to buy you a drink or making them take you to a movie. From here, you can persuade them to do larger things, such as paying a bill for you or buying you something on the pricey side. It is all about testing the waters and essentially priming your target.

• **Give some too:** If all you do is take, no matter how naïve a person is, they are going to eventually catch on to what you are doing. So, on occasion, buy them a drink, give them a compliment or offer to pay for the movie. This makes the relationship seem balanced and even, but what you are actually doing is ensuring that they continue to be available for whatever you need from them.

• **Instill fear:** This was touched on in a previous chapter, but it is actually incredibly effective for undetectable mind control. You essentially want to set up a situation that makes the person feel afraid. When people are afraid they are easier to control and make suggestions to.

• **Instill guilt:** Make the person feel guilty and they will be putty in your hands. The key here is to alleviate your guilt and reverse the roles as seamlessly as possible. This is a great mind control technique for those that are harder to break with other methods. Once you cause them to feel guilt for what they perceive is something bad happening to you, immediately act and make suggestions to get what you want from them since guilt goes away quickly when induced this way.

Principles of Persuasion

Commitment and Consistency

It is common for people to attain certain beliefs or actions and then stick with them. For example, once a person chooses a political viewpoint, they tend to stick with it. You can use this to your advantage. Have someone make a small commitment and go through with it. Then, influence them to start to do more things for you. That initial commitment develops a behavior in them that makes them prone to help you. This is the consistency.

Consistency in persuasion works this way: people are more likely to commit to bigger tasks or favors if you have convinced them to agree to smaller ones. That is, you can get someone to swim oceans for you if you first get them to jump a puddle for you. There have been some studies conducted to support this theory.

Social Proof

The victim will be influenced by the people around them; they will be more likely to want to do what others are doing instead of doing their own thing. The victim will base their beliefs and actions on what others do about them, how they act and how they believe the saying "the crowd's power" can be very effective under this belief. The victim will want to know at all times what other people around them are doing. In this country, being able to do what others are doing to fit in, despite the fact that people will say how they want to be different and be an individual, has become almost an obsession.

This is a type of persuasion you see every day on social media. Someone posts a meme, for example, that supports a specific political bias. It is not the least bit true, but people believe it anyway. This is due to the groupthink phenomenon and it is also associated with people naturally wanting to please the group they are apart of. They naturally just go with what the group wants so they are not ousted.

You can use this persuasion method to your advantage too. For example, think back to when you were a teenager. Once one friend in the group started smoking, everyone eventually tried it. There is a peer pressure in groups that naturally persuades people to do things they otherwise would not. Simply be the first in your group to do something and you will persuade the rest of the group to follow you with little effort.

Authority

A person who is an authority figure in a particular field will have an easier time influencing other when compared to a complete newbie. If you wish to persuade more people to do a particular thing, you must build your credibility by making yourself seem like you have expertise in whatever field you are playing in. This principle is a key reason why professionals display their diplomas in their field. Think about it--when you walk into a therapist's office, for instance, you are likely to consciously look out for the type of credentials they have hung on their walls. If it so happens that your therapist has a whole lot of credentials displayed, you will likely feel a sense of comfort in their expertise and experience. As such, any recommendations they have for you will be easily welcomed and implemented by you. The therapist, in essence, has managed to influence you without even saying a word.

It is a fact that your authority will not be taken very seriously if you are the only one talking about it. As such, you must ensure that you recruit others to beat the drums on your behalf, so to speak. There are subtle ways of doing this. In the office, you can identify a field that you are passionate about and become the office guru of that field. For some people, this might be the field of Microsoft Excel or reporting. The guy who is known as the office Excel guru will have an easier time getting things from people because they already know he knows what he is talking about. He has also proven himself likable and useful by solving all their Excel problems, and his colleagues will want to pay him back somehow. You do not have to learn Excel to make your mark in the world. There are numerous other fields that you can excel in and present yourself as an authority figure.

If you can make yourself appear authoritative, you can make people do things for you they otherwise would not. Just think about the things people do for the boss at work that they hate doing. However, they do them anyway simply because a person in authority asked them to. This is something you see a lot in advertising. For example, a toothpaste commercial tells you that the American Dental Association approves of it. This alone makes you automatically trust the toothpaste and want to use it. You were persuaded to use this toothpaste based on an authority recommending it.

Scarcity

In economics, the laws of demand and supply are simple and straightforward: when supply is low and demand is high, prices go up. To translate this, scarcity builds value. If you are a businessperson looking to convince people to buy your product or service, it helps to highlight the fact that the product is on offer for only a limited amount of time. Further, let your customers know that they stand to lose out significantly if they do not access this product on time. When the marketing message is packaged that way, they will be more people rushing to beat the time limitation on your product.

In the world of business and personal relationships, it is important to become a scarce product yourself. If you are always available to everyone every time they need you, you will quickly lose your value. You have got to learn the art of being inaccessible and unavailable if you wish to retain your air of mystery and influence around you. When you do finally show up, your word will be revered more than the word of a person that is constantly showing up and talking themselves out of any relevance and value.

In your life, you can use this by making your time seem scarce, for example. You want to spend more time with someone, but you want them to be the person to ask you. So, by making yourself limited in their life, you create a need for yourself. This persuades them to call you and set up a time to get together.

Reciprocation

Reciprocity is simply doing unto others as you would have them do unto you. As you go about your daily interactions, reciprocity calls for kindness and generosity. Showing kindness to others is a good thing that makes others, and yourself feel better about your interaction. Even more than that, doing good is your way of collecting chips that you can cash in later. If you have been nice and kind to another person, you stand a better chance of them being nice and kind to you.

If you are hoping to be able to persuade a person, you must behave in a decent manner towards them. Speak a kind word, do them a favor or even buy them a gift. Later on, when you need to convince them to do something, they will be more agreeable. After all, you have proven yourself to be a kind human being who has their interest at heart.

This is just a natural human instinct. If you make a person feel indebted to you, you always have them available to do something for you. In fact, you can ask just about anything of them and the natural human instinct will be for them do it without question.

You see this often with different organizations when they are seeking donations. They offer a small gift of some sort. They offer you a small gift and now you feel like you have to donate because they just gave you something.

Speaking in "We"

Part of being persuasive is to make people feel like they are not alone. When you are working to persuade someone, never use "you" when talking, but always use "we" instead. They will feel that by doing what you ask, they are helping themselves too. It also makes them feel like they are a part of something, which is a big motivating factor when someone is going to do something they normally would not.

The Principle of Liking

If a person likes you, they are more likely to meet your demands, whatever this may be. A person that is not liked and is unlikeable as well will hear no more times than a person that is well-liked. But how do you go about getting people to like you? According to science, the secret to being liked is a combination of three main factors. First, people like those who are similar to them. For you to appear similar to the person you are hoping to persuade, you must find common ground with them. For instance, many foreigners have learned that the simplest way to become more likable is by learning and speaking the local language. The other thing that you need to be aware of when making yourself more likable is flattery. Flattery will open many doors for you if you use it well. People like people who pay them compliments. If you want to ask someone to do something for you, start first by paying them a genuine-sounding compliment. Just because it's called flattery does not mean that you must be effusive about it. In fact, being too excessive in your praise will be counterproductive to your need to be liked. Last but not least, be the kind of person that is usually agreeable and cooperative towards the achievement of mutual goals, and you'll be one step closer to being likable. If you are always stepping on other people's toes in order to get what you want, you will have very few friends, and this will not help your case when you need to persuade someone in future. Remember, being agreeable and cooperative does not entail being a doormat. Sometimes, it just means putting in some little effort that helps a person achieve a goal that is significant to them. For instance, if a colleague is struggling with a due report, offer to assist them with the printing and mailing. It is not a whole lot of work, but you will go from the uninvolved, nondescript colleague to the likable colleague that is kind and helpful.

Steps to Help You Get Through Tough Times

Below is a list of steps you need to follow through to become positive and to navigate the tough times in life.

Remain Positive

When everything around you is crashing, or you have tried all you can to take out a persistent problem, the last advice you want to hear is that you should remain positive. In the first place, positivity requires you to be calm and somewhat happy, but when everything is improper, there is no much joy to go around. However, you ought to strive as hard as you can to remain happy. Positivity serves the most significant part of overcoming a challenge.

When you remain positive, you put yourself in a position to make it through the tough times by giving you hope that there is a better day at the other end of the challenge you are handling. Positivity also makes you a better person because it improves your attitude, causes you to be calmer, and gives you the agility you need to deal with future challenges.

When challenges and hard times hit you, you can choose to curl up in fetal position and play victim so that people around you pity you. You could also choose to stand, remain positive and do what you need to do to ensure that you see the light at the end of the tunnel.

Positivity does not mean that you will not be sad, shed a tear or feel a little discouraged, it means that through it all, you will have it in your mind that life must go on. You will pick up the pieces of what's left, and soldier on to the next step in life.

Embrace Creativity

There will come times when you can only stand and watch when you cannot do much to change your circumstances. When this happens, you will have to deal with the situation as it is. There will also come times when you can do two or three things, and the circumstances will suddenly improve. Most of these times, the solution to your problem won't be lying around; if it were, you wouldn't be dealing with the issue you are dealing with now. Finding a solution will require you to step back, see the bigger picture and creatively come up with a solution.

Learn from Your Experience

Life has many lessons, but the ones we surely do not forget are those that we learn when going through pain, disappointment and other difficult emotions. Amazingly, these lessons are the ones that we carry through life, and they end up being of the most significant benefit to us. Therefore, after you have gone through a negative experience, sit back and dissect the entire situation. Pull everything apart, see what went wrong, what caused it, how it affected you, how you resolved it, and what you could have done differently to avoid the situation. You will find that in every experience, there are valuable lessons to learn and to pass along to other people. You also get a clearer picture of what you need to do to prevent a reoccurrence of the same

Shift Things Up

Once you have gathered the lessons, you got from your difficult time, it's time to make changes. If you can implement the change, immediately do it. There is no point in prolonging the pain. If the change needs some time to be implemented, set a timeline by which you will have implemented the change. The lessons you have carried from your experiences you will need, and you can refer to them when the situation recurs.

You see, it would be pointless to go through a challenge and not learn from it. If you examine every difficulty you have gone through, you will see that there has been an unseen benefit in each of them. Challenges come about to sharpen us and to prepare us for the next step in life, and the higher you go, the greater the challenges you encounter.

Conclusion

To ensure that you will become a successful persuader, this book contains theoretical rules and practical techniques that you can easily use. Read this book carefully because it contains pieces of information that can potentially change your life for the better.

We have seen that the ability to persuade is one of the most crucial ingredients in our dealings with people, if we are to have any sort of influence and do not want to be relegated to the role of camp follower for the rest of our lives. The greater our ability is to persuade others, the better we will be at whatever field it is we are pursuing, be it social, business or recreational. It is not sufficient to simply persuade people to follow you once or twice. To gain influence, we need to establish ourselves as persuasive on an ongoing basis. This requires trust, credibility and a high degree of empathy for the needs of others. Not to mention, practice.

I hope this information has been beneficial to you in expanding your knowledge and sense of possibility in how you can begin to leverage the principles of persuasive language to your advantage. Keep in mind the amazing power of language, as sometimes it is your greatest tool to creating the life you desire. Remember to practice believing in your ability to influence yourself and others. Also remember that the more you practice these techniques, the more they will become part of your natural vocabulary; your secret arsenal of persuasive power!

This e-book was written to act as your personal guide to persuasion. I want this to help you change your life. It's a truly special skill to have and it can bring you tremendous power. All you have to do is start, make that first step and begin learning how to use this exciting, new power. Don't wait any longer, start right now! Good luck!

Printed in Great Britain
by Amazon